The Collected Courses of the Academy of European Law
Series Editors: Professor Philip Alston and
Professor Gráinne de Búrca,
European University Institute,
Florence

VOLUME IX/2

Peoples' Rights

Sheffield Hallam University
Learning and Information Services
Withdrawn From Stock

The Collected Courses of the Academy of European Law
Edited by Professor Philip Alston and Professor Gráinne de Búrca

This series brings together the Collected Courses of the Academy of European Law in Florence. The Academy's mission is to produce scholarly analyses which are at the cutting edge of the two fields in which it works: European Union law and human rights law. A 'general course' is given each year in each field, by a distinguished scholar and/or practitioner, who either examines the field as a whole through a particular thematic, conceptual or philosophical lens, or who looks at a particular theme in the context of the overall body of law in the field. The Academy also publishes each year a volume of collected essays with a specific theme in each of the two fields.

This book has been printed digitally and produced in a standard specification in order to ensure its continuing availability

OXFORD
UNIVERSITY PRESS

Great Clarendon Street, Oxford OX2 6DP

Oxford University Press is a department of the University of Oxford.
It furthers the University's objective of excellence in research, scholarship,
and education by publishing worldwide in

Oxford New York

Auckland Cape Town Dar es Salaam Hong Kong Karachi
Kuala Lumpur Madrid Melbourne Mexico City Nairobi
New Delhi Shanghai Taipei Toronto
With offices in
Argentina Austria Brazil Chile Czech Republic France Greece
Guatemala Hungary Italy Japan South Korea Poland Portugal
Singapore Switzerland Thailand Turkey Ukraine Vietnam

Oxford is a registered trade mark of Oxford University Press
in the UK and in certain other countries

Published in the United States
by Oxford University Press Inc., New York

Oxford is a registered trade mark of Oxford University Press
in the UK and in certain other countries

Published in the United States
by Oxford University Press Inc., New York

© P. Alston

The moral rights of the author have been asserted

Database right Oxford University Press (maker)

Reprinted 2005

All rights reserved. No part of this publication may be reproduced,
stored in a retrieval system, or transmitted, in any form or by any means,
without the prior permission in writing of Oxford University Press,
or as expressly permitted by law, or under terms agreed with the appropriate
reprographics rights organization. Enquiries concerning reproduction
outside the scope of the above should be sent to the Rights Department,
Oxford University Press, at the address above

You must not circulate this book in any other binding or cover
And you must impose this same condition on any acquirer

ISBN 0-19-924365-4

SHEFFIELD HALLAM UNIVERSITY
WL
341.48
PE
COLLEGIATE LEARNING CENTRE

Peoples' Rights

Edited by

PHILIP ALSTON

Academy of European Law
European University Institute

Peoples' Rights

Edited by

PHILIP ALSTON

Academy of European Law
European University Institute

This book has been printed digitally and produced in a standard specification in order to ensure its continuing availability

OXFORD
UNIVERSITY PRESS

Great Clarendon Street, Oxford OX2 6DP

Oxford University Press is a department of the University of Oxford.
It furthers the University's objective of excellence in research, scholarship,
and education by publishing worldwide in

Oxford New York

Auckland Cape Town Dar es Salaam Hong Kong Karachi
Kuala Lumpur Madrid Melbourne Mexico City Nairobi
New Delhi Shanghai Taipei Toronto

With offices in

Argentina Austria Brazil Chile Czech Republic France Greece
Guatemala Hungary Italy Japan South Korea Poland Portugal
Singapore Switzerland Thailand Turkey Ukraine Vietnam

Oxford is a registered trade mark of Oxford University Press
in the UK and in certain other countries

Published in the United States
by Oxford University Press Inc., New York

Oxford is a registered trade mark of Oxford University Press
in the UK and in certain other countries

Published in the United States
by Oxford University Press Inc., New York

© P. Alston

The moral rights of the author have been asserted

Database right Oxford University Press (maker)

Reprinted 2005

All rights reserved. No part of this publication may be rep
stored in a retrieval system, or transmitted, in any form or
without the prior permission in writing of Oxford U
or as expressly permitted by law, or under terms agreed
reprographics rights organization. Enquiries conce
outside the scope of the above should be sent to th
Oxford University Press, at the ad

You must not circulate this book in any
And you must impose this same con

ISBN 0-19-9

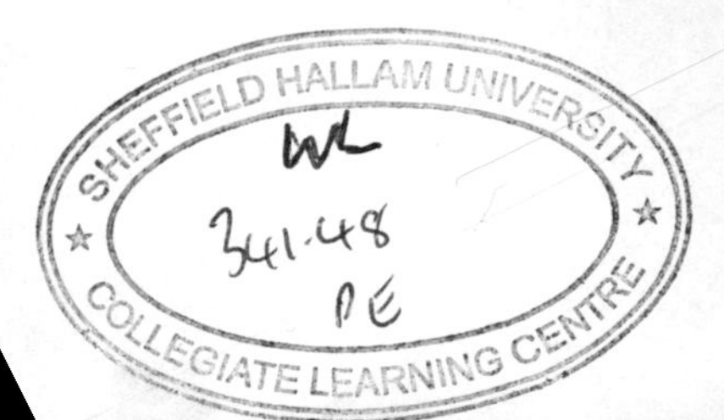

Contents

Notes on Contributors

Philip Alston is Professor of Law at New York University and Professor of International Law at the European University Institute in Florence. He has been Editor-in-Chief of the *European Journal of International Law* since 1997 and was the Chairperson of the UN Committee on Economic, Social, and Cultural Rights for eight years until 1998. He was Director of a major project on human rights policies within the European Union which resulted in a far-reaching 'Human Rights Agenda for the EU for the Year 2000' endorsed by a *Comité des sages* and a volume of essays entitled *The EU and Human Rights* published in English in 1999 and in French in 2001.

James Crawford SC FBA moved to the UK from Australia in 1992 to take up the Whewell Chair of International Law at the University of Cambridge. He was previously Professor of Law at Adelaide and Sydney Universities, and a member of the Australian Law Reform Commission. He is a member of the United Nations International Law Commission, and in that capacity chaired the Commission's Working Group on a Draft Statute for an International Criminal Court (1994). Since 1997 he has been appointed the ILC's Special Rapporteur on State Responsibility; the Commission completed that topic in 2001. In addition to his work at Cambridge (where he is Director of the Lauterpacht Research Centre for International Law) he has been counsel in many cases before the International Court of Justice and other international tribunals.

Benedict Kingsbury is Professor of Law at New York University Law School. He previously taught at Oxford University and at Duke University, and has been a visiting professor at Harvard Law School, the University of Tokyo Law Faculty, and the University of Padua. His most recent work is *Alberico Gentili e il Mondo Extraeuropeo* (2001). He is currently working on a book on indigenous peoples and international law. His co-edited works include: *Hugo Grotius and International Relations*; *The International Politics of the Environment*; *United Nations, Divided World*; and *Indigenous Peoples of Asia*. The Filomen D'Agostino and Max E. Greenberg Research Fund kindly supported his research for his chapter in this volume.

Peter Leuprecht is Dean of the Faculty of Law of McGill University. He is a member of a committee of four *sages* which prepared a Human Rights Agenda for the European Union, and in 1999 he was awarded the *Prix du civisme européen.* In August 2000 Professor Leuprecht was appointed as the UN Secretary-General's Special Representative for human rights in Cambodia. He was previously an official in the Secretariat of the Council of Europe, first as Secretary of the Committee of Ministers, then Director of Human Rights, and lastly as Deputy Secretary-General. He has been Visiting Professor at the Faculty of Law of McGill University and at the *Département*

des sciences juridiques de l'Université du Québec à Montréal, and Advisor to the Canadian Department of Justice. He has taught at the Universities of Strasbourg and Nancy and is the author of numerous publications in the field of international law and human rights.

Dr Anne Orford is a Senior Lecturer in the Law School at the University of Melbourne. She researches in the areas of human rights, international economic law, postcolonial theory, and feminist legal theory. Her publications in those areas include articles in the *European Journal of International Law*, the *Harvard International Law Journal* and the *Michigan Journal of International Law*. Dr Orford has taught courses in international economic law, international human rights law, and legal theory at the University of Melbourne, the Australian National University, and La Trobe University. She has worked with a range of NGOs on issues of human rights and economic justice. She is currently working on two books, one on humanitarian intervention to be published by Cambridge University Press, and one on the relationship between free trade, human rights, and democracy to be published by Federation Press and Zed Books.

Dinah Shelton is Professor of Law and Director of the Doctoral Program in International and Comparative Human Rights Law at the Center for Civil and Human Rights, Notre Dame Law School, USA. She has taught at numerous other universities in the United States and Europe and has spoken before scholarly groups, government bodies, and international organizations on every continent. She is on the executive council of the International Institute of Human Rights and has served in various offices in the American Society of International Law and other professional institutions. She is a member of the Court for International Environmental Arbitration and Conciliation and on the board of *Environnement sans frontières*. She has written extensively on international law, especially human rights law and international environmental law. Her book *Remedies in International Human Rights Law* was awarded the Certificate of Merit of the American Society of International Law in 2000. She is also the co-author, with Alexandre Kiss, of *International Human Rights Law* and the *Manual of European Environmental Law*.

Table of Cases

A. International

Council of the League of Nations

European Commission on Human Rights

European Court of Human Rights

Inter American Court of Human Rights

International Court of Justice

Advisory Opinion

Permanent Court of International Justice

New Zealand

Tanzania

United States

Table of Treaties, Legislation, and International Instruments

A. European Community Legislation

B. International Treaties and Other Instruments

C. National Legislation

Abbreviations

CEC	Commission for Environmental Cooperation
CHR	Commission on Human Rights
Codex	Codex Alimentarius
CSCE	Conference on Security and Cooperation in Europe
EC	European Community
ECOSOC	(UN) Economic and Social Council
ENMOD	Convention on Military or Any Other Hostile Environmental Modification Techniques
ETS	European Treaty Series
GATT	General Agreement on Tariffs and Trade
IACHR	Inter-American Commission on Human Rights
IAEA	International Atomic Energy Agency
IBRD	International Bank for Reconstruction and Development
ICCPR	International Covenant on Civil and Political Rights
ICESCR	International Covenant on Economic, Social, and Cultural Rights
ICRC	International Committee of the Red Cross
IDA	International Development Association
ILO	International Labour Organization
IMF	International Monetary Fund
IMO	International Maritime Organization
NAAEC	North American Agreement on Environmental Cooperation
NAFTA	North Atlantic Free Trade Agreement
NGO	Non-Governmental Organization
OECS	Organization of Eastern Caribbean States
OAS	Organization of American States
OAU	Organization of African Unity
OSCE	Organization on Security and Cooperation in Europe
PIC Convention	Rotterdam Convention on the Prior Informed Consent Procedure for Certain Hazardous Chemicals and Pesticides in International Trade
SPS Agreement	Agreement on the Application of Sanitary and Phytosanitary Measures
TNC	Transnational Corporation
TRIPS	Agreement of Trade-Related Measures of Intellectual Property Rights
UDHR	Universal Declaration of Human Rights
UN	United Nations
UNCC	United Nations Compensation Commission

UNCED	United Nations Conference on Environment and Development
UNCLOS	United Nations Conference on the Law of the Sea
UNCTAD	United Nations Conference on Trade and Development
UNDAF	United Nations Development Assistance Framework
UNDG	United Nations Development Group
UNECE	United Nations Economic Commission for Europe
UNEP	United Nations Environment Programme
UNESCO	United Nations Educational, Scientific, and Cultural Organization
UNPO	Unrepresented Nations and Peoples Organization
WGIP	(UN) Working Group on Indigenous Populations
WHO	World Health Organization
WTO	World Trade Organization

1

Introduction

PHILIP ALSTON

1. A Time to Take Stock

For all its vagueness and ambiguity, the right of peoples to self-determination succeeded during the second half of the twentieth century in transforming not only many of the basic tenets of international law but also in reshaping the international community. It is hardly surprising then that the proponents of the broader concept of peoples' rights, which assumed considerable importance starting in the early 1970s, aimed at provoking a similarly fundamental transformation of the way in which human rights are conceived and implemented. The principal means by which they sought to achieve this objective was through the elevation of the well-recognized, but nonetheless vague and open-ended, duty of states to cooperate to achieve the objectives of the United Nations Charter, in combination with an emerging principle of solidarity, so as to transform the correlative duties that attach to human rights into concrete obligations upon governments to transfer resources to those in need.

These initiatives reached their high point in the 1970s when a range of peoples' rights was enshrined in the African Charter of Human and Peoples' Rights. This breakthrough was followed by sustained but diverse efforts to achieve clear recognition of various peoples' rights—most notably the rights to development, peace and environment—within the United Nations context. These rights,[1] along with other established group rights such as the right of self-determination, the right to existence, minority rights, and indigenous

[1] The list has also been said to include a right to humanitarian assistance and a right to ownership of the common heritage of mankind. These rights are not dealt with in the present volume. The former, which has been the subject of extensive debate in the post-Cold War era, has consistently been examined within the existing framework of international law and individual human rights rather than being treated as a peoples' right. The latter has not been the subject of any significant scholarly or diplomatic debate. For the most recent version of a comprehensive proposal setting forth the various rights see Vasak, 'Revisiter la troisième génération des droits de l'homme avant leur codification', in *Héctor Gros Espiell Amicorum Liber: Persona humana y derecho internacional,* Vol. II (1997) 1649.

peoples' rights, make up the overall group of 'peoples' rights' that are sometimes referred to as 'third generation human rights', or 'solidarity rights'.[2]

It is now timely, at the beginning of the twenty-first century, to take stock of how far the international community has really moved in relation to these efforts to expand the notion of peoples' rights and to consolidate its status within the context of international law generally and of international human rights law in particular. It can be said from the outset that the overall verdict is not a particularly encouraging one. The concept has undergone several important phases in its evolution but the most recent phase, which began with the end of the Cold War, has seen a high level of rhetorical invocation of the various rights combined with a systematic diminution of the practical significance accorded to the great majority of them. This is not to suggest that the potential inherent in the concept is now unrealizable. Far from it. But the starting point for any effort to reinvigorate the concept is a clear appreciation of the rather dismal current state of the art and an understanding of the background to the current situation.

This volume does not seek to revisit the issues that preoccupied a great many of the analyses about peoples' rights which have appeared in the past. They include issues such as the definition of a people and the relationship between peoples' rights and human rights. Even though a decade or more has passed since most such analyses were undertaken, for the most part there is not a great deal to add to those particular debates.[3]

2. The Contributions of this Volume to the Debate

The aim of this volume is to provide an analysis of the current state of the debate both as it relates to the concept in general and to some of the key rights which are grouped within this category. The right of self-determination remains the single most important and most frequently invoked of the rights

[2] The terminology of third generation human rights has long been subject to controversy, but there is little point in the present volume in revisiting a well-worn debate which has been adequately taken care of elsewhere. For a defence see C. Wellman, *The Proliferation of Rights: Moral Progress or Empty Rhetoric?* (1999), at 29–38; and Wellman, 'Solidarity, the Individual and Human Rights', 22 *Human Rights Quarterly* (2000) 639. Cf. Cohen-Jonathan, 'Préface', in J. Matringe, *Tradition et modernité dans la Charte africaine des droits de l'homme et des peuples: étude du contenu normatif de la Charte et de son apport à la théorie du droit international des droits de l'homme* (1996) 10 where the concept is said to be both 'inappropriate and dangerous'. See also Rosas, 'So-Called Rights of the Third Generation', in A. Eide, C. Krause and A. Rosas (eds), *Economic, Social and Cultural Rights: A Textbook* (1995), at 243–6; and Alston, 'A Third Generation of Solidarity Rights: Progressive Development or Obfuscation of International Human Rights Law?', 29 *Netherlands International Law Review* (1982) 307.

[3] By far the best survey of these issues continues to be J. Crawford (ed.), *The Rights of Peoples* (1988).

in question. It has in the past, however, been the subject of a great deal of aspirational analysis which seemed to pay all too little attention to the actual practice of the international community. And where that practice has been the focus, the legacy of the era of decolonization has dominated, with the result that much of the literature has had relatively little to offer in helping us to analyse the key challenges that confront the international community at a time when it is grappling with the twin phenomena of fragmentation and globalization. James Crawford's chapter aims to make up for the shortcomings of these two approaches, both by providing an antidote to wishful thinking, and a guide to the elements that are relevant in an era when the principle of non-intervention is increasingly called into question in situations in which compelling questions of self-determination are raised. His analysis is given particular pertinence by his consideration of the 1995 decision of the International Court of Justice in the *Case Concerning East Timor*,[4] his careful recounting of the arguments that led the Canadian Supreme Court in 1998 to deny the right of the people of Quebec the right to secede from Canada[5] and his reflections on the significance for self-determination of the intervention in Kosovo in 1999. While his conclusion that, except in colonial or quasi-colonial settings, the right of self-determination is inherently non-self-executing and cannot *per se* dictate the creation of any particular outcomes or institutional arrangements, seems a far cry from the assertions often made on behalf of many of the peoples who are struggling to achieve a radical change in their political status, it can also be seen to be a more accurate reflection of the current state of the art in both international and domestic law.

The relatively modest formulation proposed by Crawford will be tested in the years ahead in the context of the work of the United Nations in drafting a UN Declaration on the Rights of Indigenous Peoples. This and a range of other efforts at the international level to promote and protect the rights of indigenous peoples is the focus of the chapter in this volume by Benedict Kingsbury. He does not describe these developments *per se* but rather focuses on the conceptual dimensions of the debate which have consistently been neglected. Going significantly beyond earlier efforts to distinguish the different grounds upon which special status for indigenous peoples has been sought,[6] he identifies five different conceptual structures which have been

[4] 1995 ICJ Reports 90.

[5] *Reference re Secession of Quebec from Canada* [1998] 2 SCR 217. For a thoughtful analysis of the case and its potential application to the United Kingdom, see Walters, 'Nationalism and the Pathology of Legal Systems: Considering the Quebec Secession Reference and its Lessons for the United Kingdom', 62 *Modern Law Review* (1999) 371.

[6] See, for example, Sanders' rather more basic analytical distinction between 'historical-legal' and 'territorial cultural minority' based claims. Sanders, 'Self-Determination and Indigenous Peoples', in C. Tomuschat (ed.), *Modern Law of Self-Determination* (1993) 55, at 71.

used, sometimes interchangeably and often without clarity, in claims brought by indigenous peoples. They are: (i) human rights and non-discrimination claims; (ii) minority claims; (iii) self-determination claims; (iv) historic sovereignty claims; and (v) claims as indigenous peoples, including claims based on treaties or other agreements between indigenous peoples and states. In determining the response to a particular claim it will matter a lot in a given context which of these structures is invoked. At present, however, there is little consistency and no significant prospect of definitively reconciling the different usages. In Kingsbury's view this is not necessarily a bad thing but it points to the importance of institutional arrangements through which the different concepts can be mediated and at least partially reconciled. It also points to the importance of international instruments such as the draft UN Declaration, and thus of the terminology which governments finally agree upon.

In her chapter on 'Environmental Human Rights' Dinah Shelton also devotes considerable attention to the rights of indigenous peoples. Her main focus, however, is on what she identifies as the four different ways in which environmental considerations and human rights law interact. They are: (i) the invocation of human rights norms in the context of international environmental instruments; (ii) the adaptation of existing human rights guarantees in response to threats of environmental harm; (iii) recognition of a human right to an ecologically-balanced and sustainable environment; and (iv) a responsibilities approach to human rights which includes respect for the environment. She evaluates the theoretical implications of each approach and acknowledges the extent of opposition in relation to each of them, including in particular the right to environment which is one of the key peoples' rights cited in the broader literature. It is noteworthy that Shelton's analysis does not focus at all on the specifically peoples' rights dimension of the right and in this respect her approach is consistent with the great majority of the analyses that have addressed the issue.[7]

The chapter by Peter Leuprecht reflects the assumption that although the protection of the rights of minorities is of ever-increasing importance in today's multicultural world, it can best be achieved within the confines of existing human rights law and without placing any particular emphasis on the notion of peoples' rights. He places considerable store in the Council of Europe's Framework Convention for the Protection of National Minorities[8] which entered into force in 1998. He also emphasizes the potential importance of the role to be played by the Advisory Committee which was established to

[7] See generally A. Boyle and M. Anderson (eds), *Human Rights Approaches to Environmental Protection* (1996); and A. Cançado-Trindade (ed.), *Human Rights, Sustainable Development and the Environment* (1992).

[8] ETS No. 157.

assist the Council's Committee of Ministers to monitor the activities of States Parties to the Convention.[9]

Anne Orford focuses on the right to development in the context of current economic theories and practices, especially those linked to the phenomena of globalization, that she sees as a threat to the enjoyment of human rights. She traces the history of the emergence of the concept and the extent to which the debate was, and still remains, mired in a struggle between North and South. She then explores the principal areas of contention that have plagued much of the debate in this area. They include the question whether individuals or states are the subjects or bearers of the right, whether the right to development trumps other human rights, and what is meant by 'development' in this context. But rather than remaining in a zone of abstraction that seems so attractive to many of the proponents as well as opponents of the right, she applies her findings to the concrete policies, projects and actions of the three international institutions that she identifies as having the greatest influence over the shape of the global development process: the International Monetary Fund, the World Bank and the World Trade Organization. She demonstrates considerable scepticism as to the extent to which either human rights norms in general or the right to development have been taken into account in most of these areas.

Orford is not, however, an unabashed proponent of the right to development. She is highly critical of the ways in which it has been used and abused in the relevant debates and concludes that it is principally useful as a 'site of international resistance' to the agenda of the international economic institutions. For this to happen, however, it is essential to move beyond the assumption that there are spheres of activity which are immune to the reach of rights discourse.

Among the key questions that emerge from this survey are whether the category of peoples' rights, which is said to be firmly established within international law,[10] is a viable one and whether it adds significantly to our capacity to address some of the key challenges confronting the international community in the twenty-first century? In some respects at least, the present volume proceeds on the assumption of an affirmative answer to both of these questions. But that does not necessarily mean that all of the contributors share the view that the various rights usually included within this category or class of rights actually make up a coherent group of peoples' rights which share certain fundamental characteristics and which are central to any 'progressive' agenda within the field of human rights. In fact, it is clear that the peoples'

[9] Pentassuglia, 'Monitoring Minority Rights in Europe: The Implementation Machinery of the Framework Convention for the Protection of National Minorities—With Special Reference to the Role of the Advisory Committee', 6 *International Journal on Minority and Group Rights* (1999) 417.

[10] Crawford, 'Some Conclusions', in Crawford, supra note 3, at 166.

dimension of each of the rights is very far from being consistent from one right and one context to the next. Perhaps the appropriate response is that there is no need for a shared conception as long as it is sufficiently clear in each context what is meant by the use of the term 'peoples'. Alternatively, it might be concluded that the term 'peoples' rights' is, in effect, a legal fiction, albeit one that has been embraced with both vigour and consistency by many of the participants in the debates over international human rights policy, whether in the legal, diplomatic, or political arenas, in the scholarly literature, or in the increasingly vocal views put forward by NGOs and their civil society cohorts.

Law has always made good use of legal fictions, generally defined as assumptions of a beneficial or at least harmless character which are intended to promote a just outcome.[11] If we accept this approach then the question is whether the cause of international human rights law is furthered by the maintenance of the fiction that there is a separate and coherent category of peoples' rights or whether the maintenance of such a fiction might actually be harmful in some ways. For example, its invocation in a particular context might prevent a more systematic and open-minded analysis of the vital issues which really need to be addressed. It might posit artificial but misleading similarities among a heterogeneous group of rights, thereby saddling each of the debates with ideological baggage which is out of date, not well founded, or of at best marginal relevance.

These and many other questions are explored in the chapters that follow. It is clear that, whatever conclusions we might draw from them, the concept of peoples' rights will continue to be a significant reference point in the future debates over international human rights law and policy.

[11] See generally L. Fuller, *Legal Fictions* (reprinted 1967, originally published in 25 *Illinois Law Review* (1930–1)); and P. Olivier, *Legal Fictions: An Analysis and Evaluation* (1975).

2

The Right of Self-Determination in International Law: Its Development and Future

JAMES CRAWFORD[1]

Introduction

The 'right of self-determination of peoples' is perhaps the most controversial and contested of the many controversial and contested terms in the vocabulary of international law. It was not of course invented by lawyers, or even by President Wilson; it goes back at least to the nationalist movements of the nineteenth century.[2] But because it was gradually incorporated in texts, was given effect to in various institutional arrangements, was the core of key disputes over the future of territory and people (disputes which had legal dimensions or which were sought to be resolved through legal procedures), it entered the language of international law, and it seems to have done so irrevocably. And yet there remain central uncertainties about the notion, which I hope to address in this chapter.

There are two parts to this account. In the first part I discuss the development of the right of self-determination. In the second part I look to the future of self-determination, with its precarious balance between respect for the identity and right to self-government of peoples, and at the same time respect for the territorial integrity of existing states, however they may have been constituted and whatever the ethnic or national affiliations or aspirations of their populations.

The underlying issue is this: to what extent is self-determination a useful element in the debates that are going on about the dissolution and re-creation of states and the protection of distinct groups within the state—whether they are ethnic groups, cultural, religious or linguistic minorities, indigenous peoples or others? Of course, that question is much broader than a merely legal

[1] Thanks to Roger O'Keefe and Tom Grant for their assistance with the research for this chapter.

[2] See A. Cobban, *The Nation State and National Self-Determination* (1968).

one. Self-determination was a battle cry long before it was a legal principle, and some would say it is only precariously a legal principle now. When lawyers talk about self-determination (and a review of the literature shows that they do only too often[3]), they usually assume that law, and in particular international law, is *relevant* to the broader question. So it is appropriate first to make some comments on that assumption.

The essential difficulty is that the various groups, communities, societies and peoples of the world are extraordinarily diverse and largely commingled. With rare exceptions, they do not exist on discrete territories, exclusive of the territories occupied by other such groups. To what extent is it useful to conceive of the aspirations for control over their affairs which such diverse groups and societies have—whether in the former Yugoslavia or in Canada or wherever else—in terms of rights? Because the appeal to the right of self-determination is precisely that, an appeal to a right, and the notion of a right has no meaning unless, first of all, we can determine the bearers of the right and the persons who are obliged to respect it and, secondly, unless we can give the right some content.

According to one view, the term 'right'—as it appears in the phrase 'right of self-determination under international law'—has a special and highly qualified sense, and this has an underlying cause, which is the special and qualified sense of the term 'law' as it occurs in the phrase 'international law'. International law may exist—that it exists in some sense seems undeniable—but if it exists, it is only because of its specific character. It exists, as it were, in a special underwater world, in which all analogies with normal life and law above ground are deceptive. According to this view, when we use the word 'law' in the context of international law, we always have to read the word in a special way. We are talking about an essentially fluid medium which does not operate in the way law does in national systems—the systems in which we live and move and have our first legal education. In the international medium, every concept or notion taken from national law carries with it an in-built error of parallax; it is impossible to treat it as unaffected by the translation.

Now up to a point this may be true. International law clearly has certain special characteristics. Its primary subjects are not ordinary people at all but a *numerus clausus* of states and the organizations they have created for various purposes, and this has profound effects on the way in which international law operates, whether you think of it as a system or as a process. Nonetheless, the tradition of international law is that these legal persons exist neither in a pure vacuum nor in a pure flux, but in a society, a society of sorts, no doubt, but a society nonetheless; that international law is the law of that society and that

[3] The best single work is A. Cassese, *Self-Determination of Peoples. A Legal Appraisal* (1995); for a review of which see Crawford 90 *AJIL* (1996) 331. See also the works contained in the bibliography.

it performs at least some of the functions of law in any human society, of limiting and constraining as well as empowering and validating. If we talk about rights, meaning legal rights, we must be talking about norms, principles or rules which are capable of having legal effects, which bind as well as guide, and which are capable of being adjudicated on. Thus if it is said—as the International Court virtually said in the *South West Africa* cases in 1966[4]—that the consistency of the apartheid system with the Mandate for South West Africa is a matter of political judgement, and is non-justiciable, we may doubt whether the basic principle of the mandate system is a legal principle at all. And indeed it might not be. Institutions can be established by law to allow orderly, non-legal judgements to be made by the competent persons, as in a trade practices commission which has to consider the case for licensing a restrictive agreement on the grounds of its overall economic efficiency. Even the rule of law does not require the rule of lawyers.

But there is a problem with a merely institutional view of self-determination (i.e. with the view that the international law of self-determination is, as it were, the administrative law of a series of institutions established to oversee the administration of particular territories on political grounds[5]). The question of apartheid, or of self-determination for the people of East Timor or Palestine, is not a question of economic efficiency, or even an issue of nice political judgement. At some level we want to say that it is a question of entitlement or right. No victim of apartheid ever argued that that system was consistent with the principle of self-determination: if that is so, how can a court of justice distance itself from the issue? The argument that it was an economically more efficient way of ruling South West Africa (even if it were true) just seems intolerable.

Alternatively, we might say that self-determination, though in some sense 'legal', does not give rise to real rights. It is not non-justiciable, but its role in reaching judgement in any matter is a qualified one. Within legal systems there can be norms or standards which have a merely directive function. These so-called 'soft' rules form part of legal discourse, they may be capable of influencing outcomes, but they do not bind in their own terms. The 'maxims' of the law—for example, who comes to equity must come with clean hands, no one can benefit from his or her own wrongful act, no right without a remedy—are of this kind. They are directive principles. It may be that self-determination is also of this kind; that it is a legal value but is not a legal norm. Whether this is so, however, cannot be decided in the abstract. We have to see how a putative norm functions in a given legal system, and, especially in the case of self-determination, this requires a historical as much as an analytical inquiry.

[4] ICJ Reports (1966) 6.

[5] This is, no doubt, part of the function of the international law of self-determination. But it is not the whole story, otherwise that 'right' would be merely a *droit de regard*. See Crawford, 'The General Assembly, the International Court and Self-determination' in A.V. Lowe and M. Fitzmaurice (eds), *Essays in honour of RY Jennings* (1996) 585.

PART A

THE DEVELOPMENT OF THE RIGHT OF SELF-DETERMINATION

1. *Lex Lata, Lex Obscura*

The development of the right of self-determination has been above all a historical process. Events have occurred in a particular order and have been responded to, to some extent, on a case by case basis. This is not to say, necessarily, that the law is in an incoherent state, but it has certainly developed in a contingent and often partial and incomplete way. So we have the paradox that the international law of self-determination both exists and is obscure. It is the subject of confident and verifiable statements of claim—the people of East Timor continue to have the right of self-determination as against Indonesia;[6] the people of Quebec have no unilateral right to secession as against Canada.[7] But it is said, and with some justice, to be radically uncertain and insecure. Can this paradox be explained—we might call it the paradox of *lex lata, lex obscura*?

Before seeking to explain it, let me explain why there is a paradox. *Lex lata* is law which is established or laid down. *Lex ferenda* is law which is in the process of being made and therefore is in some sense embryonic, uncertain, unclear, not fully established—not something a court can declare without making new law, to express the point with fine circularity. Now the general view is that the right of self-determination is, in some respects at least, *lex lata* and not *lex ferenda*. Scholars speak of it as an existing right. So did the International Court in a series of cases from 1971 onwards. So does the Human Rights Committee, in its otherwise rather evasive General Comment on Article 1 of the International Covenant on Civil and Political Rights.[8] So, for that matter, does Article 1 of the Covenant itself: 'All peoples have the right of self-determination.' But yet, as almost all would agree, self-determination is also *lex obscura*. No one is very clear as to what it means, at least outside the colonial context. There are major uncertainties about its interpretation and application, uncertainties which seem to go to the heart of the notion of self-determination itself. But how can the two coexist? How can there be a legal concept, a right no less, which is generally admitted to exist when no one knows what it means?

[6] As Australia conceded, and the Court agreed, in the *Case concerning East Timor* ICJ Reports (1995) 90.

[7] As Canada argued, and the Supreme Court held, in *Reference re Secession of Quebec from Canada* [1998] 2 SCR 217.

[8] CCPR/C/21/Add. 3, 5 October 1984.

2. A Short History of Self-Determination and its Relation to General International Law

As I have said, to understand this paradox it is necessary to go back to the history of self-determination. Only through that history can one see how the international legal system has managed to generate a 'right of self-determination' while the questions of the content and bearers of the right have remained, in important respects, open questions.

The history of the principle of self-determination is closely linked to the development of international law in general. It has been through a series of transitions from the period, in about the fifteenth or sixteenth century, when we might say that the law of nations gelled out of the ingredients of natural rights theory and the traditions of thought as to the relations between rulers in Europe. At the time when the law of nations was beginning to be thought of as a separate entity—or at least a separate sub-entity—it had certain characteristics: for example, relative underemphasis on the notion of the state, inclusiveness of various other polities and bodies, a certain emphasis on armed conflict.[9] These changed rather fundamentally with the decline of natural law theory and of belief in the intrinsic connection of law and morality in the early eighteenth century. Vattel is the classic writer of this period, because he encapsulated what international law was then thought to be with great clarity and accessibility. For Vattel, international law was substantially a set of arrangements between states and their rulers as to their mutual conduct.[10] This classical period also saw a huge growth of interstate transactions, the development of modern treaty making, the beginnings of international organization. The First World War was the apotheosis of the period of classical international law, and it was followed by the very uncertain transition of the inter-war period,[11] moving in turn (and entirely contingently, depending as it did on the outcome of the Second World War) to the post-1945 period of Charter international law.

International law in its classical period acquired its distinctive character and its separate role as a positive system of law by deliberately withdrawing from certain contentious areas of international relations. In particular, the Vattelian system withdrew from the regulation of resort to war, and allowed the powers (the states and their rulers) to resolve conflicts through power

[9] See H. Bull, B. Kingsbury and A. Roberts (eds) *Hugo Grotius and International Relations* (1992); P. Haggenmacher, *Grotius et la Doctrine de la Guerre Juste* (1983); Y. Onuma (ed.), *A Normative Approach to War. Peace, War and Justice in Hugo Grotius* (1993); Kennedy, 'Primitive legal scholarship', 27 *Harvard International Law Journal* (1986) 1.

[10] E. de Vattel, *Le Droit des Gens* (1758); F.S. Ruddy, *International Law in the Enlightenment* (1975).

[11] See, still, E.H. Carr, *The Twenty Years Crisis* (1946).

politics, ultimately through resort to force. Classical international law made no attempt to determine when states could resort to war. It only dealt with the question of *how* they would do it, if they did it. Within that system international law, when it came to fundamentals, had a predominantly descriptive role. It treated its subjects, the states, as existing while they existed but it offered no guarantees as to their future. If states ceased to exist, that was as it might be. The law of nations was, in a sense, the codified law of the jungle.

The League of Nations Covenant of 1919, which was part of the post-war peace settlements, marked the period of transition from classical to modern international law. It sought to limit the right, at least of its members, to resort to war but it did not purport to abolish war entirely. There were still residual cases under the Covenant when member states could resort to war: this was the so called 'gap' in the Covenant which it was attempted to fill by the Kellogg–Briand Pact of 1928. But the whole system broke down, step by step, in the face of the dictatorships in the 1930s. It was reconstituted in a rather different and (perhaps fortuitously) a more durable form under the Charter, which formally introduced a full-scale prohibition on resort to the use of force in international relations except in self-defence and gave the Security Council wide powers to maintain international peace and security.

For present purposes, the key point to make about classical international law was that it did not guarantee the rights of states to exist. *A fortiori*, it did not guarantee the rights of non-states to become states. All that was relegated to political processes, as the Poles found to their cost in their long nineteenth century. In that sense too, international law was profoundly descriptive: it prescribed *how* international relations were to be conducted but it was predominantly descriptive of the international relations there would be, i.e. of the outcomes that might follow. There could be international relations both of war and of peace: international law modulated both without precluding either—*temperamenta belli, temperamenta pacis*. Hence there was *jus in bello*, but no (or almost no) *jus ad bellum*: the laws of war, but no law against war. Until international law changed in this respect, it made little sense to talk about the right to become a state. Thus the reason that self-determination (despite its salience as a political value after 1789) did not fit into classical international law was that it aspired to something which classical international law precisely did not try to achieve, that is to constitute or reconstitute states. Classical international law left that to power politics, and therefore, almost by definition, it left the question of self-determination to power politics as well. *Sauve qui peut.* Self-determine *qui peut.*

The change away from classical international law in this regard after 1919 happened only gradually, just as the change of international law towards regulating resort to war between states was only gradual. A very good snapshot of the position under the League of Nations Covenant is provided in the successive decisions of two League of Nations commissions in the 1920s in

the dispute involving the Åland Islands. These islands in the Baltic were the subject of a dispute between Finland and Sweden, at a time when Finland was achieving its independence from Russia. The people of the islands sought to rely on the principle of self-determination, which inspired many of the famous 'Fourteen Points' of President Wilson, and underlay some (but by no means all) of the provisions of the Treaty of Versailles. The question was whether a group of islands, regarded as strategically essential to Finland, could nonetheless break away from Finland and become part of Sweden because their inhabitants (almost entirely Swedish speaking) wanted to do so. In other words—and it is significant that it was put in these terms—did they have a right of self-determination? If Finland was exercising that right *vis-à-vis* Russia, why could not the Ålanders exercise it *vis-à-vis* Finland? This is the recurrent pattern, the recurrent question: the Russian doll proliferates in many different national settings.

The League of Nations set up two commissions to enquire into the issue. First of all, it asked a Commission of Jurists whether this was an international question at all, or (as Finland said) one essentially within its domestic jurisdiction, within Article 15 (8) of the Covenant.[12] The Commission of Jurists said that, in a situation in which Finland itself was not definitively constituted, the issue of the future of the islands was not essentially within its domestic jurisdiction.[13] A second committee was then asked to investigate the merits of the claim, by which time circumstances had changed, and the control of Finland over its territory was much better established. The Committee of Rapporteurs denied that the Ålanders had the right of self-determination.[14] Although advocated by President Wilson, that principle was not incorporated in the Covenant, and did not apply as of right to any territory. Nor was there such a threat of abuse of Finnish sovereignty over the Islands so as to justify making an exception in their case. But the Ålanders *were* entitled to respect for their language and their identity, and a special regime protecting that identity should be established.[15] The result was that the Åland Islands remained part of Finland, but they were given a special autonomy statute in a treaty

[12] The Permanent Court of International Justice had not yet been created, so that an advisory opinion of the Court was ruled out. In fact, although the Court adopted an inclusive position on issues of legal personality and statehood (e.g. in cases involving the Free City of Danzig and Morocco under French protectorate), it never had to deal directly with issues of self-determination, unlike its successor.

[13] LNOJ, Sp Supp. No. 3 (1920).

[14] Report of the Committee of Rapporteurs, 16 April 1921: LN Council Doc. B7/21/68/106[VII]. See J. Crawford, *The Creation of States in International Law* (1979), at 85–7.

[15] Agreed Guarantees for the Autonomy and Swedish Character of the Åland Islands were annexed to the League Council Resolution of 24 June 1921, and a Convention on Demilitarization and Neutralization of the Åland Islands concluded on 20 October 1921.

which the League of Nations guaranteed. In amended form, that regime is still in force, and it seems to have worked well.[16]

Notoriously, the Treaty of Versailles and the counterpart peace treaties of 1919–23 paid regard to the principle of self-determination in some respects and not others. An important case of implicit regard for the interests of the inhabitants of a territory, and in the longer term for their right to self-government, was the mandate system. Fifteen Middle Eastern, African and Pacific Island territories were brought under that system, rather than being directly colonized.[17] The rhetoric of the 'sacred trust of civilization' in the mandate system might have been overdone, but being under that system was of long-term benefit to the peoples concerned, as witness the fact that with only one exception they achieved self-government, through independence or otherwise, either under the League of Nations or subsequently. The only exception is the Palestinians, who are, nonetheless, recognized as having the right of self-determination in respect of the remaining (post-1949) territory of Palestine.[18] Legally the reason the Palestinians have the right of self-determination now was that they had it as of 1922 under the mandate for Palestine.

To summarize, in the transitional, inter-war period of the League of Nations, the *general* issue of self-determination was regarded as political and not legal. But, at another level, self-determination could have particular effects if it was included in some particular regime and recognized, explicitly or expressly, as part of that regime.

A further element of the League of Nations/Treaty of Versailles system was the establishment of minority guarantees. These were essentially a concession made to the notion of ethnic and cultural distinctiveness in various regions of Europe, for groups whose claims to self-determination or independence had been denied. Again, however, these were established under specific treaties. There was no general right to be treated as a minority under the Covenant, but there were specific minority treaties, just as there was for the Åland Islands. Although the minority regime had some positive features, it was a source of dissent and conflict. The breakdown of the minorities treaties in the 1930s was a symptom of the breakdown of the system as a whole, but it gave the notion of minorities protection a bad name, and this was to have lasting effects in the post-1945 period.

[16] See L. Hannikainen and F. Horn (eds), *Autonomy and Demilitarisation: The Åland Islands in a Changing Europe* (1996), esp. ch. 10. For the Autonomy Statute of 1991 see ibid., at 309.

[17] See the list in Crawford, supra n. 14, at 426–8.

[18] See e.g. Dajani, 'Stalled Between Seasons: The International Legal Status of Palestine During the Interim Period', 26 *Denver Journal of International Law and Policy* (1997) 27. Jordan had previously been separated from Palestine in accordance with the terms of the mandate, and Israel had declared its independence and won the ensuing war.

The system of the United Nations Charter was constructed out of the ruins of the inter-war system. The founders of the Charter system sought to take what was valuable from the League experience (aspects of the organizational structure of the League, the mandate system, the Permanent Court) and to reject what was discredited (the veto for 'lesser powers' on the Council, the minorities treaties, a semi-automatic system of collective security based on the notion of resort to war). There was a general prohibition on the use of force in international relations, which took the League system much further. There was a much stronger role for the Security Council than the League of Nations Council had had. With these changes, international law became—potentially at least—more prescriptive.

Instead of the minority system, the Charter focus was on the principle of human rights for all. The underlying idea was that, rather than potentially divisive regimes for identified minorities, the guarantee of general human rights could fulfil that purpose and more. Rather than recognizing the rights of particular minority groups to practise their religion, to use their language, to have their own schools, etc., general rights of freedom of religion, speech and organization would suffice. General human rights had hardly been recognized at all in the League of Nations Covenant. The Charter moved the focus from minority rights to general human rights, in part because human rights had been so terribly violated in the preceding years, but also on the assumption that if you recognize general human rights, the problems of minorities will thereby be resolved. The minority treaties went into desuetude, and the principle of general human rights was endorsed in stages, starting with general references in the preamble and Article 55 of the Charter, then the Universal Declaration of 1948, and eventually the two International Covenants of 1966 with their committees and reporting and complaints procedures.

As we have seen, the principle of self-determination had been (tacitly) applied to mandates under the League, pursuant to Article 22 of the Covenant. It was maintained, in relation to essentially the same territories, in the form of the International Trusteeship System, which embodied the same principle under a new name and with new machinery.[19] But it was agreed that essentially the same principle should not only be applied to the colonial territories of the defeated powers (as in 1919), but to all colonial territories. That was done in Chapter XI of the Charter, in the form of a Declaration Regarding Non-Self-Governing Territories. So the underlying principle of the mandate system was now applied to all colonial territories.

It was thus, for purely historical reasons, that the category of colonial territories fell into two groups. The first group included those territories which had

[19] Charter, Chapter XII. Article 80 preserved the existing rights of states and peoples pending the conclusion of trusteeship agreements for the mandated territories.

been mandates and which (if they had not achieved independence) were brought under the trusteeship system. The remaining colonial territories were covered by Chapter XI. All these territories were seen as falling in some sense under the rubric of self-determination.

The Charter itself linked human rights and self-determination, in Article 1 and again in Article 55. Article 55 referred to the need for 'peaceful and friendly relations among nations based on the principle of equal rights and self-determination of peoples', and called on the United Nations to foster human rights for all in order to achieve that goal. But these references were somewhat ambiguous: what was the effect of the reference of self-determination in Articles 1 and 55 of the Charter, so far as non-colonial territories were concerned? Did this mark a change from the League of Nations? As we have seen, under the League of Nations general self-determination was regarded as essentially political, and self-determination as it applied to particular colonial territories was regulated by special instruments. Under the Charter, there were references to self-determination in the general sense, and these were new. The extension of self-determination to all colonial territories under Article 73 of the Charter was also new.

The initial view of the situation was that although self-determination had been extended to all colonial peoples, it stopped there. That view was largely held throughout the 1950s and 1960s. But the increasing third world majority in the General Assembly regarded self-determination as one of its major priorities and in a series of resolutions they insisted on it, on its generality, and on the inadmissibility of excuses put up by some of the colonial powers (especially Portugal and Spain) to prevent the application of self-determination to their territories. Portugal and Spain—and also France to some extent—claimed that their so-called colonies were not colonies at all, but were an integral part of their metropolitan territory. Algeria was simply a department of France and therefore had no separate right of self-determination. Faced with such claims, which were persisted in by Portugal and Spain, the General Assembly started to develop criteria for determining for itself which were the territories to which Article 73 of the Charter would apply. As early as 1952, it insisted that Article 1 of the draft international covenant on human rights should contain a statement that all peoples have the right of self-determination.[20] In addition, many

[20] The inclusion of the right of self-determination in a document devoted primarily to individual human rights derives from a decision of the United Nations General Assembly as long ago as 1952. In Resolution 545 (VI) the Assembly decided to include: 'in the International Covenant or Covenants on Human Rights an article on the right of all peoples and nations to self-determination in reaffirmation of the principle enunciated in the Charter of the United Nations. This article shall be drafted in the following terms: "All peoples shall have the right of self-determination" and shall stipulate that all States including those having responsibility for the administration of Non-Self-Governing Territories should promote the realization of that right in conformity with the Purposes and Principles of the United Nations and that States having responsibility for the administration of Non-Self-Governing Territories should promote the

western states were not prepared to say that self-determination was purely colonial. For various reasons, they sought to treat it as a general principle.

The most important of the General Assembly resolutions which expressed these developments was Resolution 1514 (XV). This proclaimed the right of self-determination for all colonial peoples. In the same year, Resolution 1541 (XV) sought to lay down the criteria for non-self-governing territories under Chapter XI of the Charter. It was on this basis that the General Assembly determined, for example, that East Timor was a non-self-governing territory.[21] By such processes, the principle of self-determination was extended to all colonial territories (in practice, a list of specified territories to which additional territories were selectively added[22]), and it was gradually made more stringent in its application to those territories. This process was specifically endorsed by the International Court in the *Namibia* opinion in 1971,[23] and again in the *Western Sahara* opinion in 1975.[24] It helped to ensure for example that, despite the power of South Africa at the time, Namibia eventually became independent, and that Southern Rhodesia could not sustain its claim to independence on the basis of minority rule.

At the same time there was an unwillingness to accept that self-determination would be specifically limited to colonial territories. Article 1 of the International Covenant was an illustration of that, but no one was very clear what the implications were. In the context of colonies, there was reasonable clarity: colonial self-determination meant the right of these people to determine their future, whether in the form of independence, integration in the administering state or some third state, or free association. Integration with the metropolitan state could occur (as with the people of Hawaii in relation to the United States, and much later the people of the Cocos (Keeling) Islands in relation to Australia). But it was a suspect category, because such integration, as compared with independence, closed off separate self-determination for the future. In principle in such cases, the people concerned had to be consulted through plebiscites, the process of consultation had to be internationally supervised, and their expression of will had to be genuine.[25] If the people concerned were not accorded full self-determination, they retained their special status under the Charter. If they

realization of that right in relation to the peoples of such Territories . . .' GA Res. 545 (VI), 5 February 1952. Voting on the resolution was 42–7(5). For a summary of the debate see *UN Ybk* 1951, at 435–7. For subsequent UN debate see e.g. *UN Ybk* 1952, at 439–47.

[21] GA Res. 1541 (XV), Principles which should guide Members in determining whether or not an obligation exists to transmit the information called for under Article 73e of the Charter (15 December 1960), Annex, Principle 1. GA Res. 1541 was adopted by 69–2 (Portugal, South Africa) with 21 abstentions (including Australia, Belgium, China, France, Italy, Netherlands, New Zealand, Spain, USSR, UK, USA). GA Res. 1542 (XV), 15 December 1960 applied the Principles stated in the Annex to GA Res. 1541 to determine that 9 Portuguese territories fell within the scope of Ch. XI. That resolution was adopted by 68–6 (17).

[22] See the list in Crawford, supra n. 14, at 429–36.

[23] ICJ Reports (1971) 16.

[24] ICJ Reports (1975) 12.

[25] See GA Res. 1541 (XV), Annex, Principles VI-VIII.

elected to enter into an association agreement with the metropolitan state (as did the people of Puerto Rico, and the Cook Islands), then they had the right periodically to reassess what they wanted: in such cases, at least, self-determination was a continuing right.

So far the principles I have outlined are relatively uncontroversial (although they were often controversial at the time). Despite the heavily political context, there is no reason to think that what was involved was not a system of international legal rights and responsibilities. No doubt there was a compliance problem in some cases, but that is not new in international relations, and the record of compliance over time was quite good. One of the valuable functions international law played in such cases was to keep the issue of legal status open, by maintaining the question as a dispute on the agenda of the United Nations. In some cases it did so even where the state directly concerned (e.g. in the early days, Britain in relation to Palestine; more recently Spain in relation to the Spanish Sahara) no longer administered the territory and no longer wished to do so.[26] Indeed international law fulfils that function to this day in such cases as the Western Sahara, East Timor and Palestine. There is a recognition that these situations remain open and are still to be resolved, whatever individual states may wish.

One factor which was important at the time in the reluctance of some legal authorities to accept self-determination as a legal principle was the underlying feeling that somehow self-determination (like other broad humanitarian principles which it was sought to introduce into international law) was non-justiciable. You could tell whether diplomatic immunity had been infringed, but how could you tell whether a people had been denied the right of self-determination? More important still, how could you tell whether it was a people? The notion was radically indeterminate: that was the worry. It is typified in Ivor Jennings' statement that to let the people decide is ridiculous, because first someone must decide who is the people.[27] It was the concern about justiciability, about the need for a clear distinction between international law and international politics, that underlay the decision of the 'statutory' majority of seven judges in the International Court in the *Second South West Africa* cases in 1966. For the Court to decide that the application of apartheid to South West Africa was (or was not) inconsistent with the mandate would involve a political judgement. But lawyers should not make political judgements; they should make legal judgments. Again, the implications of self-determination for the fabric of general international law were at play.

This was, no doubt, a lawyer's concern although there were numerically as many bold spirits on the Court, even in 1966, as there were timorous souls.

[26] There was an important difference: Britain's withdrawal from Palestine was sanctioned by GA Res. 181 (II), the partition resolution, whereas Spain's handover was presented as a fait accompli.

[27] See I. Jennings, *The Approach to Self-Government* (1956), at 56.

But the Court's decision, by the casting vote of the President, in favour of South Africa caused an uproar. Paradoxically it brought the Court into the political realm much more than its earlier, consistent decisions in favour of the General Assembly's position on South Africa had done—decisions which the Court in 1966 virtually refused to follow.[28] There was an immediate change in the electoral balance of the Court and, more subtly, a shift in legal thinking away from the narrow legalism of the 1966 judgment. No doubt legalism has its place. For example, there were real technical difficulties in the way of the Court's key decision in 1950, that the mandate for South West Africa had survived the disappearance of the League. But these were addressed effectively and convincingly by the Court in that opinion. In the end, judgements have to be made in the field of public law, including public international law, and underlying values about the role of law cannot be excluded. In the end, as a great Australian judge said, the question is not whether reasoning in public law matters is 'political'; the question is whether it is compelling.[29] The consideration of values cannot be excluded, whether one is dealing with the separation of powers in constitutional law, or the application of international human rights, or the notion of self-determination. Since 1966, the development of disciplined and principled reasoning in new fields such as international human rights has reinforced the change in the climate of legal thinking which followed the 1966 judgment. For these reasons, the justiciability factor—though still a consideration—has lost some of its salience.

As soon as opportunity permitted, the 'new' Court made a decisive move away from its position of 1966. First, in the *Barcelona Traction* case in 1970, it went out of its way to admit the possibility of a public interest in the enforcement of certain international law obligations, those owed to the international community as a whole (*erga omnes*). It expressly mentioned grave breaches of human rights and of self-determination—though the case had nothing to do with either.[30] Then in 1971, by a sweeping majority of 13–2, it upheld the General Assembly's decision to revoke South Africa's authority over the mandate for South West Africa, referring by way of justification to the importance of the principle of self-determination.[31] The changing balance on the Court can be seen from Judge Fitzmaurice's impassioned dissent: he had been the principal architect of the majority decision in 1966.

In short, there was a decisive move in the period from 1960 through 1971 in favour of treating self-determination as a part of international law. By another historical accident, this coincided with a prolonged attempt by the General Assembly to articulate a Declaration of Principles of International Law as embodied in the Charter, which was eventually adopted without

[28] Especially *Status of South West Africa*, ICJ Reports (1950) 128; *South West Africa Cases (First Phase)*, ICJ Reports (1962) 319.

[29] *State Banking Case* (1947) 74 CLR 31, 82 (Dixon J).

[30] ICJ Reports (1970) 32.

[31] *Namibia Opinion*, ICJ Reports (1971) 12.

a vote in 1970.[32] The principle of equal rights and self-determination of peoples was given a prominent place in the Friendly Relations Declaration, further reinforcing the view that self-determination was an established legal principle.

At the same time there were important inconsistencies in the practice in relation to self-determination. While relatively strong action was being taken against violations of colonial self-determination (sanctions against Rhodesia, the revocation of the mandate for South West Africa, increasing protests at the failure of Portugal to decolonize its African territories), the General Assembly was much more sensitive about claims to self-determination taking the form of secession outside the colonial context, and it tended to overlook even clear cases of 'third world colonialism'. A classic illustration was the case of Eritrea. This was an Italian colony, which was renounced by Italy in the Peace Treaty of 1947; its future fell to be decided by the General Assembly. Rather than being placed under trusteeship, Eritrea was placed under temporary administration. After consultation, the General Assembly decided in 1952 that it would be federated with Ethiopia but on a basis of considerable local autonomy.[33] For historical reasons, the Eritreans regarded themselves as distinct from Ethiopia, but their leaders were reluctantly prepared to join Ethiopia on the basis of a federation which respected their right to autonomy (and, incidentally, gave Ethiopia a seacoast). But within a few years, the Emperor of Ethiopia, Haile Selassie, abolished the federation and integrated Eritrea into Ethiopia. That was the beginning of a war of independence which would last for 30 years. The point is that there was no public criticism of Ethiopia on the part of the United Nations, despite the fact that the abolition of Eritrea's autonomy was a breach of the arrangements of 1952. So there appeared to be a double standard, with tolerance for third world as distinct from Western or 'salt water' colonialism. The reluctance of the General Assembly to criticize Indonesia in respect of West Irian and especially East Timor, or Morocco in respect of Western Sahara, lent support to the criticisms.

One possible justification for the position taken in respect of Eritrea was that self-determination was a once-for-all right. Once exercised, it disappeared with the separate international identity of the territory in question. Even if special arrangements had been made, or special guarantees given, these were not an expression of the continuing self-determination of the people concerned, and they did not affect the right of the state in question to govern the territory. But if that were so, the further implication might seem to follow that colonial self-determination was a special phenomenon, disconnected from any

[32] GA Res. 2625 (XXV), 24 October 1970.
[33] GA Res. 390 (V), 2 December 1950; cf. GA Res. 617 (VII), 17 December 1952.

broader 'political' principle of self-determination. All that remained, on this view, were the classical standards of sovereignty and non-intervention.[34]

Some other developments occurred in the period since 1975 which are worth mentioning in this brief historical overview.

The first was an attempt to develop a so-called 'third generation' of peoples' rights, modelled on self-determination which, at least in the context of decolonization, had been a considerable success. A group of writers and others with Third World affiliations or sympathies, who were concerned at the continuing and growing gap in economic development between North and South, sought to reconceive the history of human rights. The first generation related to individual civil and political rights, which was presented, rightly or wrongly, as being an essentially Western concern. The second generation related to economic, social and cultural rights, championed in large part by the socialist countries. The third generation was the generation of peoples' rights, and it reflected mainly the concerns of the Third World. Self-determination was a right of peoples, but if it was the first to be accepted it was by no means the only such right. For example, the principle of permanent sovereignty over natural resources could be seen as a right of peoples to long-term control over their own resources, including the right of a later generation to review earlier agreements for the exploitation of natural resources in the light of changed circumstances. Other candidate norms included the right to development.[35]

The concerns which inspired this line of thinking were important and valid, but there were always difficulties with it, not least historical. There is no sharp distinction between 'first generation' and 'second generation' rights. The two Covenants of 1966, concerned respectively with economic, social and cultural rights and with civil and political rights, were coeval in formulation if not inspiration, and both contain mainly individual rights. Indeed the distinction between individual and collective rights can be problematic; many rights (e.g. to democratic participation, to freedom of organization, especially the freedom to form trade unions, and also minority rights) have both individual and collective elements and can be formulated so as to emphasize one rather than the other. Self-determination, admittedly a collective right, is related to individual rights including freedom of speech and association and the democratic right to vote in free elections. It can also be seen as underpinning other (individual) rights, as its location as Article I in a separate part of the two 1966 Covenants implies. Above all, self-determination as a right

[34] Evidently, the people of Eritrea did not agree with this view, and the government of Ethiopia could not sustain the contrary; the civil war ended in 1992 with a peace agreement referring to the right of self-determination of the people of Eritrea, and accepting a plebiscite, as a result of which Eritrea became independent. See E. Gayim, *The Eritrean Question* (1993).

[35] See P. Sieghart, *The Lawful Rights of Mankind* (1986), at 161–8; A. Cassese and E. Jouve, *Pour un droit des peuples* (1978); J. Crawford (ed.), *The Rights of Peoples* (1988).

of peoples in international law has been in issue for as long as the classic individual rights, and Article 55 of the Charter expressly links them.

A further difficulty was that a number of the so-called peoples' rights were, at least as formulated, really rights of states, and especially of developing states against developed states. Thus the rights of peoples debate was linked with the controversy over the Charter of Economic Rights and Duties of States, and with general concerns about neo-colonialism. For example, the principle of permanent sovereignty over natural resources, which has achieved some measure of recognition in international law,[36] is highly equivocal as between a right of states and of peoples. The 1962 General Assembly Declaration on Permanent Sovereignty over Natural Resources is not clear in specifying whether the beneficiary of the principle is the people or the state.[37] If the state has permanent sovereignty over natural resources (and for normal purposes at least, it is the state which is seen as the holder of sovereignty in international law), then there was no reason to treat this as part of any 'third generation'; it was simply a new manifestation of the sovereignty of states over their natural resources in general. On the other hand, if the people of the state have permanent sovereignty over 'their' natural resources, then the possibility must be allowed of the people holding their own government internationally accountable for its stewardship of those resources, with corresponding impacts on the doctrine of non-intervention in matters of domestic jurisdiction—a doctrine firmly held by Third World countries. The key point about self-determination, and about all other human rights, is that these rights are primarily asserted against one's own state. Human rights are exceptionally denied abroad,[38] but the main place where they are violated is at home, in the state of which the victim is a national or resident. The same is true of violations of the rights of peoples. Moreover it is the violations at home which the government of the home state is likely to be least willing to address: the classical international law principle that the government represents the people works badly in that context.

This was not necessarily a reason for rejecting the idea of peoples' rights, but it acted as a check on their development. The debate over peoples' rights has, however, left its mark, notably in the language and in some of the content of the African Charter of Human and Peoples' Rights.[39]

I turn to a second and more recent development (which may still in time call for a reconceptualization of some of the ideas in the peoples' rights debate). This is the massive recrudescence, especially since 1989, of nationalism and ethnic conflict, which has itself produced, by way of reaction, a raft

[36] See N. Schrijver, *Sovereignty over Natural Resources* (1996).

[37] GA Res. 1803 (XVII), 14 December 1962. The resolution refers mostly to 'peoples and nations', but treats them as if they were states: see e.g. para. 2.

[38] Cf. *Loizidou* case ECHR Ser. A vol. 707 (1996).

[39] 21 *ILM* (1982) 59. The African Charter entered into force on 21 October 1986.

of new standards to protect minority rights. The post-war accommodation, based on the premise of universal rights, has been seen as inadequate, a rediscovery that should have come as no surprise.

Article 27 of the International Covenant on Civil and Political Rights (ICCPR) was a clear expression of the earlier approach. It provides that:

> In those States in which ethnic, religious or linguistic minorities exist, persons belonging to such minorities shall not be denied the right, in community with the other members of their group, to enjoy their own culture, to profess and practise their own religion, or to use their own language.

On the face of it, Article 27 is a completely negative right, a right pregnant with limitations. 'In those States in which . . . minorities exist' implies that there are states in which such minorities do not exist; moreover, it is the state which defines the minority, so that members of the majority enjoy no protection, even though they are locally in a minority (as English speakers in Quebec[40]); above all, the minority has to 'exist' in a state, implying that individuals who come to the state, e.g. as migrant workers, may not constitute a minority there. '[E]thnic, religious or linguistic minorities', and only those, leaving aside 'national' minorities who were the central case of minorities in earlier times. '[P]ersons belonging to such minorities', so that the right is actually an individual right of minority group members, not a right of the minority at all, with the consequence that whether the right is exercised is up to each individual; unlike the state or the nation, minority status is a form of voluntary association. '[S]hall not be denied the right', a deliberately negative formulation; no positive action is required by the state; all it must deny is the act of denial itself; moreover the right presumably comes from elsewhere—having regard to the language of Article 27, the right is an individual right the minority group member has (independently of being such a member), in which case, perhaps, all that Article 27 requires is that the rights which individuals have anyway should not be denied to them because they are members of a minority; they are not to be discriminated against on that ground (but discrimination is outlawed already, by Articles 2 and 26). '[I]n community with the other members of their group', further language emphasizing the nature of a minority as a voluntary association, although at least the state is not to prevent individual rights being exercised in the company of others (there is no trace of a suggestion, in the rest of the Covenant, that the state might lawfully do so anyway). '[T]o enjoy their own culture, to profess and practise their own religion, or to use their own language', these being things they might as individuals do in any event, and the *travaux* make it clear that these rights the state may not impede, but it need in no way assist, through funding bilingual education, for example.

[40] At least according to the majority of the Human Rights Committee in *Ballantyne, Davidson, McIntyre v Canada*, Communications Nos 359/1989 and 385/1989.

Thus Article 27 provides little more than that the rights, which the rest of the International Covenant says that everyone has, are not to be denied to members of certain minorities. But since 1989 it has become clear that universal human rights, important as they are, are not enough to address some minority situations. The problem is partly one of affirmative action, but more one of tolerance of difference. Underlying it is the fact that the state is allowed by human rights standards to impose national values and arrangements (funding schools only in the majority language, for example; insisting on the renaming of towns, if not of people). In such cases, as the Permanent Court saw long ago, the situation of a minority may require different (albeit 'equal') arrangements.[41] In short the preservation of human rights is compatible with at least the more subtle forms of assimilation, and this is resisted by minority groups.[42]

The events in the former Yugoslavia were the most visible signs of the difficulty, although it existed in other parts of Central Europe, the Middle East and elsewhere. In part the dynamic arose from the refusal of external self-determination to groups within the state, especially the sub-groups in the successor states of the former Yugoslavia and the Soviet Union. In those cases, minority guarantees (including strong forms of 'national' autonomy) were a *substitute* for what the Bosnian Serbs, the Kurds, the Kosovans, the Chechnyans, the South Ossetians sought. In other contexts (e.g. the Hungarian minority in Slovakia), secession was not an issue, but the shadow of a former sovereignty somehow fuelled the debate. Thus there has been since 1990 an immense and rapid attempt to reconstruct minority rights, through a General Assembly declaration, through the work of the Organization on Security and Cooperation in Europe (OSCE), and through various treaties, regional and bilateral.[43] At the same time there has been a spate of new states arising through the breakdown of existing state structures, in situations analogous to the older self-determination struggles. During the period 1945–89 there was hardly a single case of the successful breakaway of a state outside the colonial context; the only example (and that, quasi-colonial) was Bangladesh. In the period 1990–5, more than 20 new states came into existence or (in the case of the Baltic states) were restored to existence. The implications of this experience in the longer term remain to be

[41] *Minority Schools in Albania* PCIJ Ser. A/B No. 64 (1935).

[42] A good example of the difficulty groups within the state have, but the state does not, relates to the right to control their composition and access to their lands. Cf. ICCPR, Art. 12 (freedom of residence within the state), and compare the *Lovelace* case, Communication No. R 6/24, GAOR A/36/40 (1981) 166 and *Gerhardy v Brown* (1985) 57 ALR 472.

[43] See e.g. CSCE, Copenhagen Document, 29 June 1990, 29 *ILM* (1990) 1305; CSCE, Helsinki Decision Establishing a High Commissioner on National Minorities 31 *ILM* (1992) 1396; GA Res. 48/138, Declaration on the Rights of Persons Belonging to National or Ethnic, Religious and Linguistic Minorities, 20 December 1993; Council Of Europe, Framework Convention for the Protection of National Minorities, Strasbourg, 1 February 1995, ETS No. 157 (1995), and see further W. Kymlicka, *The Rights of Minority Cultures* (1996).

seen. At present we have the spectre of third states and international organizations intervening to insist on minority guarantees for groups whose own overriding concern is external self-determination. Whether such policies are wise, or can succeed, is an open question, but at least they have meant that the linkages between external and internal self-determination are being re-emphasized, and that the idea of minority rights has re-emerged.[44]

In a less dramatic but still important way, something of the same has been occurring in the context of indigenous rights. Indigenous peoples (increasingly vocal not only in the countries of settlement in North America and Australasia but also in places such as Brazil) reject being treated as members of a minority and seek separate recognition of their identity as the original peoples of their land, and they use the language of self-determination. The term is included, for example, in Article 4 of the Draft Declaration on the Rights of Indigenous Peoples, which is still under negotiation.[45] But it is understood, and is likely to be emphasized still more by states in the further negotiation of the Draft Declaration, that the reference to self-determination is to internal self-determination, and that indigenous peoples are to work out their future within the boundaries of the state in which they happen to be. Again, however, the new insistence by sub-state groups on their identity and rights is reinforcing the notion of internal self-determination.

The third development which needs to be mentioned here is that since 1989 the international system has begun to take the notion of democratic rights seriously. The essential democratic right is the right to participate in one's self-government, through elections and in other ways. That right was actually included in the Universal Declaration of 1948, unlike self-determination and minority rights, neither of which was mentioned.[46] It is reformulated in Article 25 of the ICCPR. If you regard self-determination as essentially a summary of other rights (as its position in a separate Part of the ICCPR might imply), then a key right to self-determination is the right to participate democratically in the political system to which you belong, and to participate in decisions as to its future. On this view, self-determination is a continuing right, the collective expression of the individual rights of the members of each political society.

Although proclaimed both in the Universal Declaration and the ICCPR, for many years the notion of democratic rights was largely ignored.[47] Most countries in the world were not democracies; if they were called 'The Democratic State of . . .', still more the 'People's Republic of . . .', that was a

[44] See also CSCE, Report of the Meeting of Experts on National Minorities, 19 July 1991, 30 *ILM* (1991) 1692.

[45] E/CN.4/Sub.2/1994/45, reproduced at 34 *ILM* (1995) 541.

[46] Universal Declaration of Human Rights, 10 December 1948, Art. 21.

[47] Cf. the International Court's very reserved treatment of democratic commitments in the *Nicaragua* case, ICJ Reports (1986) 14, at 131.

fair indication that democratic values were disregarded in the state concerned. But after 1989, democratic rights started to be taken more seriously, through various developments which have been discussed elsewhere.[48] The point was this: if the international system was going to take democratic rights seriously, was going to insist, at some level, on the illegitimacy of non-democratic governments, then it was more defensible to treat self-determination as a summary of other rights. If self-determination is a once-for-all event, its link with democratic rights is an occasional one. But democracy makes sense only as a continuing process. If it is a key component of self-determination, this in turn reinforces the idea that self-determination is a continuing right of all peoples.

But there is still a problem. It is all very well to have a vote, and even an equal vote, but if you are in a minority and you do not want to be part of the society in which the vote is occurring, your democratic rights may not mean very much to you. The denial of external self-determination could be alleviated by the development and extension of democratic rights, as by the development of minority rights. But the issue of external self-determination remains, and with it the issue of coherence I have mentioned already.

In short, through the historical and political processes I have outlined, the language of self-determination came to be fixed in the international debate and in authoritative texts, and as we will see more clearly in a moment, that language was universal in its terms. In a way this anticipated, as it now valuably reinforces, new emphases on internal self-determination, on democratic, indigenous and minority rights. But it did not, and does not, solve the problems produced by the artificiality of many state structures, the lack of regard for ethnic and national identities in boundary drawing, and above all the mixed and overlapping character of human communities in so many states. Hence *lex lata, lex obscura.*

3. Self-Determination Through the Texts and the Cases

Now it may be objected that this is an exaggerated and unduly provocative account. After all, there are international documents and decisions which express the right of self-determination in apparently canonical ways. Is it not the case that self-determination in international law is as expressed in these sources?

[48] See, e.g. Cerna, 'Universal Democracy: An International Legal Right or the Pipe Dream of the West?', 27 *NYU Journal of Int'l Law and Politics* (1995) 289; Crawford, 'Democracy in International Law', 64 *BYIL* (1993) 113; Franck, 'The Emerging Right to Democratic Governance', 86 *AJIL* (1992) 46; B. Roth, *Governmental Illegitimacy in International Law* (1999).

(a) Some basic texts

Taking first the treaties and other texts, I have already referred to the relevant provisions of the Charter (Articles 1 and 55, Chapters XI and XII).[49] Let me refer to some of the more important later instruments.

The first is common Article 1 to the two Human Rights Covenants of 1966. This reads in full as follows:

> 1. All peoples have the right of self-determination. By virtue of that right they freely determine their political status and freely pursue their economic, social and cultural development.
> 2. All peoples may for their own ends freely dispose of their natural wealth and resources without prejudice to any obligations arising out of international economic cooperation, based upon the principle of mutual benefit and international law. In no case may a people be deprived of its own means of subsistence.
> 3. The States Parties to the present Covenant including those having responsibility for the administration of Non-Self-Governing and Trust Territories shall promote the realization of the right of self-determination and shall respect that right in conformity with the provisions of the Charter of the United Nations.[50]

Its inclusion in both Covenants suggests that self-determination is both a civil and political right and an economic, social and cultural right. Its inclusion, alone, in a separate untitled Part I in each Covenant suggests that it is in some sense special, though this does not necessarily mean that it has a heightened status.[51]

Just as a matter of ordinary treaty interpretation, one cannot interpret Article 1 as limited to the colonial case. Article 1, paragraph 1 does not say that some peoples have the right of self-determination. Nor can the term 'peoples' be limited to colonial peoples. Article 3 deals expressly, and non-exclusively, with colonial territories. When a text says that 'all peoples' have a right—the term 'peoples' having a general connotation—and then in another paragraph of the same article, it says that the term 'peoples' includes the peoples of colonial territories, it is perfectly clear that the term is being used in its general sense. Any remaining doubt is removed by paragraph 2, which deals with permanent sovereignty over natural resources. It is true that there are difficulties in dealing with the notion of permanent sovereignty as a right of peoples rather than states, as I have noted. But that is not the point here. No one has ever suggested that the principle of permanent sovereignty over natural resources is limited to colonial territories. So far as the interpretation of Article 1 goes, that surely settles the point.

[49] For an analysis of the Charter *travaux*, see Quane, 'The United Nations and the Evolving Right to Self-determination', 47 *ICLQ* (1998) 537, at 541–4.

[50] See ibid., 558–62.

[51] Cf. the International Court's holding, in a quite different context, that Art. 1 of a bilateral Treatment of Amity had no independent meaning: *Case concerning Oil Platforms (Preliminary Objections)*, ICJ Reports (1996) 803.

Some governments have argued for the contrary view. The Indian government, in ratifying the ICCPR, declared that in Article 1 'the words "the right of self-determination" . . . apply only to the peoples under foreign domination and . . . these words do not apply to sovereign independent States or to a section of a people or nation—which is the essence of national integrity.' But there are many difficulties in restricting the right conferred by Article 1 to colonial countries and peoples. The term 'peoples' in paragraph 1 cannot possibly have a different and narrower meaning than it evidently has in paragraph 2.

Three objections were made to India's reservation, by the Netherlands, France and the Federal Republic of Germany. The Netherlands stated that:

the right of self-determination as embodied in the Covenants is conferred upon all peoples. This follows not only from the very language of Article 1 common to the two Covenants but as well from the most authoritative statements of the law concerned, i.e. the Declarations of Principles of International Law concerning Friendly Relations and Co-operation among States in accordance with the Charter of the United Nations. Any attempt to limit the scope of the right or to attach conditions not provided for in the relevant instruments would undermine the concept of self-determination itself and would thereby seriously weaken its universally acceptable character.[52]

France stated that the Indian reservation was objectionable because it:

attaches conditions not provided for by the Charter of the United Nations to the exercise of the right of self-determination. The present declaration will not be deemed to be an obstacle to the entry into force of the Covenant between the French Republic and the Republic of India.[53]

The Federal Republic of Germany, likewise, 'strongly' objected to the reservation:

The right of self-determination as enshrined in the Charter of the United Nations and as embodied in the Covenants applies to all peoples and not only to those under foreign dominations. All peoples, therefore, have the inalienable right freely to determine their political status and freely to pursue their economic, social and cultural development. The Federal government cannot consider as valid any interpretation of the right of self-determination which is contrary to the clear language of the provision in question. It moreover considers that any limitation of their applicability to all nations is incompatible with the object and purpose of the Covenants.[54]

In the context the fact that there were only three objections is not specially significant (there are even fewer reservations to Article 1). So far as India is concerned, the effect of its reservation will be judged objectively, it being significant that some states objected to it, so that it cannot be argued that the point went unchallenged.

[52] CCPR/C/2/Add.5 (1982), 3. [53] Ibid. [54] CCPR/C/2/Add.4 (1980), 4.

For these reasons, as a matter of interpretation the view expressed to the General Assembly's Third Committee in 1985 by the United Kingdom seems clearly correct:

It is no accident that the first Article of each of the International Covenants proclaims the right of self-determination. We should always remember that under the Covenants self-determination is a right of peoples and not of governments. Moreover, it is not only peoples suffering occupation by a foreign power which are deprived of their right of self-determination. We are all aware of appalling violations of the right of self-determination, accompanied by equally appalling violations of many other fundamental rights, perpetrated against peoples by their own countrymen. Amin's atrocities in Uganda and Pol Pot's in Cambodia are perhaps the most glaring contemporary examples. But they are by no means the only ones. Self-determination is not a single event, but a continuous process.[55]

Article 1 which formulates the right of self-determination in the context of human rights is paralleled by provisions in some other human rights instruments. There was no reference to self-determination in the Universal Declaration of Human Rights, nor for that matter in the American Convention or the European Covenant. But it is included in the African Charter of Human and Peoples' Rights,[56] which was adopted by the Organization of African Unity in 1981. As noted above, this is the first regional human rights instrument to deal in any way with 'collective' rights. The relevant provisions of the African Charter are Articles 19 and 20, which provide as follows:

Article 19
All peoples shall be equal; they shall enjoy the same respect and shall have the same rights. Nothing shall justify the domination of a people by another.
Article 20
1. All peoples shall have the right to existence. They shall have the unquestionable and inalienable right to self-determination. They shall freely determine their political status and shall pursue their economic and social development according to the policy they have freely chosen.
2. Colonized or oppressed peoples shall have the right to free themselves from the bonds of domination by resorting to any means recognized by the international community.
3. All peoples shall have the right to the assistance of the States Parties to the present Charter in their liberation struggle against foreign domination, be it political, economic or cultural.

Again it is clear from the contrast between Article 20(1) and (2), as well as from the use of the term 'peoples' elsewhere in the Charter, that the

[55] Cited in G. Marston (ed.) 'United Kingdom Materials on International Law 1985', 56 *BYIL* (1985) 460.

[56] See further D'Sa, 'Human and Peoples' Rights: Distinctive Aspect of the African Charter', 29 *JAfL* (1985) 72; and the essays of Balanda, Benedik and Kunig in K. Gunther and W. Benedek (eds), *New Perspectives and Conceptions of International Law* (1983).

principle of self-determination enunciated in Article 20 is intended to be general in its scope.

A second important formulation of the principle of self-determination is contained in General Assembly Resolution 2627 (XXV), on Principles of International Law concerning Friendly Relations and Cooperation among States in Accordance with the Charter of the United Nations (the Friendly Relations Declaration). I have already explained the historical importance of the Declaration for our purposes, but it is important also in that it seeks to spell out the implications of self-determination in more detail than other texts. As a General Assembly resolution the Declaration is of course not a binding document. But it remains indicative of widely held views on the subjects it deals with, and its formulations have been substantially followed, for example in the 1993 Vienna Statement.[57] In referring to 'The principle of equal rights and self-determination of peoples' the Declaration states, in part, as follows:

> By virtue of the principle of equal rights and self-determination of peoples enshrined in the Charter of the United Nations, all peoples have the right freely to determine, without external interference, their political status and to pursue their economic, social and cultural development, and every State has the duty to respect this right in accordance with the provisions of the Charter.
>
> . . .
>
> The establishment of a sovereign and independent State, the free association or integration with an independent State or the emergence into any other political status freely determined by a people constitute modes of implementing the right of self-determination by that people.
>
> . . .
>
> The territory of a colony or other non-self-governing territory has, under the Charter, a status separate and distinct from the territory of the State administering it; and such separate and distinct status under the Charter shall exist until the people of the colony or non-self-governing territory have exercised their right of self-determination in accordance with the Charter. . .
>
> Nothing in the foregoing paragraphs shall be construed as authorizing or encouraging any action which would dismember or impair, totally or in part, the territorial integrity or political unity of sovereign and independent States conducting themselves in compliance with the principle of equal rights and self-determination of peoples as described above and thus possessed of a government representing the whole people belonging to the territory without distinction as to race, creed or colour.
>
> Every State shall refrain from any action aimed at the partial or total disruption of the national unity and territorial integrity of any other State or country.[58]

[57] United Nations World Conference on Human Rights, Vienna Declaration and Programme of Action, 25 June 1993, 32 *ILM* (1993) 1661.

[58] See further McWhinney, 'The New Countries and the New International Law: The UN's Special Conference on Friendly Relations and Cooperation among States', 60 *AJIL* (1966) 1; Johnson, 'Towards Self-determination—A Reappraisal as Reflected in the Declaration on Friendly Relations', 3 *Georgia JICL* (1973) 145.

Apart from an inclusive reference to 'alien subjugation, domination and exploitation', the Declaration does not define the term 'peoples', but the reference to 'a government representing the whole people belonging to the territory', in the penultimate paragraph, would be unnecessary and even irrelevant if the principle of self-determination applied only to colonial territories.

The third instrument to which I want to refer is also a regional instrument, this time from Europe. The Final Act of the Conference on Security and Cooperation in Europe of 1975 (the Helsinki Declaration)[59] is again in the form of a non-binding declaration rather than a treaty. Its significance is as a statement of views rather than a formal commitment. But it had a considerable currency and influence in East-West diplomacy, and led later to the OSCE and its various institutions. For present purposes the Declaration is important because it includes the principle of 'Equal rights and self-determination of peoples'. Of course the Final Act was concerned only with Europe, which contains virtually no Chapter XI territories.[60] The argument that the principle was therefore irrelevant was expressly rejected at the Helsinki Conference.[61] The Final Act provides in part as follows:

> The participating States will respect the equal rights of peoples and their right to self-determination, acting at all times in conformity with the purposes and principles of the Charter of the United Nations and with the relevant norms of international law, including those relating to territorial integrity of States. By virtue of the principle of equal rights and self-determination of peoples, all peoples always have the right, in full freedom, to determine, when and as they wish, their internal and external political status, without external interference, and to pursue as they wish their political, economic, social and cultural development.

As Arangio-Ruiz points out, these paragraphs unequivocally adopt the broader view of self-determination, including its extension to matters of internal political status, and 'political, economic, social and cultural development.'[62] The notion of self-determination was clearly seen to be applicable to the Soviet Union, to Eastern Europe and to Western Europe.

Thus the principle of self-determination has been articulated, and has had its effects, in indisputably non-colonial contexts. A careful study of the texts leads inevitably to the conclusion that the right of self-determination is

[59] 14 *ILM* (1975) 1292.

[60] Except for Gibraltar, the only European territory on which information has been submitted under Art 73 of the Charter. See H.S. Levie, *The Status of Gibraltar* (1983), at 102–22. In recent years there has been an important clarification of the status of certain other European entities (Andorra, Monaco). Although it was never suggested that they were colonial territories, the principle of self-determination has been relevant to these debates. See J. Duursma, *Self-determination, Statehoood and the International Relations of Micro-States* (1996).

[61] See Arangio-Ruiz, 'Human Rights and Non-intervention in the Helsinki Final Act', 157 *Hague Recueil* (1977) 195, at 227–8.

[62] Ibid., at 224–31.

articulated as a right, and that it is of general application. On the other hand, with the partial exception of certain paragraphs of the Friendly Relations Declaration, the texts do little to resolve other uncertainties about the meaning and scope of self-determination, at least outside the colonial context.

(b) Some key decisions

A second category of sources for the international law of self-determination is the decisions of international courts and tribunals. It is true that these decisions do not have the same formal status as the Charter or as treaties; they are only binding on the States Parties. But nonetheless what the International Court, especially, says international law is, is influential, and may be definitive. Since 1950 the Court has had to deal with issues of self-determination, one way or another, nine times (no fewer than six decisions concerning South West Africa (Namibia), plus Northern Cameroons, Western Sahara, East Timor). In addition, such issues have arisen peripherally in a number of other cases.[63] Beginning with the *Status of South West Africa* opinion in 1950, the Court has generally favoured the solution most consistent with the self-determination of the people concerned, and since 1970 it has been verbally consistent in its pronouncements in favour of self-determination. For example in the *Namibia* opinion in 1971, the Court said that 'the subsequent development of international law in regard to non-self-governing territories, as enshrined in the Charter of the United Nations, made the principle of self-determination applicable to all of them'.[64]

In the *Western Sahara Advisory Opinion* the Court referred to Articles 1 and 55 of the Charter and stressed that:

> Those provisions have direct and particular relevance for non-self-governing territories, which are dealt with in Chapter XI of the Charter . . . The principle of self-determination as a right of peoples, and its application for the purpose of bringing all colonial situations to a speedy end, were enunciated in the Declaration on the Granting of Independence to Colonial Countries and Peoples, General Assembly Resolution 1514 (XV) . . . The validity of the principle of self-determination defined as the need to pay regard to the freely expressed will of peoples, is not affected by the fact that in certain cases the General Assembly has dispensed with the requirement of consulting the inhabitants of a given territory. Those instances were based either on the consideration that a certain population did not constitute a 'people' entitled to self-determination on or the conviction that a consultation was totally unnecessary, in view of special circumstances.[65]

[63] e.g. *Right of Passage* case, ICJ Reports (1960) 6; *Certain Phosphate Lands in Nauru*, ICJ Reports (1992) 240.

[64] ICJ Reports (1971) 3, 31.

[65] ICJ Reports (1975) 12, 31–3.

Again, and more clearly, the Court affirmed the validity of the principle of self-determination as a legal principle, although again it was concerned with a colonial-type territory.

Two cases however stand out against this general jurisprudence. One, the 1966 decision in the *South West Africa* cases, I have already discussed. The second is the 1995 decision in the *Case concerning East Timor*.[66] The case concerned a 1989 Treaty between Australia and Indonesia establishing provisional arrangements for the exploitation of continental shelf resources in the 'Timor gap', the area between Australia's north-eastern coast and the coast of the former Portuguese colony of East Timor. In 1975, following a partial Portuguese withdrawal from the colony (itself a part of the precipitate Portuguese withdrawal from its overseas territories following the 1974 revolution), Indonesian troops entered the territory and, following a spurious 'consultation' in 1976, purported to annex it as its twenty-seventh province. In 1975 and 1976 the Security Council rather mildly criticized the Indonesian action; the General Assembly also did so, but in increasingly diluted terms, between 1975 and 1982. Thereafter it was so unclear whether the relevant resolution would be passed that it was not put to the vote. Thus the principal organs of the United Nations had fallen silent, faced with a case of 'third world colonialism'. But the United Nations had retained East Timor on the list of Chapter XI territories, and was seeking to reach an agreement which would allow the people of the territory to decide on their future status.

Following the 1989 Treaty, Portugal commenced proceedings against Australia under the Optional Clause (Indonesia not being amenable to the Court's jurisdiction). It argued, in effect, that Australia was obliged not to deal with Indonesia in respect of the territory, but was obliged to respect the territory's continuing status as a Chapter XI territory and Portugal's continuing status as its Administering Authority, recognized as such (however faintly) by the United Nations. There was however a technical difficulty, which arose in the following way. It has been decided in a series of cases that the Court is unable to deal with the merits of a case against state B if, as a necessary prerequisite to doing so, it has to decide on the legal rights or obligations of state C, and state C is not a party and has not consented to this decision.[67] This impediment arises from the strictly bilateral basis of the Court's jurisdiction in contentious cases. In 1995, the Court applied these decisions to the issue of the status of East Timor *vis-à-vis* a 'third state', Australia. In the Court's words:

> Australia's behaviour cannot be assessed without first entering into the question why it is that Indonesia could not lawfully have concluded the 1989 Treaty, while

[66] ICJ Reports (1995) 90.

[67] This is the so-called *Monetary Gold* principle (after the decision in *Monetary Gold Removed from Rome*, ICJ Reports (1954) 19) as applied for example in *Certain Phosphate Lands in Nauru*, ICJ Reports (1992) 240.

Portugal allegedly could have done so; the very subject-matter of the Court's decision would necessarily be a determination whether, having regard to the circumstances in which Indonesia entered and remained in East Timor, it could or could not have acquired the power to enter into treaties on behalf of East Timor relating to the resources of its continental shelf. The Court could not make such a determination in the absence of the consent of Indonesia.[68]

Portugal sought to avoid this difficulty in a number of ways. First, it argued that self-determination was an obligation *erga omnes*, and that Australia's obligation to respect the right of self-determination of the people of East Timor was independent of the obligations of any third state. The Court accepted the premise (the status of the right of self-determination), but summarily denied the conclusion:

Portugal's assertion that the right of peoples to self-determination, as it evolved from the Charter and from United Nations practice, has an *erga omnes* character, is irreproachable. The principle of self-determination of peoples has been recognized by the United Nations Charter and in the jurisprudence of the Court . . . ; it is one of the essential principles of contemporary international law. However, the Court considers that the *erga omnes* character of a norm and the rule of consent to jurisdiction are two different things. Whatever the nature of the obligations invoked, the Court could not rule on the lawfulness of the conduct of a State when its judgment would imply an evaluation of the lawfulness of the conduct of another State which is not a party to the case. Where this is so, the Court cannot act, even if the right in question is a right *erga omnes*.[69]

Secondly, it argued that the United Nations had already decided the relevant issue, the continuing status of East Timor as a self-determination territory despite Indonesia's continuing occupation. As to this, the Court said:

it cannot be inferred from the sole fact that the . . . resolutions of the General Assembly and the Security Council refer to Portugal as the administering Power of East Timor that they intended to establish an obligation on third States to treat exclusively with Portugal as regards the continental shelf of East Timor. The Court notes . . . that several States have concluded with Indonesia treaties capable of application to East Timor but which do not include any reservation in regard to that Territory.[70]

The Court also noted that following the circulation of a Portuguese protest against the 1989 Treaty in the General Assembly and the Security Council, no action was taken by either. Accordingly it could not treat the earlier resolution as dispositive of the dispute.

Clearly the decision both gives and takes away so far as self-determination is concerned. There is verbal support, clear if not effusive, in favour both of the status of self-determination in international law and of the right of self-determination of the people of East Timor. On the other hand, the Court

[68] ICJ Reports (1995), at 102. [69] Ibid., at 102. [70] Ibid., at 103.

adhered strictly to the conditions for its contentious jurisdiction, and refused to treat self-determination as in any way special or distinctive for this purpose.

Two points may however be said in defence of a decision which has been much criticized in the literature. The first is that, evidently, the Court was sensitive to the equivocal position taken by the political organs of the United Nations in relation to East Timor. Had they given a stronger lead (as they had done prior to the *Namibia Opinion*[71]) the decision might well have been different. The second point is that the Court was not assisted by the approach of Portugal, which relied exclusively on the right of self-determination as the basis for an obligation of non-recognition, thereby necessarily calling on the Court to find, as against Indonesia, that the right was being violated. The position might, perhaps, have been different had Portugal relied instead on the obligation on states not to recognize a change of territorial sovereignty procured by the use of force. It seems to be settled that the obligation of non-recognition arises irrespective of the legality of the underlying use of force. For example, it does not matter whether Israel was acting in self-defence in occupying the West Bank and the Gaza Strip during the Six Day War, in the sense that, whether or not it was then acting lawfully, third states were obliged not to recognize its sovereignty over those territories pending a final settlement. But if that is so, it could have been argued that all the Court needed to find in relation to East Timor was that Indonesia's occupation resulted *in fact* from a use of force, whether or not that force was unlawful.[72] It is arguable that the *Monetary Gold* principle only applies to findings as to the legality or illegality of the conduct of a third state, and not to mere findings of fact involving a third state, at least if the facts are manifest and generally recognized. Facts do not of themselves determine legal responsibility, and anyway these facts were public knowledge and were not seriously in dispute.[73] By this route it is at least arguable that the Court could have dealt with the legal issue of Australia's recognition of Indonesia's sovereignty, without infringing the *Monetary Gold*

[71] ICJ Reports (1971) 12. That was an advisory opinion, so that the jurisdictional difficulty in *East Timor* did not arise, or at least not in the same way.

[72] Assume, for example, that instead of simply abandoning the territory to its fate, Portugal had actually handed it over to Indonesia (as Spain effectively did to Morocco and Mauritania in the case of Western Sahara). In such a case the legality of an Indonesian administration would certainly have been raised in a subsequent challenge by Portugal against Australia. Yet, because Portugal's argument focused entirely on self-determination, the factual basis of the Court's decision was indistinguishable in principle from this scenario: the Court could not decide that Indonesia's presence was unlawful.

[73] In the *Corfu Channel* case, ICJ Reports (1949) 4, the Court examined the facts of a dispute over mine-laying involving conduct of a third state, and was able to find Albania responsible. Cf. also *Military and Paramilitary Activities in and against Nicaragua*, ICJ Reports (1986) 14.

principle.[74] Whether it could have dealt with the validity of the 1989 Treaty is another question.

The International Court has never been directly confronted with the issue of self-determination outside the colonial context. In the *Frontier Dispute Case (Burkina Faso v Mali)*, a Chamber went out of its way to affirm the principle of respect for colonial boundaries (*uti possidetis*).[75] But there was no real issue of self-determination in that case, and it has never been suggested that boundaries between existing states should be drawn, or redrawn, by conducting a series of mini-plebiscites along a putative boundary.[76] And in the *Nicaragua* case, the Court applied rather strict, inter-state principles of intervention against the United States in a context where, it was argued, Nicaragua was in breach of certain democratic guarantees.[77] But again the issue of self-determination did not have to be confronted there.

No other international tribunal has had much experience with self-determination issues. The Human Rights Committee might well have done so, had it not held—in a decision which was understandable politically, whether or not it was satisfactory legally[78]—that communications under the

[74] Australia could have argued that, because Indonesia claimed sovereignty over East Timor not on the basis of its 1975 occupation but on the basis of the 1976 'consultation', the legality of that consultation was necessarily raised, and the *Monetary Gold* principle accordingly applied in any event. Indeed it is possible that the Court had this argument in mind, having regard to the very careful way in which it formulated the issue in dispute in para. 28 of its judgment. But it is not clear that the *Monetary Gold* principle can be relied on by a state to avoid the determination of its responsibility, when the issue in question is raised as a defence by that very state. On this assumption, Portugal would have shown all that was necessary, from its point of view, to establish Australia's responsibility, viz. an obligation of non-recognition (not dependent on a prior finding of unlawful conduct by another state) and a breach of that obligation. Arguably the onus would then have shifted to Australia to exonerate itself. Why should it be able to do so, not by showing a valid act of self-determination, or general recognition of Indonesian sovereignty, but simply by alleging such an act and then invoking *Monetary Gold*? At least, in such a case, it should have been incumbent on Australia to show that it had a *plausible* defence on the merits. Yet no one seriously believes (least of all Australia) that the 1976 consultation was plausibly an act of self-determination by the people of East Timor. Indeed Australia was on record as denying its validity, as did the General Assembly in successive resolutions.

[75] *Frontier Dispute Case (Burkina Faso v Mali)*, ICJ Reports (1986) 554.

[76] It is not impossible in principle: inter-cantonal boundaries in Switzerland have been determined on such a basis, down to village level.

[77] ICJ Reports (1986) 14.

[78] Article 41 refers to 'obligations under the present Covenant', and the Optional Protocol refers to 'violations of any of the rights set forth in the Covenant' (Preamble, Arts 1, 2), and to 'any provision of the Covenant' (Art. 4). Article 7 of the Protocol states that: 'Pending the achievement of the objective of resolution 1514 (XV) . . . concerning the Declaration on the Granting of Independence to Colonial Countries and Peoples, the provisions of the present Protocol shall in no way limit the right of petition granted to these peoples by the Charter of the United Nations . . .' Although the rights of petition referred to in Art. 7 include rights to petition about violations of individual rights, their primary focus is on self-determination. If the Optional Protocol categorically excluded communications relating to Art. 1 of the

Optional Protocol cannot be made in relation to the breaches of the right of self-determination under Article 1.[79] The Arbitration Commission set up by the Conference on Yugoslavia (the so-called Badinter Commission) had to deal with arguments relating to self-determination in the former Yugoslavia in a number of its opinions; these will be discussed in the second part of this chapter.

4. Conclusion, or, the Story So Far

As this analysis suggests, the application of the principle of self-determination to 'colonial countries and peoples' is well-established in international law. In the colonial context, disputes and disagreements concern questions of implementation (especially the identification of non-self-governing territories and the relevance of pre-existing territorial claims by other states). There is, nonetheless, general agreement that self-determination is relevant *in principle*,

Covenant it is difficult to see why Art. 7 of the Protocol was necessary. On the other hand Arts 1 and 2 of the Protocol refer only to 'communications from *individuals* . . . who claim to be victims of a violation of any of the rights set forth in the Covenant', and this was quite deliberate. Some drafts of Art. 1 would have allowed applications by or on behalf of groups and organizations: see M.E. Tardu, *Human Rights. The International Petition System* Vol. 1, 1.1A (1985), at 4–9. The possibility of an *actio popularis*, or of group applications, was deliberately rejected: ibid., Vol 2, 1.1, at 29. Consistently with this, Art. 90(b) of the Human Rights Committee's rules of procedure provides that: 'Normally, the communication should be submitted by the individual himself or by his representative; the Committee may, however, accept to consider a communication submitted on behalf of an alleged victim when it appears that he is unable to submit the communication himself.' Where a communication is made on behalf of an alleged victim, the Committee requires that the author justifies his or her authority to submit the communication, for example through demonstrating a close family connection or in some other way. The Committee has therefore rejected communications made by or on behalf of groups or associations: see Communication No. 128/1982, *LA on behalf of UR v Uruguay*, GAOR A/38/40 (1983) 239 (member of a Swedish branch of Amnesty International, who had been working on behalf of a Uruguayan detainee, denied standing to bring a communication on his behalf); Communication No. 104/1981, *J-T and the WG Party v Canada*, GAOR A/38/40 (1983) 231, 236 (rejecting an application on behalf of the WG Party, an unincorporated association); Communication No. 163/1984, *Group of Associations for the defence of the rights of disabled and handicapped persons in Italy v Italy*, GAOR A/39/40 (1984) 198; Communication No R9/35, *Aumeruddy-Cziffra v Mauritius*, GAOR A/36/40 (1981) 134, 139. It allows a single communication to be made by a number of individuals each claiming a violation of their rights in a particular respect, but both the individuals and the circumstances of the violations alleged must be specified with sufficient particularity.

[79] See Communication No. 78/1980, *AD on behalf of Mikmaq Tribal Society v Canada*, GAOR A/39/40 (1984) 200; *Ominayak & the Lubicon Lake Band v Canada*, Communication No. 167/1984, decision of 26 March 1990, para. 32.1, reproduced 11 *HRLJ* (1990) 305; *EP v Colombia*, Communication No. 318/1988, inadmissibility decision of 25 July 1990, para 8.2; *AB v Italy* (South Tyrol Case), Communication No. 413/1990, inadmissibility decision of 2 November 1990, para. 3.2.

whatever particular difficulties of implementation may arise. But the passages quoted from the advisory opinions of 1971 and 1975 have broader implications. The reference to the general language of Articles 1 and 55 of the Charter implies that the principle of self-determination is not limited to colonial territories. The distinction drawn by the Court between the principle itself and its application to colonial territories carries the same implication. Although the Court has not had to confront the issue directly, what it has said is consistent with the general approach taken in the texts, especially Article 1 of the ICCPR. In short, if 'All peoples have the right of self-determination', then it is not the case that only some peoples have that right. Nor is it the case that the only peoples in the world are peoples under colonial rule. It would be strange if self-determination was defined only by its denial. The principle of self-determination continues to be invoked now (e.g. in relation to Northern Ireland, or Kosovo, or Chechnya), at a time when only a handful of colonial territories remain. For these reasons it is clear law, *lex lata*, that the right of self-determination is a right of all peoples.

But the meaning of the principle, outside the colonial context, is still uncertain: it is still *lex obscura*. The problem with self-determination, outside the colonial context, is this: while authoritative sources speak to its existence, it is an intensely contested concept in relation to virtually every case where it is invoked. Hundreds of peoples around the world rely on the notion of self-determination as a basis for their right to respect, if not independence; their positions are usually contested by the governments of states, and almost always when questions of secession arise. Chechnya is not recognized by any state in the world, despite the fact the people of Chechnya have claimed the right of self-determination, and it even seems to have been expressly recognized by agreement with the Russian Federation.[80] Self-determination is invoked by the *Parti québécois* as a reason for the secession of Quebec from Canada and by the Cree Indians within Quebec as a reason for their staying in Canada. Canada denies that the people of Quebec have a right to secede, though it accepts that it will if necessary negotiate in the event of a successful referendum in Quebec. The *Parti québécois* denies that the Cree have the right to secede from Quebec. No doubt if there was a dissenting minority within the Cree, the Cree would deny that the dissenting minority have a right to become part of Quebec.

Kosovo is another example: the people of Kosovo assert the right of self-determination, but the international community's recognition of their rights is, while real, also distinctly qualified. Thus when NATO or the OSCE talks about

[80] Preambular para. 3 of the Joint Declaration, and Principles for Determining the Basics for Mutual Relations between the Russian Federation and the Chechen Republic, 31 August 1996, refers to 'the commonly recognized right of peoples to self-determination, the principles of equality, voluntary and free expression of will, strengthening inter-ethnic accord and the security of peoples', and self-determination is again referred to in Principle 3.

the Kosovo problem, it is stressed that there is no question of any right to independence. Yet it is precisely that right which the people of Kosovo assert.[81]

In short, we have the continued and repeated assertion of the right of self-determination by hundreds of groups, and at the same time the repeated denial of that right, at least if it takes the form of a claim to secession. Simultaneously, the same official sources assert that the right of self-determination exists for all peoples. The logical structure of the argument—whether it is for Kosovo or for Quebec—is very simple: 'we are a people'. How can one deny that the people of Kosovo or Quebec are a people? The term springs to the lips.[82] And 'all peoples have the right of self-determination'. Therefore, 'we have the right of self-determination'. 'All men are mortal, Socrates is a man . . .' We seem to have that rare thing, a legal argument in the form of a syllogism, establishing a contested legal proposition. An ethnic group, a group with a historical continuity and a consciousness, a group evidently entitled to respect, asserts: 'we are a people'. It seems to be so. And all peoples have the right of self-determination. The conclusion is obvious. But what is to be done with it?

PART B

THE FUTURE OF SELF-DETERMINATION

1. The Modern Law of Self-Determination: a Review of the Issues

We saw in the first part of this chapter how the right to self-determination has been proclaimed in quite general terms under the Charter, but that in the period from 1950 to the early 1980s, the main emphasis was on decolonization. One might call decolonization the active part of self-determination in this period, while general self-determination remained legally more a potential than an operative claim (rather like democratic rights in the same period). But the period of decolonization is now passed, leaving only a few outstanding unresolved disputes (e.g. Palestine, Western Sahara). In these cases, no one doubts that self-determination is relevant, but the problem is still to find a satisfactory solution.

In the period since 1989, self-determination has continued to be invoked, but in different ways, of which three may be singled out. First, it has been invoked as a justification for intervention in another state. Secondly, it has been invoked as a basis for secession from a state. Thirdly, it has been invoked as a ground for establishing special arrangements within the state providing

[81] For a postscript on Kosovo see below, 66–7.

[82] At least, it does so long as we think of the people of Kosovo as the Albanian-speaking people, or of the people of Quebec as the Francophone community, of the respective territories.

for autonomy or special rights, so-called internal self-determination. In the remaining part of this chapter I propose to focus on the second of these, because it is the most controversial, the most obvious and the most often denied of the three, and also because light has been shed on it by the recent decision of the Canadian Supreme Court in its *per curiam* opinion on the *Reference re Secession of Quebec.*[83] Before doing so, however, something should be said on the question of intervention in aid of self-determination.

2. Self-Determination and Intervention[84]

If the right to self-determination is a general right of peoples, it can be denied in relation to the whole people of a state, or (if they exist) to discrete peoples within the state, just as much as it can with respect to colonial territories. It is well established that the guarantee of non-intervention in the internal affairs of the state, reflected for example in Article 2, paragraph 7 of the United Nations Charter, does not prevent discussion of issues of self-determination in the colonial context. Outside the colonial context, the position is less clear. The Commission of Jurists in the *Åland Islands* case rejected the claim of domestic jurisdiction, but only on the basis that Finland was not definitively constituted at the time.[85] Indeed, the phrase 'equal rights and self-determination of peoples' in Charter Articles 1 and 55 appears to bear the primary connotation of non-intervention.

If self-determination is a general right, however, its violation is an international concern, and the breach of the right to self-determination cannot be justified on grounds of domestic jurisdiction. If self-determination is a continuing right, not exhausted at the moment of independence, then its normal manifestation will be through the exercise of civil, political and social rights (and especially democratic rights) within the framework of the relevant state, and the fundamental denial of those rights may be seen to implicate issues of self-determination, and justify at least international interest and concern, if not more. Indeed in recent practice various regional organizations and also, in some cases, the United Nations itself, have been deeply engaged in issues of the restoration of democratic government in a state. Examples include Cambodia, Somalia, Haiti, Burma, Liberia and more recently Sierra Leone.

In states where civil and political rights are respected, the principle of self-determination should reinforce the long-established principle of non-

[83] [1998] 1 SCR 217. For comment see e.g. Haljan, 'A Constitutional Duty to Negotiate Amendments: *Reference re Secession of Quebec*', 48 *ICLQ* (1999) 447.

[84] This section draws on the author's earlier analysis of this issue: see Crawford, 'Self-Determination outside the Colonial Context', in W.J.A. Macartney (ed.) *Self-Determination in the Commonwealth* (1988) 1.

[85] Supra, notes 14 and 15.

intervention in internal affairs. But there is a serious problem in simply equating the two. The principle of non-intervention was established long before the idea of self-determination gained currency in international relations. There are sound 'statist' reasons for it, quite apart from its indirect connection with popular representation or self-determination. To justify non-intervention by reference to self-determination is usually unnecessary. Moreover the notion of 'intervention' is a special one: it excludes action taken with the consent or permission of the government of the state in question.[86] If governments need not be representative, the consequence is that the people of a state may be kept in subjugation by foreign troops called in by an unpopular local government to maintain it in power. There is thus, in one important case, a fundamental conflict between non-intervention and self-determination.[87]

One possibility would be for the right of self-determination to generate modifications to the ordinary rules about intervention and the use of force in special cases. In normal situations non-intervention would be accepted as a sufficient guarantee, at the international level, of internal self-determination. But a use of force by another state to suppress a popular rebellion or to deny the population of a state the power to change its government would be unlawful, even if the government of the state consented to the use of force.[88] In the case of a civil war a rule of non-intervention would prevail in respect of both the government and the rebels. On the other hand external aid might be permissible even to opposition groups if their cause had substantial popular support and the processes of self-determination were being denied through the use of external aid. In extreme cases intervention in aid of self-determination might be permissible even where there was no previous external intervention in aid of the established government, for example in cases where the government's position was maintained solely by military force and through the widespread violation of the human rights of the people of the state.

Of the four propositions set out in the previous paragraph, the most relevant for our purposes is the last, which implies that self-determination justifies intervention in extreme cases—the denial of self-determination in such cases represented by the denial of self-determination to the people of the

[86] See e.g. I. Brownlie, *International Law and the Use of Force by States* (1963), at 317–27; ILC Draft Articles on State Responsibility (1996) Art. 29.

[87] See further B. Roth, *Governmental Illegitimacy in International Law* (1999) for a careful account of the relations between democratic values and non-intervention.

[88] Cf. Friendly Relations Declaration, Annex: 'Every State has the duty to refrain from any forcible action which deprives peoples referred to in the elaboration of the principle of equal rights and self-determination of their right to self-determination and freedom and independence. In their actions against, and resistance to, such forcible action in pursuit of the exercise of their right to self-determination, such peoples are entitled to seek and to receive support in accordance with the purposes and principles of the Charter.'

state as a whole, rather than by any issues of secession or internal self-determination. But the difficulty for proponents of this position is that it has very little support in state practice, in the very cases where it could have been relied on.

For example, in the case of the Tanzanian intervention in Uganda (1979), the armed forces of Tanzania intervened in Uganda, some months after Uganda had invaded, purportedly annexed and then withdrawn from the Kagera salient of Tanzania. Assisted by numbers of Ugandan exiles and local irregular forces, the Tanzanian forces eventually expelled the former President, Idi Amin (despite strong Libyan and other support).[89] A new Ugandan government was established, and achieved rapid and general acceptance. There was some criticism of Tanzania's action at the next OAU meeting, where the issue was discussed but no resolution was adopted.[90] But there was no United Nations discussion of the case: a telegram from Amin to the President of the Security Council was treated as defective in form and not acted on.[91]

Another example during the same period was the intervention of the United States and the Organization of Eastern Caribbean States (OECS) in Grenada (1983).[92] There a faction had seized power in October 1983, killing the Prime Minister and his supporters. It had not committed any general violations of human rights in Grenada, let alone violations on the scale of Amin in Uganda. But there was great hostility to it within Grenada as well as from other countries in the region, including fellow members of the OECS. A verbal invitation to invade Grenada is said to have been given by the Governor-General of Grenada, although a written invitation was only signed by him after the invasion had commenced.[93] It is clear that most Grenadans welcomed the overthrow of the Austin/Coard group, and that a representative government did emerge from the subsequent elections, held after the withdrawal of United States forces. But the Grenadan intervention was overwhelmingly condemned by the General Assembly,[94] and by a majority of the Security Council.[95] Moreover most writers who have discussed the Grenadan

[89] On the Tanzanian intervention see C. Thomas, *New States, Sovereignty and Intervention* (1985), at 90–121; Umozurike, 'Tanzania's Intervention in Uganda', 20 *Archiv des Volkerrechts* (1982) 301; Chatterjee, 'Some Legal Problems of Support Role in International Law: Tanzania and Uganda', 30 *ICLQ* (1981) 755.

[90] Thomas supra n. 89, at 109–12.

[91] Ibid., at 5.

[92] On Grenada see e.g. W.C. Gilmore, *The Grenada Intervention. Analysis and Documentation* (1984); Committee on Grenada (Gordon, Bilder, Rovene, Wallace), 'International Law and the United States Action in Grenada: A Report', 18 *Int L* (1984) 331; Doswald-Beck, 'The Legality of the United States Intervention in Grenada', 31 *NILR* (1984) 355; Moore, 'Grenada and the International Double Standard', 78 *AJIL* (1984) 145. For a good factual account see H. O'Shaughnessy, *Grenada Revolution, Invasion and Aftermath* (1984).

[93] O'Shaughnessy, supra n. 92, at 18, 177–8, 217–18.

[94] GA Res. 38/7 'The Situation in Grenada', 2 November 1983, adopted by 108–9 (27).

[95] Gilmore, supra n. 92, at 38, 95–6.

intervention have rejected the three justifications given by the United States (and supported by the other states involved).[96]

A justification for intervention in such cases has nevertheless been articulated by Reisman, who argues that:

Article 2(4), like so many in the Charter and in contemporary international politics, rests on and must be interpreted in terms of this key postulate of political legitimacy in the 20th century. Each application of Article 2(4) must enhance opportunities for ongoing self-determination. Though all interventions are lamentable, the fact is that some may serve, in terms of aggregate consequences, to increase the probability of the free choice of peoples about their government and political structure. Others have the manifest objective and consequence of doing exactly the opposite. There is neither need nor justification for treating in a mechanically equal fashion Tanzania's intervention in Uganda to overthrow Amin's despotism, on the one hand, and Soviet intervention in Hungary in 1956 or Czechoslovakia in 1966 to overthrow popular governments and to impose an undesired regime on a coerced population, on the other. Here, as in all other areas of law, it is important to remember that norms are instruments devised by human beings to precipitate desired social consequences.[97]

For those who adhere to self-determination as the 'key postulate of political legitimacy in the 20th century', the moral evaluation of intervention in any situation must be vitally affected by whether the intervention promoted or impeded the self-determination of the people concerned. But one difficulty with Reisman's argument as a legal justification for intervention is that often an intervention carried out for other reasons has been excused by a fictional or forced reliance on local invitation or on self-determination. States have in fact been very reluctant to condone, let alone justify, intervention on grounds such as these, as the examples of Bangladesh, Afghanistan and Kampuchea demonstrate.[98]

A further problem with Reisman's thesis, as it applies to the two cases outlined above, is that in neither case was self-determination, or indeed even

[96] See the works cited in supra n. 92 (with the exception of Moore); also Boyle and others, 'International lawlessness in Grenada', 78 *AJIL* (1984) 172.

[97] Reisman, 'Coercion and Self-Determination: Construing Charter Article 2(4)', 78 *AJIL* (1984) 642, at 643–4.

[98] On Bangladesh see Crawford, supra n. 14, at 115–17; J. Dugard, *Recognition and the United Nations* (1987), at 75–6 and works there cited. On Afghanistan see, e.g., Alaimo, 'La questione dell'Afghanistan alle Nazioni Unite e il problema del consenso nell'illecito internazionale', 64 *Rivista di diritto internazionale* (1981) 287. On Cambodia see Isoart, 'La situation au Kampuchea', 87 *Revue générale de droit international publique* (1983) 42; G. Klintworth, *Vietnam's Intervention in Cambodia in International Law* (1989); M. Martin, *Cambodia, a Shattered Society* (1994), at 215–55; Bazyler, 'Re-examining the Doctrine of Humanitarian Intervention in the Light of the Atrocities in Kampuchea and Ethiopia', 23 *Stanford JIL* (1987) 547; Franck, 'Of Gnats and Camels: Is There a Double Standard at the United Nations?', 78 *AJIL* (1984) 810; Warbrick, 'Kampuchea: Representation and Recognition', 30 *ICLQ* (1981) 234.

humanitarian intervention, relied on by the governments involved. The official justification given by the Tanzanian government for its intervention was self-defence, but it is clear its campaign to replace Idi Amin was essentially unrelated to defence against the earlier Kagera incursion. The United States gave three bases for the Grenada invasion, while declining to base the action on any one of them alone. These were the Governor-General's invitation, regional action under the OECS Treaty, and intervention to protect United States nationals in Grenada.[99] The factual basis for the third claim, the protection of nationals, was tenuous, and there were many difficulties in the way of the other two claims. For present purposes the point is that the United States expressly did not rely on broader claims to humanitarian intervention, let alone intervention in aid of self-determination. As Schachter forcefully pointed out, in a response to Reisman:

Even the democratic governments in the United Nations have not claimed a right to intervene forcibly to bring about the free choice of peoples in other countries. The United States, despite occasional 'rollback' oratory, has never justified its military interventions elsewhere on the ground suggested by Reisman. In Vietnam and currently in Central America, the legal justification for intervention has rested on the claim that foreign intervention had taken place and that U.S. action in response to the request of the government was justified on the basis of the collective self-defense provisions of the Charter. It is true the Grenada intervention was considered by many in the United States as politically desirable because it would lead to democratic rule in place of a repressive regime. However, significantly, the U.S. government did not assert that as a legal ground . . . The difficulty with Reisman's argument is not merely that it lacks support in the text of the Charter or in the interpretations that states have given Article 2(4) in the past decades. It would introduce a new normative basis for recourse to war that would give powerful states an almost unlimited right to overthrow governments alleged to be unresponsive to the popular will or to the goal of self-determination. The implications of this for interstate violence in a period of superpower confrontation and obscurantist rhetoric are ominous. That invasions may at times serve democratic values must be weighed against the dangerous consequences of legitimizing armed attacks against peaceful governments.[100]

[99] 'Letter', 18 *Int L* (1984) 381.

[100] Schachter,'The Legality of Pro-Democratic Invasion', 78 *AJIL* (1984) 645, at 648–9. For conclusions to similar effect see Werwey, 'Humanitarian Intervention under International Law', 32 *Northern Ireland Law Review* (1985) 357, at 408–11; Joyner 'Reflections on the Lawfulness of Invasion', 78 *AJIL* (1984) 131; Thomas, supra n. 89, at 115–20. Supporters of intervention on a broader basis include Sornarajah, 'Internal Colonialism and Humanitarian Intervention' 11 *Georgia JICL* (1981) 45; Suzuki, 'A State's Provisional Competence to Protect Human Rights in a Foreign State', 15 *Texas ILJ* (1980) 231; Weller, 'Access to Victims: Reconceiving the Right to "Intervene" ', in W.P. Heere, *International Law and the Hague's 75th Anniversary* (1999) 353.

In its judgment in the *Nicaragua* Case the International Court went out of its way to reject the argument that self-determination justifies intervention. The Court said:

There have been in recent years a number of instances of foreign intervention for the benefit of forces opposed to the government of another State. The Court is not here concerned with the process of decolonization; this question is not in issue in the present case. It has to consider whether there might be indications of a practice illustrative of belief in a kind of general right for States to intervene, directly or indirectly, with or without armed force, in support of an internal opposition in another State, whose cause appeared particularly worthy by reason of the political and moral values with which it was identified. For such a general right to come into existence would involve a fundamental modification of the customary law principle of non-intervention . . . In fact however the Court finds that States have not justified their conduct by reference to a new right of intervention or a new exception to the principle of its prohibition. The United States authorities have on some occasions clearly stated their grounds for intervening in the affairs of a foreign State for reasons connected with, for example, the domestic policies of that country, its ideology, the level of its armaments, or the direction of its foreign policy. But these were statements of interventional policy, and not an assertion of rules of existing international law . . . The Court therefore finds that no such general right of intervention, in support of an opposition within another State, exists in contemporary international law.[101]

Although the Court's decision is controversial in other respects, there was no disagreement in any of the dissenting or separate opinions with this reasoning. Judge Schwebel, in his comprehensive dissenting opinion, took issue with the Court's apparent exception of 'the process of decolonization':

In contemporary international law, the right of self-determination, freedom and independence of peoples is universally recognized; the right of peoples to struggle to achieve these ends is universally accepted; but what is not universally recognized and what is not universally accepted is any right of such peoples to foreign assistance or support which constitutes intervention. That is to say, it is lawful for a foreign State or movement to give to a people struggling for self-determination moral, political and humanitarian assistance; but it is not lawful for a foreign State or movement to intervene in that struggle with force or to provide arms, supplies and other logistical support in the prosecution of armed rebellion. This is true whether the struggle is or is proclaimed to be in pursuance of the process of decolonization or against colonial domination . . . Perhaps the best that can be said of this unnecessary statement of the Court is that it can be read as taking no position on the legality of intervention in support of the process of decolonization, but as merely referring to a phenomenon as to which positions in the international community differ.[102]

But clearly he too accepted the general proposition that intervention is unlawful, even in the interests of the self-determination of the people of the state concerned.

[101] ICJ Reports (1986) 14, at 108–9. [102] Ibid., at 351.

The question is whether this position has changed in the period since 1989, a decade in which it is undeniable that the value of democratic legitimacy has become internationally much more significant.[103] A review of more recent cases would not, I believe, lead to a different conclusion. In a number of cases (e.g. Haiti, and more recently Sierra Leone), elected governments have been ousted by rebels, usually elements of the armed forces, and other states have refused to recognize the rebels as a new government, and have called for the restoration of democratic rule. Indeed they have gone further and, relying on the consent of the 'legitimate' government, have sought in some cases to restore it to effective power. For example, SC Resolution 1132 (1997), passed under Chapter VII of the Charter, demanded, 'that the military junta take immediate steps to relinquish power in Sierra Leone and make way for the restoration of the democratically-elected government and a return to constitutional order'. In the case of Haiti, this principle of democratic legitimacy was applied to a government out of power and against a regime which (unlike in Sierra Leone) had relatively secure *de facto* control over the territory of the state. But in these and other cases, it was reasonable to treat the elected government as remaining the legitimate government for the time being: it had not been securely displaced, and the recent and (in the case of Haiti, internationally attested) electoral support of the people favoured international support for it. Neither case supports the proposition that an established undemocratic government is not entitled to rely on the principle of non-intervention, or that unilateral force can be lawfully used against it with a view to its displacement.

But if the proposition that a denial of self-determination justifies forceful intervention (not justified by Chapter VII of the Charter) must be rejected, self-determination remains relevant in judging situations where intervention has occurred, and especially in dealing with their aftermath. The degree of culpability or international responsibility flowing from an intervention may well depend on its consequences. Long-term military occupation of another state (as in Afghanistan or Kampuchea) is clearly a more serious violation of international law than a short-term action followed by the withdrawal of forces and leading to genuine local self-determination. The link that would normally exist between illegal intervention and non-recognition of a new 'government' formed as a result (e.g. in Kampuchea) may be avoided if the new government results from a genuine act of local self-determination and is clearly supported by the local population. This is the best interpretation of the creation of Bangladesh,[104]

[103] See Franck, 'The Emerging Right to Democratic Governance', 86 *AJIL* (1992) 46; Crawford, 'Democracy in International Law', 64 *BYIL* (1993) 113. But for a caveat see Crawford and Marks, 'The Global Democracy Deficit: An Essay in International Law and its Limits', in D. Archibugi, D. Held, M. Köhler (eds), *Re-imagining Political Community. Studies in Cosmopolitan Democracy* (1998) 72.

[104] See Crawford, supra n. 14, at 116–17; and Dugard, supra n. 98, at 75–6.

and it also helps to justify the rapid and general recognition of post-intervention governments established, for example, in Uganda and Grenada.

3. Self-Determination and Secession

A second general issue is whether the principle of self-determination has generated any more support for the idea of secession, at least in extreme cases, outside the colonial context.

This issue was extensively debated in submissions made to the Supreme Court of Canada in proceedings arising from a reference (i.e. an advisory opinion) by the government of Canada relating to the secession of Quebec. Quebec itself declined to appear before the Supreme Court, but an *amicus curiae* was appointed, in the form of a senior lawyer from Quebec assisted by a range of international law advisers, and there were interventions from some other Provinces and from a range of organizations. The proceedings were certainly not adversarial in the way they might have been had Quebec itself appeared, but on the other hand the issues were fully considered. Of particular interest were the opinions of a number of international lawyers retained by the *amicus curiae*,[105] who addressed the second question referred to the Supreme Court. That question was formulated in the following terms:

> 2. Does international law give the National Assembly, legislature or government of Quebec the right to effect the secession of Quebec from Canada unilaterally? In this regard, is there a right to self-determination under international law that would give the National Assembly, legislature or government of Quebec the right to effect the secession of Quebec from Canada unilaterally?

Question 1 asked whether Quebec could lawfully secede unilaterally from Canada as a matter of Canadian constitutional law; Question 3 asked which, of Canadian constitutional law and international law, would take precedence in Canada '[i]n the event of a conflict between domestic and international law on the right of the National Assembly, legislature or government of Quebec to effect the secession of Quebec from Canada unilaterally'.

(a) Expert opinions presented to the Supreme Court: a review

In an opinion annexed to the pleadings of the Minister of Justice of Canada, the present author reviewed modern state practice on secession and supported a negative answer to Question 2.[106] Rather than repeating that material, it

[105] They were Professors Georges Abi-Saab, Tom Franck, Alain Pellet and Malcolm Shaw. The present writer was one of two experts commissioned by the Minister of Justice for Canada in relation to Question 2; the other was Professor Luzius Wildhaber, now President of the European Court of Human Rights.

[106] For a slightly amended version of the opinion see Crawford, 'State Practice and International Law in relation to Secession', 69 *BYIL* (1998) 85.

seems useful to review the points of agreement and disagreement among the various opinions presented to the Supreme Court, before turning to what the Supreme Court itself said on Question 2.

The first point to note is that there was a considerable measure of agreement among the opinions presented, although it was not complete. In particular experts for the *amicus curiae* tended to deny the relevance of the principle of territorial integrity in relation to secession. Nonetheless there was substantial agreement on the following three key propositions.

In non-colonial territories, self-determination does not equal a right to secede

Thus Professor Abi-Saab accepted that 'le droit international ne reconnaît pas un droit de sécession en dehors du droit à l'auto-détermination', and noted that there was no question of a denial of self-determination to the people of Quebec.[107] Professor Franck likewise referred to 'exceptional situations in which a minority people may have a *right* to secession tenable in law and politics due to their demonstrable inability to achieve established rights of self-determination guaranteed by law'[108] (emphasis in original). Professor Pellet agreed that 'il ne résulte pas nécessairement de la positivité, aujourd'hui indiscutable, du principe de l'égalité de droits des peuples et de leur droit à disposer d'eux-mêmes que tout peuple a droit de faire sécession'.[109] And Professor Shaw said that:

> In the case of independent states outside of the colonial context, such choice [arising from the exercise of self-determination] would not (save in a very exceptional situation) include sovereignty as such . . . State practice is clear in positing the application of the principle of self-determination within the defined territory of the state in question and in thus precluding secession as an option. This has been achieved by reference to the principle of territorial integrity in international instruments.[110]

A state is entitled to oppose secession by all lawful means

According to Professor Abi-Saab:

> Avant que la sécession ne se traduise dans les faits en tant que réalité effective . . . la réclamation de la composante de la population qui voudrait faire sécession, ainsi que l'éventuel différend qui peut s'ensuivre entre elle et le pouvoir central de l'État, restent, au vu du droit international, une question interne relevant du domaine réservé de l'État en question. Les autres États, ainsi que les organisations internationales, doivent les traiter ainsi, sous peine de violer le principe de non-intervention. Le droit

[107] Abi-Saab Report, pp. 5, 6.

[108] Franck Report, pp. 10, 11, para. 2.13. Clearly he did not regard the people of Quebec as having this right: see ibid., p. 20, para. 3.8.

[109] Pellet Report, pp. 8, 9, para. 7; see also, p. 42, para. 38 (fourth point).

[110] Shaw Report, p. 20, paras 46, 48.

international ne s'appliquerait à cette situation que dans la mesure où le droit international humanitaire s'applique aux conflits armés de caractère non-international.[111]

Professor Shaw accepted that proportionate defence by a state of its territorial integrity against a secessionist group is lawful, but he also noted that:

if the domestic situation deteriorates beyond a certain point, perhaps characterized as a public order predicament, then the norms of international law would also apply. For example, if the governmental authorities were to launch a sustained and brutal armed attack upon those claiming secession, in a manner that far exceeds reasonable proportionality, then issues of international law relating to human rights and self-determination (in the sense of the exceptional situation) will become directly relevant.[112]

A secession, finally successful, may be acknowledged as leading to independence

Thus Professor Abi-Saab said that:

si le droit international ne reconnaît pas un droit de sécession en dehors du droit à l'auto-détermination, cela ne veut pas dire qu'il interdise la sécession. Celle-ci reste essentiellement un phénomène non réglementé par le droit international . . . Ainsi . . . le fait que le processus de création du nouvel État puisse être qualifié de sécession n'affecte et ne conditionne aucunement son existence juridique du point de vue du droit international, une fois le fait primaire, c'est-à-dire son effectivité étatique, matérialisé.[113]

Professor Pellet said that:

Il va de soi que, dans la réalisation de cette condition, l'attitude de l'État d'origine peut jouer un rôle fondamental: son opposition peut avoir pour effet d'empêcher le peuple sécessionniste de créer l'État auquel il aspire; au contraire, sa coopération, ou sa modération dans l'opposition, ou, plus souvent, sa résignation devant une issue qu'il pense inéluctable, peuvent grandement contribuer à l'affermissement de la nouvelle entité étatique; mais, si consentement il y a, il n'est pas la condition juridique de la licéité de la création de l'État issu de la sécession et demeure un simple facteur de son effectivité.[114]

[111] 'Before a secession has been translated into an effective situation of fact . . . the claim of that part of the population which wishes to secede, as well as any dispute which may in consequence arise with the central government of the State, remain, from the point of view of international law, a matter of the domestic jurisdiction of the State in question. Other States, as well as international organizations, must treat them as such, otherwise they will breach the principle of non-intervention. International law only applies to this situation to the extent that international humanitarian law applies to armed conflicts of a non-international character.' (Author's translation) Abi-Saab Report, pp. 5, 6; see also ibid., pp. 8, 9. See also Franck Report, p. 17, para. 3.3; Pellet Report, p. 42, para. 38.

[112] Shaw Report, p. 18, para. 44.

[113] Abi-Saab Report, pp. 6, 7.

[114] Pellet Report, p. 46, para. 41. See also Franck Report, para. 2.11.

Professor Shaw said that:

The fact that the secession of, for example, East Pakistan from Pakistan to form the independent state of Bangladesh and that of Eritrea from Ethiopia, were ultimately recognized by the international community emphasizes the point that secession is not against international law and will indeed be recognized in the appropriate circumstances. Of course, where a secession has taken place without the use of force or by virtue of negotiated agreement, the international community will accept the new situation and the new state that much more speedily.[115]

The second point to note, however, is that there were some disagreements, of which the following were the most important.

The issue of territorial integrity

A common theme among the experts for the *amicus curiae* was that seceding groups within the state (unlike the governments of *other* states) are not bound by the principles of the non-use of force or territorial integrity. They tended thus to treat the principle of territorial integrity as irrelevant when it comes to secession. But this significantly underestimates the salience attached to territorial integrity even in respect of purely internal challenges to the state. In particular, the reason why seceding groups are not bound by the international law rule of territorial integrity is not that international law in any sense favours secession. It is simply that such groups are not subjects of international law at all, in the way that states are, even if they benefit from certain minimum rules of human rights and humanitarian law. A group does not become a subject of international law by expressing its wish to secede. Until an advanced stage in the process, secession is a matter within the domestic jurisdiction of the affected state. Moreover, references in United Nations resolutions and other sources to the principle of territorial integrity reflect the point that the state is entitled to resist challenges to its territorial integrity, whether these challenges are internal (e.g. as a result of an attempted secession) or external. Thus international law, both in principle and as evidenced in state practice, favours the territorial integrity of the predecessor state. It does so, not in the sense of offering any ultimate guarantee against separation or dissolution, but in the sense that for significant and often very substantial periods of time, it allows the central government to seek to preserve the territorial integrity of the state. During this period, of course, that government must respect applicable rules of international human rights and humanitarian law, as well as its other international commitments. But a unilateral declaration of independence, while it may be the beginning of a process by which independence may be achieved, has no effect as such in international law. It does not trigger any international legal protection for the 'territorial integrity' of the seceding entity any more than it brings into play the international law rules relating to the use of force

[115] Shaw Report, p. 29, para. 70.

between existing states.[116] Outside the colonial context and situations tantamount to colonialism, there is no right of self-determination which entails a right of unilateral secession from the surrounding state. On the contrary the international system, in all cases short of the irreversible dissolution and fragmentation of a state, does endorse its territorial integrity against attempts at dissolution, from within or without. A secessionary entity has no such territorial integrity until it has achieved stable and effective independence.[117] Moreover international law does not endorse inter-provincial or other internal boundaries unless and until they have become the boundaries of independent states.[118]

The relevance of the 'principle' of effectiveness

A further divergence, at least in emphasis, between the different opinions related to the principle of effectiveness. It was agreed that, in the final analysis, a seceding entity which had secured and maintained its effective control over a territory to the exclusion of the former state could come to be regarded as

[116] As the Abi-Saab Report, p. 6 pointed out. Under the very wide terms of Chapter VII of the Charter, the Security Council may interest itself in a secessionary conflict which is a threat to international peace and security for some reason (e.g. refugee flows, or large-scale violence). But this is a different matter, and the Council has been very conscious of the value of territorial integrity in those cases in which it has intervened. See e.g. its resolutions in relation to the Kurdish problem: Security Council Resolutions 686 (1991), 2 March 1991; 687 (1991) 3 April 1991; 688 (1991), 5 April 1991; 949 (1994), 15 October 1994. Each of these resolutions explicitly affirmed Iraq's territorial integrity.

[117] Professor Franck accepts this point in his adoption of a dictum from the *Tinoco Arbitration* (1923) 1 RIAA 369, 375, cited in Franck Report, pp. 7, 8, para. 2.7. That case concerned an unconstitutional change of government within an existing state. International law has traditionally been, and still is, much readier to acknowledge unconstitutional coups within a state than unilateral secession from a state. There have been many hundreds of internal coups, acknowledged as effective, since 1945. Nonetheless Arbitrator Taft required that the new government should be one which 'establishes itself and maintains peaceful administration, with the acquiescence of the people, for a substantial period of time'.

[118] Professor Shaw (Report, p. 4a; also p. 35, para. 85) argued that 'the modern operation of the principle of *uti possidetis juris*' gives some special status to the boundaries of provinces or other federal units. But under international law the internal structure of the state is a question of fact, in the sense that internal units of whatever kind (whether in federations or unitary states) are just that, internal units. The notion of a 'people' in international law is not necessarily correlated with provincial or other internal boundaries. Of course, if a province or other internal unit manages to secede, by effectively and securely excluding the previous administration from that territory as a whole, its boundaries will come to be protected by international law, including, as applicable, the notion of *uti possidetis*. But the principle of *uti possidetis* does not apply before the event, or in an anticipatory way. It is, as a Chamber of the International Court pointed out, 'a retrospective principle', applying once statehood is achieved by the given entity: *El Salvador/Honduras*, ICJ Reports (1992) 351, at 388, cited in Shaw Report, p. 32, para. 77. The point about retrospectivity is important. If there is no *a priori* right to secede, then there can be no right to secede in relation to any particular boundaries either. The boundaries that emerge will be the outcome of the process of secession and are not predetermined.

independent. But this was not the issue which the Supreme Court of Canada was asked to address by Question 2. The question of the eventual effectiveness of an attempted secession is quite different from the question whether an entity has a right to independence, for example by virtue of the right to self-determination. There are at least three differences between the question of a right to secede and the principle of effectiveness. First, to say that a person or entity has a right is to say nothing about the world of fact ('effectiveness'). This logical point applies to self-determination as it does to any other right. The right to self-determination has been applied precisely in opposition to effective regimes, e.g. in South West Africa (Namibia), Rhodesia (Zimbabwe) and East Timor. Secondly, not only are the two issues analytically distinct: they address different stages of the process by which a particular group may attempt to secede. The right to self-determination applies *a priori.*[119] The issue of effectiveness can only be determined once the process has substantially run its course. And thirdly, the principle or right of self-determination only applies to 'peoples'. By contrast, *any* group resident on a particular area of land may attempt to secede, whether or not its population constitutes a 'people'. If eventually it prevails, in whole or in part, it may be regarded as independent.

The existence of a 'privilege' to secede (derived from the absence of a prohibition)

A third point was, perhaps, of more analytical interest. This was the argument that because international law does not prohibit secession, therefore a group within a state, such as the people of Quebec, have a privilege to secede.[120] Of course it is true that international law does not *prohibit* secession of any group whatever within the state. But this is not due to any particular sympathy for secession or the breakdown of states. It is for three related reasons. First, the question of secession is a matter within the domestic jurisdiction of the metropolitan state. If the state wishes to allow a secession to occur (as eventually Ethiopia was prepared to do with respect to Eritrea), then other states will accept that outcome. By the same token, if the metropolitan state wishes to oppose the secession by whatever lawful means, other states will stand aside and allow it to do so (as for a long time in the case of Eritrea[121] and most

[119] A point expressly accepted in the Abi-Saab Report, p. 3.

[120] See especially Franck Report, para. 2.6 ff.

[121] The case of Eritrea was a strong illustration of the point. This is because, with the unilateral abrogation of the autonomy which Eritrea had pursuant to General Assembly Resolution 284 (VI), and the subsequent attempt to assimilate the Eritrean people forcibly, there was a good case for arguing that the original right of colonial, external self-determination of that people had revived. Yet that argument received little or no international support. See E. Gayim, *The Eritrean Question* (1993); Goy, 'L'indépendence de l'Erythrée', 39 *Annuaire français de droit international* (1993) 337; Haile, 'Legality of Secessions: the Case of Eritrea', 8 *Emory International Law Review* (1994) 479.

recently in Chechnya[122]). Secondly, international law finds it necessary to accommodate new situations, securely established, so long as there is no violation of peremptory rules in the process. This was the basis for the eventual recognition of the secessions of the Spanish and Portuguese territories in Central and South America.[123] Thirdly, for international law specifically to prohibit secession, it would need to address the seceding entity as such, and this it generally does not do. Thus the fact that international law does not prohibit secession does not mean that it confers a legally recognized 'privilege' to secede, except perhaps in extreme cases.[124] The ultimate absence of any international law prohibition on secession arises not because international law in any sense welcomes or encourages secessionary activity: it is simply that secession is one of the many activities which are, *au fond*, referred to the domestic jurisdiction of the state concerned.[125] Thus there is no specific content to the so-called 'privilege', over and above the proposition that international law does not itself ultimately prohibit secession. To the contrary, if there is a privilege here—a legally recognized entitlement to act—it is the privilege of the metropolitan state to seek to maintain its territorial integrity by lawful means. That state has a privilege to oppose and even to suppress

[122] Russian military action in Chechnya was criticized for breaching norms of humanitarian law applicable in internal armed conflict, as well as certain arrangements relating to the movement of conventional forces in Europe. As far as I am aware, no state denied that Russia was entitled to resist the secession by lawful means. See Tappe, 'Chechnya and the State of Self-determination in a Breakaway Region of the Former Soviet Union: Evaluating the Legitimacy of Secessionist Claims', 34 *Col J Trans L* (1995) 255; Gazzini, 'Considerations on the Conflict in Chechnya', 17 *Human Rights LJ* (1996) 93.

[123] See Crawford, supra n. 14, at 249–51, 256–7, with references.

[124] Ibid., at 266–8.

[125] Professor Franck relied on the decision of the Permanent Court in *The Lotus* (1927) PCIJ Ser. A No. 10 for the proposition that 'anything not prohibited by international law is deemed to be permitted'. Thus, since the secession of Quebec is not actually prohibited by international law, it is deemed to be permitted: Franck Report, para. 2.6. This is, however, a misunderstanding of the decision in *The Lotus*. What the Permanent Court said was that '[r]estrictions upon the independence *of States* cannot be presumed': (1927) PCIJ Ser A. No. 10 at p. 18 (emphasis added, and see the whole of the preceding passage). The Permanent Court was not at all concerned with the position of non-state entities, such as secessionist groups. Indeed, the point can be illustrated from the facts of *The Lotus* itself. The question was whether Turkey could try a French officer who had been in control of a French merchant ship on the high seas and who was allegedly responsible for its collision with a Turkish ship, causing loss of life. Now the French lieutenant of the *SS Lotus* was not prohibited by international law from colliding with the Turkish ship. Negligent manslaughter at sea was not a crime under international law, and the lieutenant was not personally accountable under international law for his conduct. But it would be extremely odd to argue that therefore his act was *permitted* by international law, or that he had a *privilege* to do it. It was a matter for the relevant state or states to determine, in the exercise of their jurisdiction, whether his acts were or were not criminal. The only question for the Permanent Court was whether France was the only state with jurisdiction over the event, or whether in the circumstances Turkey also had jurisdiction. The issue of a 'privilege', as distinct from a 'right' or 'duty', simply did not arise.

unilateral secession. And in the face of this, it is seriously misleading to argue that international law 'permits' or 'privileges' secession.

The 'lessons' of the Yugoslav case

A number of the expert reports characterized the break-up of Yugoslavia as a case of secession from Yugoslavia by individual republics, including Bosnia-Herzegovina, from which the inference was drawn that the tolerance of the international community for the 'premature' independence of the constituent republics indicates a shift towards increased approval or tolerance of secession.[126] It is true that the early stages of the Yugoslav crisis were characterized, *inter alia*, by attempts on the part of several of the constituent republics to secede. Two of them, Slovenia and Macedonia, had established substantial *de facto* control over their territory to the exclusion of Belgrade by the second half of 1991. But the international community did not proceed to recognize them as states which had seceded, piecemeal, from a continuing metropolitan state of Yugoslavia. On the contrary, it came to the view that Yugoslavia as a whole was dissolving into its constituent entities, relying to some extent on the special constitutional position of the republics within Yugoslavia. This was precisely the point of the early classification of Yugoslavia as a case of dissolution, as distinct from the successive secessions of particular parts of a continuing state. The issue was directly faced in the first of the Badinter Opinions, in November 1991, and it was relevant not just to the question of state succession but to the international response to the conflict as a whole. If the Belgrade government and the Yugoslav National Army were to be treated as the government and the army of a subsisting, continuing state of Yugoslavia faced with a series of secessions, they would presumably be regarded as representing Yugoslavia as a whole. If on the other hand they were to be treated as organs of a Serb faction identified primarily with the constituent republics of Serbia and Montenegro, Yugoslavia itself would be in the course of dissolution, and different consequences would follow in terms of the status of those organs and their entitlement to control the external assets of Yugoslavia. For various reasons (and for better or worse) the latter choice was made, in December 1991. In other words, it was decided to treat Yugoslavia as being in a state of dissolution, and the Serb-dominated organs as having no authority to represent that state. This decision has informed the whole of the subsequent handling of the crisis.[127] The distinction between secession and

[126] See e.g. Franck Report, pp. 11, 12, paras 2.14, 2.15.

[127] See especially Badinter Opinion No. 1 of 29 November 1991: 92 ILR 162. It should be stressed that the recognition of Croatia and Bosnia-Herzegovina was, at the time, anything but the recognition of 'facts'. The Croatian Government did not control its territory then or for many months thereafter; the Bosnian government still does not. Nor did other states distinguish between those cases and the two cases (Slovenia and Macedonia) where the facts might well have supported prompt recognition of secession.

dissolution can thus have important consequences, even though the two may be difficult to distinguish in a given case. As Alain Pellet noted, they are 'institutions juridiques distinctes'.[128] In the case of dissolution, there is no basis for privileging any governmental actor which is opposed to the process of dissolution; there is no reason for treating the consent of any one of those actors as having greater relevance than another, and this had considerable significance, precisely in the case of Yugoslavia.[129] That case does not support the view that international law is moving towards greater tolerance or acceptance of secession.

The implications of modern state practice on secession

Indeed there is a question whether international law is moving the other way, towards some form of prohibition, although most of the expert reports discounted this. Even a cursory study of UN resolutions shows the concern often expressed at secession, and the desire of many states not to give any credence to the possibility of secession. The fact is that state practice in the matter of secession has been relatively consistent and remarkably conservative. It is a fact that no state has been admitted to the United Nations since 1945 without some accord or accommodation with the government of the former metropolitan state—not even Bangladesh, perhaps the clearest case of secession in the modern period, not even the Baltic states.[130] There is a question whether this consistent practice, and the evident aversion of the international community to anything that looks like support for secession, has made unilateral secession actually unlawful. Probably it has not done so, for two reasons: first, the lack of any articulated basis for such a change in international law; secondly, because there is ultimately no point in the refusal to recognize facts not brought about in violation of international law.[131] But this does not mean that the post-1945 practice is legally irrelevant. How rules of law are applied in practice is relevant in determining their meaning and predicting their likely application in future cases. In dozens of cases in the modern period, and not

[128] Pellet Report, p. 21, para. 20.

[129] This was seen to be the case, by late 1991, with the 'central' authorities in Yugoslavia. The key legal opinion is Badinter Opinion No. 1 of 29 November 1991. The question asked of the Arbitration Commission was whether Yugoslavia was in the course of dissolution, which involved the crucial question of classification. It was answered by reference to the criteria for statehood: see 92 ILR 162, at 165, 166. The consequences of this classification in the field of state succession at this stage were secondary: the issue was recognition, which followed shortly thereafter.

[130] The Baltic states were of course in a special position because their independence had been unlawfully suppressed in 1940, and many third states continued to recognize them as states for the 50 years of their suppression. They were not 'seceding entities' from a metropolitan state, and as far as I am aware no other state recognized them as such. But see Pellet Report, p. 40, para. 36.

[131] See Crawford, supra n. 14, at 266–8.

only those where there was external intervention, the international community has refused to recognize even fairly successful metropolitan secession movements. In a few cases (Bangladesh, the former Yugoslavia), special factors such as genocide and/or widespread civil war tending to the dissolution of the state as a whole, have persuaded the international community to take a different line. But those cases are exceptional, and they do not detract from the general value which international law attributes to the territorial integrity of independent states. It is true that internal groups seeking to secede are not bound by the 'interstate' aspects of international law, including the rules relating to the use of force between states, domestic jurisdiction and territorial integrity. The reason is precisely because they are not states. But those rules are *applicable to their situation*, and the territorial state is entitled to oppose a secession, within the framework of its domestic jurisdiction and subject only to certain limitations as to the method by which its opposition is expressed. Thus the value of territorial integrity applies even as against entities which are not bound to respect that integrity.

In a curious way, however, perhaps the central and most difficult question about self-determination leading to secession was hardly touched on in the expert reports, although it did form a part of the review of practice undertaken in the opinions tabled by the Solicitor-General for Canada. This is the question to what extent the so-called 'proviso' in the Friendly Relations Declaration really amounts to international law sanctioning the possibility of secession in extreme cases. It will be recalled that the 'proviso' reads as follows:

> Nothing in the foregoing paragraphs shall be construed as authorizing or encouraging any action which would dismember or impair, totally or in part, the territorial integrity or political unity of sovereign and independent States conducting themselves in compliance with the principle of equal rights and self-determination of peoples as described above *and thus possessed of a government representing the whole people belonging to the territory without distinction as to race, creed or colour.*[132]

The 'safeguard clause' was reaffirmed in slightly different language by the United Nations World Conference on Human Rights held in Vienna in 1993. The Vienna Declaration provides, in relevant part:

> In accordance with the Declaration on Principles of International Law concerning Friendly Relations and Cooperation Among States in accordance with the Charter of the United Nations, this [*sc* the right of self-determination] shall not be construed as authorizing or encouraging any action which would dismember or impair, totally or in part, the territorial integrity or political unity of sovereign and independent States conducting themselves in compliance with the principle of equal rights and self-determination of peoples *and thus possessed of a government representing the whole people belonging to the territory without distinction of any kind.*[133]

[132] Emphasis added. For the Declaration see the text to supra n. 58.

[133] United Nations World Conference on Human Rights, Vienna Declaration and Programme of Action, 25 June 1993, 32 *ILM* (1993) 1661, 1665 (emphasis added).

A key issue in the debate about secession is whether these paragraphs envisage secession (so-called 'remedial secession') in the case of those states which do not conduct themselves in compliance with the principle of equal rights and self-determination of peoples; for example, where they totally deny to a particular group or people within the state any role in their own government, either through their own institutions or the general institutions of the state. At any rate some (the present writer included[134]) have argued that, in extreme cases of oppression, international law allows remedial secession to discrete peoples within a state, and that the 'safeguard clauses' in the Friendly Relations Declaration and the Vienna Declaration recognize this, even if indirectly.[135]

In the arguments before the Supreme Court of Canada in the *Quebec Secession* opinion, this issue hardly figured. By no stretch of the imagination could it be said that the people of Quebec were oppressed or that Canada was not governed by a constitutional system 'representing the whole people belonging to the territory without distinction of any kind'. This was fully accepted by the *amicus curiae* and in the various legal opinions. However the government of Canada relied on what might be referred to as the 'obverse' of the safeguard clause: without actually committing itself to the idea of remedial secession, it argued that the safeguard clause was a safeguard against secession for those states which complied with it. In other words, it was said that a state whose government represents the whole people of its territory without distinction of any kind *complied* with the principle of self-determination in respect of all of its people and was entitled to the protection of its territorial integrity. In such a case, all the people (including discrete peoples within the state) exercised the right of self-determination through their participation in the government of the state on a basis of equality. It was really to combat this argument that some of the opinions presented by the *amicus curiae* argued that the principle of territorial integrity had no relevance to secession.

(b) The Supreme Court's conclusions

In its opinion in *Reference re Secession of Quebec*, the Supreme Court unanimously expressed the view that international law did not give to Quebec any right of unilateral secession. It therefore answered Question 2 in the negative. Indeed the case for a positive answer had hardly been made: essentially the *amicus curiae* argued that Question 2 should not be answered because it was a question of 'pure' international law, unrelated to internal Canadian law, and because a simple negative answer would be misleading given the *possibility* of secession under international law. The Supreme Court held that it could and should answer the question,[136] and in doing so it gave the first authoritative

[134] See the tentative view expressed in Crawford, supra n. 14, at 101.
[135] See Cassese, supra n. 3, at 109–25 for a full discussion of the 'safeguard clause'.
[136] See [1998] 1 SCR 217, 235–8 (paras 23, 27–31).

legal opinion on secession since the two League of Nations opinions on the *Åland Islands*, 75 years earlier.[137] In the end, it gave essentially the same answer to that question as the two Commissions had done.

It began, where the Commission of Jurists began in 1923, with the proposition that:

international law does not specifically grant component parts of sovereign states the legal right to secede unilaterally from their 'parent' state . . . Given the lack of specific authorization for unilateral secession, proponents of the existence of such a right at international law are therefore left to attempt to found their argument (i) on the proposition that unilateral secession is not specifically prohibited and that what is not specifically prohibited is inferentially permitted; or (ii) on the implied duty of states to recognize the legitimacy of secession brought about by the exercise of the well-established international law right of 'a people' to self-determination.[138]

The Supreme Court briskly dismissed the first of these two arguments:

International law contains neither a right of unilateral secession nor the explicit denial of such a right, although such a denial is, to some extent, implicit in the exceptional circumstances required for secession to be permitted under the right of a people to self-determination, e.g., the right of secession that arises in the exceptional situation of an oppressed or colonial people . . . [I]international law places great importance on the territorial integrity of nation states and, by and large, leaves the creation of a new state to be determined by the domestic law of the existing state of which the seceding entity presently forms a part. Where, as here, unilateral secession would be incompatible with the domestic Constitution, international law is likely to accept that conclusion. . .[139]

The second argument, based on self-determination, received more extended treatment, a treatment which deserves to become the standard modern account of the issue. The Supreme Court began by affirming that the principle of self-determination is 'a general principle of international law', citing a range of sources. It then addressed four questions: the definition of 'people'; the scope of the right; the safeguard clause and the question of 'oppressed' peoples; and the relationship of the self-determination to the so-called 'principle of effectivity'. The answers given should be briefly reviewed.

The definition of a 'people'

In argument, the *amicus curiae* had simply and starkly asserted the existence of a people of Quebec, and this was not for a moment denied by Canada. But this apparent agreement obscured a number of questions. Is the 'people' of Quebec the whole permanent population of the province, or is it the established Francophone community? Are there several peoples in Quebec, e.g. the

[137] See the text to supra nn. 12–16. [138] [1998] 1 SCR 217, 277 (para. 111).

[139] Ibid., at 278 (para. 112), citing R.Y. Jennings, *The Acquisition of Territory in International Law* (1963), at 8, 9.

Cree and other First Nations with traditional links to land there? If the answer is that the people of Quebec for international law purposes is not identical to the permanent population of a Canadian province (from which it should follow that other societies with established links to land and their own recognized identity in Quebec could also be regarded as peoples), what followed? Are all 'peoples', properly so-called, entitled to self-determination, at all or to the same extent? The briefs of the Minister of Justice for Canada, arguing for a negative answer to Question 2, had been able to avoid these questions. So, for the most part, did the briefs and opinions submitted on behalf of the *amicus curiae.* The Supreme Court began by acknowledging the uncertainty in the definition of a 'people' in international law, but it did advance matters to some extent. It said:

International law grants the right to self-determination to 'peoples'. Accordingly, access to the right requires the threshold step of characterizing as a people the group seeking self-determination. However, as the right to self-determination has developed by virtue of a combination of international agreements and conventions, coupled with state practice, with little formal elaboration of the definition of 'peoples', the result has been that the precise meaning of the term 'people' remains somewhat uncertain. It is clear that 'a people' may include only a portion of the population of an existing state. The right to self-determination has developed largely as a human right, and is generally used in documents that simultaneously contain references to 'nation' and 'state'. The juxtaposition of these terms is indicative that the reference to 'people' does not necessarily mean the entirety of a state's population. To restrict the definition of the term to the population of existing states would render the granting of a right to self-determination largely duplicative, given the parallel emphasis within the majority of the source documents on the need to protect the territorial integrity of existing states, and would frustrate its remedial purpose.[140]

In the end, however, it declined to go further:

While much of the Quebec population certainly shares many of the characteristics (such as a common language and culture) that would be considered in determining whether a specific group is a 'people', as do other groups within Quebec and/or Canada, it is not necessary to explore this legal characterization to resolve Question 2 . . . Similarly, it is not necessary for the Court to determine whether, should a Quebec people exist within the definition of public international law, such a people encompasses the entirety of the provincial population or just a portion thereof. Nor is it necessary to examine the position of the aboriginal population within Quebec . . . [W]hatever be the correct application of the definition of people(s) in this context, their right of self-determination cannot in the present circumstances be said to ground a right to unilateral secession.[141]

Despite its reticence, the passage supports both the view that self-determination applies to peoples in the ordinary sense of the term, and is not confined to the

[140] [1998] 1 SCR 217, at 281 (paras 123–4). [141] Ibid., at 281 (para. 125).

whole population of existing states, and the view that several peoples may co-exist in relation to a particular territory. At the same time the Supreme Court declined to say that the people of Quebec are a 'people' in the sense of international law, something the *amicus curiae* and the Solicitor-General for Canada had equally declined to argue.

The scope of the right to self-determination

Secondly, the Supreme Court addressed the question of the scope of self-determination, holding that this was 'normally fulfilled through internal self-determination—a people's pursuit of its political, economic, social and cultural development within the framework of an existing state'.[142] The right to external self-determination only arose in 'the most extreme of cases and, even then, under carefully defined circumstances',[143] having regard to the parallel need for respect for the territorial integrity of states. After citing the safeguard clause in the Friendly Relations Declaration and the Vienna Declaration of 1993, the Supreme Court went on to quote the final statement of the CSCE Vienna meeting in 1989, to the effect that '[n]o actions or situations in contravention of this principle will be recognized as legal by the participating States'.[144] It concluded, paraphrasing the language of the safeguard clause, by saying:

> There is no necessary incompatibility between the maintenance of the territorial integrity of existing states, including Canada, and the right of a 'people' to achieve a full measure of self-determination. A state whose government represents the whole of the people or peoples resident within its territory, on a basis of equality and without discrimination, and respects the principles of self-determination in its own internal arrangements, is entitled to the protection under international law of its territorial integrity.[145]

Colonial and oppressed peoples

This was a sufficient basis, combined with the uncontested proposition that the government of Canada does represent its whole people on a basis of equality and without discrimination, to justify a negative answer to Question 2. But the Supreme Court went on to discuss the 'positive' aspect of the safeguard clause, i.e. the issue whether external self-determination may sometimes be justified as the only method of preventing systematic oppression of a distinct people within a state. It said, again quoting Cassese's standard treatment:

> The right of colonial peoples to exercise their right to self-determination by breaking away from the 'imperial' power is now undisputed, but is irrelevant to this Reference.

[142] [1998] 1 SCR 217, at 281 (paras 123–4). [143] Ibid.

[144] Supra n. 140, at 283 (para. 129). For the text of the 1989 statement see (1989) 28 *ILM* 527.

[145] Supra n. 140, at 284 (para. 130).

The other clear case where a right to external self-determination accrues is where a people is subject to alien subjugation, domination or exploitation outside a colonial context. This recognition finds its roots in the Declaration on Friendly Relations . . .
A number of commentators have further asserted that the right to self-determination may ground a right to unilateral secession in a third circumstance . . . [T]he underlying proposition is that, when a people is blocked from the meaningful exercise of its right to self-determination internally, it is entitled, as a last resort, to exercise it by secession. The Vienna Declaration requirement that governments represent 'the whole people belonging to the territory without distinction of any kind' adds credence to the assertion that such a complete blockage may potentially give rise to a right of secession. Clearly, such a circumstance parallels the other two recognized situations in that the ability of a people to exercise its right to self-determination internally is somehow being totally frustrated. While it remains unclear whether this third proposition actually reflects an established international law standard, it is unnecessary for present purposes to make that determination. Even assuming that the third circumstance is sufficient to create a right to unilateral secession under international law, the current Quebec context cannot be said to approach such a threshold.[146]

The 'principle of effectiveness'

Finally it had been argued in a number of the opinions and by the *amicus curiae* that, while there might not be a right to secession based on self-determination by Quebec, nonetheless international recognition would readily be conferred on Quebec based upon its control over territory, i.e. on the principle of effectiveness. The Supreme Court could have avoided the issue entirely, since it had nothing to do with the questions actually asked of it. But that would have been unreal, and the Supreme Court did deal with the argument (as it also did in relation to Question 1). It said, *inter alia*:

Secession of a province from Canada, if successful in the streets, might well lead to the creation of a new state. Although recognition by other states is not, at least as a matter of theory, necessary to achieve statehood, the viability of a would-be state in the international community depends, as a practical matter, upon recognition by other states. That process of recognition is guided by legal norms. However, international recognition is not alone constitutive of statehood and, critically, does not relate back to the date of secession to serve retroactively as a source of a 'legal' right to secede in the first place. Recognition occurs only after a territorial unit has been successful, as a political fact, in achieving secession . . . [O]ne of the legal norms which may be recognized by states in granting or withholding recognition of emergent states is the legitimacy of the process by which the de facto secession is, or was, being pursued. The process of recognition, once considered to be an exercise of pure sovereign discretion, has come to be associated with legal norms. See, e.g., European Community Declaration on the Guidelines on the Recognition of New States in Eastern Europe and in the Soviet Union . . . While national interest and perceived political advantage to the recognizing state obviously play an important role, foreign

[146] Ibid., at 285, 286 (paras 132–5), citing Cassese, supra n. 3, at 334.

states may also take into account their view as to the existence of a right to self-determination on the part of the population of the putative state, and a counterpart domestic evaluation, namely, an examination of the legality of the secession according to the law of the state from which the territorial unit purports to have seceded. As we indicated in our answer to Question 1, an emergent state that has disregarded legitimate obligations arising out of its previous situation can potentially expect to be hindered by that disregard in achieving international recognition, at least with respect to the timing of that recognition. On the other hand, compliance by the seceding province with such legitimate obligations would weigh in favour of international recognition. The notion that what is not explicitly prohibited is implicitly permitted has little relevance where (as here) international law refers the legality of secession to the domestic law of the seceding state and the law of that state holds unilateral secession to be unconstitutional . . . It may be that a unilateral secession by Quebec would eventually be accorded legal status by Canada and other states, and thus give rise to legal consequences; but this does not support the more radical contention that subsequent recognition of a state of affairs brought about by a unilateral declaration of independence could be taken to mean that secession was achieved under colour of a legal right.[147]

Thus the Supreme Court deftly linked its answers to Questions 1 and 2. Under the Canadian Constitution as interpreted by the Supreme Court, a decision (by a clear majority of the electors of Quebec on a clear question put to them) favouring secession would oblige the federal government to negotiate the various outstanding issues in good faith, with a view to amending the Constitution either to redress grievances or to allow separation. The very existence of that constitutional right (even though its content would be largely non-justiciable at the time) internalizes the value of self-determination. At the same time it gives the indigenous people of Quebec their own right to be consulted and to be at the negotiating table.[148] Thus the Supreme Court made it clear, by the combination of its answers to Questions 1 and 2, that a referendum vote favouring secession (even if by a clear majority and on a clear question) would be neither automatic nor self-executing as a matter of Canadian law and international law. It would mark the beginning, not the end, of a negotiating process in which there would be substantial questions on the agenda, including even (since the position of the indigenous peoples of northern Quebec would be at stake) the territorial scope of the putative new state itself.

[147] Supra n. 140, at 289, 290 (paras 143, 144; see also para. 146).

[148] Ibid., at 287 (para. 139): 'the concern of aboriginal peoples is precipitated by the asserted right of Quebec to unilateral secession. In light of our finding that there is no such right applicable to the population of Quebec, either under the Constitution of Canada or at international law, but that on the contrary a clear democratic expression of support for secession would lead under the Constitution to negotiations in which aboriginal interests would be taken into account, it becomes unnecessary to explore further the concerns of the aboriginal peoples in this Reference'.

Taking these elements into account, the Supreme Court thus summarized its answer to Question 2 in the following terms:

> In summary, the international law right to self-determination only generates, at best, a right to external self-determination in situations of former colonies; where a people is oppressed, as for example under foreign military occupation; or where a definable group is denied meaningful access to government to pursue their political, economic, social and cultural development. In all three situations, the people in question are entitled to a right to external self-determination because they have been denied the ability to exert internally their right to self-determination. Such exceptional circumstances are manifestly inapplicable to Quebec under existing conditions. Accordingly, neither the population of the province of Quebec, even if characterized in terms of 'people' or 'peoples', nor its representative institutions, the National Assembly, the legislature or government of Quebec, possess a right, under international law, to secede unilaterally from Canada.[149]

The coherence and directness of the Supreme Court's answer to Question 2 provokes a further question. How much of a safeguard clause is the 'safeguard clause' itself? How much certainty is to be found in the inter-linked principles of self-determination and territorial integrity, as explained and rationalized by the Supreme Court? It is difficult to say, since in contexts such as these international law is operating at the extreme of its capacities to control or influence. Almost by definition such cases raise local views and feelings to their own extremes, and the temptations to external intervention too often prevail over any purely legal constraints. The Supreme Court was evidently aware of these uncertainties, as witness its careful formulations, and also, probably, its decision to go beyond the questions asked in order to speculate to a degree on the issues of effectiveness and on possible outcomes.

But there are two responses to the sceptic's doubts. The first is internal. The rule of law has been a conspicuous value of Canada and of both its principal legal traditions. One can only hope that the careful and accurate response given on Question 2 may help to focus, or refocus, the internal debate. The second is more properly a matter for the international lawyer. Although the dominant influence of international law in a given dispute cannot be assumed, neither should it be disregarded. There are strong systematic constraints favouring the principle of territorial integrity, which the lessons of the dissolution of the Soviet Union and the former Yugoslavia have powerfully reinforced.

4. Conclusion

The discussion in the preceding sections suggests the conclusion that, outside the colonial context, the primary subjects of external self-determination are

[149] Ibid., at 289, 290 (paras 143, 144).

the whole people of each state. That assumption is certainly made in the United Nations Charter, both implicitly and in its opening reference to 'the peoples of the United Nations'. Having regard to the established rules about self-defence and territorial integrity, the assumption appears to be inherent in the international system. The key difference with colonial or non-self-governing territories is that the identification of such territories involves the identification of a 'people' with rights against the metropolitan state; such territories have a separate status pending self-determination. Outside the colonial context there remains a strong presumption in favour of territorial integrity and against secession.

But this does not mean that the only 'peoples' relevant for international purposes are the whole people of each state. International lawyers should resist the conclusion that a widely-used term is to be stipulatively and narrowly defined, in such a way that it reflects neither normal usage nor the self-perception and identity of diverse and long-established human groups. That would make the principle of self-determination into a cruel deception: it may be so, but the presumption is to the contrary, and our function should be to make sense of existing normative language, corresponding to widely-regarded claims of right, and not to retreat into a self-denying legalism.

Moreover, although distinctions are sometimes drawn on the basis of classes or categories of groups (e.g. national, ethnic, religious or linguistic minorities, indigenous populations, etc.), these distinctions are imprecise at best. A more useful distinction is that between the people of the state as a whole, more or less dispersed minorities which are in some way distinctive in terms of ethnicity, language or belief, and 'concentrated' minorities forming a distinctive unit in a particular area of the state and constituting a substantial majority of the population in that area. All these groups can, depending on the circumstances, properly claim to be 'peoples'. But the consequences of the recognition of that claim must also depend on the circumstances, if the rights of others involved are not also to be denied.

The question of self-determination for whole populations was referred to earlier in this chapter. If the primary rule here remains that of non-intervention, gross violations of self-determination have given rise to legitimate international concern in many cases, and in a number of ways, the practice of non-intervention is being modified to take account of the value of self-determination.

So far as distinct groups within the state are concerned, the Canadian Supreme Court has confirmed that in normal circumstances, their right to self-government and self-determination does not extend to secession. But there remains the possibility that a particular people may be treated systematically by the central government in such a way as to become, in effect, non-self-governing with respect to the rest of the state. By analogy with GA Resolution 1541 (XV), Principle IV, if they are arbitrarily placed in a position

or status of subordination, the question of external self-determination is surely raised. Measures grossly discriminating against the people of a territory on grounds of their ethnic origin or cultural distinctiveness may effectively single out and thereby define the territory concerned as non-self-governing according to existing criteria, reinforcing or even constituting the case for external self-determination by the people of that territory.

But situations of internal colonization are very much the exception. In the normal case it is clear that ethnic or cultural distinctiveness of groups within the state, whether or not it qualifies those groups as 'peoples' for the purposes of the principle of self-determination in international law, does not entitle them to secede from the state of which they are part. Despite this, there is a growing acceptance that, for real equality to be achieved for such groups within the state, measures of a collective kind may be necessary. These can include measures of local autonomy, provisions for separate representation in legislative and executive bodies at central or regional level, land rights (especially in the case of indigenous groups with historical links to areas of land) and so on. The state's acknowledged interest in territorial integrity does not require the subjection of distinct groups within the state to a unitary government dominated by an ethnically defined majority. On the contrary, 'arithmetical' equality in such cases may involve a denial to a minority group of any adequate way of life other than that of assimilation into the majority group—in effect, a denial of their right to respect. In these ways, external and internal self-determination are linked, and the connection made by the Canadian Supreme Court between Question 1 (on constitutional law) and Question 2 (on international law) has a broader significance.

Thus, despite the difficulties and uncertainties identified earlier, the continuing vitality and potential for expansion of the principle of self-determination, at least as a directive principle, should not be underestimated. Complaints are often made about the 'international double standards' said to exist in the differential treatment of colonial and non-colonial 'peoples'. But the principle of self-determination shows no sign of disappearing from the language of international relations with the virtual demise of Western colonialism. The principle is entrenched in general terms in the United Nations Charter and in the two Human Rights Covenants, and it has been repeated in other significant international instruments adopted at intervals since 1966. It was reasonable to concentrate initially on the elimination of more obvious forms of colonial rule, but unreasonable (then and now) to treat international law as static and incapable of further development. But if the step is taken to apply self-determination outside the colonial context, the consequences of those applications inevitably become more diverse or diffuse, and the range of outcomes more various. Outside the colonial context, the legitimacy of maintaining national unity and territorial integrity must be accepted. But national unity and territorial integrity are consistent with a variety of outcomes.

This involves admitting that, at least outside colonial or quasi-colonial contexts, both self-determination and the cognate right to democratic self-government are inherently non-self-executing. They are critical standards; they do not themselves determine particular institutions or outcomes. They can be used to disqualify institutions or outcomes which are evidently inconsistent with self-determination or democratic rule, and to justify attempts to remedy them. That may be a more modest outcome than the self-executing cry for independence based on a bare majority of votes (50 per cent plus one) of a claimed constituency. It still seems to be worth having.

A Postscript on Kosovo

The lectures on which this chapter is based were delivered well before the Kosovo crisis led to the use of massive armed force in the form of the NATO bombing campaign beginning in April 1999 and ending with Security Council resolution 1244 (1999) of 10 June 1999 and the withdrawal of Yugoslav troops from the province. Prior to the conflict, the internationally agreed approach to the future of Kosovo was articulated in Security Council resolution 1199 (1998) of 23 September 1998, preambular paragraphs 12 and 13, which referred to the need for 'an enhanced status for Kosovo, a substantially greater degree of autonomy, and meaningful self-administration', while affirming 'the commitment of all Member States to the sovereignty and territorial integrity of the Federal Republic of Yugoslavia'. See also Security Council resolution 1160 (1998) of 31 March 1998.

Security Council resolution 1244 (1999), heralded as a defeat for the government of Yugoslavia, involved no change in these principles, despite some ambiguities on questions of future status. Adopted by 14–0 with China abstaining, the resolution referred to 'the grave humanitarian situation in Kosovo, Federal Republic of Yugoslavia', and to the imperative need 'to provide for the safe and free return of all refugees and displaced persons to their homes'. It referred in the preamble to 'the Kosovo population' but in paragraph 10 to 'the people of Kosovo'. It reaffirmed 'the commitment of all Member States to the sovereignty and territorial integrity of the Federal Republic of Yugoslavia and the other States of the region, as set out in the Helsinki Final Act', as well as 'the call in previous resolutions for substantial autonomy and meaningful self-administration for Kosovo'. Acting under Chapter VII of the Charter, it established an international military and civil presence in Kosovo (effective until the Security Council otherwise decides), and limited the return of Yugoslav military or police forces to token levels. At the same time it demanded the demilitarization of the Kosovo Liberation Army (KLA), and called for 'the development of provisional institutions for democratic and autonomous self-government pending a political settlement,

including the holding of elections'. A longer-term political process is to be established 'to determine Kosovo's future status, taking into account the Rambouillet accords (S/1999/648)'. Those accords, and the two annexes to the resolution, purport to affirm the territorial integrity of Yugoslavia notwithstanding the existence of autonomous self-governing institutions. For example, Annex I (a statement of G–8 Foreign Ministers adopted on 8 May 1999) formulates the following 'general principle':

> A political process towards the establishment of an interim political framework agreement providing for a substantial self-government for Kosovo, taking full account of the Rambouillet accords and the principles of sovereignty and territorial integrity of the Federal Republic of Yugoslavia and the other countries of the region, and the demilitarization of the KLA . . .

Annex II refers to 'the development of provisional democratic self-governing institutions to ensure conditions for a peaceful and normal life for all inhabitants in Kosovo'.[150]

[150] On Kosovo see further Phillips, 'Comprehensive Peace in the Balkans: The Kosovo Question', 18 *Human Rights Q* (1996) 820; Weller, 'The Rambouillet Conference on Kosovo', 75 *International Affairs* (1999) 57; Simma, 'NATO, the UN, and the Use of Force: Legal Aspects', 10 *EJIL* (1999) 1.

3

Reconciling Five Competing Conceptual Structures of Indigenous Peoples' Claims in International and Comparative Law

BENEDICT KINGSBURY*

On what conceptual foundations do legal claims made by indigenous peoples rest? Uncertainty on this issue has had the benefit of encouraging the flowering of multiple approaches, but it has also done much to heighten national dissensus on questions involving indigenous peoples, and it has been a serious obstacle to negotiation in the United Nations (UN) and the Organization of American States (OAS) of proposed Declarations on the Rights of Indigenous Peoples. This chapter seeks to clarify the debate by distinguishing and exploring five fundamentally different conceptual structures employed in claims brought by indigenous peoples or members of such groups:[1]

human rights and non-discrimination claims
minority claims
self-determination claims
historic sovereignty claims
claims as indigenous peoples, including claims based on treaties or other agreements between indigenous peoples and states.

Each of these conceptual structures has its own style of argument, historical account and canon, patterns of legitimation and delegitimation, institutional adherents, discursive community, and boundary markers. Each depends on simple premisses to define its locus. These premisses have been adopted and adapted in political struggles. Protagonists in these struggles purport to render the broad analytic distinctions between the categories as deeply cleaved boundaries, although most recognize that these distinctions are reconsidered

* In memory of Andrew Gray (1955–99), whose death in a plane crash in Vanuatu robbed the indigenous peoples' movement of a selfless chronicler, indefatigable activist, and great friend.

[1] Much of the doctrinal structure and background omitted here is explored in Kingsbury, 'Claims by Non-State Groups in International Law', 25 *Cornell International Law Journal* (1992) 481.

and the boundaries repositioned over time. Debates as to the essence of each conceptual structure, and especially as to the boundaries between them, are often proxies for clashes of political interest. The construction of conceptual structures and of lines between them is a form of political expression, but one that utilizes, and is thus conditioned by while itself affecting, languages of law and philosophy. Political interests are scarcely veiled in polar positions taken in arguments as to whether human rights can be held by groups or only by individuals, whether it is correct under the International Covenant on Civil and Political Rights that minorities have no right of self-determination but all peoples do, whether the operative concept is indigenous peoples or indigenous people. For lawyer-diplomats, by contrast, a frequent objective is to bridge these political divides, making the boundaries indistinct and permeable, so that they are not necessarily determinative at all. This latter project is shared by some lawyer-activists, but they proceed from the premiss that there are conceptual differences between the categories, and that the political impetus behind a particular category can be astutely marshalled for some other objective by extending that category's domain. This is one purpose of arguments that self-determination is actually a human right, that minority rights to culture extend to indigenous land rights, that all indigenous peoples by virtue of that designation have the right to self-determination.

In political negotiations about normative matters, the question of which concept is applicable is often set up as the key threshold issue—its resolution is seen as a key to channelling argument, determining which structure of analysis and legitimation will then prevail, and thus influencing outcomes. In initial negotiations on the UN and OAS declarations, many state representatives tended to urge that the issues be addressed as human rights or perhaps minority rights questions, while indigenous representatives often framed the core issues in terms of self-determination or historic sovereignty. Over time some convergence has occurred on the utility of a fifth category—the notion that some legal claims raised by indigenous peoples are *sui generis* and have a distinct conceptual structure. The forensic point of this chapter is that different claims made by indigenous peoples may fall into any of these five categories, or into several at once, and that the totality of these claims as a genre cannot and should not be understood as belonging exclusively to any one or other category. While genuine analytical distinctions underpin this division into categories, these distinctions do not in themselves resolve many of the more difficult problems that arise in practice. Three sets of practical problems arise for consideration in this chapter. First, how far and how successfully may the first four, well-established categories—which have in large measure been structured by norms and patterns of legal practice not related specifically to indigenous peoples—be adapted to the distinctive features of indigenous peoples' issues? Secondly, how well do these different and apparently competing concepts fit together in an

integrated legal structure? Thirdly, do the problems and limits of these processes of adaptation and integration of the first four categories suggest, against the background of the increasing salience of indigenous peoples' issues and the rapid evolution of law and policy in this area, that a new legal category of claims of 'indigenous peoples' has been established, and if so, what is its justification, structure and significance? These questions will be addressed in discussion of each of the five categories. The significance and implications of this five-fold division, including strategies it encourages and the contextual variation and legitimation this fragmentation make possible, will be considered in the conclusion.

This chapter is concerned with conceptual issues rather than doctrinal analysis or political assessment. Having been prepared as a specialized course, the outlines of the arguments about the identification, adaptation, and reconciliation of distinct conceptual structures will be illustrated to a disproportionate extent—for reasons of pedagogical practicality—by specific cases in national and international tribunals. A consequence of focusing on juridical decisions is that the lineaments of the conceptual structures are those identifiable in international jurisprudence and in a sample of those national legal systems where 'indigenous peoples' issues' are a subject of substantial litigation and express judicial articulation. It is suggested that a comparable but more ambitious analytical project could be undertaken with reference to political discourse or to non-judicial policy-making, broadening the range of actors and regions involved.

1. Human Rights and Non-discrimination

Whether issues raised by indigenous peoples can be addressed exclusively within the existing framework of international human rights law, or whether by contrast a new legal category of indigenous peoples' rights requires recognition, is a fundamental political debate that exemplifies the political tendency to polarize around questions of which legal category applies. Some state representatives in UN and OAS negotiations have suggested that the conscientious application of human rights standards is all that is necessary satisfactorily to address problems suffered by members of indigenous groups. In this view, the historic problems to be overcome are discrimination against indigenous peoples and unequal treatment by the state, and the solution is to establish effective national institutions for human rights protection where these have been lacking, and to ensure true equality of treatment between members of indigenous groups and other citizens. State representatives who take this line are often opposed to claims to collective rights, suspecting that these are incompatible with true equality among the citizenry. Some also oppose any recognition of indigenous groups as 'peoples', fearing that this

may place the indigenous group outside the national 'people' whose existence legitimizes the state and whose bounds define a limit of the equal rights-bearing community. The problems with this polar position will be considered further below. The opposite position taken by some indigenous representatives, that the human rights programme has been irrelevant in practice and is a conceptual obstacle to realization of indigenous aspirations, is animated by bitter experience of atrocities and monumental injustices in some supposedly rights-protecting countries. For some radical leaders this view represents an outright repudiation of existing state arrangements. For others it embodies critiques of rights discourse as a diversion that have been made in legal-liberal polities, for example Derrick Bell's critique of the civil rights struggle as channelling energies of black Americans into areas of symbolic success but with limited impact on underlying problems.[2] These cautions are important, and the mistrust grounded in historical experience is great, but strong repudiation of the international human rights programme is not part of the mainstream agenda of the international indigenous peoples' movement. Many indigenous groups, antagonized by the assimilationism of the 'human rights only' position and aware that such equal rights rhetoric has historically been accompanied by gross injustices, point out that the human rights programme has not worked adequately in institutional practice, and argue that it is normatively insufficient. This suggests that the human rights programme ought to be used, and that it might be made more useful by reform, but leaves for later consideration the question whether a reformed human rights programme could ever satisfactorily address all the issues, and in particular whether a distinct category of indigenous peoples' rights ought to exist alongside the human rights programme and other international legal structures.

Claims by members of indigenous peoples are often claims to respect for basic human rights, for example a claim to be free from torture or slavery. Such claims are usually made against the state, but may be substantively directed at conduct by certain non-state groups, including armed bands, mining corporations, or indigenous peoples' organizations. At issue is whether the human rights programme can be adapted and renovated to take account of distinctive issues raised by indigenous peoples. In countries where the human rights programme is not normatively important or where it is not operationalized, questions about incorporating indigenous peoples into it are rather abstract and futuristic, although indigenous peoples in some such countries may already receive some measure of state support or protection. In evaluating the adaptability of the human rights programme, the focus must be on this programme as it is enunciated and operationalized in relevant national institutions and in international institutional practice.

[2] D. Bell, *And We Are Not Saved: The Elusive Quest for Racial Justice* (1987).

A fundamental question in human rights claims made by members of indigenous groups against the state is how far the distinctive situation of the indigenous group is relevant. Issues relating to the fair treatment of groups, and the inevitable questions about individual identity and membership which any operational reference to groups entails, are entangled with standard human rights claims based on the suffering of individuals in several existing normative structures. 'Genocide' imports issues of harm to groups into the very definition of the crime committed against any individual. The concept of 'ethnocide', although not well-developed juridically, is understood by human rights advocates to extend the ambit of genocide to destruction of culture and other conditions essential for the continued distinctive existence of a group. In practice the interaction between individual rights claims and group membership is most systematically established by prohibitions of wrongful discrimination. The strong international policy against racial discrimination has been an important source of leverage in indigenous claims. In the landmark decision of the High Court of Australia on aboriginal title in *Mabo*, for example, Brennan J indicated that the unacceptability of racial discrimination or other violations of fundamental internationally-recognized human rights was a strong reason for that court to be willing to reverse the long-established principle of Australian property law that aboriginal people hold no rights to land at common law except those derived from the Crown.[3] Conversely, the identity of a particular individual *vis-à-vis* a particular indigenous group may be relevant in introducing the question of discrimination to issues that would otherwise be unproblematic. In *Means v District Court of the Navajo Nation*, for example, Russell Means, a prominent Oglala Sioux activist, was arrested by Navajo Nation police on the Navajo Reservation for alleged assault there of Navajo victims, but he argued that the US statutory provision that confers jurisdiction on the Navajo tribal court over non-members who are Indian, but not over other non-members, is contrary to the provisions for equality and non-discrimination in the US Constitution.[4]

A survey of decisions by state courts in countries formally and substantively committed to judicial enforcement of some human rights shows divergent patterns and much uncertainty in addressing the issue whether, and how, the distinctive situation of indigenous groups affects human rights arguments. One line of approach is to deny any distinctive character to indigenous claims on the ground that human rights are universal, not special. An illustration is *Lyng v Northwest Indian Cemetery Protective Association*,[5] where Indian plaintiffs challenged a proposal by the US Forest Service to build a road on public land in the Chimney Rock area of Northern California, on the ground that the road would effectively destroy the tranquillity essential to the continuation of

[3] *Mabo v Queensland* 107 ALR 1 (1992).

[4] Supreme Court of the Navajo Nation, 1999.

[5] 485 US 439 (1988).

Indian meditative religious practices on this land that had been pursued for many generations. Writing for a majority in the US Supreme Court, Justice O'Connor rejected the argument that the Indians' right to religious freedom under the First Amendment was infringed by road construction. Although federally recognized Indian tribes occupy a special place in the US legal system, and US law recognizes aspects of what is often called 'sovereignty' of Indian tribes, Justice O'Connor did not see this as relevant to a First Amendment claim. Her position was that Indians have exactly the same First Amendment rights as anyone else, and that these do not extend to controlling the use of public lands. The historic experience of Indians, including the loss of control of lands they had long used, was not material, nor was the ancient character and spatial location of this particular religious practice. Her argument was that the courts must be neutral as amongst religions, and cannot begin inquiries into the veracity or merits or historical weight of religious claims that would privilege some religious claims over others. But it might well be argued, to the contrary, that the First Amendment jurisprudence does exactly this in privileging understandings of religion that depend not on expanses that since colonization have become 'public' lands, but on private buildings protected by a property rights regime that is itself buttressed by First Amendment limits on state action. The process by which land historically used by Indians for religious observance became 'public lands', and the weakness of the property rights they enjoy, is integral to evaluating protection of their religious freedom. Supposed neutrality in human rights protection can be, as here, a distortion where the human rights question is separated from the property rights regime and from governance regimes, such as federal trust responsibilities or frameworks for self-government.

A second approach is to start with a requirement of universality but modify it to favour indigenous peoples where disadvantage or past injustices warrant. In *Gerhardy v Brown*,[6] a defendant who was not a member of the Pitjantjatjara and thus had no right to enter lands restored to Pitjantjatjara communities under the Pitjantjatjara Land Rights Act (a South Australian statute), challenged his prosecution for illegal entry onto the lands by arguing that the statutory provision limiting his access infringed the Racial Discrimination Act (a Commonwealth statute intended to give effect to provisions in the International Convention on the Elimination of All Forms of Racial Discrimination). A majority in the High Court of Australia took the view that the South Australian legislation was on its face racially discriminatory in that only Aboriginal people could be Pitjantjatjara and so entitled to free access to the land, whereas non-Pitjantjatjara (including non-Pitjantjatjara Aboriginal people like the defendant) were entitled to access only if other conditions were satisfied (e.g. if they had permission, or were a

[6] 57 ALR 472 (1985).

candidate for election to public office). A strong argument may be made that this approach to the concept of legally prohibited discrimination is misguided, and that the court should have asked whether the measures had an objective and reasonable justification, were proportionate to this justification, were not unnecessarily under- or over-inclusive, and reasonably accommodated the interests of others.[7] In the terms used in US jurisprudence, the question is whether the classification of Pitjantjatjara by reference to traditional ownership of the land, when only Aboriginal people could satisfy the requirement of being a traditional owner, and the exclusion of non-Pitjantjatjara from the land, was a measure justified by compelling state interest and was narrowly tailored to meet the legitimate objectives of the statute. In *Gerhardy*, the court failed to make such an inquiry (although in subsequent cases it has indicated that this approach might be modified in future).[8] The court held, however, that the statutory provision was saved by the provision in the International Convention excluding from the category of racial discrimination: 'Special measures taken for the sole purpose of securing adequate advancement of certain racial or ethnic groups or individuals . . . in order to ensure such groups or individuals equal enjoyment of human rights and fundamental freedoms . . .' The policy of this Convention provision is widely understood to apply even where there is no specific evidence of the effects on particular groups or persons of past discrimination. It thus diverges from, for example, current US judicial approaches to affirmative action, under which racially-based affirmative action or reverse discrimination is subject to the same requirements as to compelling state interest and narrowness of tailoring as is racial discrimination against discrete and insular minorities. Nevertheless, some members of the High Court in *Gerhardy* were strongly influenced in their finding on prima facie discrimination by concern that allowing the government to evade prohibitions of racial discrimination by reference to such criteria as traditional ownership might open a loophole for what Gibbs CJ called 'the most obnoxious discrimination'. By this he seems to have meant apartheid. His suspicions of 'traditional ownership' as a sufficient criterion for excluding non-owners overcame the argument that most owners of property can exclude non-owners; he focused on 'the vast area of the lands . . . more than one-tenth of the state' to distinguish the situation of the Pitjantjatjara from that of ordinary property holders, although Australian property law protects the exclusionary rights of non-aboriginal holders of very large tracts. This logic—that claims settlements with indigenous peoples for restoration of land to traditional owners may involve racial discrimination against non-members of these groups—is a basis for much political

[7] See e.g. Brownlie, 'Rights of Peoples in International Law', in J. Crawford (ed.), *The Rights of Peoples* (1988) 1, at 9.

[8] See e.g. *Western Australia v Commonwealth*, 183 CLR 378 (1995), esp. 451; this case upheld the Native Title Act 1993 against a challenge under the Racial Discrimination Act.

opposition to, and some judicial concerns about, land claims settlements or other historically-grounded arrangements. Some of the concerns are well-founded, most obviously where the language of 'indigenous rights' is used to justify domination and abuse of 'non-indigenous', but also where a state action purporting to favour a disadvantaged indigenous group is in fact a disguised measure to serve another sectional interest, whether a mining company or an exclusively self-serving elite. The concept of non-discrimination is thus valuable in, but also a potential obstacle to, indigenous peoples' claims. It too is often described with an air of neutrality that belies its real workings, especially its connections with property, self-government, history, and social justice.

A third approach is to uphold special measures by states that benefit indigenous groups precisely *because* of the distinctive histories and experiences of these groups. In *Morton v Mancari*, the US Supreme Court was unanimous in upholding an explicit policy of the US Bureau of Indian Affairs to give preference in its hiring and promotion policies to members of federally-recognized Indian tribes. Rejecting a due process challenge by non-Indian employees, the court held: 'The preference, as applied, is granted to Indians not as a discrete racial group, but, rather, as members of quasi-sovereign entities whose lives and activities are governed by the BIA in a unique fashion.'[9] The court here steps outside the structure of standard human rights and non-discrimination arguments, focusing on the distinctive history of Indian–US relations and on the trust obligations of the US toward Indians, elements that were to make almost no appearance in *Lyng* when the issue involved the high political stakes of public land use rather than the arcane world of the Bureau of Indian Affairs. Even in *Morton*, the court's approach is not one of judicial rights-activism; the opinion is very deferential toward congressional policy, and reaffirms the plenary power of Congress in relation to Indians. The judgment is thus suggestive of the ambivalence of state judicial recognition of a distinct body of law triggered by identities as indigenous peoples: the category may have significant effects, but state government institutions endeavour to reserve to themselves the power of shaping it.

This analysis of *Lyng*, *Gerhardy*, and *Morton* suggests that they differ significantly, representing three approaches to the use of human rights and non-discrimination arguments in indigenous peoples' claims. *Lyng* embraces a universal human rights approach in which indigenous claims receive no special consideration, *Gerhardy* allows special consideration but under careful watch as presumptive discrimination, and *Morton* permits the legislature to adopt special measures without special scrutiny for reasons of history and the historically-grounded trust relationship the US is deemed to have assumed. Nevertheless, they have much in common. In each case the questions are

[9] 413 US 535, 554 (1974).

framed in terms of state law: the meaning of the First Amendment, the Racial Discrimination Act, the Due Process clause. There is no real indigenous voice in any of the cases; the cases are about Indians and Aborigines, but they themselves do not figure greatly in the judicial opinions. The courts do not demonstrate a close grasp of indigenous experience in relation to religion, land, self-government, or state institutions such as the Bureau of Indian Affairs. This judicial pattern is changing, however, as negotiations and decisions on matters such as land, fisheries, resource management, language, education, and broadcasting evolve into general state acceptance of some degree of indigenous participation, self-government, and voice. Landmark judicial decisions in New Zealand, Canada, and to some extent Australia have pointed the way toward, without necessarily themselves accomplishing, this turn. *New Zealand Maori Council v Attorney-General* established the principles of the Treaty of Waitangi as in some way constitutional, and envisaged Maori and the Crown proceeding as treaty partners; this has since become a canon of New Zealand public policy.[10] *Delgamuuk v British Columbia* establishes that indigenous understandings of relations to land and territory, embodied often in oral history, are admissible and relevant in the construction of a concept of aboriginal title that is not simply a creation and sufferance of the state legal system, but embodies both indigenous history and indigenous aspirations. While the Supreme Court of Canada did not address forms of self-government, the Court's approach is suggestive of such a development, and its call for governments and first nations to negotiate has been understood in that context. In neither *NZMC* nor *Delgamuuk* did the court rest heavily on standard human rights concepts. Rather than stretch and adapt these, the courts focus on elaborating a body of public law in which certain types of indigenous claims are *sui generis. Mabo v Queensland* is more equivocal in this respect. Human rights considerations figure as a justification for reversing earlier authority on aboriginal title, and much of the discussion is about concepts of property in common law rather than about the terms of a public political relationship of the sort that the New Zealand Court of Appeal founded on the Treaty of Waitangi. Nevertheless, the situation of indigenous peoples' property in Australia became a substantial *sui generis* issue, with the Commonwealth government seeking at least some aboriginal input through the Australian and Torres Strait Islander Commission before adoption of the Native Title Act 1993. [11] The weakness of the public law element became manifest in the retreat from parts of the High Court's jurisprudence in the Native Title Amendment Act 1998, government recalcitrance in dealing with and funding the Commission, and the unilateral terms of government policy on matters

[10] [1987] 1 NZLR 641.

[11] For criticism, see e.g. Coe, 'ATSIC: Self-Determination or Otherwise', 35 *Race and Class* (1994) 35.

ranging from 'national reconciliation' to the restructuring of aboriginal land councils.[12]

This review indicates that the adaptation of the category of 'human rights' is of fundamental importance in addressing indigenous issues, and that courts and state institutions often prefer to address such issues within this frame, but practice and experience suggest that additional concepts are needed and are often deployed. Issues connected with distinct histories, cultures, and identities animate the search for alternative concepts of international law and national law related to, but going beyond, individual human rights and non-discrimination. These concepts, increasingly influential in judicial practice and political negotiations relating to indigenous peoples' claims, will be considered in subsequent sections.

2. Minorities

'Minorities'—or more often, a variant such as 'national minorities'—has been utilized as a juridical category in international treaty law for several centuries, and was actively promulgated and operationalized by post-World War I legal instruments and League of Nations institutions. After 1945, however, states looked to the lessons of Nazi Germany's irredentist use of disaffected German minorities in neighbouring countries, and to the imminent problems of nation-building in post-colonial states, and became reluctant to establish international law standards focused specifically on minorities, preferring instead to build the general human rights programme applicable to all individuals. Hence the lack of minority rights clauses, beyond prohibitions of discrimination, in the 1948 Universal Declaration of Human Rights, the 1950 European Convention on Human Rights, and comparable regional instruments in the Americas and Africa. The body of international legal instruments focused specifically on 'minorities' is thus an impoverished one. Recognition of a need to face this deficiency resulted in the early 1990s in the UN Declaration on Minorities (1992) and the Council of Europe Framework Convention for the Protection of National Minorities (1995), but neither is very expansive, as many state governments have continued to be unwilling to support general normative provisions that may encourage group demands or inhibit national integration. Germany, for example, is willing to grant significant legal entitlements to some long-established groups within Germany, including the Danish and Sorb minorities, but much less to other minority groups. France continues to assert that there are no minorities in

[12] An overview of public law issues in Australian courts is Clarke, '"Indigenous" People and Constitutional Law', in P. Hanks and D. Cass, *Australian Constitutional Law: Materials and Commentary*, 6th edn. (1999) 50.

France to whom international law instruments on minorities should apply, although its internal legal practice is more nuanced, especially in favouring a degree of autonomy for Corsica. Algeria, Burundi, Madagascar, Senegal, Turkey, and Venezuela are among other states that have at times taken positions similar to that of France. [13] Article 27 of the International Covenant on Civil and Political Rights (ICCPR), an instrument drafted in the early 1950s and adopted in 1966, thus remains the principal general minority rights treaty text of global application, and it is worded as an individual rights provision, phrased with an aspiration to avoid encouraging new minorities to appear, and seeking to impose only modest duties on states.[14]

If many state governments have been hesitant to see 'minorities' operate as a flourishing general legal category, wishing to subsume it into human rights, many indigenous leaders and advocates have insisted on distinguishing themselves from 'minorities', arguing that classifying indigenous peoples as minorities is belittling, missing what is distinctive about being indigenous and being a people.[15] This political struggle about categories goes to important issues of identity and philosophy. It is misleading, however, to transpose these political misgivings about the applicability to indigenous peoples' issues of a broad category of 'minorities' so as to exclude this category from the framework of forensic law as it is currently practised. Advocates, some national courts, and above all the UN Human Rights Committee have seen in Article 27 a basis and justification for addressing indigenous issues, enabling these institutions to ensure that they are not bypassed and to take an active part in responding to the rising demand for action on these issues.[16] In dealing with indigenous issues, the Human Rights Committee has increasingly interpreted Article 27 in a creative and expansive manner so as to elude some of the strictures states may have hoped to set upon it.[17] This has been reinforced by national courts, and by various national commissions and advisory bodies.

[13] For discussion see P. Thornberry, 'The UN Declaration on the Rights of Persons belonging to National or Ethnic, Religious and Linguistic Minorities: Background, Analysis, and an Update', in A. Phillips and A. Rosas (eds), *Universal Minority Rights* (1995), 13.

[14] Article 27 provides: 'In those States in which ethnic, religious or linguistic minorities exist, persons belonging to such minorities shall not be denied the right, in community with the other members of their group, to enjoy their own culture, to profess and practise their own religion, or to use their own language.'

[15] Such a distinction is partially acknowledged in Article 30 of the Convention on the Rights of the Child (1989), which broadly tracks the language of Article 27 but refers to minorities 'or persons of indigenous origin'.

[16] Article 27 has also been used even where not directly applicable as a treaty text. It was relied on, for example, by the Inter-American Commission on Human Rights as powerful evidence of the existing state of international law relevant to the interpretation of the less specific American Declaration on the Rights and Duties of Man: the *Yanomami* case, Case 7615 (Brazil), Res. 12/85, adopted 5 March 1985.

[17] For an overview, see Human Rights Committee General Comment No. 23 (50) on Article 27, UN Doc. A/49/40, p. 107.

Perhaps the most important juridical application of Article 27 for some indigenous peoples has been a series of holdings that failure of the state to protect indigenous land and resource bases, including the continuing effects of past wrongs, may in certain circumstances amount to a violation of the right to culture protected in Article 27. The leading case is the views of the Human Rights Committee in *Ominayak v Canada*, where the Committee concluded that the historical inequity of the failure to assure to the Lubicon Lake Band a reservation to which they had a strong claim, and the effect on the band of certain recent developments including oil and timber concessions, 'threaten the way of life and culture of the Lubicon Lake Band, and constitute a violation of Article 27 so long as they continue'.[18] The Committee has incorporated this understanding of Article 27 in numerous discussions of state reports, and has pressed states to adopt this expansive understanding of their Article 27 obligations in national policy. For example, the Committee weighed in to the controversy concerning dam projects on the Biobio river in Chile, expressing concern that these 'might affect the way of life and the rights of persons belonging to the Mapuche and other indigenous communities', and casting doubt on the Chilean government policy of land acquisition and resettlement: 'Relocation and compensation may not be appropriate in order to comply with article 27 of the Covenant.'[19] This view that Article 27 obligations impose constraints on government economic development policy was applied as the rule of decision by the Supreme Administrative Court of Finland in nullifying deeds for mining claims in Sami areas in a series of cases beginning in 1996.[20] The District Court of Sapporo made similar use of Article 27 in finding in 1997 that the government had improperly failed to consider Ainu culture before proceeding to build the Nibutani Dam.[21]

Notwithstanding opposition by some indigenous groups to any categorization as minorities, Article 27 may be an important source of leverage for indigenous peoples in securing recognition. The need to make periodic reports under the ICCPR spurred debate within Japan about the government line that the country is homogeneous, leading eventually in the late 1980s to the official abandonment of the view of Japan as entirely homogeneous, and agreement that Ainu are a distinct ethnic group for purposes of Article 27. This in turn paved the way in the Japanese political system for

[18] UN Doc. A/49/40, Annex IX, 1, 27 (1990). Other cases taking this approach include *Länsman* v *Finland (No. 1)*, Communication 511/1992, UN Doc. CCPR/C/57/1, p. 74; *Länsman v Finland (No. 2)*, Communication 671/1995, UN Doc. CCPR/C/58/D/671/1995; and *Kitok v Sweden* Communication 197/1985, HRC Official Records 1987–88, Vol. 2, 442.

[19] UN Doc. CCPR/C/79/Add.104, 30 March 1999, para. 22.

[20] See especially *Kasivarsi Reindeer Herders' Cooperative v Ministry of Trade and Industry*, File No. 1447, Helsinki, 15 May 1996. See also the decisions of 31 March 1999 in cases 692 and 693.

[21] *Kayano and Kaizawa v Hokkaido Expropriation Committee* (1997), translated by M. Levin, 38 *ILM* (1999) 397.

the government to move glacially toward recognition of Ainu as indigenous. Although such recognition was not included in the Ainu law of 1997, official government statements have moved in this direction, nudged significantly by the finding of the Sapporo District Court that Ainu are indigenous, in a case that was itself leveraged by Japan's acceptance of Article 27.

Another source of misgivings by some indigenous groups about Article 27 is that its complex implications go well beyond possible claims by groups against states. *Lovelace v Canada*[21a] represents on its face the use of Article 27 by a group member to challenge the group's own policy of excluding her. Under the Indian Act Sandra Lovelace had lost her status as an Indian by the act of marrying a non-Indian man, whereas Indian men who married non-Indian women did not lose their status. Her exclusion was upheld by the political representatives of her own Maliseet band on the Tobique reservation. But the Committee's handling of the case can be appreciated also as a response to a century of the Indian Act policy of assimilation. Not only did the Indian Act transform women who married out into non-Indians, and their children with them, it also ended the Indian status of men who served in the Canadian army, and of Indians who became 'enfranchised'. Marrying a white, having a white father, military service, and civic entitlement to vote were all badges of honour qualifying Indians to upgrade to non-Indian. This established pattern, of assimilation combined with gender-targeting, had structured many Indian communities.[22] The Committee's views reflect sensitivity to the problems for community decision-making and capacity of disentrenching such a longstanding identity-shaping system. The Committee did not treat the case as one of discrimination in Indian communities between men and women,[23] nor did it find simply that Article 27 entailed that all ethnic Indians wishing to do so should be entitled to move back to their band's reservation. The Committee focused narrowly on Sandra Lovelace's own circumstances as a divorcee wishing again to live on her reservation after her divorce. Partly because it chose not to confront the entire structure of the Indian Act, a paternalistic dimension is discernible in the Committee's language. This element apart, the prudence of the Committee's circumspection was borne out by the upheaval and long process of adjustment precipitated by the reform and partial rectification of the assimilationist provisions of the Indian Act in 1985.[24]

[21a] *Lovelace v Canada* (1981) 68 ILR 17 (Human Rights Committee).

[22] Turpel, 'The Women of Many Nations in Canada', in International Work Group for Indigenous Affairs, *Indigenous Women on the Move* (1990) 93.

[23] The Committee's approach may be explained more austerely as being crafted to avoid problems of the Covenant's application *ratione temporis*: Sandra Lovelace had married, and lost her Indian status, in 1970, but the Covenant entered into force for Canada only in 1976. But the Committee itself develops its reasoning as an interpretation of the substantive provisions of the ICCPR rather than as a construction of residually available provisions.

[24] Long after this amendment making excluded women and their children eligible for reinstatement, the status of future generations remains unresolved.

The regime of minority rights involves intricate dynamics and balances between individual claims, state action, community autonomy, and participation by members of a minority group in its shared cultural and economic life.

Is the status of a group as historically prior, or indigenous, relevant to the way in which these balances are struck? The US Supreme Court decision in *Santa Clara Pueblo v Martinez* confronted the question of the significance of distinct Indian history and political identity in refusing to overturn a decision of the Santa Clara tribal authorities denying membership to the children of Julia Martinez. Ms Martinez was a member of the Santa Clara Pueblo, a traditional reservation community of fewer than 1500 people in which gender was an important explicit part of the definition of social roles. Her children had grown up on the reservation and were Tewa-speaking, but were excluded from membership and thus from inheriting property or the right of residence on the reservation after her death, because Santa Clara membership rules excluded children of a female tribe-member born to a marriage with a non-member, while including children of a male tribe-member in such circumstances.[25] The argument of Justice Thurgood Marshall's opinion for the court begins by quoting with approval from Chief Justice John Marshall in *Worcester v Georgia*:[26] 'Indian tribes are "distinct, independent political communities, retaining their original natural rights" in matters of local self-government.'[27] The court affirms the power of Congress to make laws regulating Indian tribes and conferring federal court jurisdiction, but favours judicial circumspection where Congress has not clearly given federal courts the power to intervene. Finding that no such power had been granted here, the court is able to avoid consideration of the membership issue. The opinion is anchored by the court's recognition 'that the tribes remain quasi-sovereign nations which, by government structure, culture, and source of sovereignty are in many ways foreign to the constitutional institutions of the federal and State governments'.[28] This is buttressed by policy arguments that federal judicial intervention 'may substantially interfere with a tribe's ability to maintain itself as a culturally and politically distinct entity',[29] and that membership issues 'will frequently depend on questions of tribal tradition and custom which tribal forums may be in a better position to evaluate than federal courts'.[30] Thus a membership rule which on its face affronts much liberal sentiment was allowed to stand as a concession to indigenous self-government, although it is possible that the court was aware that the membership rule had

[25] Her husband was a Navajo. Navajo membership rules make Navajo membership difficult for non-resident children of such a marriage. At the time children who could not claim membership of a recognized group were in theory denied benefits such as those accorded by the Indian Health Service, although in practice such benefits have increasingly been made available to people who are Indian even if for such reasons not members of a federally recognized tribe.

[26] 6 Pet 515, 559 (1832).

[27] 436 US 49, 55 (1978).

[28] Ibid., 71.

[29] Ibid., 72.

[30] Ibid., 71.

been adopted in living memory with US government encouragement and that currents of reform were evident in the Pueblo. Justice White in dissent implies that self-government is not the issue. Where, as here, the group itself is very small, with members of the tribal government and the tribal court well acquainted with the specific situation of each family, his reasoning suggests that the real justification for federal court intervention is that the group is transgressing the fundamental liberal principle that one must not be the judge in one's own cause. The conflicting opinions in this case highlight a clash between modern liberal conceptions of the state, with a supposedly independent judiciary constraining excesses and abuses of state power, and the realities of government by some kinds of non-state groups, especially face-to-face groups or those relying on non-judicial methods of social control.

A different balance was struck by the High Court of Tanzania in *Ephrahim v Pastory and Kazilege*.[31] In this case Haya customary law allowed men to sell clan land outside the clan without consent of the clan, but allowed women only the power of usufruct, not alienation. In other Tanzanian cases state court judges had abstained from intervention, stating that in the absence of statutory provisions, needed reforms in customary law could come only by evolution of views within the particular community, but Mwalusanya J saw the judicial role as encompassing renovation of customary law to accord with the prohibition of sex discrimination in the Bill of Rights. Accordingly, sale of land by a woman was allowed on the same terms as sale by a man, which under Haya law meant that other clan members could redeem the sale by payment of the purchase price to the outside purchaser within six months. The pluralist legal system of Tanzania, in which for a large proportion of the population customary law of many different communities regulates matters of property, inheritance, family and personal law within the framework of state law, differs materially from state legal systems in European settler societies where accommodation of self-governance for numerically small indigenous groups is understood as an anomalous departure from universality. It is thus consistent for judges in local state courts to favour intervention in Tanzania but argue for abstention from the affairs of the Santa Clara Pueblo.

Comparing Bahaya and Santa Clara indicates that formulation of a non-contextual normative theory governing the striking of such balances is a challenging and probably hazardous undertaking if the theory is intended to be operational in international law. A stimulating attempt is Will Kymlicka's normative distinction, intended to be operational, between external protection that the state should help provide for minority groups to prevent domination by the wider society or other social groups, and internal restrictions that a group imposes on the freedoms of its members, which, he argues, liberalism does not permit. Thus it is consistent with liberalism to provide special

[31] Mwalusanya J, 22 February 1990, 87 ILR 106.

political representation of minorities in legislative and recommendatory bodies, self-government, and 'polyethnic' rights such as support of minority languages.[32] By contrast, the liberal state in which a minority group is located must consider intervention against persistent internal restrictions, for example against what Kymlicka regards as theocratical discrimination against protestants in some Pueblo Indian communities.[33] Non-consequentialist versions of liberalism focus on the violation of the rights of individuals whose freedom is restricted,[34] without necessarily distinguishing different impacts of comparable interventions arising from, e.g. the different historical experiences and current circumstances of Bahaya in Tanzania and Santa Clara Pueblo Indians. Extreme rights-orientation thus creates false similitude. Kymlicka is careful to avoid this, but his account is not explicitly contextual. He utilizes a preliminary distinction between multinational and polyethnic polities that is almost determinative of consequences but is much more clearcut on paper than many polities are in fact. He employs an inside/outside internal/external dichotomy that is confounded by practice and is curiously ahistorical. For the purposes of internal restrictions, a minority group is evaluated as if it were a state, rather than a focal point of identity and power within a much larger polity, a set of variegated, churning societies, and perhaps a complex of transnational markets and connections.[35] Culture is treated as coextensive with the group, simply something a group happens to have. Nor does Kymlicka distinguish liberalism as an ideal justificatory theory from the complex of justificatory theories actually prevailing in different polities. The argument for upholding external protections while considering intervention against a category of 'internal restrictions' is deceptively simple. It is stimulating as a parsimonious normative theory in one group of liberal states, but operationalizing it in these simple terms without close attention to history, context, consequences, and prevailing background norms may have unappealing or dangerous results.

Operationalizing such a normative theory involves the questions of who judges, how they judge, and what are the various impacts of different rights-protecting institutions.[36] Adjudicative approaches to minority questions have made appreciable contributions, but face inevitable limits, confronted even within the relatively circumscribed scope of Article 27.[37] The case of *Kitok v Sweden* before the Human Rights Committee typifies the problems

[32] *Multicultural Citizenship: A Liberal Theory of Minority Rights* (1995), ch. 3.

[33] Ibid., 40.

[34] Cf. Brian Barry's criticism that Kymlicka is a romantic nationalist, too well-disposed toward collectivities when there is a real tension with the rights and moral value of individuals: 'Book Review', 107 *Ethics* (1996) 153.

[35] T. Franck, *The Empowered Self: Law and Society in the Age of Individualism* (1999).

[36] Some of these issues are noted in *Multicultural Citizenship*, supra n. 32, ch. 8.

[37] Johnston, 'Native Rights as Collective Rights: A Question of Group Self-Preservation', 2 *Canadian Journal of Law and Jurisprudence* (1989) 19.

encountered by tribunals in using Article 27 as a means to redress wrongs involving land and natural resources. The diminution of areas available for reindeer pasturage due to encroachment by other users, combined with rising living standards, was interpreted by the Sami authorities, whose decisional competence was embodied in Swedish state law, as necessitating restricting some aspiring reindeer herders in order to maintain the viability of the reindeer-herding lifestyle. The decision-making system on reindeer herding among members of the Sami Village (*Sameby*) was reportedly weighted toward those who already had large herds. If it had been clear to the Committee on the complex facts that Ivan Kitok's formal exclusion from entitlement to herd reindeer was an arbitrary exercise of local power, Article 27 might well have provided a basis for intervention, the infringing conduct of the Swedish state being its failure to intervene. But in so far as the *Sameby* policy depriving those who spent more than three years away was a response to the crisis in the long-term viability of reindeer-herding lifestyle and culture, the Swedish state was much more fundamentally implicated in not securing sufficient land, pasturage, and support for the culture to Sami, yet the Committee became more hesitant to intervene. This paradox structures the result in the case, a very uneasy compromise in which no violation of the ICCPR is found because Kitok was in fact being permitted, although not as of right, to herd reindeer, and nothing is said about the systemic assimilationist effects of the diminishing resource base or other aspects of historic Swedish state policy.

Many of the most difficult systemic issues involving minorities are more effectively addressed through negotiations and policy processes, especially in deeply divided societies. In highly charged cases international oversight and conciliation may play an important role, as some of the work of the High Commissioner for National Minorities of the Organization for Security and Cooperation in Europe (OSCE) attests. In cases involving indigenous peoples, international and national regimes of minority rights may set useful minimum standards. Adjudicative or quasi-adjudicative proceedings are significant in upholding fundamental rights, and in some cases may overcome a political impasse or provide impetus to needed policy reforms.

Indigenous claims often have much in common with minority claims. Before the surge of contemporary legal activity concerning indigenous peoples, tribunals frequently conflated the categories. Dealing with (and finding inadmissible) a Sami challenge to a Norwegian government hydro-electric dam project flooding reindeer herding areas in 1983, for example, the legal basis on which the then European Commission on Human Rights proceeded was simply that 'a minority group is, in principle, entitled to claim the right to respect for the particular life style it may lead' as private life, family life, or home under Article 8 of the European Convention.[38] That

[38] *G and E v Norway, Applications* 9278/81 and 9415/81, DR 35 (1984), 30.

the distinction is not always applicable or easily drawn is attested by the hesitation of the Supreme Court of Canada in the *Quebec Secession* reference. It recognized that the protection of aboriginal and treaty rights 'is an important underlying constitutional value', but skirted the issue whether these rights should be 'looked at in their own right or as part of the larger concern with minorities'. [39]

In practice, however, tribunals facing indigenous issues have increasingly found themselves identifying or constructing distinct analytical approaches that go beyond standard minority provisions. This is especially prevalent where claims arise from the distinct historical circumstances of indigenous groups, as such claims are often *sui generis* in the national society. This applies for example to the kinds of issues addressed in the *Delgamuuk*, *Mabo*, and *New Zealand Maori Council* cases. Where claims are based on maintenance and development of a distinct culture, religion, or language, there may be substantial analogy between indigenous claims and claims of minority groups generally, and the legal techniques used will often overlap. Very often the distinct indigenous element will be integral to such claims too. But there is no universal bright line. Where the substantive differences are contestable, distinctions between indigenous claims and similar claims by other minorities may or may not be legitimate, depending in part on compliance with fundamental human rights standards, and in part on the complex dynamics of different societies.

The dynamics are well illustrated by questions relating to reindeer herding and Sami identity in Finland. Reindeer herding has a fundamental place in Sami culture, a place recognized in Protocol 3 to the accession agreements governing the entry of Sweden and Finland into the European Community.[40] This provides:

THE HIGH CONTRACTING PARTIES, RECOGNIZING the obligations and commitments of Sweden and Finland with regard to the Sami people under national and international law, NOTING, in particular, that Sweden and Finland are committed to preserving and developing the means of livelihood, language, culture and way of life of the Sami people, CONSIDERING the dependence of traditional Sami culture and livelihood on primary economic activities, such as reindeer husbandry in the traditional areas of Sami settlement, HAVE AGREED on the following provisions, *Article 1* Notwithstanding the provisions of the EC Treaty, exclusive rights to reindeer husbandry within traditional Sami areas may be granted to the Sami people. *Article 2* This Protocol may be extended to take account of any further development of exclusive Sami rights linked to their traditional means of livelihood . . .

[39] *Reference re Secession of Quebec* [1998] 2 SCR 217, para. 82.

[40] Act Concerning the Conditions of Accession of the Republic of Austria, the Republic of Finland and the Kingdom of Sweden to the European Union, as amended, Protocol No. 3 on the Sami People, OJ 1995 L1, 10, 11 (1/1/95).

In Finland, however, exclusive rights of this sort have not been accorded to Sami. Reindeer herding is practised by assorted individuals, most of whom are Sami, some of whom do not regard themselves as Sami, and some of whom claim to be Sami but are not regarded as Sami by recognized Sami organizations. A single reindeer-herding cooperative may include people in each category. Many of the special government regulations relevant to reindeer herding are applied not on the basis of ethnicity, but to geographic localities. Difficult questions thus arise as to whether reindeer herding is an activity in which preference and decision-making roles should be allocated on the basis of being Sami, or a traditional reindeer herder, or a resident of the relevant locality, or some combination of these. Some may argue, for example, that everyone who participates in traditional reindeer-herding culture is a member of a minority whose rights to culture ought to be protected under Article 27, whereas others have argued that Sami are the relevant minority, or that the operative category is membership in the Sami indigenous people and participation in its community or political organizations. As the indigenous (Sami) category becomes more significant in public discourse in Finland, efforts have been made by 'non-Sami' to broaden the category of 'Sami' to include them on grounds such as cultural affinity, kinship connection, or fairness in representation. At one level the debate takes place in terms of legal categories and texts such as Article 27; at another it is a political struggle that is part of a continuous process of construction and reconstruction of these categories and of the lines between them. Any normatively appealing solution will not simply be categorical, it must involve some balance of competing interests and rights. It is nevertheless of great importance how the power of decision is allocated. Typically this power has, in practice, rested preponderantly with state institutions, but this simple allocation is increasingly contested by reference to a competing conceptual structure, that of self-determination.

3. Self-determination

Negotiations on international normative instruments relating to indigenous peoples have repeatedly become ensnarled in the question: does the international law of self-determination apply to indigenous peoples? As in other areas, political debate has revolved around the binary issue of the complete applicability or inapplicability of an existing conceptual structure. Representatives of indigenous peoples in international negotiations have insisted, as a large group of them put it in a 1993 *démarche* to the UN Working Group on Indigenous Populations, that 'the right of self-determination is the heart and soul of the declaration. We will not consent to

any language which limits or curtails the right of self-determination.'[41] They proposed incorporation of a version of Article 1(1) of the 1966 Covenants in the UN Draft Declaration, modified to state expressly that the right of self-determination belonged to indigenous peoples. The five members of the Working Group adopted this proposal verbatim in Article 3 of the draft: 'Indigenous peoples have the right of self-determination. By virtue of that right they freely determine their political status and freely pursue their economic, social and cultural development.' A number of states met this with categorical opposition, asserting that these groups are not peoples, and have no international law right of self-determination. These binary views are accompanied by deceptively simple appraisals of what is involved. For many indigenous advocates, the core idea of self-determination is self-evident and spelled out in the draft; complaints about lack of clarity are political diversions or academic excesses. For some state governments, self-determination is a principle upholding independent states, and any application of it to groups within states would undermine the state.

Self-determination has long been a conceptual morass in international law, partly because its application and meaning have not been fully formulated in agreed texts, partly because it reinforces and conflicts with other important principles and specific rules, and partly because the specific international law practice of self-determination does not measure up very well to some of the established textual formulations.[42] The standard international law of self-determination accords to the people of certain territorially-defined units the right to determine the political future of the territory. The categories of units to which this right applies have not been precisely delineated, but in addition to states, at least five such categories are supported in the practice of states and inter-state institutions.[43] These are:

(1) mandated territories, trust territories, and territories treated as non-self-governing under Chapter XI of the UN Charter;
(2) distinct political-geographical entities subject to *carence de souveraineté* (gross failure of the duties of the state);
(3) other territories in which the principle of self-determination is applied by the parties;
(4) highest-level constituent units of a federal state where that state has dissolved;

[41] Quoted in S. Pritchard (ed.), *Indigenous Peoples, the United Nations, and Human Rights* (1998) 46.

[42] Some of the problems are surveyed in C. Tomuschat (ed.), *The Modern Law of Self-Determination* (1993).

[43] Many are discussed in *Reference re Secession of Quebec* [1998] 2 SCR 217 (Supreme Court of Canada). For more substantial treatment see James Crawford's chapter in this volume.

(5) formerly independent entities reasserting their independence with at least the tacit consent of the established state, where their incorporation into that state was illegal or of dubious legality.

A somewhat distinct body of practice confers upon such units, and especially on peoples of independent states as represented by their governments, certain economic rights relating especially to natural resources, and certain protections in relation to title to territory and the use of force.[44] While claims by indigenous peoples may in some cases fall within these categories, for the most part their acceptance would involve some rethinking of existing practice as represented in this summary. Elements of existing interpretations of self-determination, together with increasingly coherent bodies of emerging national and international practice, and the growing support among state governments for initiatives in relation to internal self-determination generally and to indigenous peoples specifically, suggest that the case of indigenous peoples may be one in which innovative normative formulations can be agreed. These will almost certainly not be exhaustive of the issues, probably will not be highly precise, will not be universally respected, and may well be somewhat incoherent. At a minimum, they must not be disastrously dangerous, and within the limits of existing imprecision and incoherence should be consistent with existing formulations relating to self-determination, human rights, and other fundamental principles. If this is to happen, it is suggested that a fundamental reorientation is called for that leaves aside the binary conceptual debate and moves closer to emerging practice. This reorientation involves shifting—not for the purpose of exhaustive statement but merely for the purpose of reaching agreement on partial formulations—from an end-state approach to a relational approach to self-determination.

The legal instantiation of self-determination upon which the claims of indigenous peoples have drawn most in the formative period of the international indigenous movement is the law established for decolonization of extra-European colonies of European states, and to a lesser extent the international law applied to special situations such as minority rule under apartheid in South Africa. The practice of decolonization did much to transform what had been in effect a political principle of self-determination into a legal right, with correlative duties for states exercising control over such units of self-determination, and more attenuated duties arising for other states as the *erga omnes* character of the right came to be recognized.[45] Arguments for the extension of the decolonization justification of the right of self-determination to indigenous peoples presuppose, and recognize, their colonized status. These arguments appeal to the

[44] See generally I. Brownlie, *Principles of Public International Law,* 5th edn. (1998), at 167 and 599–602.

[45] *East Timor (Portugal v Australia),* ICJ Reports (1995) 90, para. 29; 1966 Covenants, Art. 1(3).

logic of decolonization and urge that its unfinished business be addressed. Some of the early rhetoric of the international indigenous peoples movement referred to the 'Fourth World', and sought support from newly decolonized states of the 'Third World'. This approach has been reinforced by appeal to the principle of equality, which is explicitly associated with self-determination in the UN Charter principle of 'equal rights and self-determination of peoples'. If 'all peoples' have the legal right to self-determination, it is strongly argued that it is unjustifiable discrimination to treat indigenous peoples differently from other 'peoples'.[46] This logic leads to the view that independence should be one of the options for an indigenous people exercising self-determination, even if it is an option rarely chosen in practice.

This argument from decolonization has been reinforced by practice suggesting that self-determination in the strong form as a right to establish a separate state may be an extraordinary remedy in distinct territories suffering massive human rights violations orchestrated by governing authorities based elsewhere in the state; such an argument may explain acceptance of the secession of Bangladesh from Pakistan. Internationally-backed autonomy within the state may be an alternative remedy in such situations, much discussed in the case of Kosovo. But the far-reaching argument that self-determination in this strong form of statehood or almost complete autonomy is essential as a general precondition for human rights does not establish which groups or territories are the units of self-determination for purposes of human rights enhancement; nor does it overcome legitimate concerns about the threats to human rights and to human security posed by repeated fragmentation and irredentism.[47] The remedial human rights justification for self-determination, while persuasive in some cases, is most unlikely to become normal rather than exceptional unless the sovereignty and legitimacy of states declines precipitiously.[48]

The right to self-determination in the context of European decolonization was conceived primarily as an instrument for ending the colonial relationship by conferring freedom. The future relations between colonizer and colonized were then to be determined by free agreement, but the right to self-determination was concerned with the preconditions for such choice, not with the relationship itself. Many problems were accentuated by the rapidity and artificiality of the transformation of legal relations from colonial hierarchy to the supposed equality and freedom of relations among sovereign states; often the theory of these legal relations was grossly disconnected from economic, political and social relations as they existed in practice. The duties

[46] Daes, 'Equality of Peoples under the Auspices of the United Nations Draft Declaration on the Rights of Indigenous Peoples', 7 *St Thomas Law Review* (1995) 493.

[47] Horowitz, 'Self-Determination: Politics, Philosophy, and Law', in I. Shapiro and W. Kymlicka (eds), *Ethnicity and Group Rights* (1997) 421.

[48] Kingsbury, 'Sovereignty and Inequality', 9 *EJIL* (1998) 599.

of the colonial state correlative to the right of the people of the colonized unit to self-determination were mainly procedural, encompassing rather modest preparations of the territory for possible independence, the negotiated establishment of an environment and framework for a legitimate act of self-determination, the proper conduct of a referendum, and the orderly transfer of power. The focus was on realization of an end-state: usually independence, but occasionally some other political arrangement. Most of the groups participating in the international indigenous peoples movement, however, expect to continue in an enduring relationship with the state(s) in which they presently live. This is the expectation of leaders of the states involved. The claims of Cree in Quebec illustrate this dynamic. They have not sought independence from Canada, concentrating instead on their evolving relations with the federal and provincial governments, to which Canadian courts have increasingly contributed. But if Quebec secedes based on its existing boundaries, thus changing the nature of these relations, they insist on exercising their right of self-determination to determine their future, which might well involve their continuing in Canada.[49] Thus the claim to self-determination in the sense of a choice among internationally-sovereign entities is considered in practice by Cree leaders as relational and remedial, triggered by outside action disrupting existing relationships. In practice, assertion by the international indigenous movement of a strong form of the right of 'all peoples' to self-determination may prove double-edged for Cree in Quebec who oppose Quebec independence, as such an argument is equally well-adapted to assertions of self-determination in the name of some 'people' defined by a separatist movement able to secure a majority in Quebec.

The international indigenous movement has been reluctant in international negotiations to move away from the end-state model including possible independence, in order to maintain solidarity with groups unwilling to accept any relationship with an existing state. A representative statement of such a position is that of Mick Dodson, then a central figure in the Australian Aboriginal and Torres Strait Islander Commission and Chair of the UN Voluntary Fund for Indigenous Populations: 'Finally, even where a state meets the obligations required under the Declaration,[50] there will be some indigenous peoples whose right to self-determination will never be satisfied until they

[49] Grand Council of the Crees, *Sovereign Injustice: Forcible Inclusion of the James Bay Crees and Cree Territory into a Sovereign Quebec* (1995). The Supreme Court of Canada paid disconcertingly little specific attention to issues raised by aboriginal peoples in *Reference re Secession of Quebec* [1998] 2 SCR 217, for reasons it gives at para. 169. The Supreme Court may well imply, but does not make absolutely explicit, that aboriginal peoples should have a distinct place in negotiations were Quebec to seek independence. In a forthcoming work, Catherine Beagan Flood argues that a constitutional convention on participation by aboriginal peoples in certain types of negotiations has emerged in Canadian constitutional practice.

[50] Declaration on Friendly Relations, UNGA Res. 2625 (1970).

have a free and independent state of their own. And it would be a violation of those peoples' right of self-determination for anyone else to say that this is not an acceptable way for them to exercise that right.'[51] Similarly, a conference of 'representatives of indigenous peoples of Asia' at Baguio declared in 1999 'that although autonomy and self-government may be a way through which many indigenous peoples wish to exercise their right of self-determination . . . these are not the only ways by which indigenous peoples may exercise this right . . . they have the right to establish their own government and determine its relations to other political communities'.[52] While the international indigenous movement may well adhere to this theoretical position, it is not viable as an express formulation for a UN Declaration on the Rights of Indigenous Peoples to be adopted by states, nor does it embody the current preoccupations of most internationally active indigenous peoples. By contrast, a relational approach to self-determination captures many of the aspirations embodied in the UN Draft Declaration produced by the UN Working Group on Indigenous Populations (WGIP).[53] Such an approach might be pursued in a UN Declaration without foreclosing remedial questions that may arise in extraordinary cases.

Self-determination is about the relation between state and community. As an international programme it has complex modern origins: in efforts by nationalists to establish states for their nations, in efforts by state elites to establish a mass sense of belonging to overcome the artificiality of the modern rationalist-legal industrialized state, and in hybrid efforts to end foreign domination and create state and nation all at once.[54] It can be state-threatening or state-reinforcing, liberating or chauvinist, democratic or demagogic. In its legal operation it has since 1920 generally buttressed the states system, even when potentially a threat, as with the lift it provided to the minorities

[51] 'Towards the Exercise of Indigenous Rights: Policy, Power and Self-Determination', 35 *Race & Class* (1994) 67, at 74. Elsewhere he notes that when indigenous peoples started trying to persuade the WGIP to recognize the right to self-determination: 'The members of the Working Group thought that we were crazy. The Chairperson made it clear that there was no way that the Working Group could support recognition of such a politically contentious right. An examination of the drafts from one year to the next reveals that our perspectives were gradually accepted.' A significant group of state governments have moved in the same direction over the years, suggesting that unswerving adherence to the basic position was initially a successful strategy for indigenous negotiators. Dodson, 'Comment', in S. Pritchard (ed.), *Indigenous Peoples, the United Nations and Human Rights* (1998) 64. On the conduct of the negotiations in the first four annual sessions of the Inter-Sessional Working Group of the Human Rights Commission, see the thoughtful accounts by Andrew Gray in the *International Work Group for Indigenous Affairs (IWGIA) Yearbook*.

[52] Baguio Declaration, adopted at Baguio City, Philippines, 18–21 April 1999, mimeo.

[53] UN Doc. E/CN.4/Sub.2/1993/29, Annex I.

[54] For a review see e.g. Koskenniemi, 'National Self-Determination Today: Problems of Legal Theory and Practice', 43 *ICLQ* (1994) 241.

programme in the 1920s and 1930s,[55] and its expression in the law of mandates, trusts, and decolonization. In many states in which groups active in the international indigenous peoples movement live, maintenance of the state at present involves efforts by the state to enhance its legitimacy, engaging with forms of community that run deeper than rational-legal associations, and in some cases accommodation of pluralism and multiple identities. There is thus for the time being a convergence between indigenous peoples and state decision-makers, with sufficient overlap to make conceivable the adoption of some set of international principles, at least in the form of a UN declaration. Reconstruction of the concept of self-determination is needed to take advantage of this convergence. The end-state independence-oriented focus, established during European decolonization and still relevant in some situations, has diverted attention from the development of legal principles concerning enduring relations between indigenous peoples and states.[56]

The 1993 UN draft declaration proposed by the WGIP incorporates numerous ideas relevant to such reconstruction, but the only element explicitly connected with self-determination is the strong preference for autonomy expressed in Article 31:

> Indigenous peoples, as a specific form of exercising their right to self-determination, have the right to autonomy or self-government in matters relating to their internal and local affairs, including culture, religion, education, information, media, health, housing, employment, social welfare, economic activities, land and resources management, environment and entry by non-members, as well as ways and means for financing these autonomous functions.

The meaning of 'autonomy' and 'self-government' is not further specified, but the political connotation is one of freedom, subject to restrictions as to matters not specifically included in the powers of the autonomous entity. In practice the most conspicuous exclusions from autonomy relate to foreign affairs and military security, but Article 31 is more hesitant even than this, not providing specifically for autonomy in matters such as policing, taxation, or judicial proceedings. Article 31 does not expressly connect autonomy with a land base, leaving open the possibility of autonomy that is defined by personal affinity rather than territorial area. The kinds of autonomy regimes which indigenous peoples operate or aspire to vary enormously, influenced in part by geographical and demographic settings.[57] Almost all such regimes presuppose extensive relations between the autonomous institutions and other gov-

[55] Berman, '"But the Alternative is Despair": Nationalism and the Modernist Renewal of International Law', 106 *Harvard Law Review* (1993) 1792.

[56] Kirgis, 'The Degrees of Self-Determination in the United Nations Era', 88 *AJIL* (1994) 304.

[57] For one study of the practicalities of self-determination, far from although connected with the politics pursued in negotiations in Geneva, see A. Gray, *Indigenous Rights and Development: Self-Determination in an Amazonian Community* (1997).

ernment institutions of the state, and between indigenous people and other people within or outside the autonomous area. Relations between autonomous entities (and their institutions) and the state (and its institutions) require a complex governance framework, often embodied in a formal agreement or in constitutional or legislative provisions which, although formally unilateral, may over time be understood as requiring the consent of all affected groups before amendment.[58] Establishing the terms of such relationships, and the legal elements structuring the dynamics of their continued evolution, has become a specialized field of practice in crafting solutions in many strife-torn polities.[59] More systematic analysis of rapidly evolving autonomy arrangements involving indigenous peoples and other groups may provide part of a structure of norms to give substance to an emerging legal understanding of autonomy.[60] It is clear, however, that in the overwhelming majority of cases autonomy is not simply freedom, it is a relationship. Indeed, most of the aspirations of most groups in the indigenous peoples movement involve definition of relationships with states. The relational dimension of self-determination embodies these aspirations. Giving meaning to this element of self-determination thus requires that a central focus be on the terms and dynamics of these relational aspects.

The UN draft declaration identifies, and makes provision concerning, many further crucial issues in such relationships, but does not expressly connect these to self-determination in the way advocated here. The dynamic of the UN process has been rather the opposite, treating self-determination as an end-state issue, and separating the debate on self-determination from the structuring of relationships. The draft declaration provides much of the material from which the concept of self-determination may be reconstructed in relational terms, but does not always develop the relational aspects sufficiently. The draft envisages that indigenous groups may determine their own memberships and the structures of their own institutions (Arts 32 and 33), while indigenous individuals have rights to obtain citizenship of the states in which they live. Recourse for an individual aggrieved by a membership decision of the group is not specified—decisions are required as to the enduring responsibilities and powers of states of the sort invoked by Ms. Lovelace and Ms. Martinez. Indigenous institutions and juridical practices may be maintained and promoted, subject to internationally recognized human rights standards (Art. 33), but the relation of these institutions and practices to state

[58] See section 35 of the Canadian Constitution Act 1982. Even provisions such as the allocation of power on Indian issues to the federal government in section 91(24) of the British North America Act 1867 could not easily be amended without support from First Nations in Canada.

[59] See Y. Ghai, Vol. IX of the Collected Courses of the Academy of European Law (forthcoming).

[60] H. Hannum, *Autonomy, Sovereignty and Self-Determination*, rev. edn. (1996).

institutions, particularly the judicial system, is not explicitly addressed. The draft would require states to include the rights recognized in the Declaration in national legislation 'in such a manner that indigenous peoples can avail themselves of such rights in practice', but the role of state institutions, especially courts and administrative agencies, is not systematically addressed. The capacities and powers of states are alluded to throughout the draft. States are required, for instance, to 'take effective measures to ensure that no storage or disposal of hazardous materials shall take place in the lands and territories of indigenous peoples' (Art. 28), a formulation that deliberately did not provide for indigenous consent to receipt of such materials. Indigenous peoples have the right to effective measures by states to prevent any interference with, alienation of or encroachment upon their rights to 'own, develop, control and use the lands and territories . . . which they have traditionally owned or otherwise occupied or used' (Art. 26). This may entail some state responsibility to prevent alienation of land even where an indigenous person wishes to sell, albeit perhaps only in exceptional circumstances where the group's own political and legal structures are in disarray or where the conduct of the state (for example in wrongly individualizing communal title) has precipitated the situation. Even with qualifications, such state involvement raises complex problems, often restricting the ability of indigenous groups to raise capital by mortgage or to make their own development decisions. Further engagement between the state and indigenous people is indicated in provisions that indigenous peoples are entitled to benefit from state education (Art. 15) and health care (Art. 24) where they wish, from the full rights accorded by international labour law and national labour legislation (Art. 18), and from financial and technical assistance (Art. 37), and they have the right to special measures to improve their economic and social conditions (Art. 22) and reflection of indigenous cultural diversity in state-owned media (Art. 17). The broad philosophy of the draft is that indigenous peoples have the right to maintain and strengthen their distinct characteristics and legal systems while retaining the right to participate fully in the life of the state (Art. 4; also Arts 8, 12–14, 19–21, 23 *et al.*) The provisions concerning indigenous spiritual and material relationships to, and ownership, control and restitution of, land, territories and waters, together with provisions on environment, development, and indigenous responsibilities to future generations (Arts 25–8) provide a foundation for a land and territorial base within the state. The draft would constrain state military activities and development projects in indigenous areas except with the consent of the people concerned (Arts 28 and 30)—although specific formulations such as these will be debated, negotiation on such issues is part of relational autonomy as already widely practised. The draft is lacking in provisions on duties of indigenous peoples, and in provisions on reconciling the conflicting rights and interests of others, including non-members and dissenting members—these and other relational questions

are of immense practical importance, but do not appear to be excluded or prejudged by the draft as written.

After long hesitation about the application of the provisions on self-determination in Article 1 of the ICCPR to indigenous groups within independent states, the UN Human Rights Committee has begun, in dialogues with states parties under the reporting procedure, to express views under the self-determination rubric on the substantive terms of relationships between states and indigenous peoples. It has emphasized in particular the provisions of Article 1(2), which stipulates that all peoples may freely dispose of their natural wealth and resources, and must not be deprived of their own means of subsistence. It has criticized the Canadian government practice of insisting on the inclusion in contemporary claims settlement agreements of a provision extinguishing inherent aboriginal rights, confining aboriginal rights instead to those specified in the agreement.[61] The Committee recommended that this practice 'be abandoned as incompatible with Article 1 of the Covenant', an important indication that the Committee believes the Article 1 provisions on self-determination are applicable to indigenous peoples in Canada.[62] The Committee further recommended on the basis of Article 1 that the Canadian government implement the Royal Commission report on the need for greater allocation of land and resources to ensure institutions of aboriginal self-government do not fail.[63] Earlier the Committee on Economic, Social and Cultural Rights had made similar substantive recommendations to the government of Canada, without basing itself explicitly on self-determination and the terms of Article 1 of the International Covenant on Social and Cultural Rights (ICESCR).[64] As Article 1 is common to both Covenants, the logic of gradual convergence in interpretation is compelling, and is likely to prevail over differences in institutional dynamics. The intervention of such bodies in the dynamics of state-indigenous relations under Article 1 may be well judged in relation to Canada, where the government accepts the general principle of indigenous

[61] This policy was criticized by the Royal Commission on Aboriginal Peoples in its final report (5 vols, 1996), drawing in turn on an earlier study by Mary Ellen Turpel and Paul Joffe. See Royal Commission on Aboriginal Peoples, *Treaty Making in the Spirit of Co-existence: An Alternative to Extinguishment* (1995).

[62] For argument that harsher elements of the policy of extinguishment pursued by the Australian government infringe international law, see Pritchard, 'Native Title from the Perspective of International Standards', 18 *Australian Year Book of International Law* (1997) 127. The Native Title Amendment Act has been critically considered also by the UN Committee on the Elimination of Racial Discrimination. The New Zealand government's policy of seeking to make contemporary settlements of Maori claims 'full and final' has been criticized by Maori leaders and several scholars, including Annie Mikaere and Russell Karu.

[63] Concluding Observations on the Fourth Periodic Report of Canada, UN Doc. CCPR/C/79/Add. 105, 7 April 1999, para. 8.

[64] Concluding Observations on the Third Periodic Report of Canada, UN Doc. E/C.12/1/Add.31, 4 December 1998, para. 18.

self-determination and where the political and policy system has already developed and calibrated possible initiatives. The international bodies, which have scant ability to formulate such detailed policies themselves, are able in such a case to boost one part of a national process. The challenge for these bodies is whether to try to apply such interpretations of self-determination for indigenous peoples to states where the government and the political system are not prepared to accept any such notion, or in situations where there is no carefully crafted and politically legitimate policy document upon which the international body may seize.

The number of state governments accepting principles for relationships with indigenous peoples that incorporate elements of self-determination has gradually increased. Reasonably representative of current positions of Canada, New Zealand, Denmark and other governments is a 1995 statement by the then Australian (Labour) government, that self-determination is 'an evolving right which includes equal rights, the continuing right of peoples to decide how they should be governed, the right of people as individuals to participate in the political process (particularly by way of periodic free and fair elections) and the right of distinct peoples within a state to make decisions on and administer their own affairs'.[65] The government of Guatemala, formally committed to implementing provisions on land rights, local self-government and national participation in the 1995 Mexico City peace agreement on Identity and Rights of Indigenous Peoples, has taken the position internationally that self-determination of indigenous peoples is possible without threatening national unity.[66] A basis for comparable international positions is provided by the 1991 Colombian Constitution, which in tandem with a series of Constitutional Court decisions envisages significant indigenous autonomy as well as rights in relation to land, resources, consultation, representation, language, and education,[67] and by the Philippines Indigenous Peoples Rights Act of 1997 which expressly endorses indigenous self-governance and self-determination within the state. These legal policies often conflict with other government policies, and may fall far short in implementation and in their real effects, but their normative stance has some genuine support, and reflects a broader if uneven trend. This trend may be necessary to the future success of the state[68] as well as the vitality of indigenous peoples.

[65] UN Doc. E/CN.4/1995/WG.15/2/Add.2, para. 8, 30 November 1995.

[66] Statement at Commission on Human Rights Inter-Sessional Working Group on the Draft Declaration, 1998.

[67] For a short summary see Wiessner, 'Rights and Status of Indigenous Peoples: A Global Comparative and International Legal Analysis', 12 *Harvard Human Rights Journal* (1999) 57, at 80, 81.

[68] Cf. A. Milward, *The European Rescue of the Nation-State* (1992); A. Moravcsik, *The Choice for Europe: Social Purpose and State Power from Messina to Maastricht* (1998).

A relational approach to self-determination entails some crossing of the boundaries drawn in political debate between the self-determination programme and the human rights programme. This characteristic legal strategy has many adherents, and is juridically reinforced by the inclusion of self-determination as the first right in the 1966 ICCPR and ICESCR. Some thus justify self-determination on human rights grounds, as a necessary precondition and means to the realization of other human rights.[69] In this view, self-determination in finely nuanced forms is an embodiment of the underlying objectives of human rights—general rights to political participation, for example, or specific rights for the members of religious and linguistic communities collectively to make decisions concerning religious and language matters. This view, while plausible, is far removed from the most common ways in which the idea of 'self-determination' is presently used in international practice, although the tide may be moving in this direction. Others look behind the formal rules of self-determination and human rights to find a justification that unites both programmes, such as the realization of freedom and equality through rights accorded to human individuals or collectivities.[70] In this analysis the law of self-determination is the law of remedies for serious deficiencies of freedom and equality, just as the law of human rights is. Comparable arguments can also be made for unifying these categories with minority claims.[71]

Internationalist writing in western countries increasingly assumes conditions of unquestionable peace, participation, and respect constructed through dialogue—what some have described as the advent of the post-modern state.[72] In some such writing, the distinctions between the categories discussed here virtually disappear, along with sovereignty. The right to self-determination, human rights, minority rights, and indigenous rights all become one. But this view of the world is dangerously optimistic as a basis for global legal norms intended for serious application. It does not confront the hard cases where the human rights, minority rights, and self-determination programmes lead in different directions. The logic of self-determination is not simply the orderly negotiation of constitutional issues in a peaceful and affluent society. To illustrate from extreme cases, it is widely thought that the 'free elections' held to vindicate post-communist democratic self-determination in unified

[69] Hector Gross Espiell, 'The Right to Self-Determination: Implementation of United Nations Resolutions', UN Doc. E/CN.4/Sub.2/405/Rev.1 (1980), para. 59. McCorquodale, 'Self-Determination: A Human Rights Approach', 43 *ICLQ* (1994) 857.

[70] S. J. Anaya, *Indigenous Peoples in International Law* (1995); and Anaya, 'Self-Determination as a Collective Right under Contemporary International Law', in P. Aikio and M. Scheinin (eds), *Operationalizing the Right of Indigenous Peoples to Self-Determination* (2000) 93.

[71] Some such arguments are evaluated, and carefully sidestepped, in A. Spiliopoulou-Akermark, *Justifications of Minority Protection in International Law* (1997).

[72] P. Katzenstein (ed.), *The Culture of National Security: Norms and Identity in World Politics* (1996) 518.

Yugoslavia in 1990 encouraged ethno-nationalist campaigning and helped catalyse the ethnicization of politics that precipitated war and fragmentation. If these elections represented the self-determination programme, they did not represent the programme of human rights. Conversely, UN-authorized intervention in Somalia might be defended as protecting basic human rights, but the insertion of external force into complex militarized local politics is scarcely congruent with the standard discourse of self-determination. Less extreme cases involving indigenous peoples arise often. One of the unresolved dilemmas of basing indigenous claims on self-determination is that in encouraging groups to mobilize as 'nations', some may take what to outsiders (and to some insiders) appears the path of nationalist excess, oppressing dissenters, mistreating and even creating minorities in order to create a clear majority and reinforce the dominant identity,[73] and confronting neighbours. Some persons who are indigenous but have multiple connections may not wish to be forced to opt decisively into one group and out of others; other persons who identify as indigenous, especially in urban areas, may be living outside traditional communities and be left with no group to join. The self-determination programme can have such costs. They can be ameliorated, but not wished away; they must be evaluated in defining and determining the limits of the self-determination programme. On the other side of such evaluation, as many members of indigenous groups point out, the price of not having self-determination has been extremely high—state policy, pursued with bureaucratic rationality but little accountability, has often been very expensive for the state and dismal for indigenous people. The logic of self-determination is that 'the people' themselves should make these evaluations, not state governments; but this is not the logic of the human rights programme.

As to the relationship of self-determination to the minorities and indigenous peoples programmes, it has already been noted that the overlap between these latter categories is considerable, and a relational approach is relevant to both. For example, in advocating a view of self-determination as encompassing 'the right of distinct peoples within a state to make decisions on and administer their own affairs', the Australian government added that this is 'relevant both to indigenous peoples and to national minorities'.[74] But the terms of the relationships that evolve will often differ, for reasons that are practical, normative, and in some cases strategic. In some societies, indigenous claims to relational self-determination are legitimate and actionable in a way that comparably extensive claims of minorities might not be, whereas in other societies introducing such a distinction between certain specified groups may be irrelevant or even pernicious. The remarkable evolution of international norm-making to the point where numerous state governments

[73] This is a theme of D. Gladney (ed.), *Making Majorities* (1998).

[74] UN Doc. E/CN.4/1995/WG.15/2/Add.2, 30 November 1995.

accept some concept of self-determination as a principle broadly applicable to indigenous peoples, has not been remotely paralleled in relation to minorities in general. For many states this is because the category of 'indigenous peoples' is close-ended, politically accepted, and historically justified, whereas 'minorities' is much wider and free-ranging. This body of practice is strong evidence of the current political vitality of the distinction between these two categories, and suggests that the category of 'indigenous peoples' is operative and necessary to understanding the evolving law of self-determination.

4. Historic Sovereignty

Accounts and memories of an earlier era of political independence are widespread among indigenous peoples. In many cases this independence was initially recognized by the aspiring colonial power. Treaties between indigenous peoples and colonizing or trading states, made over several centuries, were commonly premissed on the capacity of both parties to act. In some cases, this implied recognition of the capacity of the leaders of the indigenous people to act directly in international law. The Treaty of Waitangi, for instance, was one of many such agreements included in standard nineteenth-century European treaty series.[75] The legal basis under which this independence was lost was often not accepted by the indigenous group involved, and even under the legal principles of contemporaneous international law espoused by the colonizers it may have been tainted by illegality. The international law concerning colonialism contained inconsistencies observed by many international lawyers in the nineteenth century and earlier. It is not surprising that leaders of some indigenous groups aspire to rectify wrongs by reviving the previous independence.

Claims by the three Baltic republics of the USSR to revive their prior sovereignty received some support during the rapid transition of these entities to independence in 1991.[76] It is arguable that the coercion involved in their incorporation into the USSR was of doubtful international legality in 1940–41, and that the incorporation was void or voidable. If Lithuanian sovereignty was never lawfully extinguished and could revive, why should not the

[75] Many such treaties are collected and printed in a separate section in Clive Parry's *Consolidated Treaty Series* (published in the latter part of the twentieth century), but often the original sources intimated no qualitative distinction of this sort.

[76] For discussion see Rich, 'Recognition of States: The Collapse of Yugoslavia and the Soviet Union', 4 *EJIL* (1993) 36; Warbrick, 'Recognition of States', 41 *ICLQ* (1992) 473. Some advocates of Eritrean independence espoused a variant of this argument, although the legal situation was different, not least because of UN General Assembly endorsement of the 1952 inclusion of Eritrea as a component part of the Ethiopian Federation. Cf. Eyassu Gayim, *The Eritrean Question: The Conflict between the Right of Self-Determination and the Interests of States* (1993).

same apply to Mohawk sovereignty, as some Mohawk have argued for centuries? The orthodox view has been that if any rule of international law existed prohibiting and potentially negating the forcible incorporation perpetrated by the USSR it was then very new, so that there are not necessarily legal implications for groups forcibly incorporated into existing states in earlier periods. Many states are aware of the vast implications of such retrospective invalidation, and in the cases of the Baltic states sought to avoid establishing such a precedent by insisting that the independent statehood of these entities should be recognized only once the agreement of the authorities in Moscow had been obtained. Because this programme is not well developed in practice, little attention has been given to fundamental questions. More generally, whereas self-determination is mainly a forward-looking programme, the historic sovereignty programme is organized to be concerned with restoration of the *status quo ante*. This may suggest legal responsibility for wrongful interference with sovereign rights, a class of claim raised in exceptional legal procedings such as those brought by Nauru and by the UN Council for Namibia, and in war reparations arrangements, but otherwise generally sidestepped by former colonial powers and by other military intervenors. Serious problems may also arise in relation to title to territory—little analysis has been undertaken, for example, of the relationship between historic sovereignty claims and the ordering principle of *uti possidetis juris*. Internal administrative boundaries utilized by the larger contemporary state may differ greatly from the boundaries ascribed to the historic entity, yet such internal boundaries have generally governed in the legal practice relating to decolonization and to disintegrating federations. The traditional or ethnic group associated with the historic entity may now be only a minority in the aspiring entity—a complexity illustrated by the relationship between Yakuts people and the self-proclaimed Sakha Republic in Siberia.

A different kind of concern is that the re-expression of indigenous aspirations in the language of national and international legal structures can involve serious distortion of intention. Haudenosaunee leader Oren Lyons, for example, has pointed to the chimerical element of the modern quest for 'sovereignty' among Indian nations in the US: 'somebody else has it and tells you you may have it, and so you try to find it; but every time you try to find it it is not there . . . if something serves the purpose of the state it is sovereign . . . it serves the government's purpose to recognize Indian sovereignty, because it then does not have to abide by the rules and regulations that govern nuclear wastes elsewhere in the United States'.[77] The recurrent affirmations of Indian sovereignty in US legal materials survive as a mixture of general principle, article of faith, aspiration, morality play, and illusion, so that there is a widespread interest in their maintenance, but much resistance to their full vindication.

[77] 'Remarks', 87 *Proceedings of the American Society of International Law* (1993) 190,at 196.

Reviving historic sovereignty carries the hope of reversing the consequences of wrongs. In focusing on past dispossession it incorporates a type of moral claim that resonates with liberal principles. But a general argument for independence for indigenous groups based on historic sovereignty goes much further than most groups wish. It takes little account of how things have changed, and its radical implications provoke damaging resistance from states. In practice most indigenous peoples seeking to revive autonomous power utilize more nuanced structures that incorporate some of the same justifications: self-determination, or the emerging conceptual structure of indigenous peoples claims.

5. Indigenous Peoples

The construction and affirmation of a distinct programme of 'rights of indigenous peoples', going beyond universal human rights and existing regimes of minority rights, has been one of the objectives of the international indigenous peoples movement. It has received support from some states prepared to recognize the validity of many claims made by indigenous peoples but anxious not simply to endorse the extension of the existing self-determination and historic sovereignty programmes to indigenous peoples without modification. The draft declaration on the rights of indigenous peoples completed by the UN Working Group on Indigenous Populations in 1993 embodies such an approach. While many of the provisions of this draft apply or restate existing human rights norms or other principles of international law to reflect particular concerns and experiences of indigenous communities, other provisions depart from this pattern to express specific aspirations and self-understandings of indigenous groups, often couched as 'rights'. This combination of components is characteristic of projects to constitute 'indigenous peoples' as a distinct legal category. It suggests, as has been argued here, that many of the claims indigenous peoples make, and much of the law relevant to dealing with them, does not depend on a group being an 'indigenous people'. It implies also that some elements of legal practice buttress the strong arguments of the indigenous peoples movement, supported by large numbers of states, for distinctive recognition.

Crafting substantive legal rules on the basis of their applicability in cases involving a distinct category of indigenous peoples can be a subtle and perilous task if high priority is given to reconciling them with the four existing frameworks already discussed. International Labour Organization (ILO) Conventions 107 (1957) and 169 (1989) are attempts to establish such a concept systematically, although with virtually no involvement of indigenous peoples in the drafting process of Convention 107 in the 1950s, and appreciable but nonetheless limited involvement in the Convention 169 process in

the 1980s. Although the assimilationism of Convention 107 and the circumspection of Convention 169 have caused the international indigenous movement to focus energies on the UN and OAS drafts and other evolving processes, these instruments provide significant minimum benchmarks on some issues for states and, in certain circumstances, international organizations. For example, Convention 107 has been invoked by national courts and international bodies to call attention to violations relating to indigenous land rights, displacement, and resettlement,[78] and Convention 169 has been invoked by the Colombian Constitutional Court in determining that consultation with and participation of indigenous people in an oil exploration licensing decision had been inadequate.[79] International development institutions have also begun to use 'indigenous peoples' as an operational concept, one that triggers procedural requirements and substantive standards. The logic of the indigenous peoples programme has gradually led these institutions to regard consultation with indigenous peoples as essential in formulating these standards and in certain institutional practices.[80]

The UN and OAS draft declarations, negotiated in processes in which indigenous peoples have had significant if not wholly satisfying roles, also reflect agreement on the existence of such a category, although not on its bounds and definition. These normative texts, and the growing body of legal practice, are beginning to establish some common understandings on legal issues that are not fully reached through adaptation of established categories, and must be addressed through a normative and institutional programme based on 'indigenous peoples' as a legal category. Particular normative features include: the legal regime for restitution of traditional lands and territories; historically and culturally grounded entitlements and responsibilities with regard to natural resources, to religious sites, and to spiritual or guardianship relationships with particular land, water, mountains, etc.; entitlements and responsibilities based on treaties or other agreements to which the indigenous people is party; certain constitutional arrangements for participation and political structures for membership and self-government; duties in relation to ancestors and future generations; continuance of certain kinds of economic practices; and perhaps entitlements and responsibilities in relation to traditional knowledge.

After a long period of relative neglect, the Inter-American Commission on Human Rights (IACHR) has been galvanized by the impetus of the OAS

[78] *Lal Chand* (Supreme Court of India, 1985); B. Morse and T. Berger, *Sardar Sarovar: Report of the Independent Review* (1992). See also the IACHR Ecuador Report (1997) (infra n. 85).

[79] Petition of Jaime Cordoba Trivino, Defensor del Pueblo, en representacion de varias personas integrantes del Grupo Etnico Indigena U'Wa, Sentencia No. SU–039/97 (3 Feb. 1997).

[80] Kingsbury, 'Operational Policies of International Institutions as Part of the Law-Making Process: The World Bank and Indigenous Peoples', in G. Goodwin-Gill and S. Talmon (eds), *The Reality of International Law* (1999) 323.

Draft Declaration and increasing involvement of legally-oriented indigenous peoples and interested NGOs, and has begun to take preliminary steps toward juridical operationalization of an indigenous peoples programme. It has begun referring some such cases to the Inter-American Court of Human Rights,[81] and has itself taken an active role in brokering friendly settlements in several cases, especially a 1998 settlement in which the government of Paraguay agreed to purchase a substantial and quite precisely stipulated land base for two Enxet communities, in effect conceding legal responsibility to uphold indigenous rights to ancestral lands.[82] In a settlement involving atrocities in 1993 by Guatemalan self-defence patrols against an indigenous community at Colotenango, it pushed successfully for a settlement which included not only compensation for victims and their families, but reparation for the community as a whole in the form of schools and other development projects.[83] Such settlements often involve large, US-based NGOs, as well as pressure from foreign governments and availability of financing by international development institutions or aid agencies. Problems may arise as to how they are carried out in practice, and how far the local community (whose members themselves have diverse interests and priorities) is really able to shape the settlement and its implementation. The compatibility of such large, structured settlements with human rights, the protection of minorities within communities, self-determination, and historic sovereignty may involve problems in particular cases that have not yet been fully explored.[84] The indigenous peoples programme has also begun to animate IACHR dialogues with states, although the IACHR's approach continues to vary somewhat across different country reports, reflecting some continued hesitancy in dealing with governments of states that have long resisted intrusion in this area.[85]

The views of the UN Human Rights Committee in *Hopu and Bessert v France* suggest, especially when read in conjunction with *Ominayak* and other cases, that a majority of the Committee are willing to adopt very broad interpretations of established rights in cases where some particular types of groups are involved.[86] The claim brought by native Tahitians against a French government decision to allow construction of a hotel complex in an area impinging on an ancient Polynesian grave site was not considered under Article 27

[81] Especially *Mayagna Indian Community of Awas Tingni v Nicaragua*, a case against government-approved logging operations that involves issues of control of land, natural resources, and development projects.

[82] Case No. 11713, friendly settlement of 25 March 1998.

[83] Case No. 11212 (Report 19/97, 1997).

[84] A useful overview by a lawyer active in several of these cases is Dulitzky, 'Los pueblos indigenas: jurisprudencia del sistema interamericano de proteccion de los derechos humanos', 26 *Revista IIDH* (1998), 137.

[85] Note the extensive discussion in IACHR, *Informe sobre la Situacion de los Derechos Humanos en Ecuador* (1997), esp. at 103–28.

[86] UN Doc. CCPR/C/60/D/549/1993, views adopted 29 July 1997.

because a majority of the Committee had decided to treat France's declaration on the non-applicability of Article 27 as a comprehensive and effective reservation.[87] This removed the most obvious basis for the claim. But the Committee found that the rights to family and to privacy of the Tahitian complainants were violated, notwithstanding that the graves were reportedly of people who had died several generations earlier, and that no direct kinship relationship between the complainants and the forebears in the grave site had been established. The Committee decided that 'family' must be interpreted by reference to the social practices and cultural traditions of the particular society, and accepted the contention of the applicants that their relationship to their ancestors was an essential element of their identities and significant in their family lives. Specifically, the burial grounds 'play an important role in the authors' history, culture and life'. Like *Lyng*, this case was precipitated by lack of control by indigenous peoples of land. Unlike the US Supreme Court in *Lyng*, the Human Rights Committee was prepared to read general human rights provisions in a special way so as to accommodate the non-standard situation of an indigenous group. The Committee's broad interpretation would have been strengthened by more systematic recourse to standard international law methodology of treaty interpretation, particularly the means set forth in Articles 31 and 32 of the Vienna Convention on the Law of Treaties. In the absence of textual or drafting evidence it would certainly have been perverse to interpret 'family' in Articles 17 and 23 as bounded by a single social pattern all over the world. As a strong dissent points out, the Committee's views treat 'family' as almost boundless, and scarcely analyse the meaning and limits of the concept of 'privacy' in applying it. The Committee thus does not specify the analytical structure and limits of the concepts on which it relies, so that these could potentially cover an almost infinite variety of cases in many kinds of societies. It might be inferred, however, that the Committee is here according special respect to indigenous societies whose traditions, culture, lands, and beliefs have been ignored and impaired by, in this case, a state established and still dominated by colonizers. If this speculative explanation of the Committee's unarticulated premisses is correct, the Committee is drawing sustenance from the developing international commitment to rights of indigenous peoples. Whether the Committee's mandate under the Optional Protocol includes carrying forward such an agenda outside Article 27, or even under Article 27, remains contentious within the Committee. One member has argued strongly for interdependence between different provisions of the Covenant—so that even a provision that is procedurally unavailable is relevant in interpreting a procedurally available provision—and more generally

[87] Whether this decision is consistent with the Committee's General Comment 24 on Reservations was not discussed. However a strong dissenting opinion on the French declaration suggests that the declaration in its own terms does not apply to the French overseas possessions.

for interdependence between express ICCPR rights and other fundamental human rights including rights pertaining particularly to indigenous peoples.[88] Strong forms of such a position were clearly rejected by the dissenters in *Hopu and Bessert*, and it is to be expected that some states will take similar views. This debate is overlain by the wider problem for the Committee of whether to enunciate only standards capable of global application, or to try to nudge some governments in a positive direction where the local political and legal climate is receptive. The Committee pursued the latter strategy in this case, with some success, as France subsequently changed the law applicable in the future to be consistent with its interpretation of the Committee's views.

The evidence is that a category of claims made by indigenous peoples is emerging as a distinct conceptual structure, although it is certainly not the case that any claim by an indigenous group or person therefore falls into this category. Is such a category justified, and how does it relate to the structures of other established international law categories? For some, more than enough justification lies in the existence and common experiences of the indigenous peoples movement, for whom it is an essential form of self-expression, mutual recognition, and leverage for legal and political change. Amongst the ambient population, and many persons who may count themselves as members of indigenous groups, the most powerful argument for a distinctive legal category based on special features of indigenous peoples is wrongful deprivation, above all of land, territory, self-government, means of livelihood, language, and identity. The appeal is thus to history and culture.[89] This justification works well in specific contexts, where it is reasonably clear in broad terms who is indigenous, who is not, what wrongs were done in the past, and why it now seems morally obligatory to respond. But formulating this justification as a rule for hard cases, or as a global abstraction capable of working across different types of societies with intricate identity politics and rapid cultural and economic change, is immensely difficult. Efforts to express culture and history as legal tests have tended to produce feeble and ultimately unconvincing searches to find or not find essentialized culture, and searches to find or not find modern majorities and minorities and peoples and owners as artefacts on the surface of history. Other justifications appeal to special historic and cultural relations with land, or to enduring disadvantage, or to systematic discrimination. These provide strong arguments, but are not exclusively justifications for an indigenous peoples category.

The construction and justification of a conceptual structure of indigenous peoples claims is political as well as legal, and threatens to exclude or make

[88] Scheinin, 'The Right to Enjoy a Distinct Culture: Indigenous and Competing Uses of Land', in T.S. Orlin, A. Rosas and M. Scheinin (eds), *The Jurisprudence of Human Rights Law: A Comparative Interpretive Approach* (2000) 159.

[89] Rosen, 'The Right to be Different', 107 *Yale Law Journal* (1997) 227.

difficult other political and legal projects. The indigenous peoples movement is part of a wider identity politics that may clash with other politics, such as women's movements. As tribal identity becomes more important and a tribe seems more beleaguered, women may feel forced to choose tribal identity and step back from pan-tribal women's movements that were more effective at reforming unequal traditions.[90] Designation of some set of people as 'indigenous' may be a simplistic social construction that creates an antonymic identity of 'non-indigenous', setting up a structure in which some are privileged and others disadvantaged for unappealing reasons. The justification of history and culture may trigger a search for authenticity that helps some who seem to meet, and may in effect set, such criteria, while taking from others who do not. Resources may go to parts of groups able to maintain a strong political leadership appealing to tribal tradition, rather than to people whose grandparents or parents drifted to urban areas. Or resources may go to new kinds of elites who are able to claim to represent regeneration and revitalization, as opposed to more traditional but less glamorous members of the same descent group. More generally, the indigenous peoples programme implies the insufficiency of other programmes for certain purposes, but its justifications imply more than simply supplementing the other programmes in special cases. The boundaries between this and other programmes are highly permeable in law as in present politics, but hard cases where the programmes clash will continue to arise, perhaps with increasing frequency.

If a distinct conceptual structure of claims as 'indigenous peoples' is emerging, how is 'indigenous peoples' defined? No general agreement has been reached in the UN, although bodies such as the ILO and the World Bank have adopted definitional criteria that function for specific purposes. Because this programme has a substantial practical existence but does not have consensus on a simple global justification, a constructivist approach to the concept is urged. This has been developed and defended at length in a separate paper, which concludes by proposing that a possible way forward for the UN on the specific problem of definition might be to establish a combined list of requirements and indicia.[91] In addition to the suggested requisites, some of the indicia would ordinarily be expected but not required in special circumstances, while other indicia would be simply relevant factors to be evaluated and weighed in cases of doubt or disagreement. As suggested in that paper, the list might be:

[90] Sunila Abeysekera has made this point in relation to the North-East Network of North-East Women, an inter-tribal women's network in north-east India.

[91] Kingsbury, '"Indigenous Peoples" in International Law: A Constructivist Approach to the Asian Controversy', 92 *AJIL* (1998) 414, at 455.

(1) essential requirements:
  (a) self-identification as a distinct ethnic group;
  (b) historical experience of, or contingent vulnerability to, severe disruption, dislocation, or exploitation;
  (c) long connection with the region;
  (d) the wish to retain a distinct identity;
(2) relevant indicia:
  (a) strong indicia
    (i) non-dominance in the national (or regional) society (ordinarily required);
    (ii) close cultural affinity with a particular area of land or territories (ordinarily required);
    (iii) historic continuity (especially by descent) with prior occupants of land in the region;
  (b) other relevant indicia
    (i) socioeconomic and sociocultural differences from the ambient population;
    (ii) distinct objective characteristics: language, race, material or spiritual culture, etc.;
    (iii) regarded as indigenous by the ambient population or treated as such in legal and administrative arrangements.

6. Conclusion

The increasingly rich body of practice in the presentation and negotiation of claims raised by indigenous peoples or members of such groups, and the burgeoning jurisprudence of some national and international courts and tribunals, has not established agreed conceptual foundations for legal analysis and political understanding of indigenous peoples' issues. It has been argued that at least five distinct conceptual structures operate. They make a difference to legal outcomes. Thus Ms Martinez would probably have won had her claim been treated as human rights, but lost because the US Supreme Court treated the issue in effect as one of Santa Clara Pueblo's self-determination with regard to membership. Ms Lovelace's claim succeeded as one for her rights as a member of a minority, although not as a human rights challenge to sex discrimination—and the Human Rights Committee was not willing to see the Band's resistance as a claim to self-determination, despite Article 1. The Lubicon Lake Band attempted to raise their claim as one for self-determination, but were rebuffed under the Optional Protocol and under Canadian law as it then was, ending up with a minority rights holding by the Human Rights Committee that was nevertheless buttressed by their position as an indigenous people. By contrast, the successful Indian claimants in

Delgamuuk obtained a Supreme Court of Canada ruling on property rights as indigenous peoples that shades into self-determination. Haudenosaunee in upstate New York might be able to employ a somewhat comparable strategy, but on past experience and observation of others they are very sceptical of such compromise solutions; many believe instead that the only satisfactory solution is recognition of the continuation of their historic sovereignty.

The absence of a singly unifying structure opens many possibilities in the law of the claims of indigenous peoples, but not just for indigenous peoples. Claimants may choose structures based on the competence and likely receptivity of the forum, looking in some cases for a structure that does not overreach, in others for one that may open paths for future lines of argument in the same or other fora. Respondents must decide whether to counter a claim within the same structure of argument as it has been made, or to recharacterize it, or to raise a competing claim based on another conceptual structure. Bodies with powers of recommendation or decision may calibrate their approaches in one of several different systems of measure, or jump between two or more structures to avoid unpalatable implications, or integrate two or more conceptual structures in seeking to craft far-sighted and workable approaches. Within liberal societies, the multiplicity of concepts offers a way beyond the limits that liberalism repeatedly confronts in coping with issues raised by indigenous peoples.[92] Such multiplicity may thus be a basis of legitimacy.

Globally, the range of concepts, and the host of ways in which they can be connected and reconciled, renders unconvincing any insistence on a single homogenizing structure that is alien to the political discourse and social patterns in some societies, or simply unpopular with the regime. If in China the concept of indigenous peoples is not accepted, and human rights discourse has clear limits, the concept of national minorities is well established in the constitutional structure and provides a structure for possible innovation and reform. If in Finland official law and policy does not recognize extensive Sami land rights, state land-use actions incompatible with Sami culture may be controlled under the minority rights programme. If in the US strong minority rights and multiculturalism are viewed with suspicion, attenuated forms of historic sovereignty and self-determination have legal endorsement and political legitimacy, albeit fragile. If New Zealand has also hesitated to move far toward official multiculturalism, biculturalism has been established on the basis of the indigenous peoples programme and the Treaty of Waitangi. This flexibility is far from the absolutism of rights, and allows for evasion and abuse. The risks of delegitimation of indigenous claims jurisprudence through incoherence, and polarization between political forces rallying around competing and utterly unreconciled concepts, are real. But the global

[92] Cf. J. Tully, *Strange Multiplicity: Constitutionalism in an Age of Diversity* (1995).

system of international law probably does not have the capacity to precisely resolve by agreement difficult questions about the connections between and limits of these conceptual structures.

Strengthened international institutions, such as the Permanent Forum for Indigenous Peoples in the UN and the increasing role of the IACHR and ILO oversight systems, can play an important role in monitoring and consciousness-raising. Specialist bodies such as the Conference of the Parties of the Biodiversity Convention can enunciate norms and action programmes in difficult areas that provide valuable guidance to states, indigenous peoples, and epistemic communities of professionals. Functional international institutions, the United Nations Development Programme for example, may be in awkward positions in formulating clear justifications for policies on the issues of indigenous peoples, because of the lack of clarity in member states and limited familiarity and experience of staff. The international indigenous peoples movement has played an important role in many institutions in raising issues and formulating proposals, and has influenced texts ranging from Agenda 21 to the World Conservation Strategy. But the number of institutions involved far exceeds the present capacities of this movement, and each institution has its own dynamic and its own pressures toward other priorities. General normative instruments such as the draft UN and OAS declarations have thus played, and if momentum is sustained may continue to play, a fundamental role in articulating norms and justifications that provide a shared reference and source of validation, even while leaving unresolved the more recondite problems of concepts and categories that have been the subject of this chapter.

4

Minority Rights Revisited: New Glimpses of an Old Issue

PETER LEUPRECHT

The subject of minority rights is not only a highly topical one, it also raises fundamental issues, and not only of a legal nature; in particular, the question of how individuals, groups and societies deal with others, with otherness, with difference. Mahatma Ghandi once said that our civilization will be judged by the way in which it treats its minorities.

One of the most alarming phenomena of our time is the resurgence of aggressive nationalism, ethnocentrism, racism, xenophobia, anti-Semitism, religious fanaticism, intolerance and irrationality. At the root of these disruptive and destructive currents, in my view, is a twofold rejection: rejection of that which is universal in human beings and humanity, and rejection of the other, of otherness, of difference.

Most conflicts of our time are internal conflicts and many of these are due to ethnic or religious strife, to an incapacity of societies and political systems to manage difference and diversity. These conflicts threaten peace and security; they are commonly accompanied by massive violations of human rights and bring about untold human suffering. The tragedies of Rwanda and former Yugoslavia are still fresh in our memories and our conscience. They should lie heavily on the consciences not only of certain warlords and political leaders, but also on the conscience of what we call the international community, which, in spite of much talk about early warning and conflict prevention, was unable to avert those tragedies.

In revisiting minority rights, my intention here is to examine first the 'oldness' of the issue and to demonstrate that the burden of history weighs heavily on it. I will then put forward some reasons for going back over this old issue and offer some new glimpses into it. Without overestimating the novelty of these insights, I shall at least try to view the question of minority rights in a broader context. Although I happen to be a lawyer, my approach in this chapter is far from exclusively legal, and is certainly not legalistic. It is my general belief that law is both a mirror of society and a means of shaping society; this certainly applies to the area of minorities.

1. The 'Old Issue'

It would be outside the scope of this chapter to give a complete historical overview of the problem of minorities. I shall therefore limit myself to what may be regarded as some salient aspects of its historical development.

In international law, religious minorities appeared as a subject of concern before national or ethnic minorities. The Treaty of Westphalia (1648) can be considered the first international law instrument dealing with (religious) minorities. International protection of national or ethnic minorities began with the Treaty of Warsaw of 1773 (the first partition of Poland). A more comprehensive protection of national or ethnic minorities was provided for by Article 1, para. 2, of the Final Act of the Congress of Vienna (1815).

Nationalism entered history at the end of the eighteenth and in the nineteenth centuries. This powerful ideology was to have a tremendous impact on the perception and actual situation of minorities. Ethnocentric nationalism had an overwhelming influence on political thinking and practice, on both the right and the left of the political spectrum. It provided a justification not only for assimilating minorities within European states, but also for colonizing other peoples overseas.

J.S. Mill wrote in 1861:

> Experience proves it is possible for one nationality to merge and be absorbed in another: and when it was originally an inferior and more backward portion of the human race the absorption is greatly to its advantage. Nobody can suppose that it is not more beneficial to a Breton, or a Basque of French Navarre, to be brought into the current of the ideas and feelings of a highly civilised and cultivated people—to be a member of the French nationality, admitted on equal terms to all the privileges of French citizenship . . . than to sulk on his own rocks, the half-savage relic of past times, revolving in his own little mental orbit, without participation or interest in the general movement of the world. The same remark applies to the Welshman or the Scottish Highlander as members of the British nation.[1]

Some years earlier, in 1849, Friedrich Engels had written:

> There is no country in Europe which does not have in some corner or other one or several fragments of peoples, the remnants of a former population that was suppressed and held in bondage by the nation which later became the main vehicle for historical development. These relics of nations, mercilessly trampled down by the passage of history, as Hegel expressed it, this ethnic trash always became fanatical standard bearers of counterrevolution and remain so until their complete extirpation or loss of their national character, just as their whole existence in general is itself a protest against a

[1] Mill, 'Considerations on Representative Government', in H.B. Acton (ed.), *Utilitarianism: On Liberty; Considerations on Representative Government* (1972) at 395, quoted in W. Kymlicka, *The Rights of Minority Cultures* (1995).

great historical revolution. Such in Scotland are the Gaels . . . Such in France are the Bretons . . . Such in Spain are the Basques.[2]

Although these authors were writing from opposing ideological camps, the similarity of these two quotations is striking. 'The half-savage relic of past times' (according to J.S. Mill) or the 'ethnic trash' (in Engels' words) was doomed to be 'absorbed' or 'extirpated'. Under the predominant nationalist ideology, both liberal individualism and socialist internationalism led to a systematic denial of the most fundamental rights of minority cultures, including their very right to exist.

Although the concept of 'la nation' as it was originally used in the French Revolution had little to do with subsequent nationalist programmes, there has been a marked insistence on linguistic uniformity in France since the Revolution. In his report on languages to the Committee on Public Safety, Barère wrote:

Who, in the Departments of Haut-Rhin and Bas-Rhin, has joined with the traitors to call the Prussian and the Austrian on our invaded frontiers? It is the inhabitant of the (Alsatian) countryside, who speaks the same language as our enemies, and who consequently considers himself their brother and fellow-citizen rather than the brother and fellow-citizen of Frenchmen who address him in another language and have other customs.[3]

As far as Marxism is concerned, Marx wrote in *The Communist Manifesto* that the proletariat have no nationality; they are workers of the world. However, for both Marxists and liberals in the nineteenth century, the 'great nations' were the carriers of historical development. The smaller nationalities were regarded as backward and stagnant. They were expected to abandon their national character and to assimilate into a 'great nation'. Attempts to maintain minority languages were regarded as reactionary and misguided; for German was the 'language of liberty' for the Czechs in Bohemia, just as French was the 'language of liberty' for the Bretons, and English was the 'language of liberty' for the Québécois in Canada. J.S. Mill opposed the idea of a distinct francophone society in Canada and encouraged the assimilation of the Québécois into the more 'civilized' English culture. He also wrote:

Free institutions are next to impossible in a country made up of different nationalities. Among a people without fellow-feeling, especially if they read and speak different languages, the united public opinion, necessary to the working of representative government, cannot exist.[4]

[2] F. Engels, *Hungary and Panslavism*, reprinted in full in Marx and Engels, *The Russian Menace to Europe*, P. Blackstock and B. Hoselitz (eds) (1952) quoted in Kymlicka supra n. 1.

[3] Quoted in E.J. Hobsbawm, *Nations and nationalism since 1780* (1992) at 21.

[4] Mill, supra n. 1, at 35.

Unfortunately, certain politicians in Europe and in other parts of the world continue to share the views advanced by J.S. Mill, although they have been shown to be misplaced, as evidenced, for instance, by the experience of multilingual Switzerland.

Engels' writings are particularly revealing. In his opinion, it was not only the right of the German nation to 'subdue, absorb and assimilate' smaller nationalities, but also its historical 'mission' and a proof of its 'vitality'.

> By the same right under which France took Flanders, Lorraine and Alsace, and will sooner or later take Belgium—by that same right Germany takes over Schleswig; it is the right of civilization as against barbarism, of progress as against stability . . . [This] is the right of historical evolution.[5]

According to the *air du temps* of the nineteenth century, progress and civilization required the assimilation of 'backward' minorities into 'energetic' majorities.

It is well worth giving emphasis to this historical background because the influence of nineteenth-century ethnocentric nationalism is far from having vanished; it has had a strong and lasting impact on political thinking and practice in Europe. Indeed, not only does it remain with us today, we even witness a resurgence of nationalism and ethnocentrism in certain European countries. In France, even in recent years, it is still possible to hear people praising 'la noblesse de l'assimilation'. Fashions have changed more with regard to terminology than substance; the term 'integration' is now regarded as 'politically correct'; but it is by no means certain whether the change of language reflects a corresponding change in fundamental attitudes.

It is also interesting to note that some of the present debates in North America on the status of indigenous peoples bear striking resemblance to earlier discussions concerning the status of minorities in Europe. Some still argue that modernization requires assimilation of the first nations in North America.

In the nineteenth century and well into the twentieth, the prevailing political thinking and practice of ethnocentric nationalism were basically hostile to minorities and to cultural and linguistic diversity. There existed some countervailing trends; not surprisingly, they were present mainly in the multinational Austro-Hungarian empire and, perhaps more surprisingly, in England, among the Pluralists such as Figgis and Laski. In Austria, and particularly in Vienna, there was a strong anti-nationalist current. As early as 1849, the great Austrian poet and playwright Franz Grillparzer, who was to be the prophet of the European tragedy, wrote in a dramatic and desperate epigram: 'Der Weg der neuen Bildung geht von Humanität über Nationalität zur Bestialität' (the way of the new culture goes from humanity through nationality to bestiality). The Austro-Marxists and, in particular, Otto Bauer opposed the prevailing trend of ethnocentric nationalism.

[5] F. Engels, *Democratic Panslavism*, quoted in Kymlicka, supra n. 1, at 23.

In the legal field, the Austrian *Staatsgrundgesetz* (Fundamental Law of the State) of 21 December 1867 stipulated in Article 19:

All ethnic groups (*Volksstämme*) of the State enjoy the same rights and each of them has an inalienable right to preserve and promote its nationality (*Nationalität*) and language.

It is interesting to note that this provision guaranteed collective rights of ethnic groups. However, this quite progressive provision applied only to one of the two parts of what had become the dual monarchy; namely, to Cisleithanien (the territories west of the river Leitha), but not to the territories under the Hungarian crown. Those who ruled in Budapest at the time were more inclined than their counterparts in Vienna to practise a policy of assimilation, i.e. magyarization.

This historical background explains, at least to a certain extent, why minority problems in this particular region have remained or have once again become hot issues and why efforts aiming at the settlement of these problems have encountered considerable difficulties. On the whole, these problems seem to have been overcome between Hungary and Romania, while tensions remain between Hungary and Slovakia.

In Cisleithanien, Article 19 of the *Staatsgrundgesetz* gave rise to a rich case law of the *Reichsgericht* (Tribunal of the Empire), which remains a source of inspiration for all those interested in minority issues.

After the First World War, the League of Nations devoted considerable attention to minority protection in a Europe whose political landscape had radically changed. President Wilson proposed that a provision be included in the Statute of the League of Nations which would obligate the 'new states' to respect minorities. This proposal was not retained. Wilson was actually concerned about the rise of chauvinism and, in particular, about reports concerning pogroms against Jews in Poland. At the Paris Peace Conference, Wilson questioned the Polish delegate, Roman Dmowski about this. His response was not at all reassuring: ten per cent of the population of Poland were Jews, he said, and 'this is at least eight per cent too many'.[6]

The system of minority protection of the League of Nations was limited to Central and Eastern Europe. Treaties concerning minorities were concluded with Poland, Yugoslavia, Czechoslovakia, Romania and Greece. Provisions on minority protection were included in the Peace Treaties with Bulgaria, Hungary, Turkey and Austria. These different treaties did not guarantee rights to individuals, but laid down state obligations. Minorities and persons belonging to them had a right of petition. The Permanent Court of International Justice could be seized; indeed, it rendered a number of

[6] Quoted in G. Brunner, I. Camartin, H. Harbich and O. Kimminich, *Minderheitenschutz in Europa*, Rechtsstaat in der Bewährung Band 17 (1985) at 20.

interesting opinions, including its famous opinion on minority schools in Albania.

The relative ineffectiveness of the system of minority protection established by the League of Nations may be traced to two factors: on the one hand, the fact that it only applied to certain countries and to certain minority situations and, on the other hand, the general weakness of the League.

The weakness of the League of Nations and its system of minority protection was strikingly demonstrated by the Bernheim case.[7] In 1933, Franz Bernheim, a German citizen of Jewish origin, made a complaint to the Council of the League of Nations about breaches by Germany of the German-Polish Treaty of 1922. He relied on the section protecting minorities in Upper Silesia, which at the time formed part of Germany. He had lived there from 1931 to 1933 and had been dismissed by a German firm, as had been the fate of all Jewish employees. He therefore complained about the measures taken against Jews.

The record of the debate to which this complaint gave rise in the League of Nations is alarmingly revealing. Germany's delegate raised a number of procedural objections; as to the merits, he did not deny the measures taken, and argued that 'the anti-Semitic movement was not directed against the Jewish religion, but only against the race'. He further argued that the Jewish problem in Germany was *sui generis* and 'could not be treated like an ordinary minority question'; this was 'a domestic matter in respect of which Germany had no commitment under international law'.

The Bernheim case probably marked the beginning of the end of the League of Nations and its system of minority protection. Another terrible war was to come down on Europe—a war which was European and particularly German in its origins and worldwide in its effects.

It is hardly necessary to go in any detail here into the celebration by the Nazi regime of the 'rupture of nationalism' and of the 'national myth which blossoms from the blood',[8] which logically led to the justification, indeed the glorification and practice, of elimination of the other, the *Untermensch*, and particularly the Jews and Gypsies. What Grillparzer had predicted 100 years earlier was to become a terrible reality: the reign of bestiality and barbarity. In his last work, *The World of Yesterday—Memoirs of a European*, written shortly before his tragic end in exile, Stefan Zweig, an Austrian, refers to 'nationalism—that dire scourge which has blighted the flower of our European culture' and to 'mankind's inconceivable relapse into a kind of barbarism presumed long dead, with its deliberate, programmatic denial of human values'.

[7] References to the Bernheim case in A. Cassese, *Human rights in a changing world* (1990), at 18 *et seq.*, and in F. Ermacora, *Menschenrechte in der sich wandelnden Welt*, Vol. I (1974), at 357, 408 and 427 *et seq.*

[8] F.G. Jünger, *Der Aufmarsch des Nationalismus* (1926), at 21.

After the Second World War, the issue of minorities became taboo for quite some time. One reason for this was the fact that, in the years leading up to the war, Nazi Germany had brutally exploited the situation of German-speaking minorities as a justification of its policy of expansion and aggression. After 1945, there was also a widely-held belief that the general protection of universal human rights would be sufficient to protect minorities.

This brief historical survey shows that the protection of minorities and minority rights is indeed an old issue and that the burden of history, particularly the history of ethnocentric nationalism, weighs heavily on it. In recent years, the old issue has been revisited, and there are good reasons for that.

2. Reasons for Revisiting the 'Old Issue'

For quite some time after the Second World War, minority rights were excluded from the emerging international law of human rights—despite some efforts to include them—within the United Nations and the Parliamentary Assembly of the Council of Europe.[9] However, the claim to self-determination appeared on the human rights agenda in the context of decolonization. The human rights approach of the international community proved to be a powerful means which helped to break down the colonial empires. Other evolving human rights concepts came into play, especially the concept of cultural integrity. Something in the nature of a human right to cultural survival and development appeared in international law. This is signalled in particular by the Convention against Genocide of 1948, which defines genocide as *inter alia* 'acts committed with intent to destroy, in whole or in part, a national, ethnical, racial or religious group, as such'; it is also illustrated by Article 27 of the International Covenant on Civil and Political Rights as well as the 1966 UNESCO Declaration of Principles of Cultural Cooperation, which affirms a right and duty of all peoples to protect and develop all cultures of humankind. Two International Labour Organization (ILO) conventions on indigenous and tribal peoples were also adopted; namely, Convention No. 107 (1957) and Convention No. 169 (1989). On 18 December 1992, the UN General Assembly adopted the Declaration on the Rights of Persons Belonging to National or Ethnic, Religious and Linguistic Minorities.[10]

These documents mark a radical departure from the earlier ideology and practice of ethnocentric nationalism and assimilation which had brought about massive human rights violations. The international community seemed to have drawn the lessons from this bitter experience. The new thinking and

[9] Cf. Leuprecht, 'Der Europarat und das Recht der nationalen Minderheiten', *Europa Ethnica* (1961) 146.

[10] United Nations General Assembly Resolution 47/135, 3 February 1993.

increasing awareness of the value of diversity can also be seen as a reaction against the process of globalization, whose effects were beginning to be felt in the economic as well as the cultural fields and which tends to force people and peoples into a homogeneous mould. Globalization and a related sense of powerlessness have probably contributed to a longing for identity, and a fear of losing one's identity. People and peoples are asking, 'Who are we? What are we?' And they want to be recognized with their identity. While this is an understandable reaction, it is not without risks. An obsession with identity, narrowly defined, could indeed bring us back to aggressive nationalism and ethnocentrism.

Another important factor which contributed to a revisiting of the issue of minorities and minority rights was the radical geo-political change which occurred after 1989 and which has affected Europe in particular. The reactivation of the minorities question in Europe is the result of the developments—positive and negative—sparked off by the downfall of the Soviet empire and the communist regimes. Among the positive developments, we can point, in the first place, to the process of democratization; among the negative ones, there is an alarming resurgence of aggressive nationalism and ethnocentrism in many parts of Europe. In some countries of Central and Eastern Europe, the progress of nationalism and ethnocentrism has been much more rapid than that of democratization, which goes some way to explaining a number of the very serious problems with which Europe is struggling today.

Under the communist regimes which were officially internationalist, national sentiment was, as Bronislav Geremek has said,[11] the most simple expression of resistance. At the same time, it is also true that politicians in regimes of decaying totalitarianism frequently used, and continue to use, nationalism as a means of clinging to power. The switch from communism to nationalism seems to have been easy for many of them. We also witness examples of alliances between the two, the so-called 'red-brown' coalitions between former communists and nationalists.

In certain quarters of Europe there seems to be a terrible and perhaps sometimes deliberate confusion between *demos* and *ethnos*, between democracy and ethnocracy. Ethnocracy is the negation of democracy. It is obvious that nationalism and ethnocentrism—whether of the majority or the minority—are not conducive to the peaceful and harmonious solution of minority problems.

It is highly significant that at the Vienna Summit in October 1993, the heads of state and government of the member states of the enlarged Council of Europe, 'alarmed by the development of aggressive nationalism and ethnocentrism', adopted important decisions on minorities as well as on a policy for

[11] B. Geremek, synthesis of debates, Council of Europe Seminar on Intercultural Learning for Human Rights, Klagenfurt (Austria), 28–30 October 1991 (Council of Europe publication), at 43.

combating racism, xenophobia, anti-Semitism and intolerance.[12] It is essential, in this author's view, to read and implement together these two sets of decisions.

There has been considerable progress in and around Europe over the past few years in relation to the recognition of minority rights. In the framework of the Organization for Security and Cooperation in Europe (OSCE), participating states have undertaken important political commitments, particularly in the Copenhagen document of 1990.[13] Since 1993, the OSCE High Commissioner for National Minorities, Max van der Stoel, has played a very constructive role.

Within the Council of Europe, two important legal instruments have been concluded:

(1) The European Charter for Regional and Minority Languages[14] was opened for signature on 5 November 1992 and entered into force on 1 March 1998. Its preamble states that 'the protection of the historical regional or minority languages of Europe, some of which are in danger of eventual extinction, contributes to the maintenance and development of Europe's cultural wealth and traditions'. 'The right to use a regional or minority language in private and public life' is described as 'an inalienable right'. The preamble also stresses 'the value of interculturalism and multilingualism' and emphasizes that 'the protection and promotion of regional or minority languages in the different countries and regions of Europe represent an important contribution to the building of a Europe based on the principles of democracy and cultural diversity'. The Charter lays down objectives and principles to be respected by states and proposes concrete measures to put them into effect in the fields of education, courts of law, administrative authorities and public services, the media, cultural facilities and economic and social life.

(2) On 1 February 1995, the Framework Convention for the Protection of National Minorities[15] was opened for signature; it entered into force on 1 February 1998. This is the first ever legally binding multilateral instrument devoted to the protection of national minorities, and contains provisions covering a wide range of issues. States parties are to undertake programmes, making use of legislation and appropriate governmental policies, in order to attain defined objectives. The Committee of Ministers of the Council of Europe, with the assistance of an advisory committee, monitors the programmes and measures adopted by states parties through a mechanism of periodic reports.

[12] Vienna Declaration of 9 October 1993, reprinted in 14 *Hum Rts LJ* (1993) 373.

[13] On the work of OSCE, cf. V.-Y. Ghebali, *L'OSCE dans l'Europe post-communiste, 1990–1996. Vers une identité paneuropéenne de sécurité* (1996). With regard to the Copenhagen Conference on the Human Dimension of OSCE, see Ghebali, supra n. 12, at 451–2. The provisions concerning minorities are contained in Section IV of the Copenhagen document. See ibid., at 502–3.

[14] Europ. TS No. 148.

[15] Europ. TS No. 157.

On 17 September 1997, the Committee of Ministers adopted the Rules on the Monitoring Arrangements under Articles 24–6 of the Framework Convention.[16] Rule 6 stipulates that 'the members of the Advisory Committee shall serve in their individual capacity, shall be independent and impartial, and shall be available to serve the Committee effectively'. In accordance with Rule 23, 'the Advisory Committee shall consider the state reports and shall transmit its opinions to the Committee of Ministers'; it may receive information from sources other than state reports (Rule 30). Following receipt of the opinion of the advisory committee, 'the Committee of Ministers shall consider and adopt its conclusions concerning the adequacy of the measures taken by the Contracting Party concerned to give effect to the principles of the Framework Convention'. It may also adopt recommendations in respect of the party concerned, and set a time limit for the submission of information on their implementation (Rule 24).

Thus, we may see that there have been considerable developments during recent years in relation to the international law concerning minority rights. There is a bitter irony, however, in the fact that it should have been the Arbitration Commission of the Conference for Peace in Yugoslavia which stated in its opinions of 29 November 1991 and 11 January 1992 that the obligation of states to ensure respect for the rights of minorities has become a peremptory norm of international law.[17]

3. New Glimpses

It seems essential to approach the issue of minorities and minority rights within a broader context, particularly that of democracy and human rights. At the same time, certain lessons can be drawn from the minority issue for human rights and democracy. In this regard I make eight points below, which may be regarded as 'new glimpses'.

(1) A first and, in my view, important lesson can be drawn from the real life experience of minorities: it is not sufficient to protect the general human rights of some kind of abstract human being. Human rights are also, and must also be, rights of 'l'homme situé', the 'situated' human being, the human being living in certain conditions which may affect his or her enjoyment of fundamental rights. Belonging to a minority is such a condition, which justifies the granting of specific rights. I am therefore not convinced by the arguments of those who claim that the idea of minority rights is incompatible with the principles of universality of human rights and of equality. This is largely

[16] Committee of Ministers Resolution (97) 10.

[17] Opinions Nos 1 and 2 in: International Legal Materials, Documents 1992 (Volume XXXI), at 1496 and 1498.

a French argument, whose origins go back to the French Revolution. The attitude of the revolutionaries is perfectly well reflected in the following statement by Count Clermont-Tonnerre:

Il faut tout refuser aux juifs comme nation et tout accorder aux juifs comme individus; . . . il faut refuser la protection légale au maintien des prétendues lois de leur corporation judaïque; il faut qu'ils ne fassent plus dans l'Etat ni corps politique, ni ordre; il faut qu'ils soient individuellement citoyens.18

This statement reflects, of course, an absolutely individualistic concept of rights. Those who share this way of thinking regard the concept of minority, and indeed of any kind of 'community' apart from the national community of citizens, with the greatest suspicion. In my opinion, this view confounds formal and genuine equality and easily leads to the assimilation of minorities. To treat in the same way human situations that are different is also a form of discrimination. Human rights law has increasingly come around to recognizing not only rights that belong to every human being, but also rights of 'l'homme situé', for instance, the accused, the worker, and so forth. Thus, it makes clear sense to guarantee rights to human beings belonging to a minority. I would, however, argue that the same rights must be guaranteed to all those who are in the same situation. It is for this reason that I reject certain definitions of the concept of minority which imply discrimination or exclusion. I am thinking, for example, of those who propose reserving minority rights to nationals of the state concerned or to those belonging to 'historic minorities'. It is unfortunately true that the word 'exist' was included in Article 27 of the International Covenant on Civil and Political Rights[19] at the request of countries receiving immigrants with the explicit purpose of excluding 'new minorities'. I do not, however, share the view that only persons belonging to 'historic minorities' or only nationals of the state concerned are entitled to minority protection. The distinction between 'historic' and 'new' minorities seems highly arbitrary; after what period of time does a minority qualify as 'historic'? As to the alleged requirement of citizenship, it is significant that the Human Rights Committee referred, in its General Comment No. 15/27,[20] to 'those cases where aliens constitute a minority within the meaning of Art. 27'. I would certainly agree that aliens can belong to a

[18] Editor's translation: 'One must deny everything to the Jews as a nation and accord everything to them as individuals; . . . legal protection for the maintenance of the would-be laws of their Jewish corporation must be refused; they must no longer form within the state either a political body or a(n) (legal) order; they must be citizens individually.' Quoted in B. Philippe, *Etre juif dans la société française* (1981), at 43.

[19] Cf. M. Bossuyt, *Guide to the 'travaux préparatoires' of the International Covenant on Civil and Political Rights* (1987), at 495 *et seq.*

[20] General Comment No. 15/27 on the position of aliens under the Covenant (22 July 1986).

minority and therefore be entitled to minority rights; they may be a particularly vulnerable minority and therefore be in particular need of minority protection.

(2) It is essential to understand and practise human rights for what they are: not only the rights of each and every one of us, but also and above all the rights of others. This vision of human rights is not easily accepted and even less easily practised, particularly in our Western societies which suffer from an essentially egoistic, individualistic and acquisitive approach to human rights.

(3) Although there seems to be a widespread verbal consensus on the indivisibility of all human rights, in practice the social and cultural dimension of human rights is badly neglected. In my view, this is largely due to the predominant pan-economic ideology and to the narrow concept of the human being it promotes; namely, the human being reduced to *homo oeconomicus*, debased to an economic factor (or, a little more optimistically, to an economic actor). This, in turn, leads to a singularly constricted view of human rights which allows no room for social and cultural rights. As far as minorities are concerned, it is surprising to note that the importance of economic and social rights is largely overlooked. Cultural rights, which unfortunately remain an underdeveloped category of human rights, are of particular importance for minorities. This was acknowledged by the 1993 Vienna Summit of Heads of State and Government of the Council of Europe member states, which decided to instruct the Committee of Ministers to draft a framework convention on minorities as well as 'to begin work on drafting a protocol complementing the European Convention on Human Rights in the cultural field by provisions guaranteeing individual rights, in particular for persons belonging to national minorities'.[21] This work was indeed begun, but has not been completed due to far-reaching disagreements among member states regarding the nature and scope of the rights to be guaranteed. It is to be hoped that this is no more than a temporary failure. Cultural rights must cease to be a forgotten category of human rights. The interesting and promising reflection on cultural rights conducted by the 'Groupe de Fribourg' points in the right direction.[22]

(4) One inevitably comes across the argument of individual versus collective or group rights in discussions on minority rights. It must be admitted that there still exists quite a strong individualistic bias in international human rights law resulting from the traditional Western liberal political philosophy. There is at the same time, however, a movement towards greater realization of collective or group rights. This is apparent in documents such as the draft Declaration on the Rights of Indigenous Peoples, the ILO Convention on

[21] Vienna Declaration (supra n. 12) Appendix II.

[22] *Projet relatif à une déclaration des droits culturels*, 'Groupe de Fribourg', Actes et documents 3 (Editions Universitaires, Fribourg (Suisse), 1997).

Indigenous and Tribal Peoples (No. 169) and the African Charter on Human and Peoples' Rights, which recognizes rights of the family and of peoples.

I believe that human rights law must take into account both the individual and the social dimension of the human being. The fulfilment of both of these dimensions is necessary for human beings to be able to live in dignity. The question which must be addressed is whether there are groups and group rights, the recognition of which is essential for the self-fulfilment of the human being as a social being and for the achievement of an effective and genuine universality of human rights. We must seriously consider whether and how we can reconcile individual rights and group rights. They can be complementary, but they may also be conflicting or mutually exclusive. An individual can hardly be free if he or she belongs to an oppressed group. On the other hand, there is an obvious and real danger that rights of the group may be used against the individual and his or her fundamental rights. It is indispensable that these problems be analysed much more profoundly and that we find ways out of the sterile and often futile ideological debates of the past and the present, for instance, the controversy currently raging, especially in North America, between communitarianism and individualism. At the same time, it must be strongly underlined that one should not force the individual into a group and that belonging to a group must be based on the free choice of the individual.

For a long time, the political and legal instruments drawn up by international organizations on behalf of minorities have been based on the principle that the beneficiaries of the rights in question are individuals. At most they have recognized that rights relating, for instance, to the use of language, the practice of a religion or cultural activities will often be exercised in community with others. This approach clearly has its limitations, particularly when it comes to certain kinds of measures in favour of minorities. Rights to a specific territory, to administrative autonomy or to special forms of participation in public decision-making are difficult to conceive as other than group rights. We would therefore do well to rethink our concepts in this field, including that of group rights.

(5) A further concept in need of clarification is that of self-determination. This principle, in my opinion, need not correspond to separation and can be accommodated in multinational states; it should not be equated with a right to independent statehood. Under a human rights approach, the concept of self-determination is capable of embracing much more nuanced interpretations and applications; it may be understood as a right of cultural groupings to the political institutions necessary to allow them to exist and develop according to their distinctive characteristics.

(6) In today's world there is much talk of identity. This is an extremely complex concept. Indeed, the meaning it is given is rather paradoxical. Etymologically speaking, it has its root in the Latin word 'idem' which means

'the same'; however, in our modern understanding it defines what makes each of us different—different from any other human being.

We are witnessing today numerous forms of manipulation and abuse of the concept of identity. People kill each other in the name of their identity and deeply disturbing phenomena of obsession with identity may be perceived.

I strongly believe in the virtues of an open and multiple identity. Antonio Perotti, one of the great 'intercultural' thinkers and actors, uses the beautiful image of the daisy: like the flower, our identity is made up of many petals. One cannot reduce the daisy to one of its petals; in the same way, one cannot reduce our identity to one of its facets, be it the ethnic, national, linguistic or religious facet. Our identity is essentially composite; it reflects the multitude and diversity of our belongings; it is a serious error to reduce it to one of these many aspects. It is also true that we construct our identity during the course of our lives; it is not immutable; we cannot deep-freeze it, nor can we put it into a museum. We constantly define and redefine our identity through contact, dialogue and exchange, and sometimes also through conflict with others. Emmanuel Lévinas, who places ethics at the heart of his philosophy, maintains that the fundamental experience of the human being consists in 'meeting the other's face'; we should be constantly aware of what he calls 'the ethical significance of the other'. Abel Martin has rightly emphasized 'the essential heterogeneity of being'; and Octavio Paz has powerfully reminded us, in his *Labyrinth of Loneliness*, that the human being is the only being that is in 'quest of the other'.

(7) In this spirit, difference and diversity should be perceived not as a handicap or barrier, but as what they really are: a tremendous enrichment, a treasure to be preserved. In today's world, cultural diversity is threatened by the strong impact of 'an all-encompassing Americanised, global culture'.[23] According to Edward W. Said, 'rarely before in human history has there been so massive an intervention of force and ideas from one culture to another as there is today from America to the rest of the world'.[24] Europe, in particular, seems to be torn between two conflicting trends: on the one hand, a recognition of 'the rich heritage of diverse languages and cultures in Europe' as 'a valuable common resource to be protected and developed'[25] and, on the other hand, the pressure of paneconomic ideology, globalization and the 'market'; determination to preserve one's 'identity', sometimes even an obsession with 'identity', on the one hand, and powerful forces of standardization and uniformity on the other.

[23] *In from the margins*, Report prepared for the Council of Europe by the European Task Force on Culture and Development (Council of Europe publication, June 1997), at 18.

[24] E.W. Said, *Culture and Imperialism* (1994), at 319.

[25] Council of Europe, Committee of Ministers Recommendation No. R (82) 18, adopted on 24 September 1982.

(8) The solution of minority problems requires the creation of a political environment in which minorities can feel safe. The best way to achieve this aim is to build a genuinely democratic society or, as Karl Popper put it, an open society which is 'a way of living together in which individual freedom, non-violence, protection of minorities and protection of the weak are important values'.[26] A genuine pluralistic democracy is infinitely more than just majority rule; it is certainly not brutal or ruthless majority rule, oppression of the minority by the majority. Respect for minorities and for others, for difference, is an essential component of any genuine democracy. Therefore, we must try to strengthen pluralism and democracy at all levels, not only at the level of the state but also at the regional and local levels. At the same time, it will be increasingly necessary to accept and practise not only political, but also cultural, pluralism.

Pluralism and democracy should be strengthened within minorities too. This is undoubtedly an important objective; however, pluralism within the minority becomes more difficult when the minority feels threatened from the outside.

Decentralization and a genuine application of the principle of subsidiarity facilitate the solution of minority problems. The traditional concept of the nation-state needs to be reviewed and demystified.

In the effort to build a genuinely democratic society, it is of fundamental importance that we come to grips with a very difficult issue, that of citizenship. In a number of countries, particularly in Europe, the question arises of who is a citizen and on what criteria citizenship should be based. I strongly believe that citizenship is not the same thing as nationality, *Staatsangehörigkeit* (belonging to a state). One can be a citizen without being a national of the state in which one happens to live. Citizenship must be a means of inclusion in a democratic society, not a means of exclusion; and neither citizenship nor nationality should be based on ethnicity.

It is essential that the multicultural character of most modern societies be given full consideration. Some do not like it, but it is a reality, not a doctrine or ideology. Any dreams of a culturally, ethnically or nationally 'pure' society are not only out of touch with reality; they are also extremely dangerous and, as we have tragically witnessed in former Yugoslavia, are bound to lead to disaster and to appalling human suffering.

Intolerance must be combated in all its forms, including aggressive nationalism, ethnocentrism and religious fanaticism. Intercultural learning and human rights education must be promoted. I do not believe in Samuel Huntington's alarming scenario of the inevitable clash of civilizations and cultures, but rather in the necessary dialogue between them. Peace and harmony must be built on the basis of respect for the other, for otherness, difference

[26] K.R. Popper and K. Lorenz, *Die Zukunft ist offen* (1994) at 135.

and diversity, on the basis of a shared ethic of humanity—that of the equal dignity of every human being. As is stated in the very first sentence of the Universal Declaration of Human Rights, 'recognition of the inherent dignity and of the equal and inalienable rights of all members of the human family is the foundation of freedom, justice and peace in the world'. It is also the key to the peaceful solution of minority problems.

5

Globalization and the Right to Development

ANNE ORFORD

The changes to the international system that have taken place since the break up of the Soviet Union have significantly altered the capacity of international law to protect and promote human rights. In particular, the increase in the speed and scale of trade and financial liberalization poses major challenges to international human rights law. Developments such as the Asian financial crisis, protests about the impact of the World Trade Organization (WTO), the controversy surrounding the negotiation of the Multilateral Agreement on Investment, the activities of the International Monetary Fund (IMF) and the World Bank and the re-emergence in many states of economic nationalism and protectionism have all contributed to putting globalization on trial.[1] Human rights activists and scholars argue that a focus on economic globalization, the power of transnational corporations and the effects of the activities of international economic institutions must be placed at the centre of campaigns to promote and protect human rights. This chapter considers the right to development in the context of economic globalization, in particular in light of the impact of trade and investment agreements and of the activities of international economic institutions.[2] The aim of the chapter is twofold: first, to assess the impact of economic globalization on the right to development and secondly, to consider the utility of the right to development as a means for resisting some of the more destructive effects of economic restructuring in the post-Cold War era.

Part I outlines the history of the emergence of the right to development in the late 1970s and 1980s, and gives a sense of the political and economic

[1] The representative of the International Confederation of Free Trade Unions at a round table on the WTO and Human Rights said that the Asian crisis had 'put globalization on trial'. See 'All Countries Bound by International Law to Take Human Rights With Them into the WTO', 2 *UDHR News* (15 May 1998).

[2] For analyses that focus on the use of unilateral rather than multilateral trade sanctions, including their use by the United States to coerce states into making concessions at the multilateral level, see C. Raghavan, *Recolonization: GATT, the Uruguay Round and the Third World* (1990), at 83–9; Drahos, 'Global Property Rights in Information: The story of TRIPS at the GATT', *Prometheus* (1995) 6; Alston, 'Labour Rights Provisions in International Trade Law: "Aggressive Unilateralism"?', 15 *Human Rights Quarterly* (1993) 1.

background to the emergence of that right. The right to development has become an increasingly important part of the United Nations (UN) human rights agenda, but as I will suggest, it has not been adopted with equal enthusiasm by the international economic institutions that affect 'development' in its broadest sense. Debates over the right to development at the intergovernmental level have for the large part remained polarized along a North/South axis, and I discuss in turn some of the ways in which that right has been deployed politically.

Part II outlines and explores the key features of the right to development, as established in the 1986 Declaration on the Right to Development.[3] I focus on some of the features of the right that have attracted controversy, such as whether individuals or states are subjects or bearers of the right, whether the right to development trumps other human rights, and what is meant by 'development' in the context of the right. I point to aspects of the right that remain particularly useful, such as the emphasis on participation in development as the basis of the right and the focus on operation of the right at both the national and international levels. Part II also notes the ways in which different aspects of the right are emphasized by states according to their national interests.

Part III analyses the relationship between the right to development and the policies, projects and actions of the three international institutions that perhaps more than any others shape the development process in many states. Those institutions are the IMF, the World Bank and the WTO. I assess the extent to which the actions of those institutions are informed by a recognition of the right to development, or whether their activities in fact violate the right to development in particular and human rights obligations more generally. I should stress that I am not suggesting that those institutions somehow impose conditions on states in situations where governments or elites are not willing to accept such conditions. Very often, economic liberals or self-interested rulers in such states support and stand to benefit from IMF or World Bank programmes. I am interested, however, in testing the extent to which the right to development can be used as a tool to measure the effects of the activities of such institutions.

Finally, Part IV asks whether a focus on the right to development is a useful means of challenging the more destructive aspects of economic globalization. Can the right to development provide a framework to challenge the activities of international economic institutions? Should human rights scholars and activists, or states seeking to adopt alternative models of development, invest time, energy and resources into attempting to develop mechanisms for

[3] Declaration on the Right to Development, adopted 4 December 1986, GA Res. 41/128 (Annex), UN GAOR, 41st Sess., Supp. No. 53, at 186, UN Doc. A/41/53 (1987). The Declaration was adopted by a vote of 146 to 1 (the US), with 8 abstentions (including the GFR, Japan and the UK).

implementing the right to development? I feel some ambivalence about the utility of focusing on a right to development in the post-Soviet era, for reasons that I outline fully in the conclusion.

I THE EMERGENCE OF THE RIGHT TO DEVELOPMENT

In order to understand the right to development, it is necessary to know something of the political and economic context in which it was first envisaged. The emergence of a numerically dominant group of developing countries in the international arena as a result of decolonization led to the elevation of economic development issues to the top of the international agenda in various fora during the 1960s and 1970s.[4] After the initial flush of independence, many former colonies became disillusioned with the international order, and with the agenda of various international economic and development organizations.[5] While most states joined the IMF and the World Bank in the initial phase of decolonization, many soon became dissatisfied with the prescriptions of the Bretton Woods institutions.[6] Many of those states took longer to join the General Agreement on Tariffs and Trade (GATT), and those who did received few benefits from the initial GATT rounds.[7]

Initially, states sought to address those problems through attempting to reform international economic institutions, with only limited success. Attempts to address development issues through the Economic and Social Council (ECOSOC) led to the formation of the United Nations Conference on Trade and Development (UNCTAD) as an organ of the General Assembly, where wider issues of international economic relationships were to be addressed. Efforts to have development issues addressed in an integrated way through the major international economic institutions, however, did not succeed. Attempts to reform the IMF, the World Bank and the GATT were remarkably unsuccessful.[8]

The 'reformist' phase involved attempts to seek minor amendments to the international economic system, with no fundamental challenges to that system. By the early 1970s, the reformist phase had given way to a 'restructuring'

[4] Alston, 'Revitalising United Nations Work on Human Rights and Development', 18 *Melbourne University Law Review* (1991) 216, at 218.

[5] Raghavan, supra n. 2, at 52. [6] Ibid. at 51. [7] Ibid.

[8] While in 1964, special provisions on Trade and Development were added to Part IV of GATT, decolonized states still gained no real commitments. Part IV is expressed in the language of best endeavours, and was never translated into binding obligations. While decolonized states made some other minor gains in GATT, such as the acceptance of the generalized system of preferences, there were basically few amendments to a system that still excluded trade in agriculture, textile and tropical products from overall commitments to trade liberalization. Ibid., at 52.

phase.[9] Decolonized states determined that special treatment was not sufficient, and that it was necessary to change the asymmetry in international economic relations and systems in order for conditions to improve. The Declaration on the Establishment of a New International Economic Order and the Charter of Rights and Duties of States were adopted by the UN General Assembly in 1974 and 1975.[10] UNCTAD took up a number of platforms of the New International Economic Order, and at Nairobi in 1976 fashioned mandates for negotiating changes in the systems and rules relating to commodities, trade, shipping, money, finance and debt. Those commitments were taken up by some other UN agencies such as the International Labour Organization, the Food and Agricultural Organization and the World Health Organization, which began to convene conferences on those issues. The major international economic institutions of the IMF, the World Bank and the GATT, however, steadfastly ignored the call for a new international economic order.[11]

The situation for states in the South worsened with the two oil price rises in 1973/4 and 1979, which led to a far more adversarial approach to economic relations by industrialized states, particularly the United States.[12] During the 1980s, economically powerful states increasingly resorted to multilateral institutions to further foreign policy goals in the economic and trade areas.[13] The Reagan administration, for example, strongly influenced the approach of the IMF and the World Bank. From 1986 onwards the World Bank, under the Reagan appointee and former United States Republican Congressman, Barber Conable, began to attach conditions to structural adjustment or policy-based loans requiring privatization and trade and investment liberalization. In the human rights area, a related policy development of the Reagan administration was to deny that economic, social and cultural rights were human rights at all.[14] Industrialized states, particularly the US, also sought to expand trade and financial liberalization through the GATT,

[9] Ibid. at 53.

[10] Declaration on the Establishment of a New Economic Order, adopted 1 May 1974, GA Res. 3201 (S-VI), 6 (SPECIAL) UN GAOR, 6th Spec. Sess. Supp. No. 1, at 3, UN Doc. A/9559 (1974), reprinted in 3 *ILM* (1974) 715; Charter of Economic Rights and Duties of States 1974, adopted 12 December 1974, GA Res. 3281, UN GAOR, 29 Sess., Supp. No. 31, at 50, UN Doc. A/9631 (1975), reprinted in 14 *IML* (1975) 251.

[11] Raghavan, supra n. 2, at 54.

[12] T. Wheelwright, *Oil & World Politics: From Rockefeller to the Gulf War* (1991) 25.

[13] Raghavan, supra n. 2, at 54–8.

[14] Alston, 'The Shortcomings of a "Garfield the Cat" Approach to the Right to Development', 15 *California Western International Law Journal* (1985) 510, at 516 [hereinafter Alston, 'Garfield the Cat']; Alston, 'US Ratification of the Covenant on Economic, Social and Cultural Rights: The Need for an Entirely New Strategy', 84 *American Journal of International Law* (1990) 365, at 372–7 [hereinafter Alston, 'US Ratification'].

and since 1995 the WTO, in order to gain access to the markets, resources and labour of countries in Asia, Africa and now Eastern Europe.

It was against that background of a changing and contested international political order that the notion of a right to development emerged. The political and economic context which led to the push for the recognition of such a right may explain why, to Jack Donnelly's evident bemusement, the right to development 'moved through the usually labyrinthine United Nations system with incredible speed'.[15] In the human rights field, the concerns of decolonized states were translated into demands for greater recognition of economic, social and cultural rights, international recognition that colonialism and neo-colonialism were gross violations of international and human rights law, and the push to recognize development cooperation as an obligation owed by former colonial powers, rather than as an act of charity.[16]

The notion of a right to development was first recognized in those terms by the UN Commission on Human Rights in 1977.[17] In 1981, the debate on the right was institutionalized in the UN system, through the establishment of a Working Group of Government Experts on the Right to Development.[18]

[15] Donnelly, 'In Search of the Unicorn: The Jurisprudence and Politics of the Right to Development', 15 *California Western International Law Journal* (1985) 473, at 475.

[16] Alston, (supra n. 4), at 218–19. Eastern European states supported the right to development although, as Alston notes, that support was premised upon the assumptions that those states had never engaged in colonization, that centrally-planned economies provided the best method of guaranteeing economic, social and cultural rights, and that large scale aid was owed by colonizers rather than by industrial powers generally. Western states supported the obligation to cooperate with respect to development, but did not acknowledge that there was any duty to do so. Those states stressed that respect for civil and political rights was necessary for all human development. That group were not prepared to accept that a right to development could require any change in their own policies.

[17] Commission resolution 4 (XXXIII) of 21 February 1977. The Commission there decided to pay special attention to consideration of the obstacles hindering the full realization of economic, social and cultural rights, particularly in developing countries, as well as of the actions taken at the national and international levels to secure the enjoyment of those rights. The Commission recognized the right to development as a human right, and recommended to the Economic and Social Council that it should invite the Secretary-General to undertake a study on the subject, 'The international dimensions of the right to development as a human right in relation with other human rights based on international cooperation, including the right to peace, taking into account the requirements of the New International Economic Order and the fundamental human needs'.

[18] Commission resolution 36 (XXXVII) of 11 March 1981. Upon the recommendation of that Working Group, the Commission on Human Rights in its resolution 1989/45 of 6 March 1989 invited the Secretary-General to organize a global consultation on the realization of the right to development as a human right. The Global Consultation on the Right to Development as a Human Right took place in Geneva from 8 to 12 January 1990. The Consultation reaffirmed that the right of individuals, groups and peoples to take decisions collectively, to choose their own representative organizations and to have freedom of democratic action, free from interference, was fundamental to democratic participation. The concept of participation was of central importance in the realization of the right to development. The Consultation also

The right was included in 1981 in Article 22 of the African Charter on Human and Peoples' Rights, otherwise known as the Banjul Charter.[19] That article provides:

1. All peoples shall have the right to their economic, social and cultural development with due regard to their freedom and identity and in the equal enjoyment of the common heritage of mankind.
2. States shall have the duty, individually or collectively, to ensure the exercise of the right to development.

The right to development was subsequently enshrined in the 1986 Declaration on the Right to Development.[20] That Declaration sets out the substance of the right in some detail, and I will outline the key features of the Declaration in the next part of the chapter. The World Conference on Human Rights, held in Vienna in 1993, reaffirmed the right to development as established in the Declaration, as a universal and inalienable right and an integral part of fundamental human rights.[21] In 1993, the Commission on Human Rights established a second working group on the right to development for a three-year period,[22] and in 1996, the Commission reaffirmed the right and established an intergovernmental working group of experts on the right to development for a two-year period.[23] The right to development is regularly reaffirmed in resolutions of the General Assembly and of the Commission on Human Rights.

It is not possible to finish an introduction to the emergence of the right to development without some reference to the politics of that right. The

considered that development strategies oriented only towards economic growth and financial considerations had failed to a large extent to achieve social justice and that there was no one model for development applicable to all cultures and peoples. The UN should take the lead in the implementation of the Declaration on the Right to Development and set up mechanisms for ensuring the compatibility of all UN activities and programmes with the Declaration.

[19] The African Charter on Human and Peoples' Rights, concluded at Banjul, 26 June 1981, OAU Doc. CAB/LEG/67/3 Rev. 5; reprinted in 21 *ILM* (1982) 59.

[20] Declaration on the Right to Development, adopted by the UN General Assembly, 4 December 1986, GA Res. 41/128 (Annex), UN GAOR, 41st Sess., Supp. No. 53, at 186, UN Doc. A/41/53 (1987).

[21] Article 10, Vienna Declaration and Programme of Action, adopted by the UN World Conference on Human Rights, 25 June 1993, UN Doc. A/CONF.157/24 (Part I), at 20–46 (1993), reprinted in 32 *ILM* (1993) 1661. See also Articles 11 and 12.

[22] Commission resolution 1993/22. The working group was composed of 15 experts and had a mandate to identify obstacles to the implementation and realization of the Declaration on the Right to Development and to recommend ways and means towards the realization of the right to development by all states. The working group held five sessions from 1993–95.

[23] Commission resolution 1996/15, approved by the Economic and Social Council in its decision 1996/258. The intergovernmental working group was composed of 10 experts nominated by governments and appointed by the Chairman of the Commission, with the mandate to elaborate a strategy for the implementation and promotion of the right to development in its integrated and multidimensional aspects.

right to development has become something of a mantra for states seeking to justify the privileging of economic development over human rights and to legitimize repressive or authoritarian policies. The right is equally systematically resisted by industrialized states seeking to ensure that their corporations and investors are not constrained in their operations in the South. Yash Ghai notes that the right to development has been 'a matter of considerable contention internationally, with developing countries arraigned on the side supporting it, and most developed countries united in their opposition to it'.[24] What is striking about the political debate concerning the right to development is the absence of a sustained attempt at the intergovernmental level to develop and promote a strong, human-rights based, alternative to the repressive interpretation of the right to development that has been pushed by authoritarian regimes. While a more progressive reading of the right to development has been the focus of the scholarship of a small group of commentators, and is certainly available as an interpretation of the Declaration of the Right to Development and other resolutions, there has been a lack of political commitment or meaningful foreign policy support amongst industrialized states for an alternative approach to the right. Instead, many industrialized states seem to have been ready to leave the interpretation of the right to development to repressive leaders, and to use the resulting narrow and dangerous interpretation as a basis for rejecting the right out of hand.

It may be, however, that this polarization is shifting to some extent. A broader level of support for the right to development appears to have emerged at the 54th session of the Commission for Human Rights, held in April 1998. The General Assembly resolution on the right to development had affirmed that the inclusion of the Declaration on the Right to Development in the International Bill of Rights would be an appropriate means of celebrating the 50th anniversary of the Universal Declaration of Human Rights (UDHR).[25] At the 1998 session of the Commission on Human Rights, Colombia on behalf of the non-aligned movement put up a resolution that would have given effect to the General Assembly resolution, but subsequently withdrew the proposed resolution for lack of support. A different resolution on the right to development was then adopted by consensus by the Commission. That resolution recognized that the 50th anniversary of the UDHR provides an important opportunity to place all human rights at the top of the global agenda and, in this context, the right to development in particular. It welcomed the high priority devoted by the UN High Commissioner for

[24] Ghai, 'Human Rights and Governance: The Asia Debate', 15 *Australian Year Book of International Law* (1994) 1.

[25] General Assembly resolution 52/136, adopted 12 December 1997, UN Doc. A/RES/52/136 (1997) (adopted by a vote of 129 in favour, 12 against, 32 abstaining).

Human Rights to activities relating to the right to development, and urged her Office to continue to accord priority to the right to development. The resolution also provided for the establishment of a follow-up mechanism on implementation of the right to development. The Commission recommended to the Economic and Social Council the establishment of a three-year open-ended working group on the right to development, to meet after the next two sessions of the Commission on Human Rights.[26] In addition, the Commission recommended that the working group be supported by an independent expert.[27] While those recommendations are not as dramatic as including the right to development within the International Bill of Rights, they do appear to represent a less divided approach to promoting the right to development and economic, social and cultural rights.

Those moves have been paralleled by the Secretary-General's decision to mainstream human rights within all UN activities, including those in the development area.[28] The right to development forms a central part of those reforms to UN development programmes and funds. As part of that process of reform, a UN Development Group (UNDG) has been established which comprises the major UN development programmes and funds as well as departments and relevant entities.[29] The aim of the Group is to coordinate development policies and decision-making. At the regional and country levels, all UN programmes will be integrated within a UN Development Assistance Framework (UNDAF). Those reforms have included the establishment of a UNDG ad hoc working group on the right to development, which aims at developing a common approach for enhancing the human

[26] That working group would have a mandate to monitor and review progress made in the promotion and implementation of the right at the national and international levels, to review reports and other information submitted by states, UN agencies, other relevant international organizations and non-governmental organizations on the relationship between their activities and the right to development, and to provide a report to the Commission on Human Rights including advice to the Office of the High Commissioner for Human Rights on implementation of the right.

[27] Commission resolution 1998/72 of 22 April 1998 (recommending to the Economic and Social Council the establishment of a three-year open-ended working group on the right to development and the appointment of an independent expert with high competence in the right to development to present to each session of the working group a study on the current state of progress in the implementation of the right to development). See also Commission resolution 1998/24 of 17 April 1998 (resolving *inter alia* to appoint, for a three-year period, a special rapporteur on the effects of foreign debt on the full enjoyment of economic, social and cultural rights, and urging governments, international organizations, international financial institutions, non-governmental organizations and the private sector to cooperate fully with the Special Rapporteur in the discharge of his or her mandate).

[28] Report of the Secretary-General on Renewing the United Nations: A Programme for Reform, A/51/950, issued on 14 July 1997, para. 78.

[29] Ibid., para. 73.

rights dimension of development operations in the process of elaborating country-level development frameworks.[30]

It is thus fair to say now that the right to development is not merely a dangerous 'delusion of well-meaning optimists', as Jack Donnelly could argue in 1985, but rather a secure part of the framework of international human rights at the turn of the century.[31] Yet despite the support for the right to development in UN human rights and development fora, the right continues to be absent from the agenda of a number of the institutions that have a major effect on development and trade issues, namely the IMF, the World Bank and the WTO. Before turning to look at some of the activities of those institutions, I want first to outline some of the key features of that right, particularly as set out in the 1986 Declaration.

II KEY FEATURES OF THE RIGHT TO DEVELOPMENT

While I am not an advocate of plain meaning theories of textual interpretation, it is useful to return to the text of the Declaration on the Right to Development in order to move beyond what has become a sterile debate. As I have already noted, both governments seeking to use, and those seeking to discredit, the right to development have adopted a dangerous interpretation of its meaning. It has become accepted by many states and some commentators that the right to development is a right of states to pursue a narrow economic model of development over the human rights of the people of the state invoking the right. The right to development is presented as allowing states where necessary to put the interests of investors over the interests of other human beings. While the Declaration on the Right to Development does not provide all the answers to that problem, it certainly offers a different interpretation of the right. This Part looks at some of the key features of the Declaration that might be of use in developing a more productive jurisprudence on the right for the post-Cold War era.

[30] The creation of the ad hoc working group is one manifestation of the commitment of the Secretary-General to ensure that as part of that process of UN reform, human rights will be included as part of the mainstream of all UN activities. For a criticism of the focus of the UNDAF process on the right to development at the operational level, rather than proceeding upon the operational principles found in the core human rights treaties, see 'The incorporation of economic, social and cultural rights into the United Nations Development Assistance Framework (UNDAF) process', Comments adopted by the Committee on Economic, Social and Cultural Rights, 15 May 1998.

[31] Donnelly, supra n. 15, at 478. The part of Donnelly's article devoted to showing that there is no source of the right to development in the international bill of rights is not now relevant, if it ever was. It is not possible to argue that human rights are necessarily limited to those enumerated in the international bill of rights. Donnelly himself recognized that even if there were no existing right to development, such a right could be created through the ordinary processes of law creation (at 489).

1. The Subject of the Right to Development

The first question to ask about the right to development is: to whom does the right to development attach? Donnelly argues that the major problem with the right to development is in determining who holds the right.[32] The right-holder is not a physical person; an institutional person must exercise the right. Donnelly suggests that '[i]n the case of a right held by a people, or by society as a whole, the most plausible "person" to exercise the right is, unfortunately, the state'.[33] He argues that this represents a radical reconceptualization of human rights and an especially dangerous one. The state can simply claim to be exercising the right on behalf of the people, sometimes at the same time as infringing other human rights.[34] That is certainly a danger that is inherent in recourse to the right to development by some multinational corporations and by some Asian governments, who at times claim to be legitimately privileging the human right to development over civil and political rights.[35] Ghai, for example, has questioned the championing of the right to development by Asian governments. Ghai suggests that the support of the right by those governments is part of a broader agenda of establishing 'the primacy of economic development over human rights'.[36] Ghai argues that their support for the right to development must be understood in the context of a broader perspective, according to which '[i]t is implied that economic development may well require restrictions on human rights, both to provide a secure political framework in which it can be pursued and to remove obstacles in its way'.[37] Through the support for the right to development, 'Asian governments seek to promote the ideology of developmentalism which justifies repression at home and the evasion of responsibility abroad'.[38]

That is not, however, the manner in which the right was formulated in the 1986 Declaration or subsequently. While the right to development is a collective right, the Declaration makes clear that the right must accrue not only to the community or to the collective, but also to the individual human person. Article 2(1) provides: 'The human person is the central subject of development and should be the active participant and beneficiary of the right to development.'

[32] Donnelly, supra n. 15, at 498–9. [33] Ibid.

[34] Cf. Bedjaoui, 'The Right to Development' in M. Bedjaoui (ed.), *International Law: Achievements and Prospects* (1991) 1177, at 1184 (arguing that the right to development 'is much more a right of the State or of the people, than a right of the individual, and it seems to me that it is better that way').

[35] It is interesting to note that few of those commentators who criticize collective rights comment upon the ease with which corporations, in reality collectivities of investors or capitalists, are granted rights, often in priority over the rights of so-called natural persons.

[36] Ghai, supra n. 24, at 9. [37] Ibid. [38] Ibid., at 10.

The World Conference on Human Rights, in reconfirming the right to development in the Vienna Declaration, also stresses that 'the human person is the central subject of development'.[39]

The Declaration on the Right to Development also refers to the right to development as a right of states. In Article 2(3), it provides that:

> States have the right and the duty to formulate appropriate national development policies that aim at the constant improvement of the well-being of the entire population and of all individuals, on the basis of their active, free and meaningful participation in development and in the fair distribution of the benefits resulting therefrom.

That formulation, however, makes clear that the state is a holder of the right to development as the agent 'of the entire population and of all individuals'. By implication, the right is exercisable by the state against those with the power to deny or constrain the capacity of the state to formulate national development policies that benefit the entire population and all individuals. As Philip Alston suggests, here the state acts as the 'medium through which the rights of individuals are able to be effectively asserted vis-à-vis the international community'.[40] Thus despite the concern of critics like Donnelly prior to the passing of the Declaration, and despite the claims of some state leaders since 1986, the right to development is not in my view a right of states, except where those states are asserting, as against the international community, their right to develop human rights-based development policies in the interests of their people.[41]

Critics of that aspect of the right to development argue that it moves away from the appropriate focus on the individual as the proper subject of human rights, to groups as subjects of rights.[42] Donnelly, for example, argues that human rights should derive from the 'idea of innate personal dignity' rather than from notions of solidarity or community, dependent as such notions are upon relations among persons or groups.[43] He suggests that membership of a community or group is not necessarily an aspect of being human, and that thus collective human rights are not logically possible.[44] Many commentators, however, have argued that an 'excessively individualistic approach to

[39] Vienna Declaration, Art. 10.

[40] Alston, 'Garfield the Cat', supra n. 14, at 512.

[41] For concerns about the right to development as a right of states, see Donnelly, supra n. 15, at 499, and the citations there of those who support that view.

[42] Ibid., at 492.

[43] Ibid.

[44] Ibid., at 493, 497. It seems to me that members of a dominant group or community are the only people capable of such a perspective. As critical commentators have shown, being human has never been a sufficient criterion for holding rights—instead, that privilege has depended on community membership of a dominant group, such as men, colonizers, property-owners or citizens. Conversely, exclusion from the category of rights-holder has also been a function of belonging to a particular group, such as women, colonized peoples or slaves. See further Orford, 'Liberty, Equality, Pornography: The Bodies of Women and Human Rights Discourse', 3 *Australian Feminist Law Journal* (1994) 72.

human rights' is not productive, and that, as Alston points out, collective rights are 'reflective of the extent to which we live in communities and to which our fate as individuals is bound up with the fate of the others in whose social context we find ourselves'.[45] Where members of a group or community suffer disadvantage, oppression or exploitation as a result of membership of that group or community, the case is even stronger for the proposition that such group members should be able to exercise collective rights against more powerful groups or communities responsible for exploitation or domination.[46]

2. The Human Right to Participate in Development

A second feature of the right to development as formulated in the Declaration is the emphasis on participation as the basis of the right. In its first article, the Declaration states that by virtue of their inalienable human right to development, 'every human person and all peoples are entitled to participate in, contribute to, and enjoy economic, social, cultural and political development'. Thus each human person and all peoples are entitled to participate in all forms of development, and equally to enjoy the benefits of that development.

The Declaration qualifies the legitimacy of state development policies by reference to participation. Article 2(3) provides that:

> States have the right and the duty to formulate appropriate national development policies that aim at the constant improvement of the well-being of the entire population and of all individuals, on the basis [inter alia] of their active, free and meaningful participation in development.

The Declaration thus stresses that for such a right to be enjoyed by individuals, it must be on the basis of a free, active and meaningful participation in and enjoyment of the benefits of development. Article 8 states further that '[e]ffective measures should be undertaken to ensure women have an active role in the development process'.

The right to development can thus be characterized as a 'participatory right'.[47] A human rights perspective gives 'participation' a meaning that is different from participation in a managerial sense. As the Human Rights Council of Australia argues, participation as a right means that people should have control over the direction of the development process, rather than simply being

[45] Alston, 'Garfield the Cat', supra n. 14, at 526.

[46] For an argument in favour of collective rights for groups who suffer disadvantage due to membership of that group, see N. Lacey, *Unspeakable Subjects: Feminist Essays in Legal and Social Theory* (1998), at 34–45.

[47] Ginther, 'Participation and Accountability: Two Aspects of the Internal and International Dimension of the Right to Development' *Third World Legal Studies* (1992) 55, at 57.

consulted about projects or policies that have already been decided upon.[48] Participation in a human rights sense means having the power to direct or to exercise authoritative influence over the development process, rather than simply being consulted about pre-determined results. According to the Human Rights Council:

> Participation understood as control cannot easily be confused with 'involved', 'consulted', 'empowered' or even 'ownership'. To ask who has control, authority, direction over a particular aspect of the development program is a much tougher question than to ask who is involved or empowered by it. It also leads to significantly more meaningful answers.[49]

Implicit in this aspect of the right to development is the recognition that peoples have the right to determine their model of development. Mohammed Bedjaoui suggests that the right to development can thus be seen as incorporating the notion of economic and social self-determination.[50] According to Bedjaoui, the right to development itself flows from the right to self-determination:

> There is little sense in recognizing self-determination as a superior and inviolable principle if one does not recognize *at the same time* a 'right to development' for the peoples that have achieved self-determination. This right to development can only be an 'inherent' and 'built-in' right forming an inseparable part of the right to self-determination.[51]

According to this interpretation, the most important aspect of the right to development is thus 'the right of each people to choose freely its economic and social system without outside interference or constraint of any kind, and to determine, with equal freedom, its own model of development'.[52]

3. Equitable and Fair Access to Benefits

The Declaration focuses on the right to equal access to the benefits of development. Article 8, for example, provides that states should 'ensure equality of opportunity for all in their access to basic resources, education, health services, food, housing, employment and the fair distribution of income . . . Appropriate economic and social reforms should be carried out with a view to eradicating all social injustices.' Article 2(3) provides that states have the right and the duty to formulate appropriate national development policies that aim at the fair distribution of the benefits resulting from development.

[48] Human Rights Council of Australia Inc., *The Rights Way to Development: A Human Rights Approach to Development Assistance* (1995) 118–21.

[49] Ibid., at 120. [50] Bedjaoui, supra n. 34, at 1184. [51] Ibid.

[52] Ibid., at 1188.

The importance of equitable access to the benefits of development is reaffirmed in the Vienna Declaration. Article 11 extends the notion of equitable access to the benefits of development to embrace the notion of intergenerational equity. It states that 'the right to development should be fulfilled so as to meet equitably the developmental and environmental needs of present and future generations'.

4. The Relationship between the Right to Development and Other Rights

The Declaration on the Right to Development makes clear that priority should *not* be given to the right to development over other human rights. Instead, it confirms the indivisibility of rights. Article 1 states that the right to development involves the realization of human rights and fundamental freedoms, and implies the full realization of the right of peoples to self-determination. The Declaration stresses that all human rights and fundamental freedoms are indivisible and interdependent, and that equal attention and urgent consideration should be given to the implementation, promotion and protection of civil, political, economic, social and cultural rights.[53] All aspects of the right to development itself are indivisible and interdependent, and each should be considered in the context of the whole.[54] According to Article 9(2), nothing in the Declaration should be construed as contrary to the purposes and principles of the UN or as in violation of the rights set out in the UDHR and human rights covenants. The indivisibility principle was strongly reaffirmed in the Vienna Declaration. Article 10 states that '[w]hile development facilitates the enjoyment of all human rights, the lack of development may not be invoked to justify the abridgement of internationally recognized human rights'.

Donnelly criticizes what he sees as the tendency to treat the right to development as a 'synthesis of more traditional human rights'.[55] Similarly, Ghai has argued that the right to development 'takes attention away from specific rights, for example, speech, assembly, social welfare, to an ambiguous portmanteau right to development, for which in the nature of Third World affairs, the State must take the responsibility in defining and implementing it'.[56] I would argue, however, that the focus on the indivisibility of rights is an important aspect of the right to development for two reasons. First, it is important to stress that the right to development does not justify the violation of other human rights, particularly in light of attempts by some governments and multinational corporations to use the right to development as an

[53] Article 6(2). [54] Article 9(1). [55] Donnelly, supra n. 15, at 481.
[56] Ghai, supra n. 24, at 10.

excuse to deny rights such as the right to freedom of association, freedom of expression or the right to political participation. That argument has no basis in the framework of the Declaration. No state can use the Declaration as authority for the argument that other human rights can be put on hold or violated while development is achieved. Similarly, international organizations are too often ready to treat human rights as if they were secondary to the economic goal of development as measured only by growth, debt repayment, foreign investment and economic liberalization, as I will discuss in more detail later. The Right to Development makes clear that development cannot be treated as a priority that justifies the infringement of human rights.

Secondly, the stress on the indivisibility of rights will remain necessary as long as states continue to treat economic, social and cultural rights as a lesser form of human rights.[57] In the context of a human rights approach to development, it continues to be important to argue that human rights are indivisible, and that economic ends do not justify exploitative means. As Bedjaoui argues:

> There is no universality of human rights without the development of all human beings. The development of individuals and peoples, and of all individuals and of all peoples, is the fundamental precondition for the effective realization of such universality.[58]

5. Against Whom is the Right to Development Exercisable?

International human rights law has traditionally been conceived of as a means of constraining one form of power, that exercised by the state. The international human rights law system that developed after 1945 treats the state as the principal threat to the freedom of the individual, human dignity and human well-being. The human rights enshrined in the UDHR and in later international covenants are designed to restrain the ability of the state to infringe the liberty of the citizen, to guarantee the participation of all citizens in government, and to ensure that the state promotes the economic, social and cultural rights of all those living within its borders.

The focus of the Declaration is broader. It recognizes that actors other than states can be responsible both for protecting human rights, and for human rights violations. The Declaration sets out a number of parties against whom the right is exercisable. First, it provides that states have an obligation to respect and promote the right to development. States must ensure that 'national development policies aim at the constant improvement of the well-being of the

[57] That opposition began in earnest with the Reagan administration. See the discussion in Alston, 'US Ratification', supra n. 14.

[58] Bedjaoui, supra n. 34, at 1199.

entire population and of all individuals, on the basis of their active, free and meaningful participation in development and in the fair distribution of the benefits resulting therefrom'.[59] The obligation to formulate appropriate and equitable national development policies is expressed both as a duty of states, presumably towards their own peoples, and as a right of states, presumably towards outside actors.[60] The notion that states have a right *and* a duty to formulate appropriate national development policies focused on participation and equitable sharing of the benefits of development is one that I will return to in considering the activities of international economic institutions.

Under the Declaration, states have the responsibility for the creation of not only national, but also international, conditions favourable to the realization of the right to development.[61] States must 'take steps to *eliminate obstacles* to development resulting from the failure to observe civil and political rights, as well as economic, social and cultural rights'.[62] While the Declaration does not explicitly address the extent to which international organizations bear responsibility for assisting states in protecting and promoting the right to development, a number of Articles can be read as applying to states acting as members of international organizations. For example, Article 3(3) provides that:

> States have the duty to cooperate with each other in ensuring development and eliminating obstacles to development. States should fulfil their rights and duties in such a manner as to promote a new international economic order based on sovereign equality, interdependence, mutual interest, and cooperation among all states, as well as to encourage the observance and realization of human rights.

Article 4(1) provides that:

> States have the duty individually *and collectively* to formulate international development policies with a view to facilitating the full realization of the right to development.

Article 4(2) states that effective international cooperation is essential in providing developing countries with the appropriate means and facilities to foster comprehensive development. Each of those Articles can be interpreted as requiring states to act to further the right to development as members of international economic institutions.

Finally, the Declaration also treats human beings as having individual and collective responsibility for development. Article 2(2) provides that individuals should 'promote and protect an appropriate political, social and economic order for development'. The Declaration there foreshadows calls such as those by the Commission on Global Governance in 1995 for recognition

[59] Article 2(3).

[60] See also Article 8, which provides that states must undertake 'at the national level all necessary measures for the realization of the right to development'.

[61] Article 3(1).

[62] Article 6(3).

that 'governments are only one source of threats to human rights' and that 'all citizens . . . should accept that obligation to recognize and help promote the rights of others'.[63]

The extension of the obligation to protect the right to development to actors other than states is not, however, without its critics. Donnelly, for example, argues that according to traditional conceptions of human rights, such rights are held primarily against the state. For him, human rights 'are essentially instruments to protect the individual against the state or to assure that the state guarantees to each individual certain minimum goods, services and opportunities'.[64] Donnelly criticizes the focus of the right to development on violators other than states, arguing that this shift functions as a means of avoiding state responsibility for human rights violations. The emergence of the right to development is part of a trend in which repressive regimes attempt 'to shift attention from particular rights to general issues, and from the primary role of the state as a violator of human rights to external forces that also contribute to human rights violations'.[65] According to Donnelly, it is essential that we do 'not lose sight of the fact that most human rights violations are directly perpetrated on people by the governments of their own countries. Discussions of the right to development, however, seem to have the effect, and perhaps even the intent, of obscuring this central point.'[66] Thus Donnelly suggests that the right to development lends itself 'to use as an excuse not to act on human rights now'.[67] Yash Ghai is also critical of this aspect of the right to development, arguing that it is an attempt to 'provide an alternative framework for the international discourse on human rights'.[68] According to Ghai, the right to development 'shifts the focus from domestic arenas (where most violations of rights take place) to the international'.[69]

Such arguments seem persuasive at first glance. The danger that Donnelly foresaw in the use of the right to development as an excuse for avoiding human rights responsibilities has certainly eventuated in some instances. Some repressive governments and their supporters amongst multinational corporations have argued that the right to development must be achieved before human rights considerations can be addressed. States might appear to be, as Donnelly argues, the principal violators of human rights, due to the power that they exercise over the destinies and lives of their people. States would be the only actors capable of violating human rights if states had the sovereign power to determine the economic, social and cultural conditions in which people live, to make policy-decisions that shape access to resources and services and to determine the nature of constitutional and governmental

[63] Cited in H. Steiner and P. Alston, *International Human Rights Law in Context: Law, Politics and Morals* (1996), at 488.

[64] Donnelly, supra n. 15, at 499. [65] Ibid., at 502. [66] Ibid., at 506.

[67] Ibid. [68] Ghai, supra n. 24, at 10. [69] Ibid.

systems, in addition to having a monopoly over the legitimate use of force within a given territory.

States, however, are no longer sovereign in that way, if they ever were.[70] Economic globalization has made the fictitious nature of state sovereignty apparent to all but the most myopic observer of international relations and international law.[71] The arguments of critics like Donnelly fail to address situations where individuals or peoples do not need protection only or even primarily against the state, but also from other powerful states, transnational corporations (TNCs) or international institutions. Nor do such arguments address situations where actors other than states make decisions about the provision of goods, services and opportunities, and thus about the protection of economic, social and cultural rights. In many cases in the globalized economy, other states, international organizations or foreign investors will be in a position to deny or effect those protections or guarantees. Thus the focus on the human rights obligations of states at the international as well as the national level is an important element of the right to development, and one that I will return to in analysing the activities of international economic institutions.

6. What is Meant by 'Development' in the Right to Development?

The final element of the right that I want to consider is the meaning it gives to the notion of 'development'. As many of you will be aware, the meaning of development is a highly contested area, and the subject of much political activism and scholarship.[72] The notion of what is meant by development is one I will return to at the end of the chapter, when I come to consider the utility of the right to development in the post-Cold War era. I want simply to note here

[70] That is not to say that *states* are weakened through economic restructuring. Indeed, certain areas of state activity must be strengthened in order to provide secure and stable conditions for foreign investment. Instead, many aspects of what we once understood as *sovereignty* are now vested, not with 'the people' however understood, but with economic experts. For the argument that states never were sovereign in that sense, and that state sovereignty has always been a fiction, see Orford, 'The Uses of Sovereignty in the New Imperial Order', 6 *Australian Feminist Law Journal* (1996) 63.

[71] For the argument that some international lawyers continue to be obsessed with technical rules related to subjects and doctrines that are no longer relevant in the rapidly shifting conditions of the late twentieth century, see Alston, 'The Myopia of the Handmaidens: International Lawyers and Globalisation', 8 *European Journal of International Law* (1997) 435.

[72] For an introduction to criticisms about the dominant models of development, see W. Sachs (ed.), *Global Ecology: A New Arena of Political Conflict* (1993); V. Shiva (ed.), *Close to Home: Women Reconnect Ecology, Health and Development Worldwide* (1994); R. Braidotti *et al.*, *Women, the Environment and Sustainable Development: Towards a Theoretical Synthesis* (1993); R. Chambers, *Poverty and Livelihoods: Whose Reality Counts?* (1995); D.C. Korten, *When Corporations Rule the World* (1995).

that the Declaration supports a fairly flexible but nonetheless people-centred approach to what is meant by development. Alston argues that the Declaration is 'unusually open-ended and indeterminate', and that this is the 'inevitable result of the conflicting interests and perspectives of its drafters' and 'the range and complexity of the interests which it sought to address'.[73] Rather than being seen as weakness, Alston argues that this should be welcomed as a strength that enables the concept to evolve with the times and to be interpreted and applied with a 'degree of flexibility that is indispensable in such an area'.[74]

Other commentators have been less than impressed with the approach to development enshrined in the Declaration. Hilary Charlesworth, for example, has argued that it is a highly contested, purely economic model of development upon which the right to development is based. According to Charlesworth:

> While the formulation of the right to development does not rest on a simple economic model of development, and includes within it a synthesis of all recognized human rights, redress of economic inequality is at its heart. An assumption of the international law of development is that underdevelopment is caused by a failure to meet the model of a capitalist economy. Development means industrialization and westernization.[75]

Despite some fluidity, the meaning of development in the Declaration includes as already mentioned the right to participation in determining the model of development, control over the process of development, and equitable access to enjoyment of the benefits of development. The Declaration also recognizes in the preamble that 'development is a comprehensive economic, social, cultural and political process which arises at the constant improvement of the well-being of the entire population'. As we will see, these features of the right to development provide a very different model from that imposed through economic restructuring and by international economic institutions.

III ECONOMIC RESTRUCTURING AND THE RIGHT TO DEVELOPMENT

Having looked at the key features of the right to development, I want now to consider the extent to which the project of economic globalization has been informed by the right to development. In particular, this Part examines whether the right has informed the policies, projects and actions of international economic institutions or whether, on the contrary, the actions of

[73] Alston, supra n. 4, at 221. [74] Ibid.

[75] Charlesworth, 'The Public/Private Distinction and the Right to Development in International Law', 12 *Australian Year Book of International Law* (1992) 190, at 196–7.

those institutions have violated the right to development. My argument is that while the right to development has become a part of the human rights agenda of the UN, it has been far from central to the work of the World Bank, the IMF and the WTO. I explore in particular the impact of the activities of those institutions in light of the key commitments of the right to development: first, that human beings and communities have the right to participate in and thus control the direction of development, and secondly, that human beings and communities have the right to participate fully and equally in enjoying the benefits of development.

While I focus on the activities of those three economic institutions, my aim is to address the process of economic globalization which they are pursuing. There are many actors involved in formulating and implementing that process, including elites in the South, elites in industrialized states, international institutions, TNCs and investors (often but not always the same bodies). While I could equally focus here on the activities of those actors, I look particularly at the activities of international economic institutions because it is through those institutions that much of the agenda of economic restructuring or multinational capitalism is being pursued in the aftermath of the Cold War. By focusing on those institutions, I do not mean to suggest that the other actors I have mentioned are innocent victims of those institutions, nor do I mean to suggest that those institutions are principally accountable for the human rights violations that result from economic globalization. I will return to the difficulties raised by the issue of blame and responsibility in Part IV. It is, however, often easier to see the ways in which economic restructuring is operating and being legitimized by focusing on the policies and actions of the IMF, the World Bank and the WTO, perhaps because at this point those institutions are still quite open about the programmes they are implementing, and quite systematic in setting out their goals and assumptions. In addition, it is useful to focus on international economic institutions as they are the key agents of economic restructuring in the post-Cold War era. Economic and investment liberalization is largely carried out multilaterally, with unilateral or bilateral initiatives threatened or resorted to in order to strengthen multilateral negotiations and regulations.

I have one further reason for focusing on those institutions. Their actions are often represented, at least in countries such as Australia, as unquestionably positive and well-intentioned. The IMF, for example, has been described regularly in the context of the Asian financial crisis as a benevolent doctor, administering bitter medicine to the people of Asia in order to heal their weak or sick economies. The WTO is presented as an agent of freedom, in the form of the free market, guaranteeing such positive norms as non-discrimination, growth, competition and higher living standards. It is unusual to see connections made between the activities of such institutions and the unrest and suffering that follow their interventions. It therefore remains useful in

industrialized states to remember that the international level of governance is as likely to be a site of repressive and exploitative actions as is the national.

1. Human Rights and Development—The IMF and the World Bank

The IMF and the World Bank are the two international economic institutions that have to date had the greatest impact on human rights. The institutions were established at the conclusion of the Second World War. Their goal was to address the economic problems that led to the depression of the 1930s, to avoid the reintroduction of measures such as protectionist trade practices or competitive currency devaluations as responses to an unstable international economic system, and to assist in the reconstruction and development of Europe and its colonies after the Second World War. The roles and functions of the Bretton Woods institutions have changed dramatically since their original creation, and they have become a significant source of financial assistance for many African, Asian, Latin American and Eastern European states. Both institutions have a major influence on the development of domestic policies in those states. As a result in part of their increased power and influence, both institutions have received increasing scrutiny and criticism from human rights scholars and activists.[76]

The IMF has been a central institution in international governance for decades, although it has achieved a new visibility due to its role in the Asian financial crisis of 1997–8. It was established to play a macroeconomic role by promoting international currency exchange stability and aiding short-term balance of payments problems which might be encountered by states in the post-war period. Its creators planned that the IMF would provide machinery for consultation and collaboration on international monetary problems and thus promote international monetary cooperation. The existence of such an institution was designed to facilitate the expansion and balanced growth of international trade, and contribute as a result to the promotion and maintenance of high levels of employment and real income. The IMF was intended to give confidence to member states by 'providing them with the opportunity to correct maladjustments in their balance of payments without resorting to measures destructive of national or international prosperity'.[77]

The system established under the IMF had three bases.[78] First, a fixed linkage between the currencies in the system was established by assigning

[76] Skogly, 'The Position of the World Bank and the International Monetary Fund in the Human Rights Field', in R. Hanksi and M. Suksi (eds), *An Introduction to the International Protection of Human Rights* (1997) 193, at 194.

[77] IMF Articles of Agreement, Article 1.

[78] For a general overview, see Skubik, 'International Economic Institutions', in K.C.D.M. Wilde and M.R. Islam (eds.), *International Transactions: Trade and Investment, Law and Finance* (1993) 417.

each currency a par value against gold. Once fixed, the value of the currency would be allowed to fluctuate only within a narrow band. Secondly, the convertibility of currencies within the system was guaranteed. The value of currencies was not only fixed to gold, but currencies were redeemable at gold value. The US dollar operated as the reserve currency of global commerce. Any dealer could trade any currency linked to the IMF system for US dollars, which were 'as good as gold'. The quotation of prices for goods and services in international trade could be denominated in US dollars. It was thought that the growth of international trade would therefore be possible, due to the freely convertible nature of currencies. Thirdly, the system aimed at assisting countries experiencing short-term balance of payment problems, by establishing a pool of currencies and gold for short-term purchase by members experiencing deficits. While called a loan, a member in trouble in fact places an agreed amount of its own national currency into a pool of currencies and gold, in exchange for some other currency held by the IMF which the member requires to meet immediate balance of payment needs.[79] The theoretical basis of such an arrangement was that in such a way a member's deficit could be dealt with efficiently without requiring that member to disrupt the value of its own currency by entering the open market to borrow the currency it required. IMF economists would then meet with representatives of borrowing countries, determine the reasons for the shortfall and counsel policy makers concerning future directions for economic plans and activities.[80]

The role and function of the IMF has, however, changed dramatically from that imagined for it in 1945. The system of monetary cooperation and exchange controls failed from the 1960s. As early as 1962, countries ceased adhering to fixed exchange rates in order to manage domestic economic needs. The episode that officially brought to an end the system envisaged at Bretton Woods was the withdrawal of the US dollar from convertibility on 15 August 1971. In that year, the US showed its first trade deficit, and with foreign holdings of US $80 billion outstanding, only US $10 billion in reserves and a run on the US dollar by speculators imminent, President Richard Nixon withdrew convertibility to protect the dollar. That withdrawal fractured the basis of the IMF. While the IMF does still exist, its capacities have changed. Par values have been eliminated and currency values are established largely through currency markets. The IMF no longer directly influences the monetary policies of the world's developed economies.[81] Developed countries

[79] IMF Articles of Agreement, Article 5, section 3(b).

[80] Ibid., section 3(c), (d), sections 5 and 7.

[81] In its earliest years, the greatest demand for use of the IMF's financial resources came from industrialized countries including the United Kingdom, France, Italy, Japan and on one occasion the United States. Over the last twenty years, however, those countries have met balance of payments problems either through capital markets, or in the case of the European

no longer use the IMF's pool of extended resources which expose them to IMF conditions and advice.[82] The IMF has a significant impact, however, on the policies of governments of developing countries. It has changed its focus from promoting exchange stability and international monetary cooperation amongst the richest countries to managing and monitoring the economies of the poorest.

The role of the World Bank has also changed over the past fifty years. The World Bank Group in fact comprises a number of institutions. The two with which I am principally concerned here are the International Bank for Reconstruction and Development (IBRD) and the International Development Association (IDA).[83] The IBRD, like the IMF, was established at the conclusion of the Second World War. It was designed to provide monies to assist in reconstruction and development projects in Europe and former European colonies in the post-war period. The monies to be loaned were to be gathered by subscriptions, and from the sale of bonds guaranteed by the IBRD and sold on the open market to investors. Under the Marshall Aid programme, however, significant sums of money were also made available by the US to western Europe for post-War reconstruction. As a result, the focus of the IBRD changed very quickly, and it became a major source of loans for developing countries needing capital. The IDA was established in 1960, supposedly as a soft loans body for the neediest countries. It provides loans at nominal interest rates, for periods of up to fifty years, usually with a ten-year period before repayments are required to begin. Loans made by the IDA can be used to support social programmes as well as infrastructure projects. As Susan George and Fabrizio Sabelli point out, while the terms of such loans are soft, the loan principal must nevertheless be repaid.[84] Thus the monies are made available as credits not gifts. A significant proportion of debt owed by the poorest countries consists of money owed to the IDA.

The role of the World Bank changed during the 1980s, in ways that increased its impact on human rights. From 1986 onward the World Bank began to attach conditions to structural adjustment or policy-based loans, requiring privatization and trade and investment liberalization. While some commentators argue that those conditions were inspired by the debt crises

Union, through arrangements with fellow members. See IMF Study Group, *IMF Study Group Report: Transparency and Evaluation,* 1998, section 2.

[82] The last time any OECD country drew such loans was in 1977, when the UK and Italy drew from the fund. In those cases, conditions were not attached in order to save the governments from political embarrassment. No such sensitivity operates with respect to the governments of developing countries.

[83] The other members of the World Bank Group are the International Finance Corporation, the Multilateral Investment Guarantee Agency and the International Centre for the Settlement of Investment Disputes.

[84] S. George and F. Sabelli, *Faith and Credit: The World Bank's Secular Empire* (1994) 11.

and the need to ensure that borrower countries had export-oriented economies that were able to honour debt repayments, others suggest that the Reagan and Bush administrations were determined to impose their own monetarist policies on developing countries. Certainly, the restructuring of the World Bank in 1987 under Conable signalled a shift away from project lending and toward lending organized around requiring a commitment to 'effective macroeconomic management and a sound policy environment' by developing countries.[85] One lending policy that facilitated that shift was the move to integrated lending, according to which all loans made to a particular country are designed to contribute to the achievement of broader policy objectives determined by World Bank officials.[86] Project lending for infrastructure, sector lending, institutional lending to reorganize government institutions and structural adjustment lending are all coordinated to achieve policy goals in a particular country.[87]

Since the early 1990s, the World Bank has begun to concentrate on issues of governance, defined by the Bank as 'the manner in which power is exercised in the management of a country's economic and social resources for development. Good governance, for the World Bank, is synonymous with sound development management.'[88] The World Bank now attaches conditions concerning governance to its loans, despite the explicit prohibition in the Articles of Agreement of the IBRD against interference in the political affairs of any member state.[89]

Thus the IMF and the World Bank operate at the turn of the century in a manner very different from that first imagined for those institutions by their creators. The aims and policies of the two institutions have in many ways converged. They have a significant impact on the policies of governments in those states seeking to make use of their resources in two ways. First, the IMF and the World Bank influence government policy through the imposition of conditions on access to credits and loans.[90] The IMF imposes economic targets

[85] *Reorganizing the Bank: An Opportunity for Renewal*, Report to the President from the Steering Committee on Reorganization of the World Bank, April 1987, para. 2.05, 2.06, discussed in George and Sabelli, supra n. 84, at 126.

[86] George and Sabelli, supra n. 84, at 19–20.

[87] Ibid., at 16–18.

[88] The World Bank, *Governance and Development* (1992) 1.

[89] Article IV section 10 of the Articles of Agreement of the IBRD provides: 'The Bank and its officers shall not interfere in the political affairs of any member; nor shall they be influenced in their decisions by the political character of the member or members concerned. Only economic considerations shall be relevant to their decisions . . .' For a critical analysis of the World Bank's recent interest in good governance, see George and Sabelli, supra n. 84, at 142–61. For a defence of World Bank policy in that area, see I. Shihata, *The World Bank in a Changing World: Selected Essays* (1991) 53 (arguing that the World Bank can involve itself in political matters where they bear on economic issues).

[90] See generally J. Williamson (ed.), *IMF Conditionality* (1983).

and structural reforms as a condition on the use of IMF resources.[91] The World Bank will not lend to a country in breach of IMF conditions or under IMF sanction. In addition, no country can become a member of, and receive loans from, the World Bank unless it also becomes a member of the IMF and becomes susceptible to IMF conditions.

The most infamous of those conditions attach to 'structural adjustment' loans and 'shock therapy' economic stabilization programmes. Structural adjustment conditions have been attached to the use of IMF and World Bank resources since the 1980s, and generally require countries to adopt policies of foreign investment deregulation, privatization, cuts to government spending on health and education, labour market deregulation, lowering of minimum wages, and a focus on production of goods for export rather than domestic production.[92] The so-called 'shock therapy' programmes that have been implemented since the late 1980s throughout Eastern Europe have been aimed at achieving a shock transition to capitalism. The conditions required by the IMF and the World Bank to further that goal have included currency devaluation, swift dismantling of protectionist trade barriers, the fragmentation of existing trade arrangements with former communist states, massive cuts to government spending, increased exports, privatization, constitutional reform and increased foreign direct investment in target states.[93] As those readers who have followed the recent IMF interventions in Asia will be aware, those conditions are increasingly aimed at finance sector reform.

The IMF and the World Bank are also able to influence government policies indirectly. Due to the weight that private banks place on the IMF's approval, such approval determines a country's creditworthiness and thus its ability to access private capital markets.[94] The IMF also exercises influence due to its role in organizing debt rescheduling. Since 1982, the IMF has played a central role in arranging for private banks to take part in concerted or coordinated lending packages.[95] The involvement of the IMF is seen as desirable, not only because

[91] While conditionality was considered legally problematic under the original Articles of Agreement, it has been sanctioned by custom and expansive interpretations of the provisions of the Articles relating to the oversight of member countries.

[92] George and Sabelli estimate that 15–20% of World Bank loans are structural adjustment loans. George and Sabelli, supra n. 84, at 13.

[93] For a strong critique of those programmes, see Gowan, 'Neo-Liberal Theory and Practice for Eastern Europe', 213 *New Left Review* (1995) 3.

[94] Tyson *et al.*, 'Conditionality and Adjustment in Hungary and Yugoslavia', in J.C. Brada *et al.* (eds), *Economic Adjustment and Reform in Eastern Europe and the Soviet Union* (1988) 72, at 74.

[95] W.R. Cline, *International Debt Reexamined* (1995) 206; M. Milivojevic, *The Debt Rescheduling Process* (1985) 43–5 (discussing the role played by the IMF in Paris Club debt reschedulings from the 1950s to the 1980s. The Paris Club, a group of creditor governments and multilateral institutions, would only agree to meet with a debtor government to discuss debt rescheduling if it had come to an agreement with the IMF to implement an economic adjustment programme prior to the meeting).

it provides extra liquidity, but more importantly because private banks assume that a lending package that includes the imposition of IMF conditionality will guarantee better and more stable economic policies in the debtor country.[96] Critics argue that the combination of these factors enables major creditor governments and multilateral institutions to use the debt burdens of states as an instrument to impose policy.[97] In countries subject to IMF and World Bank conditionality, economic restructuring limits choices available to peoples through their governments. Decision-making power over many areas of policy is thus effectively exercised by IMF and World Bank officials.

The approach adopted by the IMF and the World Bank has serious implications for the right to development. The conditions imposed by those institutions lead directly and indirectly to violations of that right. That is evident in several ways. First, the policies of those institutions clearly fail to ensure that 'every human person and all peoples . . . participate in, contribute to, and enjoy economic, cultural and political development'.[98] Decision-making over ever larger areas of what was once considered to be central to popular sovereignty and substantive democracy is now treated as legitimately within the province of economists in institutions such as the IMF and the World Bank. The supposedly economic and technocratic changes required by those institutions shape the policy choices available to governments, alter existing constitutional and political arrangements, determine the extent to which people in many states can access health care, education, pensions and social security, shape labour markets and thus affect functions that go to the heart of political and constitutional authority. The detail of the prescriptions imposed by the IMF and the Bank make it impossible for the people of target states to determine the nature of the economic, and thus the political, system in which they live. People in such states are not free to choose forms of economic or social arrangements that differ from the models chosen by those who work for the IMF or the World Bank.

The failure of those institutions to develop mechanisms by which they could be held accountable to local people further limits the right to participate in and contribute to development. The World Bank has made some moves to address that lack of accountability. In 1993, it established an Inspection Panel, which can investigate and review complaints from any group of two or more people who allege that they have been harmed by breaches of the Bank's operating procedures, including breaches of guidelines relating to resettlements or environmental impact assessments.[99] While the panel is independent

[96] Cline, supra n. 95, at 206. [97] Gowan, supra n. 93, at 58.

[98] Declaration on the Right to Development, Article 1.

[99] Bradlow, 'International Organisations and Private Complaints: The Case of the World Bank Inspection Panel', 34 *Virginia Journal of International Law* (1994) 553; Bradlow and Grossman, 'Limited Mandates and Intertwined Problems: A New Challenge for the World Bank and the IMF', 17 *Human Rights Quarterly* (1995) 411, at 432–3.

of Bank management, it has few resources, no power to enforce compliance with its recommendations, and its reports are not made public until after the Bank's response to the advice of the Panel is determined.[100] As the World Bank has no policies dealing with human rights, complaints about the human rights effects of projects are in theory not admissible before the Panel.[101] While the constitution of the panel is a step in the direction of greater accountability, much more needs to be done to ensure that a truly independent process of challenge to Bank policies and projects is available. Critics continue to call for the establishment of an independent appeals and review commission, with power to investigate complaints against the Bank, full access to internal files, power to review and investigate violations of international law in World Bank-funded projects, and with findings and recommendations that are binding unless reversed by a significant majority of the Bank's directors.[102]

The IMF has traditionally operated on the principle that, since it is an institution owned and controlled by its member states, it is sufficient for it to be accountable to those states. It is up to its members to seek the informed consent of their peoples to the positions they take in the decision-making bodies of the IMF. A 1998 IMF Study Group Report on transparency and evaluation, contributed to by IMF Executive Directors, management and staff as well as NGO members and academics, recognized some need for increased accountability by the IMF to people affected by its decisions.[103] On April 20 2000, the IMF's Executive Board agreed to set up an independent evaluation unit (EVO), to conduct objective and independent evaluations on issues of relevance to the mandate of the Fund. The IMF, however, continues to argue that the human rights effects of its policies are not relevant to that mandate. Thus while the EVO promises to address some of the more blatant problems arising from lack of an independent evaluation mechanism, it appears to be constrained in its ability to address human rights issues.

Secondly, the IMF and the World Bank do not comply with the obligation to ensure that the model of development adopted by states is one in which 'all human rights and fundamental freedoms can be fully realized'.[104] The model of development imposed by the IMF and the World Bank impacts upon the promotion and protection of civil and political rights and of economic, social and cultural rights. That model privileges the imposition of a narrow version of economic theory over any commitment to ensuring that people have access

[100] For criticisms of the limited powers of the panel, see B. Rich, *Mortgaging the Earth: The World Bank, Environmental Impoverishment and the Crisis of Development* (1994) 307.

[101] Skogly, supra n. 76, at 198.

[102] See the discussion of NGO proposals for a review body in George and Sabelli, supra n. 84, at 237–8.

[103] See IMF Study Group, supra n. 81, section 3.

[104] Declaration on the Right to Development, Article 1.

to food, health, education, social security or employment. Structural adjustment conditions, requiring the cutting of public expenditure on health and education, labour market deregulation, export-oriented production and privatization, have led to increased income disparity and the marginalization of women, the poor and rural populations in many countries.[105] Economic, social and cultural rights, such as the right to health or the right to adequate food, are made significantly less relevant in states required to engage in those forms of economic restructuring.[106]

The imposition of 'structural adjustment' and 'shock therapy' programmes also creates a climate in which abuses of human rights such as the right to freedom from torture or the right to life are more likely to occur. Such programmes have led to increased levels of insecurity and political destabilization in target states.[107] The effect of IMF and World Bank policies is to strip the state of most of its functions, except maintaining law and order and facilitating private investment. At the same time, the interests of investors are protected and secured. In situations where the state appears to address only the interests of international economic institutions and corporate investors, the insecurity, vulnerability and frustration of people increases. Violent protests, political destabilization, attempted succession and populist nationalism emerge as responses to governments that appear to be accountable only to foreign investors. The increase in insecurity of people in states targeted by structural adjustment and shock therapy programmes is further exacerbated by the refusal of the IMF and the World Bank to require cuts to military budgets.[108] According to Vito Tanzi of the IMF, excessive military budgets place a heavy burden on countries, leading to increases in budget deficits and a decline in public investment. Yet, while IMF advice 'often calls for reviewing military expenditures to identify potential fiscal savings', the Fund is 'cautious

[105] Sadasivam, 'The Impact of Structural Adjustment on Women: A Governance and Human Rights Agenda', 19 *Human Rights Quarterly* (1997) 630; *The Realization of Economic, Social and Cultural Rights,* Final Report Submitted By Danilo Turk, Special Rapporteur, UN ESCOR Hum Rts Comm, Sub-Comm On Prevention of Discrimination and Protection of Minorities, 44th Sess., Provisional Agenda Item 8, UN Doc. E/CN.4/Sub.2/1992/16 (1992) (outlining human rights violations including an increase in infant and child mortality rates as a result of Bank-IMF policies and projects).

[106] See generally 'Globalisation and Economic, Social and Cultural Rights', Statement by the Committee on Economic, Social and Cultural Rights, May 1998.

[107] For analyses of the ways in which World Bank and IMF activities have contributed to increased levels of insecurity and destabilization, see Orford, 'Locating the International: Military and Monetary Interventions after the Cold War', 38 *Harvard International Law Journal* (1997) 443; P. Uvin, *Development Aid and Conflict: Reflections from the Case of Rwanda* (1996), at 1–3, 13–35; Hippler, 'Democratisation of the Third World After the End of the Cold War', in J. Hippler (ed.), *The Democratisation of Disempowerment: The Problem of Democracy in the Third World* (1995) 1, at 25.

[108] D.L. Budhoo, *Enough is Enough: Dear Mr Camdessus . . . Open Letter of Resignation to the Managing Director of the International Monetary Fund* (1990) 69–72.

not to claim expertise in evaluating the proper level of military spending in a given country'.[109] That caution is quite remarkable given the detailed nature of the advice that the IMF and the World Bank are prepared to offer in other areas. The dangerous practice of imposing conditions that increase poverty, food scarcity, unemployment and insecurity, while failing to recommend cuts to military budgets, is a recipe for human rights abuses. When governments attempting to comply with IMF or World Bank programmes are faced with riots and protests, such protests are too readily met with repressive state action. The impact of the IMF programmes in the former Yugoslavia and currently in Indonesia are testimony to the political upheaval, insecurity and repression that can develop as a response to the dangerous combination of such policies.[110]

Thirdly, the model of development championed by the IMF and the World Bank does not guarantee equitable and fair access to the benefits of development. Instead, global economic restructuring is producing increased inequality at an alarming rate. Particular groups are asked to bear a disproportionate burden of the costs of development. Women, for example, have been described as the 'shock absorbers' of shock therapy and structural adjustment programmes, often the first to face the loss of employment security when the IMF or the World Bank require the public sector to reduce the number of employees, or when the workforce is casualized.[111] Women are likely to be required to pick up the burden of caring for sick, homeless or mentally ill family or community members when the state divests itself of those responsibilities.[112] Rural and indigenous peoples have been displaced and resettled without adequate compensation or resettlement plans in order to make way for major development projects. Those groups rarely benefit from the promised riches flowing from foreign direct investment, and instead experience economic restructuring as cuts to public sector services or employment, or as the destruction of communities and livelihoods.

As I noted above, one of the significant features of the right to development is that it imposes obligations on states acting at the international as well as the national level, and thus on states acting through international institutions. Yet the IMF and the World Bank show little if any awareness of their obligation to protect the right to development and human rights more broadly as part of

[109] V. Tanzi, *The Changing Role of Fiscal Policy in Fund Policy Advice*, paper presented at an IMF seminar on 'Asia and the IMF', Hong Kong, China, 19 September 1997, 9, reprinted at <http://www.imf.org/external/np/apd/asia/TANZI.HTM>.

[110] For further analysis of the impact of IMF structural adjustment programmes in the former Yugoslavia, see Orford, supra n. 107.

[111] Hill, 'From Nairobi to Beijing', in S. Mitchell and R. Das Prahran (eds), *Back to Basics from Beijing: An Australian Guide to the International Platform for Action,* 104, at 106.

[112] Sadasivam, supra n. 105. See generally Orford, 'Contesting Globalization: A Feminist Perspective on the Future of Human Rights', 8(2) *Transnational Law and Contemporary Problems* (1998) 171.

the development process.[113] There is no sign of any tendency to use human rights obligations as a means for determining or evaluating their actions in their recent activities or policy documents. The World Bank has never accepted that it has any legal obligations to promote human rights, has no human rights policy and has never undertaken a systematic human rights evaluation of any of its programmes.[114] While the World Bank's legal counsel, Ibrahim Shihata, states that the Bank does promote economic, social and cultural rights in a general sense through the promotion of economic development, most human rights commentators argue that the 'segments of the population most vulnerable and at risk in human rights abuses . . . rarely benefit from World Bank activity'.[115]

Some of the NGOs, activists and academics who had been concerned about the impact of World Bank policies on human rights were initially buoyed by the apparent shift in policy signalled by the 1997 World Development Report.[116] That report claims to '[refocus] on the effectiveness of the state',[117] provide a guide to 'reinvigorating institutional capability'[118] and suggest ways to bring 'the state closer to people'.[119] A closer reading of the report, however, reveals little shift in the World Bank's commitment to policies of privatization and state restructuring, based on a narrow model of economic development.[120] While the World Bank there adopted the language of participation and accountability, participation is referred to very much in a managerial sense.[121] The report is premised upon a narrow vision of the extent to which people have the right to participate in decision-making about the conditions that affect their lives. There seems little recognition in the report of the fact that collective participation in decision-making means more than participating as a consumer of public services, or of the right to participate in determining the nature of the political and thus economic system under which people live. There is no suggestion in the report, for example, of the possibility that the people of states targeted by World Bank policies

[113] Perhaps related to this failure is the limited involvement that human rights NGOs report with either the IMF or the World Bank. In a recent survey, most human rights NGOs reported no contact with international financial institutions. More than one-third reported some contact with the World Bank, and about one-fifth reported some contact with the IMF. Those figures can be compared with the four-fifths of NGOs who reported some contact with a UN body or UN agency. More than one-third reported frequent contact with a UN body or agency. See Smith and Pagnucco with Lopez, 'Globalizing Human Rights: The Work of Transnational Human Rights NGOs in the 1990s', 20 *Human Rights Quarterly* (1998) 379, at 397.

[114] Skogly, supra n. 76, at 195–6.

[115] Ibid., at 195.

[116] The World Bank, *World Development Report 1997: The State in a Changing World* (1997).

[117] Ibid., ch. 2.

[118] Ibid., part 3.

[119] Ibid., ch. 7.

[120] Orford and Beard, 'Making the State Safe for the Market: The World Bank's *World Development Report 1997*', 22 *Melbourne University Law Review* (1998) 195.

[121] Ibid., at 201–11.

have a right to reject the World Bank's model of development entirely, to decide that particular development projects or policies should not be implemented at all, to choose to participate in the development process by deciding to nationalize all private investment, or to decide that the state should guarantee full public funding for food, health, education or social security. At best, the report envisages processes by which people are consulted about the way particular projects and policies which have been controlled and decided upon by the World Bank should be implemented. The World Bank thus continues to recommend a model of development in which communities and individuals have no real capacity to participate in or control the development process, as required by the right to development. Of course, very often the regimes governing such states may in any case seek to deny such rights to the people. The World Bank, however, despite the fact that it is controlled by states who present themselves as liberal and democratic, is no less repressive than many authoritarian regimes in that respect.

The IMF continues to deny that human rights protection is an area of activity with which it should legitimately concern itself. The IMF remains 'adamant that human rights is an area completely outside the scope of the Fund's activities, and one which remains the responsibility of the individual government'.[122] Even when the IMF is considering the impact of its own policies, it treats human rights as 'a matter of domestic redistribution and outside the Fund's mandate'.[123] For example, in a recent response to a request from the High Commissioner for Human Rights for information concerning the relationship between its activities and the realization of the right to development, the IMF stated that it had difficulties in commenting on the Declaration on the Right to Development owing to its mandate which, it says, lies primarily in the area of macroeconomic surveillance.[124] Given the range and nature of IMF conditions, that appears to be a rather disingenuous statement. While the IMF now claims to attempt to mitigate the impact of adjustment on poor or vulnerable groups within a target state, it is difficult to see that the IMF in fact puts such a policy into practice.[125]

2. Trade and the Right to Development—the Agenda of the WTO

Trade and financial liberalization conducted through multilateral and regional trade agreements has also begun to limit the extent to which people in all states are able to shape the economic, social and cultural policies of their

[122] Skogly, supra n. 76, at 198.

[123] Ibid.

[124] Report of the Secretary-General submitted in accordance with Commission resolution 1997/72 on the question of the realization of the right to development, 16 February 1998, E/CN.4/1998/28, para. 39.

[125] Skogly, supra n. 76, at 198.

governments. Criticisms of the potential human rights impact of the agenda for trade, financial and investment liberalization pursued by the WTO began to surface in the aftermath of the Uruguay Round of GATT trade negotiations.[126] The Uruguay Round outcomes significantly expanded the range of activities brought within the scope of the GATT regime to include trade-related aspects of intellectual property,[127] trade in services[128] and trade-related investment measures,[129] and greatly increased the enforcement powers of the regime through the establishment of the WTO.[130] The new agenda of the WTO significantly narrows the areas of political, economic and social life in which people can participate in making decisions.[131] According to Chakravarthi Raghavan, such agreements 'curb the right to governments to intervene in the economy for the benefit of their people while expanding the "space" for TNCs'.[132] I am going to look at the effects of two trade agreements on the right to development, in order to illustrate something of the broad-reaching impact of the Uruguay Round agreements. The first is the Agreement on the Application of Sanitary and Phytosanitary Measures (the SPS Agreement),[133] and the second is the Agreement on Trade-Related Aspects of Intellectual Property Rights (TRIPS).[134]

The SPS Agreement received little attention from human rights lawyers in the aftermath of the Uruguay Round, but provides a good illustration of the way in which apparently technical free trade agreements impact upon human rights obligations. The SPS Agreement sets out obligations and procedures relating to the use of sanitary and phytosanitary measures, including those aimed at protecting human or animal life or health, and applies to all sanitary and phytosanitary measures which may directly or indirectly affect international trade.[135] Members of the WTO are obliged to ensure that any

[126] The Final Act Embodying the Results of the Uruguay Round of Multilateral Trade Negotiations was ratified by over 120 countries at Marrakesh on 15 April 1994.

[127] See Agreement on Trade-Related Aspects of Intellectual Property Rights, 15 April 1994, 108 Stat. 4809, 4815; reprinted in 32 *ILM* 1197 [hereinafter TRIPS].

[128] See General Agreement on Trade in Services, 15 April 1994, 108 Stat. 4809, 4815; reprinted in 33 *ILM* 1167.

[129] See Agreement on Trade-Related Investment Measures, 15 April 1994, 108 Stat. 4809, 4815, reprinted in J.F. Denin (ed.), *Law and Practice of the World Trade Organization, Treaties Booklet 1, Release 95–1* (1995) 161.

[130] See Agreement Establishing the World Trade Organization, 15 April 1994, 108 Stat. 4809, 4815; reprinted in 33 *ILM* 1144. See also Understanding On Rules and Procedures Governing the Settlements of Disputes, 15 April 1994, 108 Stat. 4809, 4815; reprinted in 33 *ILM* 1226.

[131] See generally Raghavan, supra n. 2.

[132] Ibid., at 40.

[133] Reprinted in Denin, supra n. 129, at 59, 61.

[134] See supra n. 127.

[135] Key terms including 'sanitary or phytosanitary measure' are defined in Annex A to the SPS Agreement. Such measures had theoretically been allowable as exceptions to the non-discrimination provisions of GATT, particularly under Article XX(b). The aim of the Agreement was, *inter alia*, to establish a framework of rules within which such exceptions would apply.

such measure is applied only to the extent necessary to protect human, animal or plant life or health, is based on scientific principles and is not maintained without scientific evidence.[136] The only exception to the obligation to base such measures upon scientific evidence occurs where relevant scientific evidence is insufficient. In that situation, members can provisionally adopt measures on the basis of pertinent information, but must seek to obtain additional information necessary for a more objective assessment of risk within a reasonable period of time.[137] Under the Agreement, members also agree to base their measures on international standards, guidelines or recommendations where they exist.[138] Members may introduce or maintain standards which result in a higher level of protection than would be achieved by measures based on such international standards, if there is a scientific justification for such increased protection or where the member has engaged in a process of risk assessment as laid down in Article 5 of the Agreement.[139]

The 1998 decision of the Appellate Body of the WTO in the *EC Measures Concerning Meat and Meat Products (Hormones)* dispute provides an example of the reach of the SPS Agreement into areas of domestic policy-making and of its impact upon human rights protection.[140] That dispute involved parallel complaints brought against the European Community (EC) by Canada and the US. The complaints concerned an EC ban on the sale of meat from animals that had been treated with any of six growth hormones.[141] Three of the banned growth hormones were 'natural' hormones, that is derived from animals, and the other three were synthetic hormones. A series of EC directives operated to ban the sale of such meat within the EC, and included a ban on the importation of meat treated with such growth hormones.[142] The

[136] SPS Agreement, Article 2. [137] Ibid., Article 5(7). [138] Ibid., Article 3(1).

[139] Ibid., Article 3(3). According to a footnote to Article 3, there is a scientific justification for adopting a higher standard if, on the basis of an examination and evaluation of available scientific information, a member determines that the relevant international standards, guidelines or recommendations are not sufficient to achieve the appropriate level of protection.

[140] Appellate Body Report, *EC Measures Concerning Meat and Meat Products (Hormones)*, adopted 16 January 1998, WT/DS26/AB/R [hereinafter the Meat Hormones Report].

[141] The hormones at issue were the 'natural' hormones oestradiol–17β, progesterone and testosterone, and the 'synthetic' hormones trenbolone acetate, zeranol and melengestrol acetate (MGA).

[142] The import prohibition was set out in three directives of the Council of Ministers enacted before the SPS Agreement came into effect: Council Directive 81/602/EEC of 31 July 1981, Council Directive 88/146/EEC of 7 March 1988 and Council Directive 88/299/EEC of 17 May 1988. As of 1 July 1997, those directives were repealed and replaced with Council Directive 99/22/EC of 29 April 1996. The effect of those directives was to prohibit the administration to farm animals of substances having hormonal or thyrostatic action. The Directives prohibited the placement on the market, or the importation from third countries, of meat and meat products from animals to which such substances, including the six hormones at issue in the dispute, were administered. Member States were allowed to authorize the administration,

complainants argued that the EC had introduced measures that differed from the voluntary standards proposed by the relevant international body, the Codex Alimentarius (the Codex).

The EC argued that the standards developed by the Codex were out of date, that it wished to maintain standards that resulted in a higher level of protection than would be achieved by measures based on the Codex standards and that for one of the hormones, no Codex standards existed. The decision by the EC to ban the use of such hormones had resulted from wide-ranging public and scientific discussion and debate about the issue over a ten-year period. Consumers had become worried about the effects on human health of residues of growth hormones in meat, and consumer confidence in meat had suffered as a result. The EC had commissioned a series of scientific inquiries into the issue, culminating in a round table on the use of growth hormones with scientists, consumer groups, industry workers and other interested parties in 1995.[143] While most scientists agreed that use of the 'natural' hormones in controlled conditions under veterinary supervision appeared to pose no threat to human health, the EC decided that it was not possible to monitor and regulate the conditions under which hormones were administered, nor was it possible to stop the black market trade in such hormones without imposing a total ban on their use. Accordingly, three directives were passed by the European Parliament enacting a ban on the use of those hormones.[144] Those directives applied both to meat produced within the EC and that imported from third countries.

The Appellate Body of the WTO found that, while the measures in dispute did not result in discrimination between domestic and foreign producers or in a disguised restriction on international trade, the ban on importation of meat treated with hormones was nevertheless in breach of the SPS Agreement. It held that the EC was not entitled to regulate the use of growth hormones as its decision to do so was not based on sufficient scientific evidence. With respect to the synthetic hormone MGA, for which there was no relevant international standard, the Appellate Body held that there was not sufficient scientific evidence to support the maintenance of even provisional measures to protect human health. With respect to the other five growth hormones, the Appellate Body held that there was not sufficient scientific evidence to support the maintenance of food safety standards that were higher than those

for therapeutic or zootechnical purposes, of certain substances having a hormonal or thyrostatic action, and under certain conditions meat and meat products treated in that way could be placed on the market or imported from third countries. See Meat Hormones Report, supra n. 140, para. 1–5.

[143] For a history of events, see Panel Report, *EC Measures Concerning Meat and Meat Products (Hormones)*, complaint by Canada, adopted 18 August 1997, WT/DS48/R/CAN, para. II.26–II.33.

[144] See supra n. 142.

set by the Codex. It held that there must be a risk assessment based on detailed scientific data in order for such measures to be enacted, even where there is no clear scientific opinion regarding the risks posed by a product and even where the measures had been enacted before, but maintained after, entry into force of the SPS Agreement.

From a purely economic perspective, the decision in the *Meat Hormone* case is unremarkable. States Parties to the SPS Agreement agree to pass laws or regulations that protect animal and human health and welfare only where there are recognized and agreed international scientific standards necessitating such protection. Where there are no such standards, states agree to pass such laws or regulations affecting foreign producers only where the state can provide scientific evidence proving that a new technology is dangerous when used in animal or plant development. In that way, profits are maximized, scientific entrepreneurialism is encouraged, and barriers to trade are only created where their necessity can be proved according to rigorous scientific standards. Otherwise, states could use a non-trade excuse, such as protecting consumer safety or environmental protection, to justify restrictive policies that inhibit the capacity of foreign producers to maximize their access to global markets. It is irrelevant that the same standards may be applied to both foreign and domestic producers, as the aim is to maximize trade.

The right to development allows a focus away from purely economic considerations, in order to address the impact that such apparently technocratic and economic decisions in fact have on broader human rights commitments. As the *Meat Hormone* decision illustrates, the SPS Agreement impacts upon the obligation to respect and promote the right to development in a number of ways. First, that Agreement infringes the central requirement that 'every human person and all peoples are entitled to participate in, contribute to, and enjoy economic, social, cultural and political development'.[145] Participation is radically constrained by that decision. The effect of the SPS Agreement is to require states to base all public policy decisions about human or animal health or welfare on a narrowly defined form of scientific evidence, which excludes from consideration any other community concerns or knowledge. The requirement that states privilege the interests of scientists, who are often paid and employed by interested corporations, over the knowledge of local consumers, workers, industry groups or farmers operates to limit the scope for contesting and debating particular policies and laws. By restricting the bases upon which states can introduce laws relating to consumer safety, animal health and welfare or sustainable farming practices, the right of peoples and communities to participate in and shape their economic, social and cultural development is effectively negated. Only those recognized as scientific experts, often working for multinational corporations, are recognized

[145] Declaration on the Right to Development, Article 1.

as legitimate sources of authorized knowledge upon which government policies can be based without breaching trade agreements.[146]

The SPS Agreement thus limits the right to participate by enshrining a particular form of knowledge as the basis upon which public policy decisions about health, safety and environmental issues can legitimately be made. Only scientific knowledge about the value of biotechnology or the impact of using patented hormones or genes in food production is admitted as legitimate. The absence of certain extremely expensive forms of scientific evidence invalidates decision-making processes. The effect of the SPS agreement is to institutionalize hierarchies of knowledge, and thus of participation.[147] Only those people who are able to participate in producing, or paying for the production of, such scientific knowledge, are able to participate in decision-making about complex and broad-ranging issues. The privileging of science as a basis for decision-making is itself premised upon a gendered and racialized hierarchy of knowledges, in which Western science is treated as value-free, objective, impartial and rational, while other forms of knowledge are dismissed as emotive, partial, subjective and irrational.[148] There are many perspectives that cannot be addressed adequately within that scientific framework. Questions about the effects of gene or hormone patenting on farmers in less powerful states or on sustainable development cannot be taken into account by policy-makers within the rules established by the SPS Agreement, as those policy-makers are restricted to basing their decisions upon narrowly defined scientific bases. Under the SPS Agreement, scientific modes of reasoning trump any other views on the legitimacy of biotechnology, without any need

[146] A different argument relating to the undemocratic nature of the process established under the SPS Agreement was made during US Congressional hearings prior to the implementation of the agreement. Critics argued that the process was undemocratic as individual citizens would not be able to appear before dispute settlement panels. See Trade Agreements Resulting from the Uruguay Round of Multilateral Trade Negotiations: Hearings Before the Committee on Ways and Means, 103rd Cong., 2nd Sess. 305 (1994) (statement of Robert Housman, Sierra Club), cited in Johansen, 'Commentary on the Agreement on the Application of Sanitary and Phytosanitary Measures' in Denin, supra n. 129, *Commentary Booklet* 5 (1995) at 1, 16.

[147] That ordering of knowledge does not exist in some ideal space outside of conquest and domination, but as an integral part of such processes. For the argument that hierarchies of knowledge were used to justify imperialist conquest, see Winant, 'Behind Blue Eyes: Whiteness and Contemporary US Racial Politics', 225 *New Left Review* (1997) 73, at 79. Winant argues that doctrines of European superiority used to justify the conquest of supposedly uncivilized or lesser peoples were based on notions of 'detached and impartial Reason': 'the supposed possession of this faculty provided a warrant for domination of the natural world, and a principle for classification of human subjects—and human bodies—according to attributions about their closeness to or distance from this ideal'. That principle for classification of human subjects and bodies is in operation in the SPS Agreement.

[148] See generally D. Haraway, *Simians, Cyborgs, and Women: The Reinvention of Nature* (1991).

to negotiate with other forms of knowledge about, or ways of valuing, such technology. That agreement limits the bases upon which states can introduce laws relating to health, safety and environmental issues, and limits the extent to which states can take into account the perspectives and values of actors other than the organized scientific research community and businesses who fund them.[149]

Secondly, the decision impacts upon the obligation to ensure that the model of development adopted by states is one in which 'all human rights and fundamental freedoms can be fully realized'.[150] That indivisibility principle is a central feature of the right to development. As I noted above, the Declaration on the Right to Development stresses that all human rights and fundamental freedoms are indivisible and interdependent, and that equal attention and urgent consideration should be given to the implementation, promotion and protection of civil, political, economic, social and cultural rights.[151] The SPS Agreement, however, limits both civil and political rights and economic, social and cultural rights.

The *Meat Hormones* decision, for example, has a subtle but significant impact on the right to health. In its argument to the WTO Appellate Body, the EC relied upon scientific opinion that ingestion of the hormones in dispute is potentially carcinogenic. In particular, the EC presented scientific evidence that the synthetic hormone MGA increases the risk of breast cancer.[152] Although the EC was not able to produce scientific research conducted on the narrow question of the relationship between breast cancer and residues of MGA in meat when used as a growth promoter, it did produce scientific evidence relating to the broader relationship between levels of progesterone—

[149] For a strikingly different model of the way in which technoscience might be subjected to public participation and critical discourse, see D.J. Haraway, *Modest_Witness@Second_Millennium* (1997), at 94–7. Haraway there compares the US approach to 'technoscientific democracy' with that of Denmark. Three groups 'essentially control how technoscience is done in the United States: the Pentagon, the organized scientific research community, and business'. Haraway points to the 'conspicuous absence of serious citizen agency in shaping science and technology policy'. In Denmark, by comparison, panels of citizens, 'selected from pools of people who indicate an interest, but not professional expertise or a commercial or other organized stake, in an area of technology', are established to guide policy on scientific and technological issues. Those panels hear testimony and cross-examine experts, read briefings prepared by a range of scientific and technical experts and representatives from trade unions, environmental organizations, women's groups and others with a stake in the issues raised, deliberate together and issue reports on the topic to a national press conference. Haraway suggests that while the process is not perfect, '[t]he degree of scientific and technical literacy encouraged in ordinary people—as well as the degree of respect for citizens' considerations encouraged among technical and professional people . . . is stunning to anyone inhabiting the depleted democratic air of US technoscience' (at 96).

[150] Declaration on the Right to Development, Article 1.

[151] Ibid., Article 6(2).

[152] See the discussion of the evidence of Dr Lucier in the Meat Hormones Report, supra n. 140, at para. 198.

the hormone MGA mimics—and increased rates of breast cancer.[153] While the complainants, Canada and the US, had scientific data relating to the health risks posed by MGA residues, the report of the Appellate Body notes that those parties 'declined to submit any assessment of MGA upon the ground that the material they were aware of was proprietary and confidential in nature'.[154] That information was presumably owned as intellectual property by the company producing the hormone.[155] The Appellate Body found that as 'there was an almost complete absence of evidence on MGA in the panel proceedings', the EC could *not* justify banning the use of that hormone.[156] While the EC had provided evidence relating to the general question of the carcinogenic potential of the hormones at issue, the Appellate Body held that the scientists upon whose opinion the EC was relying had not evaluated the carcinogenic potential of those hormones when used *specifically* as growth promoters.[157] In an extraordinary footnote, the Appellate Body held that even if the scientific evidence concerning the risk to women was correct, only 371 of the women currently living in the member states of the European Union would die from breast cancer as a result of trade in hormone-related beef, while the total population of the member states of the European Union in 1995 was 371 million.[158] The reader is left to assume that the health risk posed to those women is considered minimal and insignificant by the members of the Appellate Body, and that the potential sacrifice of the lives of a group of women can be conceived of as appropriate and necessary to achieve the greater good of competitiveness.

The EC argued unsuccessfully that, when dealing with a risk to public health of such a potentially serious nature, and when faced with conflicting and inadequate scientific research, states should be permitted to take a cautious approach to allowing the unregulated use of such hormones. As a result of the *Meat Hormones* decision, however, the onus of proof as to the safety of a particular growth hormone rests, not with the agrochemical corporations

[153] The EC provided evidence that included studies of the carcinogenic properties of the category of progestins of which the hormone progesterone is a member. The EC argued that because MGA is an anabolic agent which mimics the action of progesterone, those studies were relevant to its risk assessment regarding MGA. Supra n. 140 at para. 201. One estimate before the Appellate Body was that for every million women alive in the United States, Canada and Europe, about 110,000 of those women would get breast cancer (ibid., footnote 181). Of those 110,000 cases of cancer, one would be related to the eating of meat containing residues of progesterone or MGA.

[154] Ibid., para. 201.

[155] Giant multinational corporation Monsanto, dubbed 'the Microsoft of biotechnology', was one of the companies involved in manufacturing the growth hormones in question in the dispute. There has been heated debate over the accuracy of the scientific evidence Monsanto's scientists did provide regarding the safety of its growth hormone Posilac. See Monbiot *et al.*, 'How Monsanto Reaps a Rich Harvest', *Guardian Weekly*, 21 December 1997, at 19.

[156] Meat Hormones Report, (supra n. 140), at para. 201.

[157] Ibid., para. 199–200.

[158] Ibid., footnote 182.

who profit from the use of such hormones, but with the consumers in the states where the resulting products are to be sold.[159] Under the SPS Agreement, the lack of scientific research into the health risks posed by a novel product, process or technology acts as a barrier to consumer protection legislation, rather than as an indication that such protection is necessary. A more cautious approach would suggest that states should be free to regulate such products or processes until the corporation seeking to profit from new technologies can show by reliable scientific studies that such products or processes are safe. The history of corporate carelessness about consumer safety should make clear that governments are well advised to adopt a precautionary approach that privileges human and animal health and welfare over corporate profits where possible.[160] Instead, under the SPS Agreement, the right to health is subordinated to the imperatives of TNCs, who in this instance failed to release the information that they held concerning the health risks posed by the hormones in question. According to the logic of the *Meat Hormones* dispute, the failure of a corporation to provide any scientific evidence relating to the safety of a novel product or technology is no barrier to that corporation selling its product in foreign markets. In such a way, the investment liberalization agenda of the WTO shifts the boundary between public good and private interest in favour of the private interests of transnationals, a shift that has profound implications for the utility of liberal concepts of democracy and human rights operating in the public sphere.[161]

The right to food is also affected by the SPS Agreement. That right is dependent upon a state's capacity to ensure that economic conditions exist in which food can be produced and distributed, and upon the state's willingness to regulate industries engaged in food production. Decisions such as that of the Appellate Body in the *Meat Hormone* case mean that it will be more difficult for

[159] The Appellate Body formally held that the evidentiary burden of showing that the measure adopted was consistent with the SPS Agreement does not rest with the member imposing the measure, but with the member bringing the complaint: ibid., para. 253(a). Nevertheless, it is clear from the Report that in practice the burden of proving the existence of scientific evidence sufficient to justify the measures in dispute rested with the EC. As noted above, the complainants, for example, were not even required to make available the scientific data to which they had access relating to the health risks posed by one of the hormones in question.

[160] The EC argued that the precautionary principle had emerged as a principle of customary international law or at least as a general principle of law, and as such should be taken into account in determining its obligations regarding risk assessment. The EC argued that in the context of interpreting Articles 5.1 and 5.2 of the SPS Agreement, the precautionary principle meant that it was not necessary for all scientists to agree on the possibility or magnitude of the risk against which a measure was designed to protect consumers, nor was it necessary for all members of the WTO to perceive the risk in the same way. For the Appellate Body's discussion and rejection of that argument, see ibid., para. 120–5.

[161] Frow, 'Information as Gift and Commodity', 219 *New Left Review* (1996) 89, at 105.

small-scale farmers producing organic meat or dairy products to maintain a market for those products.[162] By limiting the extent to which consumers in the EC can demand laws that regulate the sale of meat treated by hormones, for example, corporations can limit the means available to those consumers to resist the dominance of large-scale farming by multinational corporations in other parts of the world.[163] Such corporations are also seeking to make 'eco-labelling' illegal, arguing that such labelling should properly be characterized as a technical barrier to trade. If successful, such bans on labelling would make it impossible for consumers to choose to buy organic products. Corporations are thus seeking to limit both the capacity of states to regulate genetically modified food or food treated with hormones, and the ability of consumers to exercise the choice not to buy such food. The effect of the combination of such moves at the international level is that it will be far more difficult for consumers to support organic and sustainable farming practices, whether for reasons of health, safety, animal welfare, environmental protection or solidarity with Third World farmers. As Ralph Nader and Lori Wallach note:

> It's a very neat arrangement. European corporations target US laws they do not like. US corporations target European laws they do not like. Then European and US corporations attack Japanese laws and vice versa—the process can go on until all laws protecting people and their environment have either been reversed or replaced by weaker laws that do not interfere with the immediate interests of the corporations . . . Corporations are poised to win at both ends, while citizens and democracy lose.[164]

Finally, the *Meat Hormone* decision also illustrates the ways in which trade agreements impact upon civil and political rights. Civil and political rights such as the right to political participation and the right to self-determination, are weakened where international agreements operate to remove decisions about consumer safety or environmental protection from the political arena. Attempts to criticize such practices are themselves subject to increased control

[162] According to one report, organic farming poses a threat to the globalized operation of monopolistic agrochemical firms. The consumption of organic produce is rising by 20 to 30 per cent per year. See Monbiot, 'Give us this day our daily toxic bread', *Guardian Weekly*, 22 March 1998, at 14.

[163] Multinational corporations have increased their control over agriculture through increasing the integration of seeds with chemicals and animal products with hormones. As a result, farmers are becoming increasingly dependent on biotechnology corporations. For analyses of that process and its effects, see Shiva, 'The Seed and the Earth: Biotechnology and the Colonisation of Regeneration', in V. Shiva (ed.), *Close to Home: Women Reconnect Ecology, Health and Development Worldwide* (1994) 128; Shiva, 'Biotechnological Development and the Conservation of Biodiversity' in V. Shiva and I. Moser (eds), *Biopolitics: A Feminist and Ecological Reader on Biotechnology* (1995) 193.

[164] Nader and Wallach, 'GATT, NAFTA, and the Subversion of the Democratic Process', in J. Mander and E. Goldsmith (eds), *The Case Against the Global Economy: And for a Turn Toward the Local* (1996) 92, at 98.

by legal systems responding to the interests of multinational corporations.[165] By denying civil and political rights such as the right to participate in decision-making to people in one part of the world, TNCs can more easily deny the economic, social and cultural rights of those people in other parts of the world seeking to develop sustainable means of producing food. Food production becomes increasingly tied to the profits and interests of monopolistic corporations. States signing on to such trade agreements to further economic development substantially weaken the human rights guarantees of people within their states and globally.

The impact of trade agreements on the protection and promotion of the right to development is also well illustrated by the operation of the Agreement on Trade-Related Aspects of Intellectual Property Rights (TRIPS).[166] That agreement obliges states to have in place laws or regulations protecting a broad range of intellectual and industrial property rights.[167] In addition, states agree to provide the legal and administrative infrastructure necessary to ensure that intellectual property rights can effectively be enforced under domestic law, both by their own nationals and by foreign rights holders.[168] TRIPS is of particular interest as it is one of the Uruguay Round agreements that marks a major shift away from the traditional GATT goal of liberalizing trade in goods. TRIPS uses the language of free trade to facilitate the reconceptualization and international protection of information as private property.

Prior to TRIPS, intellectual property rights had not been linked with trade. Intellectual property had a long history in industrialized countries. The use of patents in particular had developed as a form of government regulation aimed at rewarding inventive work, enabling the spread of knowledge useful to society and ensuring that inventions were widely available for productive use.[169] The granting of patents was aimed at achieving a balance between the goals of granting a monopoly right to the holder of a patent to make use of or produce a particular invention, and ensuring that such inventions could be widely used to develop industries in the patent-granting country. That balance was met by, *inter alia,* granting patent holders the right to exploit their invention exclusively only for a short term, requiring that the patent actually

[165] The 'McLibel' trial in the United Kingdom, and the growth of 'food disparagement' laws in American states, are attempts to prevent people from questioning the practices adopted by such corporations. Monbiot, supra n. 162. For an analysis of the McLibel trial, see J. Vidal, *McLibel: Burger Culture on Trial* (1997).

[166] TRIPS Agreement, supra n. 127.

[167] Ibid., Part II.

[168] Ibid., Part III. For an examination of the legal and administrative changes required by developing countries to provide protection for patents relating to pharmaceutical and agricultural chemical products under TRIPS, see Appellate Body Report, *India—Patent Protection for Pharmaceutical and Agricultural Chemical Products,* adopted 19 December 1997, WT/DS50/AB/R.

[169] Raghavan, supra n. 2, at 116–17.

be exploited within the territory of the country granting the patent, and limiting the nature of inventions over which patents could be granted.[170]

While originally designed as a means of fostering the technological and industrial progress of the state granting the patent, there has been a trend towards internationalizing intellectual property rights, thus allowing the owners of such rights to exploit them not only at the national but also at the international level. The Uruguay Round of trade negotiations saw the forum for this internationalization shift to the trade regime. The globalization of intellectual property rights, however, appears conceptually at odds with the ideas underlying free trade regimes. A patent right over DNA or a copyright over software is a 'property right over an abstract object that gives the owner the power to determine the physical reproduction of that object, thus creating monopoly privileges over the reproduction of objects'.[171] The creation of monopoly rights to exploit inventions is further strengthened when there is an attempt to create a global property regime. As Peter Drahos argues, such a regime 'offers the possibility that abstract objects come to be owned and controlled by a hegemonic state'.[172] The related weakening of the obligation to exploit the patent in all countries where it is granted leads to patents being used to secure exclusive rights over export markets. Within a world economy, the existence of a system of global monopoly privileges may constitute a serious threat to a given state's capacity to shift its comparative advantage through efficient manufacture of new products. The holder of monopoly privileges has the power to change the costs of production.[173] Indeed, when states like the US began to push to have intellectual property added to the Uruguay Round agenda, many trade negotiators and the GATT Secretariat itself had little familiarity with intellectual property regimes, and saw a conceptual tension between free trade and the monopoly privileges that intellectual property rights represent.[174] The US was nevertheless able to make use of a process of economic coercion involving the threat and use of trade sanctions to ensure that the TRIPS agreement was finally agreed to as part of the Uruguay Round of reforms.[175]

[170] For example, many European countries refused to grant patents over medicines: ibid., at 124–5.

[171] Drahos, supra n. 2, at 16. [172] Ibid., at 16. [173] Ibid., at 14.

[174] Ibid.

[175] Ibid., at 14, 15. Drahos reveals that the US made use of a range of coercive trade mechanisms at the bilateral level to ensure that states complied with US negotiating objectives relating to intellectual property protection. In addition, the US government in concert with major US corporations made use of an 'information' campaign in various countries to instil the idea that inventions and ideas were 'property' and that their 'theft' was a serious issue. The outcome of the negotiations over TRIPS was particularly remarkable given that most countries other than the US are net importers of technological and cultural information, and yet have agreed to pay more for that information under TRIPS.

The TRIPS agreement will have a significant impact on the development model available to many states, and limits the capacity of people to participate in making decisions about an extremely wide range of issues and interests. One illustration of the impact of those limitations on the right to development is provided by the requirement in Article 39 that contracting parties establish legal and institutional protection for trade secrets of investors. That requirement operates to entrench the unaccountability of TNCs to local communities.[176] Internationalizing the protection of the trade secrets of such corporations leads to a corresponding increase in the secrecy of production and manufacturing processes. As a result, the right to participate in development is constrained. Such an increase in secrecy makes it difficult for local peoples to have knowledge of the likely risks of processes conducted in their communities, thus increasing the likelihood that they will have to bear the burden of damage when accidents occur. Article 39 thus limits the capacity of individuals and communities to participate in making decisions about whether or not hazardous industries should be allowed, where they should be located, and on what terms. By denying local people the capacity to make informed decisions about the nature of foreign investment, corporate interests are privileged over human rights.

TRIPS also impacts upon the obligation to ensure that the model of development adopted by states is one in which 'all human rights and fundamental freedoms can be fully realized'.[177] That agreement privileges economic interests over the protection and promotion of a range of economic, social and cultural rights. For example, the nature of the intellectual property regime embodied in TRIPS is such that traditional, community-based knowledge about seeds and plants is not patentable, while innovative, individually-based knowledge produced by scientific researchers but derived from traditional knowledge *is* patentable.[178] Corporations patent the genetic properties of seeds developed over generations as insect resistant or for medical properties, and are then able to exploit the intellectual property rights to that genetic material as a commodity in the countries from which the knowledge and seeds were first taken.[179] That practice is particularly widespread in the agrochemical and pharmaceutical industries. As a result, access to information about food and medicines is privatized and those goods are made more expensive.[180] Human rights such as the right to health or the right to adequate food thus become significantly less relevant.[181]

[176] Jaising and Sathyamala, 'Legal Rights . . . and Wrongs: Internationalising Bhopal' in Shiva, supra n. 163, at 88.

[177] Declaration on the Right to Development, Article 1.

[178] Frow, supra n. 161, at 98.

[179] Ibid.

[180] Lindsay, 'GATT: Development and Intellectual Property', 3 *Arena Journal* (1994) 33, at 38.

[181] See further the discussion of the impact of TRIPS upon human rights in Orford, supra n. 107, at 473.

Finally, TRIPS represents one of a new breed of trade and investment agreements that substantially limit the autonomy of the states who sign on to those agreements to determine the nature of their domestic legal systems. One of the assumptions of much discussion in the trade and development area is that states and peoples are free to choose the development model, and in particular the legal and administrative system, that they believe best suits their conditions, and that if the choice is a bad one, it will be punished by foreign markets or investors. Agreements like TRIPS fundamentally unsettle that assumption. Here, a powerful state, the US, was able to make use of its market power to ensure that states signed on to a far-reaching agreement relating to a form of property that will be at the heart of economic development into the next century. That agreement goes further than perhaps any other international agreement to date in terms of stating in detail the kinds of laws and administrative systems that states must have in place. For example, Part II of the agreement sets out the minimum standards of intellectual property protection that states must provide, relating to matters such as the length of the term of patent protection to be guaranteed.[182] Part III deals with the enforcement of intellectual property rights in great detail. It provides that states must implement enforcement procedures that are fair and equitable, and which are not to be 'unnecessarily complicated or costly, or entail unreasonable time limits or unwarranted delays'.[183] Decisions relating to intellectual property matters are preferably to be in writing with reasons, and rights of judicial review are to be provided in the case of judicial decisions.[184] States are obliged to provide for criminal procedures and penalties, at least in the case of wilful trademark counterfeiting or copyright piracy on a commercial scale, and the remedies to be available under criminal procedures are to include 'imprisonment and/or monetary fines sufficient to provide a deterrent'.[185]

As trade lawyers Michael Trebilcock and Robert Howse note, these provisions create an 'unprecedented degree of control by an international regime over domestic civil and administrative procedures'.[186] Such requirements are a 'massive intrusion into domestic legal systems, and especially the balance that those systems strike between the rights of defendants and those of plaintiffs'.[187] When considered in the light of the coercive methods resorted to by powerful states during negotiations of TRIPS, it is difficult to see how the right to development is in operation in the area of global intellectual property rights. States and peoples are increasingly limited by such agreements in their capacity to choose models of development that do not suit the interests of powerful states such as the US.

[182] Under Article 33, patents are to be granted for a term of twenty years, longer than that granted in most states at the time of signing TRIPS.

[183] Article 41:2. [184] Articles 41:3 and 41:4. [185] Article 61.

[186] M.J. Trebilcock and R. Howse, *The Regulation of International Trade* (1995), at 270.

[187] Ibid.

IV THE UTILITY OF THE RIGHT TO DEVELOPMENT IN THE POST-COLD WAR ERA

I want to finish by considering whether the right to development is a useful way of addressing the problems posed by globalization, and particularly by the activities of international economic institutions. I continue to feel some ambivalence about that question. I am going to frame my inquiry into the utility of the right to development by reference to two uses of the language of rights noted by Philip Alston in his defence of the right to development.[188] One use is to provoke a sense of outrage, to mobilize people in support of a particular goal.[189] Once people feel a sufficient sense of injustice and entitlement that they can say 'we have a right to that and you can't take it away from us', they are in a better position to overcome the injustice oppressing them.[190] The second use of rights language 'is to facilitate access to a range of legal norms and enforcement mechanisms through which to seek the vindication, in a particular setting, of important claims, the essential legitimacy of which is widely recognized'.[191] Alston stresses that it is important to allow the interplay between those two approaches to rights: the inspirational and creative aspects of rights discourse and the legalistic approach. To what extent then is the right to development useful legally and creatively as a means of challenging the current project of economic liberalization?

1. Rights as Legal Mechanisms

First, what role can the right to development play as a legal mechanism for constraining the operations of international economic institutions? As the creature of resolutions and declarations, the right to development arguably does not yet exist as a binding legal obligation upon states. More importantly, no treaty organ or similar body exists to monitor state compliance with the right to development, although the Commission on Human Rights in 1998 recommended the establishment of a working group to investigate mechanisms for implementing the right to development. It is important to

[188] Alston, 'Garfield the Cat', supra n. 14, at 512–13.

[189] Ibid., at 512. See also Mansell and Scott, 'Why Bother About a Right to Development?', 21 *Journal of Law and Society* (1994) 171, at 177 (pointing to 'the role of law, and specifically the language of rights, in both locating development issues firmly on the international political agenda and in providing a means of enhancing the visibility and credibility of the claims of the poor, both at home and within global institutional structures').

[190] Alston, 'Garfield the Cat', supra n. 14.

[191] Ibid., at 513.

acknowledge the limitations that would apply even if a mechanism were to be created for monitoring compliance with the right to development. Existing mechanisms for monitoring other international human rights obligations lack enforcement capacity and resources. That lack of resources is particularly problematic in the areas of economic, social and cultural rights, and can be compared to the resources available to the institutions whose activities impact upon those rights, such as the IMF.[192]

The Declaration on the Right to Development in its current form would be difficult, if not impossible, to implement. As the Committee on Economic, Social and Cultural Rights has recently noted, the Declaration on the Right to Development was not designed to be of use in an 'operational' context: 'Its great strength lies more in stating broad principles rather than identifying specific measures to be taken at the country level.'[193] The Declaration points instead to the international dimensions of human rights obligations, while relying upon existing categories of rights and existing core human rights treaties as the basis for addressing human rights concerns at the operational level. Thus the utility of the right to development at this level may lie in the fact that it points to aspects of human rights protection that have been in danger of being forgotten or discarded: the emphasis on both individual and collective rights, the need to address interstate behaviour, and equal treatment of economic, social and cultural rights and civil and political rights.[194]

The broader limitations of rights as a mechanism for constraining the activities of international economic institutions are made visible by the attention that the right to development places on the activities of international institutions. The extent to which international human rights law can offer tools for resisting human rights violations caused by the activities of actors such as multinational corporations, international economic institutions, privatized government agencies or foreign investors is limited at present. The destructive effects of the activities of international economic institutions pose a challenge to the areas of international law that have been developed to protect individuals against abuses by states.[195] Indeed, it may be that states are willing to divest themselves of many areas of what was once recognized as sovereignty in

[192] Alston, supra n. 71, at 444.

[193] 'The incorporation of economic, social and cultural rights into the United Nations Development Assistance Framework (UNDAF) process', Comments adopted by the Committee on Economic, Social and Cultural Rights, 15 May 1988, para. 5.

[194] Some of the useful developments in the area of influencing the actions of international economic institutions focus on economic, social and cultural rights rather than the right to development. See, for example, the dialogue between the High Commissioner for Human Rights and the World Bank, the IMF and other financial institutions with a view to their incorporating the principles of the right to development in their policies, programmes and projects.

[195] Orford and Beard, supra n. 120, at 215.

order to avoid the network of obligations that have developed to constrain state activity in the areas of environmental protection, labour standards and human rights.

The right to development does point to the human rights obligations of states acting at the international level as members of international organizations. No straightforward mechanism exists to date, however, for enforcing such obligations. International human rights law may provide citizens with the means to challenge the steps taken by states to implement IMF conditions or World Bank programmes. Yet as the recent events in Indonesia make clear, the far-reaching nature of the conditions imposed by international institutions, and the speed with which change occurs as a result, mean that appeals to under-resourced human rights bodies are not an adequate method of preventing or responding to potential human rights abuses. In addition, there is no existing mechanism which makes it possible to challenge states about decisions they make as members of international institutions where such decisions violate the human rights of people in other states.[196]

International human rights law must attempt to develop methods for holding actors other than states accountable for human rights abuses, or for holding states accountable for the human rights abuses of those actors whose activities they make possible.[197] Human rights lawyers need to develop an approach to human rights protection that is sufficiently subtle to deal with situations where state functions are privatized in order to limit accountability for the effects of particular activities,[198] or where actions are carried out in private or covertly. One example of a secretive activity that has an impact on human rights is derivatives trading.[199] Commentators have argued that such trading was implicated in the Mexican and related Latin American currency crises of 1994.[200] Given the increases in the trade in derivatives in Asia during the 1990s,[201] the contribution of investors and currency speculators to

[196] Cf. Skogly, supra n. 76, at 200, arguing that as states constitute the decision-making bodies of international organizations, those states that have undertaken international human rights obligations cannot neglect those obligations simply by acting through an international organization. While those obligations usually relate to the human rights of people within the territory or jurisdiction of the state concerned, the right to development does extend the obligation to promote and protect rights to states acting in international fora.

[197] Orford and Beard, supra n. 120, at 216.

[198] Ibid., at 208–12; Chinkin, 'Feminist Interventions into International Law', 19 *Adelaide Law Review* (1997) 13, at 21; Duncanson, 'Unchartered Lands in an Age of "Accountability" ', III(1) *Res Publica* (1997) 3.

[199] For a discussion of the secretive nature of over-the-counter derivatives trades, see D. Henwood, *Wall Street: How it Works and for Whom* (1997) at 34–7.

[200] S. Griffith-Jones, *The Mexican Peso Crisis* (1996) at 21–5; F. Partnoy, *F.I.A.S.C.O.: Blood in the Water on Wall Street* (1997) at 189–205.

[201] International Monetary Fund, *International Capital Markets: Developments, Prospects, and Key Policy Issues* (1996) 72 (noting that 'market participants report that the largest future growth area for derivatives is in the emerging markets, particularly Southeast Asia, as government

the destabilization of South-East Asian economies should be seriously discussed. While the crises arguably fuelled by derivatives trading or the actions of international economic institutions have human rights effects, the difficult challenge facing human rights lawyers is to envisage ways of holding particular actors accountable for human rights abuses in such instances.

The 1997 Report of the Intergovernmental Group of Experts on the Right to Development suggests some ways in which international economic institutions might be involved in a consultative process regarding the right to development.[202] It proposes, for example, that the High Commissioner for Human Rights should pursue dialogue with the World Bank, the IMF and other financial institutions with a view to their incorporating the principles of the right to development in their policies, programmes and projects. It also recommends that the content of and procedures for structural adjustment programmes and policies should be reviewed in terms of their effects on the realization of the right to development. It encourages recent joint efforts by the World Bank and NGOs to review the effects of structural adjustment programmes, and states that the international community should adopt more effective measures to resolve the external debt problem of developing countries for a more effective promotion and realization of the right to development. The workings of the international financial market should be reviewed, to determine the effects of unregulated financial speculation on the right to development.

Yet the fact remains that such proposals seem to have little influence on the ways in which institutions like the IMF or the WTO conceive of their responsibilities and mandates. The implication of such programmes of action is that it is the responsibility of underfunded human rights bodies and non-governmental organizations to determine the effects of the actions of international economic institutions and international financial markets, rather than the responsibility of those actors to take account of the impact of their policies and programmes on human rights. The lack of any discussion of the legal obligations of such organizations points to the lack of political will to raise such issues at the intergovernmental level.[203]

restrictions on foreign exchange and stock ownership are eased'); Lynch, 'Growth in Asia-Pacific Markets', in E. Sheedy and S. McCracken (eds), *Derivatives: The Risks that Remain* (1997) 3, at 16–24; Sheedy, 'The Risks that Remain', in ibid., 332, at 333. See also Cline, supra n. 95, at 423–64.

[202] 'Question of the Realization of the Right to Development', Report of the Intergovernmental Group of Experts on the Right to Development on its second session, E/CN.4/1998/29, 7 November 1997, ch. 1.

[203] In July 1998 the Director-General of the WTO announced a plan for enhanced co-operation with NGOs. The proposed changes are to include the initiation of informal meetings between the Director-General and NGO representatives 'with the goal of improving and enhancing our mutual understanding', and the creation of an 'NGO Forum' on the WTO Website to make available information of particular interest to NGOs. It remains to be seen

2. The Inspirational Aspect of Rights

To what extent can the right to development operate at the inspirational or motivational level, to provide a form of critique that can challenge prevailing ways of being and understanding? Let me start with the concerns I have about the extent to which focusing energy and resources on the right to development can assist in mobilizing resistance to the injustices of economic restructuring. One set of concerns I have relates to the conceptual framework offered by human rights as a basis for responding to globalization, and the second relates to the framework of development.

(a) The limitations of human rights

Human rights are concerned principally with constraints on the exercise of one form of power: power that operates publicly, through repressive or coercive means, largely at the level of the state. Human rights instruments are arguably less suitable to resisting other forms of power. Theorists have argued that power operates today not only or perhaps even principally through coercive mechanisms, but in other more private and personal ways. So, for example, we could see the desire that is produced in people to own commodities, or the desire to become a consumer, as an effect of power, a different productive kind of power.[204] The operation of that kind of power

whether this announcement signals a shift towards a greater respect for international obligations in areas like human rights on the part of the WTO. See 'Statement made by the Director-General on Transparency and Inter-action with Civil Society to the General Council', 15 July 1998, reprinted at <http://www.wto.org/wto/new/dgspnote.htm>.

[204] One theorist who has contributed a great deal to the articulation of this shift in understanding the operation of power is Michel Foucault. In his influential text, *The History of Sexuality Volume 1,* Foucault challenges the assumptions about the operation of power in liberal states. In that introductory volume, Foucault rethinks the relationships between power and knowledge in late capitalist societies. He argues that power operates in liberal states in ways that differ from what he terms the juridical model of power that is accepted in much political and legal theory. That juridical model presents power as a centralized commodity, operating in a top-down fashion, and as essentially repressive rather than productive. Foucault suggests that under liberalism, coercive juridical power is no longer the dominant form of power. As a result, an analysis of power 'must not assume that the sovereignty of the state, the form of the law, or the over-all unity of a domination are given at the outset; rather, these are only the terminal forms power takes'. Power does not operate from the top down, as something seized by an all-powerful sovereign and then used to oppress those with less power. Particular agents of the state or of some other powerful body do not have a monopoly on power. Rather, power exists in relations between people rather than as a commodity that can be held by an entity. That reconceptualization of power allows a shift away from the image of particular structures, institutions or entities as all-powerful. The vision of power as something held by entities like sovereign states is only the end point of the processes of exercises of power at many levels. Foucault argues that we should not mistake these 'terminal forms power takes' for the whole field of operations of power generally. The effect of focusing only on the terminal, juridical form of power is to mask the operation of power in its 'liberal' form, and thus to make that form of power all the more effective. See M. Foucault, *The History of Sexuality, Volume 1: An Introduction* (trans. R. Hurley) (1981), at 92–102.

can be seen in countries targeted for 'development' projects or for transition from communist to market economies.[205] Corporations spend a great deal of time and money ensuring that new consumers are created in such countries. Indeed, corporations may use the tools of law and economics to ensure that there is no restriction on the use of advertising to produce the desire for their products in human beings.

One example of the recognition by corporations that power operates at the personal and intimate level, as well as at the level of government, is provided by the recent 'McLibel' case.[206] That case involved a defamation action and was brought by McDonald's against activists in Britain who distributed pamphlets questioning the effect of the activities of McDonald's on the environment, labour standards, animal welfare and human health and safety. The fact that McDonald's was ready to engage in costly, time-consuming and arguably damaging litigation in order to ensure control over the message that reaches consumers about its products indicates the importance of the operation of power in the private sphere. The profits of such corporations are dependent upon successfully influencing the way in which individuals understand the world.

Similarly, tobacco manufacturers have engaged in well-planned attacks on advertising bans in developing countries, in order to ensure increased markets for tobacco.[207] The US government, for example, has acted on behalf of US manufacturers by threatening trade sanctions against states like Taiwan, Korea and Japan if markets are not opened to US tobacco products and laws restricting cigarette advertising are not lifted.[208] Such campaigns indicate the complicated ways in which power operates in the globalized economy, with the operation of power at the state and international level functioning to ensure the successful operation of power at the personal level through corporate advertising. Demand for cigarettes in China, for example, is created through the depiction of tobacco products as examples of Western sophistication and affluence, with powerful images of Western lifestyles used to create a desire for cigarettes as symbols of status and success.[209] Patricia Williams has suggested that global capitalism operates as a kind of 'seductive humiliation' in its creation of and appeal to the desires of human beings:[210]

> Western flashing of cash and its ability to generate massive realignments troubles me less as ideology than as a deep discourtesy, a seductive humiliation, which teaches that self-worth derives from appearances and material possessions.[211]

[205] Williams, 'Law and Everyday Life', in A. Sarat and T.R. Kearns (eds), *Law in Everyday Life* (1993) 171.

[206] See further Vidal, supra n. 165.

[207] Gruner, 'The Export of US Tobacco Products to Developing Countries and Previously Closed Markets', 28 *Law and Policy in International Business* (1996) 217.

[208] Ibid., at 218–19. [209] Ibid., at 229. [210] Williams, supra n. 205, at 190.

[211] Ibid.

The operations of development agencies and international economic institutions also operate in part at that private and intimate level, converting 'ordinary lives into a set of problems to be solved'.[212] Aid agencies and the World Bank reinterpret the most intimate aspects of the lives of human beings as development issues, with aid recipients told that their lives and ways of being act as problems for development or barriers to their salvation.[213]

Human rights instruments and institutions are not designed or equipped to subvert the operation of that form of power. The right to development does not provide a language or a structure for responding to the ways in which human beings are persuaded to desire the products of power. Nevertheless, human rights mechanisms can respond to the more coercive aspects of the operation of the free market, by pointing to the ways in which sales of tobacco are a human rights issue as well as a trade issue, for example, or challenging the denial of freedom of speech in the interests of protecting the corporate profits of McDonald's. Rights must, however, be seen as only one means for resisting power. The areas of action that rights can address are only one site of political activity or the operation of power. We are left then with a rather chastened form of rights discourse. Rights offer one potential form of legal resistance to the power of states and potentially of international institutions, but only one form of resistance and to only one kind of institutionalized and visible form of power.

Rethinking the operation of power in this area complicates arguments about the use of rights to resist globalization in another way. Human rights law depends upon particular actors, traditionally states, being vested with human rights obligations and required to promote and protect human rights. Yet economic restructuring is a process conducted at many different levels and by the actions of many different actors—some characterized as national, some international, some public and some private. In order for human rights to offer any response to the process of economic restructuring, a more flexible approach to considering which actors are exercising power and potentially violating human rights is necessary. The right to development does appear to allow an approach to economic restructuring that does not involve preconceptions as to which actors are exercising power. Instead, the right to development as currently formulated allows a more flexible spirit of inquiry, one which is extremely useful in making sense of and resisting globalization.

One further issue arises with respect to the use of the human rights framework to contest economic globalization. Critics from Karl Marx onwards have argued that the language and concept of rights provides no purchase for resisting the excesses of capitalism.[214] The essence of that argument is that human rights discourse takes as its subject a particular conception of what it is to be

[212] Stamp, 'Foucault and the New Imperial Order', 3 *Arena Journal* (1994) 11, at 19, 20.

[213] Ibid., at 18, 20. See also Uvin, supra n. 107.

[214] See Marx, 'On the Jewish Question', in J. Waldron (ed.), *Nonsense Upon Stilts: Bentham, Burke and Marx on the Rights of Man* (1987) 137.

a human being—that is, property-owning, self-sufficient, atomistic, competitive and individualistic. The capacity of civil and political rights to represent broader needs is limited by a history of being granted only to property-owners. As a result, rights discourse does not readily allow for the recognition of the need for 'collective control over common resources and a common heritage'.[215] The language of civil and political rights provides limited tools for attempting to 'change the terms of the discourse from that of private rights vested in individuals, to public rights over common resources, vested in communities, and from individual ownership to collective control'.[216] Thus rights discourse may not be capable of contributing to the political practice of marginalizing the Western economy, precisely because it is central to constituting the subject of that economy.[217]

As the criticisms made by Donnelly illustrate, however, the right to development does potentially operate outside the purely individualistic framework developed in relation to the civil and political rights that were the subject of critique by Marx. The right to development focuses on the economic sphere, and on responsibility for developing an appropriate social, political and economic order for a version of development that does not simply maintain exploitation. It is arguably not only limited to the public realm of liberal individuals, and does address the material and private conditions of people's lives. Thus the less atomistic approach offered by the right to development may offer a useful counterweight to the excessive individualism of some more traditional approaches to human rights.

(b) Development as an alibi for exploitation

The second and more serious set of concerns I have relates to the broader development discourse upon which any notion of a right to development must draw. As Arturo Escobar has shown, the basic premise upon which developmentalism is based is that all states should aim to develop or progress

[215] Jaising and Sathyamala, supra n. 176, at 96. [216] Ibid.

[217] For feminist critiques which argue that human rights law misrepresents the operation of power in ways that reinscribe and celebrate a particular version of 'humanity' as the subject of rights, see Orford, supra n. 44; Davies, 'The Heterosexual Economy', 5 *Australian Feminist Law Journal* (1995) 27. Commentators have responded to that critique in a number of ways. Jeremy Waldron, for example, argues that the broader international human rights regime developed under the UN does not suffer from the same limitations as those revolutionary Declarations of Rights criticized by Marx and others. For example, as a result of economic crises of the 1930s and the influence of the Socialist bloc, many states and peoples supported the inclusion of rights to economic and social security in the international covenants, on the basis that 'the structure of the economy and the fundamental distribution of wealth and power over the means of production could not be exempted from the sort of urgent moral scrutiny associated with a commitment to human rights'. See Waldron, 'Nonsense upon Stilts?—a reply' in Waldron, supra n. 214, 151, at 158.

to the standard set by developed or industrialized states.[218] Development theory assumes that the central goal of states should be to develop from a state of poverty or underdevelopment to an advanced state of prosperity and industrialization. That idea was used to justify and humanize the processes of intervention conducted by international institutions, beginning in the era of decolonization.[219] Escobar argues that after the Second World War, the 'perception of poverty on a global scale' was produced in the developed world for the first time through the use of statistical surveys of populations in decolonized countries.[220] People living in industrialized states were able to imagine whole populations as lacking the wealth and material goods that they possessed. The shift that made it possible to imagine two-thirds of the world's peoples as poor subjects had other effects. It made it possible to believe, for example, that if 'the essential trait of the Third World was its poverty . . . the solution was economic growth and development'.[221] Through such practices of representation, the 'Third World' was progressively inserted 'into a regime of thought and practice in which certain interventions for the eradication of poverty became central to the world order'.[222] Escobar's argument is that the intervention that occurred in the name of development was itself a form of exploitation, but that the idea of development served to make such exploitation palatable to those who profited from such intervention.[223] Development functioned largely to provide an 'alibi for exploitation'.[224]

One response to the use of development as an alibi for exploitation is that many popular or grassroots organizations and social movements in Africa, Asia and Latin America are now focusing on resisting development and refusing altogether the language of development and the framework within which developmentalism is practised.[225] Activists are engaged in developing alternatives to development, rejecting its paradigm and language. Scholars engaged on such projects write of working '[b]eyond, in spite of, against development'.[226] They attempt to 'imagine alternatives to development and

[218] See generally A. Escobar, *Encountering Development: The Making and Unmaking of the Third World* (1995).

[219] See the argument in Orford and Beard, supra n. 120, at 201.

[220] Escobar, supra n. 218, at 24. [221] Ibid. [222] Ibid.

[223] Much profit has been made from such intervention, for as Susan George, Bruce Rich and other critics of development have famously shown, the net result of the narrow economic model of development imposed by international economic institutions over the past fifty years has been an increased net capital flow from developing states to those states whose governments or bankers act as developers or lenders. See Stamp, supra n. 212, at 14; S. George, *The Debt Boomerang: How Third World Debt Harms Us All* (1992) xiv–xvi; Rich, supra n. 100, at 109, 110, 175, 309.

[224] See Spivak and Plotke, 'A Dialogue on Democracy' in D. Trend (ed.), *Radical Democracy: Identity, Citizenship, and the State* (1996) 209, at 212.

[225] Escobar, supra n. 218, at 215. [226] Ibid.

to "marginalize the economy"—[a] metaphor that speaks of strategies to contain the Western economy as a system of production, power, and signification'.[227]

The strategic utility of the right to development is questionable on two grounds in light of the directions taken by Third World activism. First, the right to development has itself been criticized for enshrining the notion of development that has been so thoroughly critiqued and contested. If it is only possible, or if it is too easy, to understand development in narrow economic terms, it may be of no use to speak of a right to 'development'. Secondly, not only does advocating a right to development appear to go against the grain of much Third World activism today, but using the language of development risks legitimizing the very agendas and programmes that the right is aimed at subverting. In other words, talking about a right to development may act to prop up the whole edifice of developmentalism as practised by the World Bank and other international economic institutions. As Michel Foucault notes, 'to speak is to do something—something other than to express what one thinks; . . . to add a statement to a pre-existing series of statements is to perform a complicated and costly gesture'.[228] The issue that arises for human rights lawyers is whether the act of making a statement about the right to development is 'to perform a complicated and costly gesture'—by appearing to offer resistance without in fact transforming the discourse as a whole.[229]

Thus I am left with a sense of caution or concern. The right to development does provide a means of engaging with the economic framework that I have argued is dominating the new world order. Yet by adopting the language of development, human rights lawyers and activists risk reproducing the legitimacy of developmentalism as a set of institutional practices, a framework for understanding the world and as an alibi for exploitation.

(c) The utility of the right to development

In such a context, what does it mean for human rights activists to continue to insist on speaking about a right to development? Does it have any utility in such an environment? Can the right to development provide a language or mechanism for challenging the activities of international economic institutions?

The notion of a right to development does retain some utility in the realm of inspiration. Its most important use is that it engages directly with the language and concerns of neoclassical economics, while attempting to renegotiate the meaning of that language and those concerns. Many areas of progressive activity at the international level fail to engage adequately, or at all, with economic globalization and its effects.[230] The strength of a notion like

[227] Escobar, supra n. 218, at 216.
[228] M. Foucault, *The Archaeology of Knowledge* (1972) 209.
[229] Escobar, supra n. 218, at 216.
[230] Orford, supra n. 107; Alston, supra n. 71.

the right to development is that it is directly engaged with such ideas, and requires human rights lawyers in particular to engage closely with the whole business of development as carried on by international institutions. As my overview here has shown, the agenda of international economic institutions is widespread, complicated and has far-reaching implications. The notion of a right to development is one site of international resistance to that agenda.[231]

The right to development focuses on the international implications of a national commitment to human rights.[232] That focus makes it more difficult for states to separate their human rights commitments from foreign policy decisions and from activities as members of international organizations. The right to development operates at that level particularly when it comes to challenging or scrutinizing the activities of international economic institutions. International lawyers are at a stage where it is still radical to focus on the activities of international institutions as potential violators of human rights. As I have argued elsewhere, there is a tendency to treat internationalism as the realm of only progressive values and institutions.[233] Despite the growth in the power and efficacy of multilateral institutions in the post-Soviet era, commentators continue to treat such actors as essentially benevolent, able to bring peace, security, development, human rights and democracy to the world. As Ruth Wedgwood argues:

> (I)n international law circles, an enthusiasm for multilateralism sometimes brings a suspension of judgment. Even international lawyers who admit the deep interweaving of law and morality, drift towards a 'multilateral positivism'—the presumption that if a decision is reached multilaterally, it can't be wrong . . . The ordinary inquiry appropriate to the intervention of one country into another country's affairs, a scepticism or burden of persuasion for unilateral intervention, turns into credulity if the action is multilateral.[234]

Thus the language of rights may be useful in contributing to an awareness, particularly in industrialized states, that it is both possible and desirable to resist economic globalization, particularly, but not only, where it is carried out under the auspices of the international economic institutions. The language of rights helps to make clear that such institutions are capable of human rights violations and also capable of being constrained just as states are.

A rights-based commitment to participation in the development process could be used to inspire an increased scrutiny into how it is that technoscience and economics have become privileged forms of knowledge. I have pointed to

[231] Another powerful site of resistance is international environmental law and politics. It may be that those areas of international activity provide a more far-reaching and useful method for contesting economic intervention.

[232] Alston, 'Garfield the Cat', supra n. 14, at 516.

[233] Orford, supra n. 107.

[234] Wedgwood, 'The Evolution of United Nations Peacekeeping', 28 *Cornell International Law Journal* (1995) 631.

some of the subtle ways in which the institutionalization of expert knowledge operates as a means of limiting the capacity of communities to participate in decision-making. That is true both of economic expertise, as evidenced by the fetishization of such expertise in World Bank documents, and of scientific expertise in the case of agreements like the SPS Agreement. As Ashis Nandy argues:

> [B]efore envisioning the global civilization of the future, one must first own up to the responsibility of creating a space at the margins of the present global civilization for a new, plural, political ecology of knowledge.[235]

The right to development, with its focus on participation in decision-making about development, can play a role in the move towards creating such a plural, political ecology of knowledge, where different forms of knowledge are negotiated on the basis of equality.

An approach to the right to development that acknowledges the multiple sites of resistance to economic globalization may also allow scholars and activists to move away from the state-sponsored North/South polarization over which level of governance is responsible for human rights violations. The strength and the weakness of the current formulation of the right to development is that it allows for recognition of the many ways in which states and human beings may operate to violate human rights. Rather than using that recognition of different forms of agency as an excuse for avoiding responsibility for human rights violations, NGOs and scholars working in the area can attempt to ensure that no level of governance or actor is able to avoid acknowledging their role in contributing to such violations.

While the right to development may have the potential to be used in ways that could begin to address the effects of economic restructuring, lawyers seeking to make use of it must reckon with the way in which it serves a multitude of political ends. The polarization of the right to development along a North/South axis serves many interests. For example, repressive governments can make use of the right to development as an excuse for violating other human rights of their populations. Powerful industrialized states benefit from refusing to develop the alternative accounts of the right to development clearly included in the Declaration. By seeking only to denounce and delegitimize that right, those states are not required to take responsibility for the obligations that it places upon them, and leave the field open to repressive governments to develop a dangerous jurisprudence on the right to development. Both sets of interests serve to hurt the people who suffer as a result of a commitment to economic globalization that ignores human rights.

[235] Nandy, 'Shamans, Savages, and the Wilderness: On the Audibility of Dissent and the Future of Civilizations', 14 *Alternatives* (1989) 263, at 266.

The choice between national and international versions of capitalism, between repressive national governments or exploitative international institutions, is no choice. At this moment, in many parts of the world, both levels of governance are equally repressive, equally destructive, equally violent. The right to development has become a mantra for those states seeking to justify the use of repressive domestic policies in order to enhance the wealth and prestige of their leaders, while the opposition to the right to development serves equally as a means of justifying the use of international economic institutions to facilitate a process of globalization that enhances the wealth and prestige of the elites and leaders of both industrialized and target states. The only way in which NGOs and scholars seeking to work in this field can avoid that politicized and self-serving polarization is to refuse to be drawn into the game of demonizing one level of governance while celebrating another.

Finally, Mohammed Bedjaoui argues that the notion of having a right to, rather than a need for, development takes the notion of development out of the realm of charity, and into the realm of obligations:

> [T]he State seeking its own development is entitled to demand that all the other states, the international community and international economic agents collectively *do not take away from it what belongs to it, or do not deprive it of what is or 'must be' its due in international trade* . . . The claim of such a State goes something like this: 'Before giving me charity or offering me your aid, give me my due. Perhaps I shall then have no need of your aid. Perhaps charity is no more than the screen behind which you expropriate what is due to me. Such charity does not deserve to be so called; it is my own property you are handing back to me in this way and, what is more, not all of it.'[236]

Solidarity on the part of people in industrialized states involves the recognition that human rights violations in states targeted by economic restructuring are the condition of prosperous and consumer lifestyles. Perhaps the most important task facing human rights lawyers in industrialized states in this century will be moving away from the triumphalist liberalism that is creeping into post-Cold War international law literature, and towards a commitment to working in solidarity with activists in other parts of the world to challenge exploitation and inequality.

V CONCLUSION

As an ever-increasing number of people around the world are subjected to decisions made by the IMF, the World Bank and the WTO at the international level, and to support for such decisions by oppressive governments at the national level, the need for a means of contesting the commitment to

[236] Bedjaoui, supra n. 34, at 1191–2.

economic globalization becomes urgent. There is a growing awareness of the need to develop multilateral mechanisms capable of controlling the destructive impact of economic restructuring. A focus on the right to development may assist in helping people to realize that globalization is a political, public and contestable process, rather than an unstoppable force that will inevitably overtake all states. International human rights lawyers will need to harness creatively both the inspirational and the legalistic aspects of the right to development if they are successfully to use that right to effect change in the current agendas of states, international economic institutions and foreign investors.

6

Environmental Rights

DINAH SHELTON

International law for the promotion and protection of human rights and international environmental law reflect two of the fundamental values and aims of modern international society. The primary objective of human rights law is to secure the self-actualization of every person, to protect each individual from abuse of power by state agents and to assure that basic needs can be met. States must also exercise due diligence to ensure that human rights are not violated by non-state actors. Environmental law, in turn, seeks to protect and preserve the basic living and non-living resources and ecological processes on which all life depends. It can thus be seen as an inherent part of the human rights agenda or as a broader and sometimes competing goal. In either case, unlike human rights law, international environmental law is primarily concerned with controlling the activities of non-state actors who are the predominant cause of environmental harm.

The development of human rights law in the aftermath of the Second World War[1] preceded the emergence of international environmental law by some two decades. In the 1960s,[2] public opinion first manifested concern with the environment, stemming in large part from scientific findings regarding the harmful consequences of widespread pesticide use, and from reaction to large and destructive oil tanker accidents.[3] Considerable apprehension was also expressed about potential damage to the environment from nuclear radiation and industrial pollutants.

[1] As is well-known, specific human rights issues, e.g. abolition of slavery and the protection of religious minorities were addressed far earlier. See L. Sohn and T. Buergenthal, *International Protection of Human Rights* (1968) 1–337.

[2] Earlier agreements concerning specific natural resources were primarily concerned with economic exploitation rather than conservation or protection. See e.g. the 1902 Convention for the Protection of Birds Useful to Agriculture. A few texts before the Second World War attempted to combat pollution of specific rivers and lakes and in the 1950s limited efforts were made to combat marine pollution.

[3] The publication of Rachel Carson's *The Silent Spring* (1962) is largely credited with first bringing environmental concerns to public consciousness. The *Torry Canyon* oil pollution disaster in 1967 was a major event inciting public action against environmental degradation. See A. Kiss and D. Shelton, *International Environmental Law* (2nd edn. 2000), at 438–9.

While each area of law has developed rapidly and in large part independently of the other, the earlier evolution of human rights law has influenced and sometimes inspired innovations in international environmental law. In addition, the emergence of concern for the environment has stimulated interest in exploring the relationship between human rights and environmental protection. As recognition of an interdependence has increased, the two fields have experienced a degree of convergence. Differences in goals and priorities have also become apparent, however, demonstrating the difficulty of merging or fully integrating either subject into the other.

When environmental protection became a major international issue, there was little international law on the topic. At the time of the 1972 Stockholm Conference,[4] whose full title made clear that it was devoted to the 'human environment', human rights law furnished an existing means to address issues of environmental harm, despite of the absence of reference to the environment in earlier-drafted human rights texts.[5] Significantly, preparations for the Stockholm Conference coincided with the convening of the 1968 Teheran Conference on Human Rights, which was the first international human rights conference organized by the United Nations and marked the twentieth anniversary of the adoption of the Universal Declaration of Human Rights. The Teheran Conference, overcoming the long-standing political debate that led to the adoption of two human rights covenants rather than a single instrument, proclaimed that all human rights are interdependent and indivisible,[6] opening the door for consideration of complex issues such as the right to development and environmental rights.

Human rights as an approach to environmental protection also served to induce developing countries to participate in the environmental movement. Up to and including the Stockholm Conference, many economically less-developed states viewed environmental degradation as a problem of rich, industrialized countries.[7] They were, however, vitally concerned with human rights, particularly in the context of self-determination and economic development. The Teheran Conference, which proclaimed the interdependence of peace, development and human rights stimulated interest in the Stockholm Conference among poorer countries concerned with resource depletion and its impact on development.

Today, it is accepted that on the one hand 'adequate protection of the environment is essential to human well-being and the enjoyment of basic human

[4] See, *Report of the United Nations Conference on the Human Environment*, Stockholm 5–16 June 1972, UN Doc. A/CONF.48/14/Rev. 1.

[5] See Part III below.

[6] *Final Act of the International Conference on Human Rights*, UN Doc.A/CONF.32–41; UN Pub. E.68.XIV.2. The United Nations proclaimed 1968 as International Human Rights Year.

[7] Kiss and Shelton, supra n. 3, at 624.

rights, including the right to life itself',[8] and, on the other hand, that the fulfilment of human rights, especially the right to information and procedural guarantees of participation and access to remedies, is crucial to preventing environmental harm. Legal instruments of international environmental law increasingly refer to such rights. In turn, human rights bodies have studied the links between the two subjects and human rights organs with the requisite jurisdiction have considered petitions alleging human rights violations related to environmental harm.

Human rights law and environmental protection interrelate at present in four different ways. First, those primarily interested in the environment utilize or emphasize relevant human rights guarantees in drafting international environmental instruments. They select from among the catalogue of human rights those rights that can serve the aims of environmental protection, independent of the utility of such protection for the enjoyment of other human rights. Recognizing the broad goals of environmental protection, the emphasis is placed on rights such as freedom of association for members of non-governmental environmental organizations and the right to information about potential threats to the environment, which may be used for nature protection not necessarily related to human health and well-being. The weakness of compliance mechanisms in nearly all international environmental agreements raises questions about the short-term effectiveness of this method in achieving the goals of environmental protection, at least when compared with recourse to the more developed human rights supervisory machinery.

A second approach invokes existing human rights law and institutions, recasting or applying human rights guarantees when their enjoyment is threatened by environmental harm. This method is unreservedly anthropocentric. It seeks to ensure that the environment does not deteriorate to the point where the human right to life, the right to health, the right to a family and private life, the right to culture, the right to safe drinking water, or other human rights are seriously impaired. Environmental protection is thus instrumental, not an end in itself. As Judge Weeramantry of the International Court of Justice asserts:

> The protection of the environment is . . . a vital part of contemporary human rights doctrine, for it is a *sine qua non* for numerous human rights such as the right to health and the right to life itself. It is scarcely necessary to elaborate on this, as damage to the environment can impair and undermine all the human rights spoken of in the Universal Declaration and other human rights instruments.[9]

[8] UN/ECE, Convention on Access to Information, Public Participation in Decision-Making and Access to Justice in Environmental Matters (Aarhus, 25 June 1998), Preamble.

[9] *Gabcikovo-Nagymaros Case (Hungary-Slovakia),* ICJ, Judgment of 25 September 1997 (Separate Opinion of Judge Weeramantry), at 4.

With a focus on the consequences of environmental harm to existing human rights, this approach can serve to address most serious cases of actual or imminently-threatened pollution. The primary advantage it offers, compared to pursuing the environmental route, is that existing human rights complaint machinery may be invoked against those states whose level of environmental protection falls below that necessary to maintain any of the guaranteed human rights. From the perspective of environmental protection, however, this human rights approach is deficient because it generally does not address threats to non-human species or to ecological processes.[10] Alan Boyle does not find the limited focus a deficiency:

> [t]he virtue of looking at environmental protection through other human rights, such as life or property, is that it focuses attention on what matters most: the detriment to important, internationally protected values from uncontrolled environmental harm. This is an approach which avoids the need to define such notions as a satisfactory or decent environment, falls well within the competence of existing human rights bodies, and involves little or no potential for conflict with environmental institutions.[11]

The third approach aims to incorporate the environmental agenda fully into human rights by formulating a new human right to an environment that is not defined in purely anthropocentric terms, an environment that is not only safe for humans, but one that is ecologically-balanced and sustainable in the long term. Various international efforts have been undertaken in this direction, as discussed below, and some have proved successful. Nonetheless, despite the inclusion of ecological concerns in various formulations of the right, strict environmentalists continue to object to the anthropocentrism inherent in taking a human rights approach to environmental protection.[12] In addition, the notion of a right to environment has met resistance from others who claim that the concept cannot be given content, who assert that the inherent variability of environmental conditions and qualities means no justiciable standards can be developed.[13]

Finally, a fourth approach questions claims of rights in regard to environmental protection, preferring to address the issue as a matter of human

[10] See e.g. K. Bosselmann, *When Worlds Collide: Society and Ecology* (1995) for a critique of anthropocentrism.

[11] Boyle, 'The Role of International Human Rights Law in the Protection of the Environment', in A. Boyle and M. Anderson (eds), *Human Rights Approaches to Environmental Protection* (1996) 43.

[12] Bosselmann, supra n. 10; see also Redgwell, 'Life, the Universe, and Everything: A Critique of Anthropocentric Rights', in Boyle and Anderson, supra n. 11, at 71.

[13] See Handl, 'Human Rights and Protection of the Environment: A Mildly "Revisionist" View', in A. Cançado-Trindade (ed.), *Human Rights, Sustainable Development and the Environment* (1992) 117, at 120–2; Boyle, supra n. 11.

responsibilities. Several projects to draft declarations of human responsibilities are underway, and most have a strong environmental focus.[14] Even some human rights texts that proclaim environmental rights balance these with a statement of human duties.[15] Following a discussion of the theoretical issues raised by linking human rights and environmental protection, each of the four approaches will be discussed, with a review of relevant texts and jurisprudence. The related topics of the rights of local communities, including indigenous peoples and farmers, and environmental rights in international humanitarian law complete the chapter.

I HUMAN RIGHTS AND ENVIRONMENTAL PROTECTION IN THEORY

The interrelationship of human rights and environmental protection is undeniable. First, the enjoyment of internationally recognized human rights depends upon environmental protection. Without diverse and sustained living and non-living resources, human beings cannot survive. The problem can be demonstrated by the example of freshwater. Only 2 per cent of the water of the earth is accessible for human use. Any loss of water resources, especially pollution of underground aquifers, poses dangers for generations to come. According to the UN Water Council between 5 million and 10 million people die each year as a result of polluted drinking water, most of them women and children in poverty.[16] Severe water shortages exist in 26 countries and by 2050, two-thirds of the world's population could face water shortages. Sixty per cent of the world's drinking water is located in just 10 countries and much of it is polluted. Freshwater shortages are already raising tensions and threaten to be a cause of future interstate conflicts. Air pollution, contaminated soil and loss of food sources[17] add to the problems of health and survival. Maintenance of the earth's cultural diversity, in particular the preservation of

[14] A group of former heads of state, joined in the InterAction Council, proposed such a text, for adoption on the 50th Anniversary of the adoption of the Universal Declaration of Human Rights. The responsibilities it discusses are little more than an extension of human rights obligations to individuals and other non-state actors.

[15] See Draft Declaration on Human Rights and the Environment, E/CN.4/1994/Sub.2/9 (Annex).

[16] UN, Report of the United Nations Water Council (1998). The WHO estimates at least 5,000,000 deaths a year. Comparative Assessment of the Freshwater Resources of the World, Report of the Secretary-General, E/CN.17/1997/9 (1997) 21. At any given time, an estimated one-half of the people in developing countries suffer from water-borne and food-related diseases caused either directly by infection, or indirectly by disease-carrying organisms that breed in water and food: ibid., at para. 5.

[17] Virtually all the world's fish stocks are declining. See FAO, *The State of the World's Fisheries and Aquaculture* (1998) 8.

indigenous peoples and local communities, requires conserving the areas in which they live.

In turn, environmental protection is enhanced by the exercise of certain human rights, such as the right to information and the right to political participation. Unlike the field of human rights, where most violations are committed by state agents, environmental harm largely stems from actions of the private sector. Effective compliance necessitates knowledge of environmental conditions and norms. In addition, local communities play a vital role in preserving the resources upon which they depend. Allowing those potentially affected to participate in decision-making processes concerning harmful activities may prevent or mitigate the threatened harm and contribute to public support for environmental action, as well as lead to better decisions. In the event the activity goes forward and harm is suffered, remedies can provide for restoration or remediation of the damaged environment.

Despite a common core of interest, the two topics remain distinct. Environmental protection cannot be wholly incorporated into the human rights agenda without deforming the concept of human rights and distorting its programme. Ecologists are concerned with the preservation of biological diversity, including species not useful or even harmful to humans, as well as with ecological processes whose full significance may not be fully known or understood. The central concern is the protection of nature because of its intrinsic value, not because its protection will provide immediate benefits to humans.[18]

Further, not all human rights are immediately relevant to environmental protection, e.g. the right to a name and the right to marry are not crucial to achieving the environmental agenda. From the human rights perspective, neither does it appear that the enjoyment of these rights is negatively affected by environmental harm.

The view that mankind is part of a global ecosystem may reconcile the aims of human rights and environmental protection, because both ultimately seek to achieve the highest quality of sustainable life for humanity within existing natural conditions.[19] Potentially conflicting differences of emphasis still exist, however, because the essential concern of human rights law is to protect individuals and groups alive today within a given society, an aim that might be referred to as intragenerational equity. Environmental law adds to the goal of human rights the additional purpose of sustaining life globally by balancing the needs and capacities of present generations of all species with those of the future; it is thus also concerned with intergenerational equity and interspecies equity. Together, the three aims can be seen to comprise the concept

[18] The 1982 World Charter for Nature proclaims that 'every form of life is unique and merits respect regardless of its worth to man'.

[19] See Shelton, 'Human Rights, Environmental Rights, and the Right to Environment', 28 *Stanford Journal of International Law* (1991) 103.

of environmental justice. Clearly, the broad protection of nature at times may conflict with preservation of individual rights, such as the right to property. It is not surprising, then, that international environmental law and international human rights law have at times placed emphasis on different components of environmental protection and human rights.

The proposal to guarantee a right internationally to an environment of a specified quality raises additional considerations. Some argue that it is unlikely that environmental protection will be accepted as a human right and efforts in this direction divert attention from other more worthy causes.[20] Yet, laws often respond to perceived social problems by restraining the exercise of power and establishing agreed norms of public conduct. Viewed from this perspective, laws protecting human rights respond to threats to human dignity and existence by upholding the immutable foundations of human rights as recognized in international instruments. Formulations of rights reflect emerging social values. Thus, as environmental protection comes to be perceived as fundamental to human dignity and well-being, it moves towards the requisite acceptance. The growing awareness of the breadth and depth of the environmental crisis can be seen in increasing recourse to rights language.

An immediate, practical objective of international human rights law is to gain international recognition of specific human rights. Successfully placing personal entitlements within the category of human rights preserves them from the ordinary political process. Rights may thus significantly limit the political will of a democratic majority, as well as a dictatorial minority. The limitation on domestic political decisions is an important consequence of elaborating a right. In the environmental field, the high short-term costs involved in many environmental protection measures often make environmental decisions unpopular with economically affected communities. The recognition that environmental protection is a core value and right can be particularly valuable in countering this disapproval and ensuring that the long-term needs of humanity are not sacrificed to short-term interests.

In legal doctrine, the issue of a right to an environment of a certain quality is complicated by both temporal and geographic elements absent from other human rights protections. While most human rights violations affect only specific and identifiable victims in the present, environmental degradation harms not only those currently living, but future generations of humanity as well. The harm can take various forms. First, an extinct species and whatever benefits it would have brought to the global ecosystem are lost forever. Secondly, economic, social, and cultural rights cannot be enjoyed in a world where resources are inadequate due to the waste of prior generations. Thirdly, the very survival of future generations may be jeopardized by sufficiently

[20] Handl, supra n. 13, at 142.

serious environmental problems. A right to environment thus implies significant, constant duties toward persons not yet born.

The other unusual aspect of a right to environment is the potentially vast expansion of the territorial scope of state obligations. Present human rights instruments generally require each state to respect and ensure guaranteed rights 'to all individuals within its territory and subject to its jurisdiction'.[21] This geographic limitation reflects the reality that a state normally will have the power to protect or the possibility to violate human rights only of those within its territory and jurisdiction. However, nature recognizes no political boundaries. A state polluting its coastal waters or atmosphere may cause significant harm to individuals thousands of miles away. States that permit or encourage depletion of the tropical rain forest can contribute to global warming which threatens to disrupt the world's climate.

Ultimately, the definition of a right to environment must refer to substantive environmental standards that quantitatively regulate harmful air pollution and other types of emissions. Some see this as undermining any claim that environmental protection can be considered a human right. In their view, it cannot be considered inalienable, defined as the impermissibility of derogations, because the constant reordering of socio-economic priorities involved in setting environmental policies precludes its having a fixed character.[22] However, this same evolution and reordering of priorities and values is seen in respect to other internationally recognized human rights: education, equality and non-discrimination—especially in regard to what constitutes impermissible distinctions and therefore who benefits from the right—and in defining what constitutes cruel, inhuman or degrading treatment or punishment. Few if any rights are absolute or fixed in content and most are subject to limitations and even suspensions or derogations. Recognizing a particular interest or claim as a human right is one means of establishing an order or priority, in setting the right above other competing interests and claims not deemed rights.

To say that environmental entitlements have been and will continue to be susceptible to restrictions for the sake of other, socio-economic objectives, such as ensuring continued 'development' or 'saving jobs' is to establish the conclusion as a criterion. If there is no right to a safe and healthy environment, environmental considerations will be balanced against other social interests on an equal basis. Alternatively, if there is both a right to development and a right to environment, the same balancing of juridically equal interests is required. Only if one of the interests is designated a right does it

[21] International Covenant on Civil and Political Rights, Art. 2, GA Res. 2200A (XXI) Annex, UN Doc. A/6316 (1966), 999 UNTS 171, reprinted in 6 *ILM* (1967) 368.

[22] Handl, supra n. 13, at 129–32.

have what Dworkin refers to as a 'trumping' effect requiring that the balance be presumptively resolved in its favour.[23]

Although establishing emission or quality standards requires extensive international regulation of environmental sectors based upon impact studies, such regulation is by no means impossible. Adoption of quality standards demands extensive research and debate involving public participation, but substantive minima are a necessary complement to the procedural rights leading to informed consent. Otherwise, a human rights approach to environmental protection would be ineffective in preventing serious environmental harm.

Establishing the content of a right through reference to independent and variable standards is often used in human rights, especially with regard to economic entitlements, and need not be a barrier to recognition of the right to a specific environmental quality. Rights to an adequate standard of living and working conditions and to social security are sometimes further defined in international accords such as the European Social Charter or Conventions and Recommendations of the International Labour Organization. States implement these often flexible obligations according to changing economic indicators, needs and resources. The 'framework' of the human rights treaty contains the basic guarantee to be supplemented by further international, national and local regulations, laws and policies.

A similar approach could be utilized to give meaning to a right to environment. Both the threats to humanity and the resulting necessary measures are subject to constant change based on advances in scientific knowledge and conditions of the environment. Thus, it is impossible for a human rights instrument to specify precisely what measures should be taken, i.e. the products that should not be manufactured or the precise balance of land uses. These technical details can be negotiated and regulated through international environmental norms and standards, where the necessary measures to implement the right to environment can be determined by reference to independent environmental findings and regulations capable of rapid amendment. The variability of implementing demands imposed by the right to environment in response to different threats over time and place does not undermine the concept of the right, but merely takes into consideration its dynamic character.

Finally, it is claimed that there are political risks to recognizing a right to environment because different conditions require different solutions and it 'might turn into an extremely effective legal platform for internationalizing

[23] R. Dworkin, *Taking Rights Seriously* (1977). For an indication of the trumping value of property rights over environmental protection see *Lucas v South Carolina Coastal Council*, 60 *United States Law Week* (1992) 4842. Of course, rights may be restricted or overridden for a 'compelling state interest' or through definitional exceptions; e.g. the right to be free from slavery does not exempt individuals from compulsory public service during periods of natural disaster.

national decision-making in areas that represent the core of traditional state sovereignty'.[24] This is true, but all international human rights law involves an invasion of 'the core' of traditional state sovereignty. The law exists precisely for that reason and reflects the fact that the content of the reserved domain of states is constantly evolving. The sovereignty or domestic jurisdiction objection was raised by Mexico when the Inter-American Human Rights Commission considered a complaint regarding alleged election fraud; by the former Soviet Union when the United Nations began to discuss its failure to permit the emigration of Soviet Jews; by South Africa in response to criticisms of apartheid. States have always been reluctant to adopt and implement international human rights norms. They have done so in response to public pressure, especially from non-governmental organizations, which became convinced that decisions about how governments treat human beings should not be exempt from international scrutiny and accountability.

II INTERNATIONAL ENVIRONMENTAL LAW AND HUMAN RIGHTS

In the relatively short history of international environmental law, its lawyers and activists have sought to use human rights discourse to express the importance of the issues at stake. International texts have included references to environmental rights such as freedom of association, the right of access to information, the right to public participation, and due process rights. More rarely, they have proclaimed a right to an environment of a certain quality.

In the preparations for the 1972 Stockholm Conference on the Human Environment, emerging environmental awareness led the United Nations to consider the interdependence of environmental protection and human rights. Several proposals were made to cast environmental protection in human rights terms. At Stockholm, the United States supported adoption of the following language:

> Every human being has a right to a healthful and safe environment, including air, water and earth, and to food and other material necessities, all of which should be sufficiently free of contamination and other elements which detract from the health or well-being of man.

Although the proposal was supported by non-governmental organizations, conference participants did not accept it. Instead, in the Stockholm Declaration they proclaimed the oft-quoted Principle 1:

[24] Handl, supra n. 13, at 130.

Man has the fundamental right to freedom, equality and adequate conditions of life, in an environment of a quality that permits a life of dignity and well-being, and he bears a solemn responsibility to protect and improve the environment for present and future generations.[25]

In addition, Principle 2 declared protection of the human environment a precondition for the well-being of peoples.

The Stockholm Declaration stops short of proclaiming a right to environment, but it clearly links human rights and environmental protection, with the latter viewed as instrumental to achievement of the former. Thus, the Declaration sees human rights as fundamental and environmental protection as an essential means or precondition to achieving the 'adequate conditions' for a 'life of dignity and well-being' that are guaranteed.

Ten years after Stockholm, in 1982, the United Nations General Assembly proclaimed the World Charter for Nature, the first general environmental instrument adopted after the Stockholm Declaration. The Charter makes no reference to human rights; instead it gives both a rationale and an ethical foundation for environmental protection that attempts to merge concern for human well-being with recognition of the intrinsic value of nature. Its preamble recognizes that 'Mankind is a part of nature and life depends on the uninterrupted functioning of natural systems which ensure the supply of energy and nutrients' while also expressing its conviction that 'every form of life is unique, warranting respect regardless of its worth to man, and, to accord other organisms such recognition, man must be guided by a moral code of action'. The Charter is described as a set of 'principles of conservation by which all human conduct affecting nature is to be guided and judged'. The principles require that nature be respected and its essential processes not be impaired.

Subsequently, the World Commission on Environment and Development (Brundtland Commission) issued its report. The Commission's Expert Legal Group proposed as its first legal principle that '[a]ll human beings have the fundamental right to an environment adequate for their health and well-being'.[26] The Brundtland Report led the United Nations to convene a second world environmental conference, to focus on environment and development. The World Charter for Nature provided the international code of conduct leading into this meeting, the United Nations Conference on Environment and Development (UNCED) (Rio de Janeiro, 1992).

[25] Declaration of the United Nations Conference on the Human Environment, UN Doc. A/CONF.48/14/Rev.1, UN Pub. E.73.II.A.14, reprinted in 12 *ILM* (1972) 849.

[26] Expert Group on Environmental Law of the World Commission on Environment and Development, Environmental Protection and Sustainable Development: Legal Principles and Recommendations, 25; UNGA Res. 42/187, 11 December 1987, A/42/427 and Annex of Legal Principles.

UNCED adopted five instruments, which contain only isolated references to human rights.[27] The term 'human rights' is used only three times in the Rio texts: once in calling for an end to human rights abuses against young people,[28] a second time in stating that 'indigenous people and their communities shall enjoy the full measure of human rights and fundamental freedoms without hindrance or discrimination',[29] and finally, in referring to the right to housing.[30]

Working Group III of the Preparatory Committee considered a number of proposals for including a right to environment in the final Rio Declaration. The consolidated draft[31] contained several provisions referring to a human right to a healthy environment. However, none of these proposals achieved the consensus necessary for approval during the Rio meeting. Instead the final text reflects, but retreats, from, the language of a December 1990 resolution of the UN General Assembly, Resolution 45/94, which:

> Recognizes that all individuals are entitled to live in an environment adequate for their health and well-being; and calls upon Member States and intergovernmental and non-governmental organizations to enhance their efforts towards ensuring a better and healthier environment.

The final text of Principle 1 of the Rio Declaration provides:

> Human beings are at the center of concerns for sustainable development. They are entitled to a healthy and productive life in harmony with nature.

The text changes the formulation of the Stockholm Declaration. Instead of referring to human rights, Principle 1 speaks of entitlement, a term sometimes used in law to indicate revocable or terminable government benefits, but which can also mean having a right to claim something.[32] The language leaves a sense of ambiguity about the intention of the drafters, increased by

[27] UNCED adopted the Rio Declaration on Environment and Development, A/CONF. 151/26 (Vol. I) 8, reprinted in 31 *ILM* (1992) 874; Agenda 21, A/CONF.151/26 (Vol. III); the Non-Legally Binding Authoritative Statement of Principles for a Global Consensus on the Management, Conservation, and Sustainable Development of all types of Forests, A/CONF./151/26 (Vol. I) 6 reprinted in 31 *ILM* (1992) 881; the United Nations Framework Convention on Climate Change, A/CONF.151/26 (Vol. I), reprinted in 31 *ILM* (1992) 849 and the Convention on Biological Diversity, A/CONF.151/26 (Vol. I), reprinted in 31 *ILM* 818 (1992).

[28] Agenda 21, United Nations Conference on Environment and Development, UN Doc. A/CONF.151/26, Vol. III, Ch. 25, para. 25.8 at 12.

[29] Ibid., Ch. 26, para. 26.1 at 16.

[30] Ibid., Ch. 7, para. 7.6 at 74.

[31] Principles on General Rights and Obligations, Chairman's Consolidated Draft, Preparatory Committee for the United Nations Conference on Environment and Development, UN Doc. A/CONF.151/PC/WG.III/L.8/Rev.1, 20 August 1991.

[32] Black's Law Dictionary defines entitle as 'to furnish with proper grounds for seeking or claiming'. The French version of Principle 1 states that 'Les êtres humains . . . *ont droit* à une vie saine et productive en harmonie avec la nature' (emphasis added).

the fact that the Rio Declaration uses the term 'right' in proclaiming the sovereign right of states to exploit their resources (Principle 2) and the right to development (Principle 3). In later principles, the Rio Declaration refers to and discusses subjects contained in human rights instruments, such as adequate standards of living and meeting needs of the majority of the people of the world (Principle 5), but consistently does not use the term 'human rights'. Even with regard to well-established environmental rights, such as public participation, the Declaration avoids rights terminology, but, as shown below, calls for public participation in terms of efficiency.

Agenda 21 discusses the social and economic dimensions of environment and development while generally omitting references to human rights. It focuses on trade, finance, and combating poverty. Chapter 3, on combating poverty, calls for eradicating hunger without citing existing human rights guarantees regarding freedom from hunger or the right to food.[33] It does state, however, that 'an effective strategy for tackling the problems of poverty, development and environment simultaneously should begin by focusing on resources, production and people, and should cover demographic issues, enhanced health care and education, the rights of women, the role of youth and of indigenous people and local communities and a democratic participation process in association with improved governance'.[34] In further passages related to women, Agenda 21 calls on states to implement measures to ensure equal rights of men and women to decide freely and responsibly the number and spacing of their children, and provide access to information, education and means to enable them to exercise the right.[35]

The Agenda 21 discussion of housing contains the only references to human rights instruments. It calls for protecting people by law against unfair eviction from their homes or land. Chapter 7.6 states that:

> access to safe and healthy shelter is essential to a person's physical, psychological, social and economic well-being and should be a fundamental part of national and international action. The right to adequate housing as a basic human right is enshrined in the Universal Declaration of Human Rights and the International Covenant on Economic, Social and Cultural Rights.[36]

Similar references might have been expected in regard to food, health, life, and property, but are absent in the texts.

It is possible that human rights issues were overlooked in the multitude of problems facing the UNCED negotiators. For the most part, the participants

[33] See e.g. Art. 11, International Covenant on Economic Social and Cultural Rights, GA Res. 2200A (XXI), 21 UN GAOR Supp., No. 16 at 49, UN Doc. A/6316 (1966), 993 UNTS 3.

[34] Agenda 21 (supra n. 27), at Ch. 2, para. 2.32, at 28.

[35] Ibid., Ch. 3, para. 3.8(k) at 34. References to women's reproductive rights are repeated in Ch. 5, para. 5.17.

[36] Ibid., Ch. 7, para. 7.6 at 74.

were not drawn from the human rights community. Many were not legally trained, nor specialists in international law in general.

The decision to reject proposals for including a right to environment cannot be seen as inadvertent, however; rather there was a lack of consensus on the issue and its relevance to the matters under consideration. UNCED focused on North–South issues of economic development and global environmental protection. Unlike human rights, the linkage of environmental protection and economic development presents the possibility of reciprocal trade-offs and bargaining. In contrast, most states feel that they gain little from advancing human rights concerns. For this reason, among others, human rights leadership generally comes from NGOs and victim groups. Apart from women's and some indigenous organizations, human rights groups were generally absent from UNCED. In addition, some developing countries may have felt they lacked the capacity to tackle human rights and environmental protection simultaneously and preferred to emphasize environmental protection because of its closer perceived link to economic development. Finally, any focus on rights of indigenous peoples, closely linked to environmental protection, may have been unappealing to the host state and its neighbours, whose treatment of indigenous peoples was open to considerable criticism.

During and after Rio, the absence of support for a human right to an environment of a specified quality led activists to shift attention away from this broad approach to one of identifying those human rights whose enjoyment could be considered a prerequisite to environmental protection. In general, the emphasis was placed on procedural rights, especially those of environmental information, public participation, and remedies for environmental harm. Already in paragraph 23 of the 1982 World Charter for Nature, it was agreed that '[a]ll persons, in accordance with their national legislation, shall have the opportunity to participate, individually or with others, in the formulation of decisions of direct concern to their environment, and shall have access to means of redress when their environment has suffered damage or degradation'. In the Rio Declaration, Principle 10 similarly provides:

> Environmental issues are best handled with the participation of all concerned citizens, at the relevant level. At the national level, each individual shall have appropriate access to information concerning the environment that is held by public authorities, including information on hazardous materials and activities in their communities, and the opportunity to participate in decision-making processes. States shall facilitate and encourage public awareness and participation by making information widely available. Effective access to judicial and administrative proceedings, including redress and remedy, shall be provided.

It is notable that neither the World Charter for Nature nor the Rio Declaration speaks of 'rights' to information and participation. The World

Charter speaks of 'opportunity' while the Rio Declaration seems to take a utilitarian view that information, participation and remedies are useful for environmental protection, without being grounded in human rights law. In spite of this limitation, rights of public information, participation and access to remedies have become widely recognized in international environmental law.

1. Access to Information

The duty to provide environmental information or a right to information is found in many environmental instruments. The Framework Convention on Climate Change, Article 6, provides that its parties 'shall promote and facilitate at the national and, as appropriate, subregional and regional levels, and in accordance with national laws and regulations, and within their respective capacities, public access to information and public participation'.[37] Other recent multilateral treaties contain broad guarantees of public information. These include the Helsinki Convention on the Protection and Use of Transboundary Watercourses and International Lakes (Article 16),[38] the Espoo Convention on Environmental Impact Assessment in a Transboundary Context (Article 3[8]),[39] and the Paris Convention on the North-East Atlantic (Article 9).[40] The last mentioned is typical in requiring the contracting parties to ensure that their competent authorities are required to make available relevant information to any natural or legal person, in response to any reasonable request, without the person having to prove an interest, without unreasonable charges and within two months of the request.

Other recent environmental treaties include obligations on States Parties to inform the public of environmental hazards. The International Atomic Energy Agency (IAEA) Joint Convention on the Safety of Spent Fuel Management and on the Safety of Radioactive Waste Management[41] is based to a large extent on the principles contained in the IAEA document, *The Principles of Radioactive Waste Management.* The Preamble of the treaty recognizes the importance of informing the public on issues regarding the safety of spent fuel and radioactive waste management. This is reinforced in Articles 6 and 13, on siting of proposed facilities, which require each State Party to

[37] Climate Change Convention (supra n. 27).

[38] Convention on the Protection and Use of Transboundary Watercourses and International Lakes (Helsinki, 17 March 1992), UN Doc. E/ECE/1267, reprinted in 31 *ILM* 1045 (1992).

[39] Convention on Environmental Impact Assessment in a Transboundary Context (Espoo, 25 February 1991), 30 *ILM* (1991) 800.

[40] Convention for the Protection of the Marine Environment of the North-East Atlantic (Paris, 22 September 1992), 32 *ILM* (1993) 1069.

[41] Vienna, 5 September 1997, reprinted in 36 *ILM* (1997) 1431.

take the appropriate steps to ensure that procedures are established and implemented to make information on the safety of any proposed spent fuel management facility or radioactive waste management facility available to members of the public.

Two 1998 conventions are somewhat divergent in regard to the right to environmental information. The Aarhus Convention on rights of information, participation and remedy (see Section 4 at the end of Part II) contains very broad guarantees. In contrast and despite its name, the Rotterdam Convention on the Prior Informed Consent Procedure for Certain Hazardous Chemicals and Pesticides in International Trade (PIC Convention)[42] is vague and rather tentative on the obligations of States Parties to ensure that information on chemical and pesticide hazards is made available to the public. The prior informed consent referred to is that of the government of the importing state. Although the ultimate aim of the PIC Convention is to protect human health and the environment, including the health of consumers and workers, there are few direct references to the duty to inform.

Despite the absence of state obligations to provide information to the public, the objectives of the PIC Convention cannot be carried out in the absence of informed persons. The Preamble expresses the desire of the States Parties to ensure that hazardous chemicals that are exported from their territory are packaged and labelled in a manner that is adequately protective of human health and the environment. Similarly, the objective of the PIC Convention expressed in Article 1 is:

> to promote shared responsibility and cooperative efforts among Parties in the international trade of certain hazardous chemicals in order to protect human health and the environment from potential harm and to contribute to their environmentally sound use, by facilitating information exchange about their characteristics, by providing for a national decision-making process on their import and export and by disseminating these decisions to Parties.

Article 10(8), which applies to importing states, requires that decisions on permitting or rejecting importation of items be made available to persons concerned under its jurisdiction 'in accordance with its legislative or administrative measures'. The concerned persons referred to apparently means companies and individuals engaged in importation and sale of the regulated items, although the obligation could be read more broadly. Similarly Article 11(1) requires that exporting states inform those concerned within its territory of decisions taken by all States Parties in regard to hazardous chemicals and pesticides, information that the secretariat must distribute every six months.

[42] 10 September 1998. 38 *IML* (1999).

Article 13 contains the most detailed obligations on information and implicitly places the duty to inform primarily on the manufacturer or packager of the export. Each party shall require that, whenever a customs code has been assigned to such a chemical by the World Customs Organization, the shipping document for that chemical bears the code when exported.[43] Each party also shall require that exported chemicals listed in Annex III of the Convention as well as those chemicals banned or severely restricted in its territory are subject to labelling requirements that ensure adequate availability of information with regard to risks and/or hazards to human health or the environment, taking into account relevant international standards. Further, each party may subject exported chemicals to environmental or health labelling requirements in its territory that ensure adequate availability of information. Article 13 requires that exporting parties include for the importer a safety data sheet following an internationally-accepted format with the most up-to-date information available on the listed chemicals.

The only provision imposing a direct duty on States Parties to make information available to the public is found in Article 15 on implementation. Paragraph 2 requires each State Party to ensure, 'to the extent practicable' that the public has 'appropriate' access to information on chemical handling and accident management and on alternatives that are safer for human health or the environment than the chemicals listed in Annex III to the Convention.

Regional environmental texts also contain formulations of a right to information or a corresponding state duty. Within the European Community, the right to information generally means that the individual has the right to be informed about the environmental compatibility of products, manufacturing processes and their effects on the environment, and industrial installations. Specific directives vary in regard to public rights to information. Some air pollution directives, for example, make no reference to public information[44] while others[45] provide that information shall be made available to the public concerned in accordance with the national legal procedures. The European Community also requires information to be provided to those who may be particularly at risk from certain activities or products. For example, framework Directive 89/391 of 29 June 1989 on the protection of workers against risks at the workplace includes provisions for employee information and consultation. Other directives apply to specific industries, such as mining

[43] Article 13(1)(a) calls on the Conference of the Parties to encourage the World Customs Organization to assign specific Harmonized System customs codes to the individual chemicals or groups of chemicals listed in Annex III, as appropriate.

[44] Directives: 80/779/EEC, OJL 229/30 of 30 August 1980; 82/884/EEC OJL 378/15 of 31 December 1982; 85/203/EEC, OJL 87/1 of 27 March 1985.

[45] See e.g. Directive on Combating Air Pollution from Industrial Plants, 84/360/EEC, OJL 188 of 16 July 1984.

and fishing, or to specific hazards, such as asbestos.[46] In all cases, the directives require information to be given to workers about the risks they face.

Two general directives address rights of information. The duty to provide information is made explicit in Council Directive 85/337 concerning environmental impact assessment.[47] Finally and most pertinently, on 7 June 1990 the European Community adopted a Directive on Freedom of Access to Information on the Environment.[48]

The Freedom of Information Directive covers information held by public authorities which relates to the state of the environment; and activities or measures adversely affecting or likely so to affect the environment; activities or measures designed to protect the environment (Article 2(a)). The provision thus includes virtually all environmental data. The term 'public authorities' means all administrations with responsibilities relating to the environment (Article 2(b)). In addition, Article 6 extends the directive's coverage to all bodies having responsibilities for the environment which derive from public authorities; thus anyone delegated environmental functions is included. Judicial and legislative bodies are excluded provided they act 'in a judicial or legislative capacity'.

Access to information is available to any 'natural or legal person' (Article 3(1)) without distinction according to the nationality of the requesting person. Thus, individuals in another member state or even those from outside the European Community may have access to information. The applicant need not 'prove an interest' in order to obtain the information.

The directive allows member states to refuse a request for information when it affects the confidentiality of proceedings of public authorities, international relations and national defence; public security; matters which are or have been in litigation or under inquiry, or which are the subject of preliminary investigation proceedings; commercial and industrial confidentiality, including intellectual property; the confidentiality of personal data and/or files; material supplied by a third party without that party being under a legal obligation to do so; material the disclosure of which would make it more likely that the environment to which such material relates would be damaged; where it involves a supply of unfinished documents or data or internal communications, or where the request is manifestly unreasonable or formulated in too general a manner. The state may, but is not obliged to, refuse information in the cases listed. It is unclear if the scope of the grounds for refusal, e.g. public security, is subject to review by the European Court of Justice or if they are within the discretion of member states.

[46] See e.g. 83/477/EEC, OJL 263 of 24 September 1983.

[47] Council Directive 85/337 of 27 June 1985 concerning the Assessment of the Effects of Certain Public and Private Projects on the Environment, 85/337/EEC, OJL 175 of 7 July 1985.

[48] Council Directive 90/313/EEC of 7 June 1990 on the Freedom of Access to Information on the Environment, OJL 158 of 23 June 1990.

Procedural guarantees in the directive include requiring a response within two months to any request for information. Reasons must be given for any refusal. Finally, there should be a judicial or administrative review of the decision in accordance with the relevant national legal system.

Other organizations or meetings have issued non-binding declarations proclaiming a right to environmental information. The World Health Organization's European Charter on the Environment and Health states that 'every individual is entitled to information and consultation on the state of the environment'.[49] The states participating in the Organization on Security and Cooperation in Europe (OSCE) have confirmed the right of individuals, groups, and organizations to obtain, publish and distribute information on environmental issues.[50] The Bangkok Declaration, adopted 16 October 1990, affirms similar rights in Asia and the Pacific[51] while the Arab Declaration on Environment and Development and Future Perspectives of September 1991 speaks of the right of individuals and non-governmental organizations to acquire information about environmental issues relevant to them.[52]

2. Public Participation

Obtaining information is a prerequisite for the major role played by the public, which is participating in decision-making, especially in environmental impact or other permitting procedures. Public participation is based on the right of those who may be affected to have a say in the determination of their environmental future. This may include foreign citizens and residents. In human rights instruments the right to participate in public affairs is widely recognized as part of democratic governance.[53] In environmental texts, as well, rights of participation are found. The right to participate has two

[49] European Charter on Environment and Health, adopted 8 December 1989 by the First Conference of Ministers of the Environment and of Health of the Member States of the European Region of the World Health Organization.

[50] Conference on Security and Cooperation in Europe, Sofia Meeting on Protection of the Environment (October–November 1989) (CSCE/SEM.36, 2 November 1989).

[51] Ministerial Declaration on Environmentally Sound and Sustainable Development in Asia and the Pacific (Bangkok, 16 October 1990), A/CONF.151/PC/38. Paragraph 27 affirms 'the right of individuals and non-governmental organizations to be informed of environmental problems relevant to them, to have the necessary access to information, and to participate in the formulation and implementation of decisions likely to affect their environment'.

[52] Arab Declaration on Environment and Development and Future Perspectives, adopted by the Arab Ministerial Conference on Environment and Development (Cairo, September 1991), A/46/632, cited in UN Doc. E/CN.4/Sub.2/1992/7, 20.

[53] See Part III below.

components: the right to be heard and the right to affect decisions. Principle 23 of the 1982 World Charter for Nature provides most explicitly:

All persons, in accordance with their national legislation, shall have the opportunity to participate, individually or with others, in the formulation of decisions of direct concern to their environment, and shall have access to means of redress when their environment has suffered damage or degradation.

The Rio Declaration, Principle 10, recognizes the need for public participation. The Declaration stresses the participation of different components of the population: women (Principle 20), youth (Principle 21), indigenous peoples and local communities (Principle 22).

Agenda 21 also strongly emphasizes the importance of public participation. Agenda 21 encourages governments to create policies that facilitate a direct exchange of information between the government and the public in environmental issues, suggesting environmental impact assessment procedures as a potential mechanism. In the Preamble to chapter 23, the Agenda states:

One of the fundamental prerequisites for the achievement of sustainable development is broad public participation in decision-making. Furthermore, in the more specific context of environment and development, the need for new forms of participation has emerged. This includes the need of individuals, groups, and organizations to participate in environmental impact assessment procedures and to know about and participate in decisions, particularly those that potentially affect the communities in which they live and work. Individuals, groups and organizations should have access to information relevant to environment and development held by national authorities, including information on products and activities that have or are likely to have a significant impact on the environment, and information on environmental protection measures.

Most recent multilateral and many bilateral agreements contain references to or guarantees of public participation. The Climate Change Convention, Article 4(1)(i) obliges parties to promote public awareness and to 'encourage the widest participation in this process including that of non-governmental organizations'. The Convention on Biological Diversity allows for public participation in environmental impact assessment procedures in Article 14(1)(a). Outside the UNCED context, the 1991 Espoo Convention on Environmental Impact Assessment in a Transboundary Context requires States Parties to notify the public and to provide an opportunity for public participation in relevant environmental impact assessment procedures regarding proposed activities in any area likely to be affected by transboundary environmental harm. In a final decision on the proposed activities, the state must take due account of the environmental impact assessment, including the opinions of the individuals in the affected area.

The UN Desertification Convention goes furthest in calling for public participation, embedding the issue throughout the agreement.[54] Article 3(a) and (c) begin by recognizing that there is a need to associate civil society with the action of the state. The treaty calls for an integrated commitment of all actors—national governments, scientific institutions, local communities and authorities and non-governmental organizations, as well as international partners, both bilateral and multilateral, to achieve the aims of the convention.[55]

Other agreements referring to public participation are the:

- Protocol to the 1979 Convention on Long-Range Transboundary Air Pollution Concerning the Control of Emissions of Volatile Organic Compounds or Their Transboundary Fluxes (Geneva, 18 November 1991), Article 2(3)(a)(4);
- Convention on the Protection and Utilization of Transboundary Rivers and Lakes (Helsinki, 17 March 1992), Article 16;
- Convention on the Transboundary Effects of Industrial Accidents (Helsinki, 17 March 1992), Article 9;
- Convention for the Protection of the Marine Environment of the Baltic Sea (Helsinki, 9 April 1992), Article 17;
- Convention for the Prevention of Marine Pollution of the North-East Atlantic (Paris, 22 September 1992), Article 9;
- Convention on Civil Responsibility for Damage resulting from Activities Dangerous to the Environment (Lugano, 21 June 1993), Articles 13–16;
- North American Convention on Cooperation in the Field of the Environment (Washington, DC, 13 September 1993), Article 2(1)(a), 14;
- Convention on Cooperation and Sustainable Development of the Waters of the Danube (Sofia, 29 June 1994), Article 14;
- Protocol to the 1975 Barcelona Convention on Specially Protected Zones and Biological Diversity in the Mediterranean (Barcelona, 10 June 1995), Article 19;
- Joint Communiqué and Declaration on the Establishment of the Arctic Council (Ottawa, 19 September 1996), Preamble and Articles 1(a), 2, 3(c);
- Kyoto Protocol to the United Nations Framework Convention on Climate Change (10 December 1997), Article 6(3).

There are exceptions to the general trend towards including rights of public participation in multilateral environmental agreements. The United Nations Convention on the Law of the Non-Navigational Uses of International Watercourses (New York, 21 May 1997) and recent regional agreements for water management provide for interstate cooperation, but do not include

[54] UN Convention to Combat Desertification in those Countries Experiencing Serious Drought and/or Desertification, in Particular in Africa (Paris, 17 June 1994), UN Doc. A/AC.241/15 Rev. 7, reprinted in 33 *ILM* (1994) 1328.

[55] See also ibid., Arts 10(2)(e), 13(1)(b), 14(2), 19 and 25.

provisions for the public to participate in decisions regarding the uses and management of international watercourses.[56]

The North American Agreement on Environmental Cooperation (NAAEC) contains institutional arrangements for public participation.[57] It is also the first environmental agreement to establish a formal procedure through which individuals, environmental organizations and business entities can file complaints. NAAEC is designed to complement the existing environmental provisions of the North American Free Trade Agreement (NAFTA). NAAEC allows individuals and non-governmental organizations to make submissions alleging that a State Party is failing to enforce its environmental law effectively (Article 14). The procedure is not designed to provide a remedy for individual environmental harm, but rather to enlist the public in ensuring that the parties abide by their NAFTA obligation to enforce their environmental laws. Anyone residing or established in North America can bring a submission. The identity of the submitter must be established and the party must have been given prior notice of the matters alleged in the submission. Sufficient facts must be alleged to allow the secretariat to review the submission.

The secretariat determines if the submission merits making a request for a response from a party based on criteria in Article 14(2).[58] The submission must aim at promoting enforcement rather than at harassing industry.[59] According to Article 14, the secretariat will solicit a response from a party if the complaint raises matters whose further study in the process would advance the goals of NAFTA. The party must respond to the complaint, refer

[56] See e.g. Kenya–Tanzania–Uganda, Final Act of the Conference of Plenipotentiaries on the Establishment of the Lake Victoria Fisheries Organization (Kisumu, Kenya, 30 June 1994); Bangladesh-India, Treaty on Sharing of the Ganges Waters at Farakka (New Delhi, 12 December 1996); India-Nepal, Treaty Concerning the Integrated Development of the Mahakai River (New Delhi, 12 February 1996).

[57] Canada–Mexico–United States, North American Agreement on Environmental Cooperation (Washington, Ottawa, Mexico City, 13 September 1993), 32 *ILM* 1480 (1993). The Agreement creates a permanent trilateral body, the Commission for Environmental Cooperation (CEC), composed of a Council, a Secretariat and a Joint Public Advisory Committee (Art. 8). The Joint Public Advisory Committee includes fifteen members from the public, five from each member country, and advises the Council as well as provides technical, scientific, or other information to the secretariat. The Committee also may advise on the annual programme and budget as well as reports that are issued. It meets annually, along with the regular meetings of the Council.

[58] In reviewing submissions, the secretariat should decide whether: (A) the submission alleges harm to the person or organization making the submission; (B) the submission, alone or in combination with other submissions, raises matters whose further study in this process would advance the goals of the NAAEC; (C) private remedies available under the law of the party concerned have been pursued; and (D) the submission is drawn exclusively from mass media reports.

[59] NAAEC, Art. 14(1)(d).

the matter to relevant judicial proceedings, or advise that private remedies are available. The secretariat may dismiss the submission on the basis of the response or may recommend to the Council the creation of a Factual Record of the submission and the response. The Council must approve the recommendation by a two-thirds vote, after which the secretariat is authorized to create the Factual Record (Article 15(2)). In the preparation of the Factual Record, there is considerable opportunity for public participation. The secretariat is mandated to consider information furnished by a party and any relevant technical, scientific or other information that is (a) publicly available; (b) submitted by interested non-governmental organizations or persons; (c) submitted by the Joint Public Advisory Committee; or (d) developed by the secretariat or by independent experts. No judgment issues nor are remedies directly afforded.

In the first four years after NAAEC came into force on 1 January 1994, the secretariat received seven submissions from NGOs and private persons. [60] The secretariat recommended the preparation of a Factual Record only in a matter involving Mexico, submitted by Mexican environmental groups. They alleged that the government had failed to enforce its environmental law by not requiring the preparation of an environmental impact assessment in connection with a port and related works on the island of Cozumel near the Paraiso coral reef. The submission was accompanied by extensive factual documentation. Among the points raised in response, Mexico challenged the jurisdiction of the CEC because the acts complained of occurred prior to NAAEC's entry into force and because the submitters had not alleged that they suffered any harm. The secretariat adopted the notion of 'continuing effects', well-known in human rights jurisprudence, in deciding that the submission was admissible in regard to lack of enforcement that continued after 1 January 1994, the date the treaty entered into force. In regard to standing, the secretariat took a broad view, rejecting the argument that national tests for standing should be applied to the international procedure. While the secretariat noted that the submitters 'may not have alleged the particularized, individual harm required to acquire legal standing to bring suit in some civil proceedings' in domestic courts, it found that the matter should go forward given 'the specially public nature of marine resources'. It found that the submitters' concerns were within the 'spirit and intent' of the NAAEC. Looking at the submission as a whole, the secretariat affirmed that the object and purpose of the Agreement

[60] The submissions are: Biodiversity Legal Foundation *et al.*, Submission (30 June 1995); Sierra Club *et al.*, Submission (30 August 1995); Comite para la Proteccion de los Recursos Naturales, A.C. *et al.*, Submission (17 January 1996); Sr. Aage Tottrup, Submission (20 March 1996); Friends of the Old Man River, Submission (9 September 1996); Southwest Center for Biological Diversity, Submission (14 November 1996); British Columbia Aboriginal Fisheries Commission *et al.*, Submission (2 April 1997). All documents related to submissions made under Article 14 are available at <http://www.cec.org/>.

is the overriding consideration in deciding whether or not to recommend the preparation of a Factual Record. The Council concurred and ordered the preparation of the Record.

The fact that only one submission led to the preparation of a Factual Record should not be taken as a signal that the process is without effect; the act of submitting a matter publicizes the lack of state enforcement of environmental laws and may be sufficient to impel a government to address the matter. Through this process the interested public may communicate its views and information to the officials of the state concerned, without regard to borders or traditional standing limitations of domestic courts.

Recent bilateral agreements also increase the possibilities for public participation. The 1991 Canada–United States Agreement on Air Quality[61] provides that the International Joint Commission previously established shall invite comments, including through public hearings as appropriate, on each progress report prepared by the Air Quality Committee established to assist in implementing the agreement. A synthesis of public views shall be submitted to the parties and, if requested, a record of such views. After submission to the parties, the synthesis shall be released to the public. The parties agree to consult on the contents of the progress report based in part on the views presented to the Commission. Further, in Article XIV, the parties shall consult with state or provincial governments, interested organizations, and the public, in implementing the Agreement.

The Agreement on Environmental Cooperation between Canada and Chile[62] lists among its objectives the promotion of transparency and public participation in the development of environmental law, regulations and policies. The obligations of the parties include periodically preparing and making publicly available reports on the state of the environment. In more detail, Article 4 provides that each party shall ensure that its laws, regulations, procedures and administrative rulings of general application respecting any matter governed by the agreement are promptly published or otherwise made available to enable interested persons and the other party to become acquainted with them. To the extent possible, each party is to publish in advance any such measure that it proposes to adopt and provide interested persons and the other party a reasonable opportunity to comment on the proposed measures.

The multitude of provisions on public participation are very important to the effectiveness of international environmental law. The process by which rules emerge, how proposed rules become norms and norms become law, is highly important to the legitimacy of the norms. To a large extent, legitimacy

[61] Canada–United States Agreement on Air Quality (Ottawa, 13 March 1991), 30 *ILM* (1991) 676.

[62] Ottawa, 6 February 1997, reprinted in 36 *ILM* (1997) 1193.

is an issue of participation: the governed must have and perceive that they have a voice in governance through representation, deliberation or some other form of action. In the domestic arena participation takes place indirectly through election of representatives and directly through lobbying and grass-roots action. Various interests and communities participate in shaping the final legislative product. The interests of the various stakeholders are balanced as they participate in the legal process.

Legitimacy in turn affects compliance. Norms that are perceived to be legitimate are more likely to be effective, as each participant has invested in the process and contributed to the outcome. Without public participation, coercive enforcement often becomes the primary means of ensuring compliance, rather than voluntary acceptance of norms adopted through a process viewed as fair. The lack of resources to monitor and enforce myriad norms undermines the effectiveness of norms that fail to attract public support. Participation thus makes for better and more effective regulation. From the human rights perspective, as discussed further below, participation is part of democratic governance and an essential part of self-expression.

3. Access to Justice

Environmental instruments frequently proclaim the need for effective remedies. Principle 10 of the Rio Declaration provides that 'effective access to judicial and administrative proceedings, including redress and remedy, shall be provided'. Agenda 21 calls on governments and legislators to establish judicial and administrative procedures for legal redress and to remedy actions affecting the environment that may be unlawful or infringe on rights under the law, and to provide access to individuals, groups and organizations with a recognized legal interest. The United Nations Convention on the Law of the Sea (UNCLOS) also provides that states shall ensure that recourse is available for prompt and adequate compensation or other relief in respect of damage caused by pollution of the marine environment by natural or juridical persons under their jurisdiction.[63] The right to a remedy is not limited to nationals of a state. Some international agreements contain obligations to grant a potential or *de facto* injured person a right of access to any administrative or judicial procedure equal to that of nationals or residents. Equal access to national remedies has been considered one way of implementing the polluter pays principle. Implementation of the right of equal access to national remedies requires that states remove jurisdictional barriers to civil proceedings for damages and other remedies in respect of environmental injury. Both the Espoo

[63] United Nations Convention on the Law of the Sea (Montego Bay, 10 December 1982), Art. 235(2), UN Doc. A/CONF. 62/122 (1982), reprinted in 21 *ILM* (1982) 1261.

Convention and the Helsinki Convention on the Transboundary Effects of Industrial Accidents call for equality of access.

The 1997 Agreement between Canada and Chile concerning Environmental Cooperation contains broad remedial guarantees in addition to obligations of state enforcement of environmental laws and regulations. Article 6 requires each state party to ensure that interested persons may call on authorities to investigate alleged violations of the state's environmental laws and regulations. In addition, each party must ensure that affected persons have access to administrative, quasi-judicial or judicial proceedings for the enforcement of the applicable environmental laws and regulations. Private access shall include, in accordance with local law, rights to sue for damages, to seek sanctions or remedies such as penalties, emergency closures or orders to mitigate the consequences of violation, and to request that appropriate enforcement actions are taken by authorities to protect the environment or avoid environmental harm.

4. Aarhus Convention on Access to Information, Public Participation in Decision-Making and Access to Justice in Environmental Matters

The various international efforts to promote environmental rights in environmental instruments produced a landmark agreement on 25 June 1998, when 35 states and the European Community signed a Convention on Access to Information, Public Participation and Access to Justice in Environmental Matters.[64] The Convention builds on prior texts, especially Principle 1 of the Stockholm Declaration. Indeed, it is the first treaty to incorporate and strengthen the language of Principle 1. The Preamble expressly states that 'every person has the right to live in an environment adequate to his or her health and well-being, and the duty, both individually and in association with others, to protect and improve the environment for the benefit of present and future generations'. The following paragraph adds that to be able to assert the right and observe the duty, citizens must have access to information, be entitled to participate in decision-making and

[64] The Convention was sponsored by the United Nations Economic Commission for Europe (UNECE). The signatory countries are: Albania, Armenia, Austria, Belgium, Bulgaria, Croatia, Cyprus, Czech Republic, Denmark, Estonia, Finland, France, Georgia, Greece, Iceland, Ireland, Italy, Kazakhstan, Latvia, Liechtenstein, Lithuania, Luxembourg, Monaco, Netherlands, Norway, Poland, Portugal, Republic of Moldova, Romania, Slovenia, Spain, Sweden, Switzerland, Ukraine, United Kingdom of Great Britain and Northern Ireland and the European Community. The Convention is open for signature by the 55 members of the UNECE, which includes all of Europe as well as the United States, Canada, and states of the former Soviet Union. States having consultative status with the UNECE may also participate.

have access to justice in environmental matters. These provisions are repeated in Article 1 where States Parties agree to guarantee the rights of access to information, public participation, and access to justice. The Convention acknowledges its broader implications, expressing a conviction that its implementation will 'contribute to strengthening democracy in the region of the UNECE'.

The Convention obliges States Parties to collect and publicly disseminate information, and respond to specific requests (Articles 4 and 5). Each party is to prepare and disseminate a national report on the state of the environment at three to four year intervals. In addition, it is to disseminate legislative and policy documents, treaties and other international instruments relating to the environment. Each party must ensure that public authorities, upon request, provide environmental information to a requesting person without the latter having to state an interest. Public authorities means, in addition to government bodies, any natural or legal person having public responsibilities or functions or providing public services. The information has to be made available within one month, or in exceptional cases up to three months. In addition to providing information on request, each state party must be pro-active, ensuring that public authorities collect and update environmental information relevant to their functions. This requires that each State Party establish mandatory systems to obtain information on proposed and existing activities which could significantly affect the environment. This provision is clearly aimed at the private sector and is supplemented by Article 5(6) which requires States Parties to encourage operators whose activities have a significant impact on the environment to inform the public regularly of the environmental impact of their activities and products, through eco-labelling, eco-auditing or similar means. States Parties are also to ensure that consumer information on products is made available.

To enhance the effectiveness of the Convention, the States Parties must provide information about the availability of and access to information, i.e. the type and scope of information held by public authorities, the basic terms and conditions under which it is made available and the procedure by which it could be obtained. The Convention also foresees the establishment of publicly-accessible electronic sites that should contain reports on the state of the environment, texts of environmental legislation, environmental plans, programmes and policies, and other information that could facilitate the application of national law.

The treaty provides numerous exceptions in Article 4(4) to the duty to inform, in the light of other political, economic and legal interests. The state may refuse to provide the information if the information is not in its possession; the request is manifestly unreasonable or too general; concerns material not completed or internal communications of a public authority; or if the disclosure would adversely affect:

- the confidentiality of public proceedings;
- international relations, national defence or public security;
- criminal investigations or trials;
- commercial and industrial secrets; however, information on emissions relevant to the protection of the environment shall be disclosed;
- intellectual property rights;
- privacy, i.e. personal data;
- the interests of a third party;
- the environment, such as the breeding sites of rare species.

The Convention also states that all exceptions are to be read restrictively and the state may provide broader information rights than those contained in the Convention. In addition, where non-exempt information can be separated from that not subject to disclosure, the non-restricted information must be provided. In spite of these interpretative provisions, many environmental groups have expressed concern that the exceptions will result in the withholding of extensive and crucial information. Any refusal to provide information must be in writing and with reasons given for the refusal. Reasonable fees may be charged for supplying information. The government has special disclosure obligations in case of any imminent threat to human health or the environment.

Public participation is guaranteed in Articles 6–8, and is required in regard to all decisions on whether to permit or renew permission for industrial, agricultural and construction activities listed in an Annex to the Convention as well as other activities which may have a significant impact on the environment. The public must be informed in detail about the proposed activity early in the decision-making process and given time to prepare and participate in the decision-making. During the process, the public must have access to all relevant information on the proposal including the site, description of environmental impacts, measures to prevent and/or reduce the effects, a non-technical summary, an outline of the main alternatives, and any reports or advice given. Public participation can be through writing, hearings or inquiry. All public comments, information, analyses or opinions shall be taken into account by the party in making its decision. All decisions shall be made public, along with the reasons and considerations on which the decision is based.

In addition to providing for public participation regarding decisions on specific projects, the Convention calls for public participation in the preparation of environmental plans, programmes, policies, laws and regulations. Further, States Parties are to promote environmental education and to recognize and support environmental associations and groups.

The provisions of Article 9 on access to justice mirror many human rights texts in requiring proceedings before an independent and impartial body established by law. Each State Party must provide judicial review for any

denial of requested information, and a remedy for any act or omission concerning the permitting of activities and 'acts and omissions by private persons and public authorities which contravene provisions of its national law relating to the environment'. Standing to challenge permitting procedures or results is limited to members of the public having a sufficient interest or suffering impairment of a right; however, the Convention provides that environmental non-governmental organizations 'shall be deemed' to have sufficient interest for this purpose. Standing to challenge violations of environmental law is open to the public, including NGOs 'where they meet the criteria, if any, laid down in national law' (Article 9(3)).

The Convention's topic has induced the drafters to take small steps towards the creation of compliance procedures and enhancement of public participation on the international level. Primary review of implementation is conferred on the Meeting of the Parties, at which non-governmental organizations 'qualified in the fields to which this Convention relates' may participate as observers if they have made a request and not more than one-third of the parties present at the meeting raise objections (Article 10). This is a common provision in international environmental agreements. The Convention adds, however, a provision on compliance review (Article 15) which mandates the establishment by the Meeting of the Parties of a 'non-confrontational, non-judicial and consultative' optional arrangement for compliance review, which 'shall allow for appropriate public involvement and may include the option of considering communications from members of the public on matters related to this Convention'. This tentative language marks the first time a petition procedure has been contemplated in an international environmental agreement.

If the compliance procedure is established when the Aarhus Convention comes into force, it will mark an important step in enhancing the effectiveness of international environmental agreements. At present, nearly all environmental agreements vest authority over issues of implementation and compliance in the Conference or Meeting of the Parties, a plenary and political body. In some cases small secretariats are created, but which lack broad competence. It is largely due to the weaknesses in existing environmental compliance mechanisms that many persons concerned with environmental rights have turned to human rights law.

III INTERNATIONAL HUMAN RIGHTS LAW AND THE ENVIRONMENT

The human rights community increasingly views environmental protection as an appropriate part of the human rights agenda. In turn, the use of international complaints procedures has become an accepted means to achieve the

ends of environmental protection. Given the general absence of petition procedures in environmental treaties and institutions, it is not possible to choose between bringing an international human rights case or an international environmental case because almost no forum exists for the latter. Human rights tribunals provide the only international procedures currently available to challenge government action or inaction regarding environmental protection: thus the continued pressure to sensitize human rights tribunals to broad environmental concerns.

International human rights law, which began by recording the fundamental human rights which are internationally guaranteed, along with the state duties to respect and ensure them, had largely completed its codification efforts when environmental issues became matters of international concern. Largely due to this, almost no global human rights treaty contains a specific mention of environmental rights or a right to environment. The United Nations Convention on the Rights of the Child[65] is the only United Nations human rights treaty to refer to aspects of environmental protection, linking it to the right to health. It specifies in Article 24 that:

> 1. States Parties recognize the right of the child to the enjoyment of the highest attainable standard of health and to facilities for the treatment of illness and rehabilitation of health. . . .
> 2. States Parties shall pursue full implementation of this right and, in particular, shall take appropriate measures:
> . . .
> (c) To combat disease and malnutrition . . . through *inter alia* the application of readily available technology and through the provision of adequate nutritious foods *and clean drinking water, taking into consideration the dangers and risks of environmental pollution* (emphasis added);
> . . .
> (e) to ensure that all segments of society, in particular parents and children, are informed, have access to education and are supported in the use of, basic knowledge of child health and nutrition, . . . hygiene and *environmental sanitation* and the prevention of accidents (emphasis added).

United Nations human rights organs began annually considering environmental issues as they relate to human rights in the late 1980s, when the issue was raised by African countries concerned about transboundary movements of hazardous and toxic wastes. In 1988, the UN Sub-Commission on Prevention of Discrimination and Protection of Minorities considered this specific question under its agenda item concerning human rights and scientific and technological developments. It adopted resolution 1988/26, drafted and cosponsored primarily by its African members. The resolution refers to

[65] United Nations Convention on the Rights of the Child (20 November 1989), GA Res. 44/25, 44 UN GAOR, Supp. (No. 49), UN Doc. A/44/49, 166 (1989) reprinted at 28 *ILM* (1989) 1448.

the right of all peoples to life and the right of future generations to enjoy their environmental heritage. It notes that the movement and dumping of toxic and dangerous wastes endangers basic human rights, such as the right to life, the right to live in a sound and healthy environment, and consequently the right to health. To help remedy these environmental problems, the resolution calls for both a ban on the export of toxic and dangerous wastes and a global convention on that subject. In March 1989, the Commission approved the Sub-Commission text.[66] Two months later the Basel Convention on the Control of Transboundary Movements of Hazardous Wastes and Their Disposal was adopted,[67] but African states expressed disappointment at what they viewed to be a weak agreement. As a consequence the topic remained on the human rights agenda and gradually expanded to include dangerous products as well as wastes.

At its 51st session in 1995, the Commission adopted a proposal to appoint a special rapporteur to study the adverse effects of the illicit movement and dumping of toxic and dangerous products and wastes on the enjoyment of human rights. [68] The mandate of the Special Rapporteur is broad. In addition to investigating the human rights effects of illegal dumping of toxic and dangerous products and wastes in developing countries, the Special Rapporteur is given explicit authority to receive and examine communications and do fact-finding on illicit traffic and dumping. This authority has been given to a few other UN special rapporteurs and allows the development of an individual complaints procedure on the subject under study. The Rapporteur may make recommendations to states on measures to be taken and is also to produce an annual list of the countries and transnational corporations engaged in illicit dumping, as well as a census of persons killed, maimed or otherwise injured due to the practice.

In her progress report,[69] the Special Rapporteur described the process for considering communications as similar to that used by other thematic

[66] Res. 1989/42, UN ESCOR, 44th Sess., Supp. No. 2, at 111, UN Doc. C/CN.4/1989/86 (1989).

[67] Convention on the Control of Transboundary Movements of Hazardous Wastes and Their Disposal (Basel, 22 March 1989), UN Doc. UNEP/WG.190/4, reprinted at 28 *ILM* (1989) 657.

[68] Res. 1995/81. The vote was 32 to 15, with six abstentions. The division was geographic, with all developing countries of the South voting in favour of the proposal and all Northern states expressing opposition. France, on behalf of the European Union, argued that the question could be dealt with much more effectively through instruments such as the Basel Convention on the Control of Transboundary Movements of Hazardous Wastes and their Disposal. Consequently, the study 'would lead to needless duplication of international mechanisms and to dissipation or wastage of resources'.

[69] Adverse effects of the illicit movement and dumping of toxic and dangerous products and wastes on the enjoyment of human rights, Preliminary report submitted by Mrs Fatma Zohra Ksentini, Special Rapporteur, E/CN.4/1996/17 (1996).

rapporteurs and working groups. Given the existence of a wide variety of international and domestic legal instruments and procedures that address movement and dumping of toxic and dangerous products and wastes, the Special Rapporteur announced that the human rights dimension is the focus of the procedure, including the issue of vulnerable groups and the perspective of victims.

In a 1997 report[70] the Special Rapporteur noted that she had received information on allegations of countries and enterprises engaged in illicit traffic which were sent to governments. The government replies were summarized in an addition to the 1998 report.[71] Given the transboundary nature of the problem, the information was sent both to the country of origination and the country where the alleged victims were found. The replies indicate the controversial nature of the entire venture. Some questioned the jurisdiction of the Special Rapporteur or described legal measures to combat illicit trafficking, without reference to the specific case that was the subject of the communication. Some of the allegations involved incidents that pre-dated the establishment of the procedure and before changes in national legislation, raising issues of retroactivity in the applicable norms. Some states indicated they had recovered and brought back wastes, while others indicated the matter was under investigation. The communications included some well-known cases where human violations have been linked to environmental harm, although it is not clear that they concern illicit transboundary movement of hazardous wastes or products. One complaint was based on activities of Shell Oil Company in the Ogoni region of Nigeria and appears to have been a broad-based attack on activities of the government and the company in the region. The government reply claimed that all oil companies in Nigeria conform to local environmental laws. The US reply on this and similar cases of US companies' investment operations in developing countries asserted that the allegations were not based on illicit trafficking and dumping of hazardous wastes, but rather with pollution and treatment of local populations. As such they exceeded the mandate of the Rapporteur. Similar complaints from NGOs about the practices of particular companies in a single country were met with hostile responses by the government that approved the company's presence. In response to allegations about the operations of Texaco's Caltex company in Indonesia, for example, the government said it 'considers it possible that anti-Indonesian elements working in collaboration with certain NGOs are behind the allegations'.[72] Similarly, the government of Myanmar responded to an allegation concerning its construction of a natural gas pipeline with the participation of French and US oil companies by calling it

[70] Adverse effects of the illicit movement and dumping of toxic and dangerous products and wastes on the enjoyment of human rights, Progress report submitted by Mrs Fatma Zohra Ksentini, Special Rapporteur, E/CN.4/1997/19 (1997).

[71] E/CN.4/1998/10/Add. 1 (1998).

[72] Ibid., 4.

'unfounded and totally untrue, emanating from the opponents of the Government of Myanmar who aim at denigrating the Government and the armed forces'.[73]

The 1998 report of the Special Rapporteur contained information on additional specific cases and incidents. Most of them involved chemical companies in Europe exporting contaminated waste to Asia and the Middle East. In many cases, the government replies indicated prosecutions were initiated and the waste returned to the place of origin. The Special Rapporteur found that the communications showed that the right to life and security of person, health, an adequate standard of living, adequate food and housing, work and non-discrimination, were implicated by the acts denounced. In certain cases the reported incidents had led to sickness, disorders, physical or mental disability and death. In other instances, the right of association and the freedom of access to information were ignored or curtailed, hampering the ability of individuals or groups to prevent dumping or obtain a remedy. Most communications alleged violation of the right to information which led to often irreversible consequences to the environment and rights of individuals. Information had been withheld not only prior to but after incidents. According to the Special Rapporteur, the most vulnerable groups in society are the main targets of illegal dumping, with discrimination often occurring.

Unlike many international human rights procedures, the mechanism appears to have generated inter-state complaints or state-initiated communications. In the 1998 report, for example, the government of Paraguay informed the Special Rapporteur that it was investigating a serious case of illicit movement and dumping of toxic waste that might have occurred in its territory. The government asked the Special Rapporteur for assistance in the investigation. Similarly, the government of Thailand informed the Special Rapporteur of a 1991 fire in warehouses in the port of Bangkok, causing loss of life and property in the surrounding areas.

The procedure holds promise but thus far has been hampered by lack of resources and full information, as well as difficult issues of defining the scope of jurisdiction of the Special Rapporteur. Complaints are often vague, fragmentary or incomplete because those making complaints lack access to information or are obstructed in their activities. It is thus difficult to identify incidents, measure their magnitude or discover their consequences. Even governments often have only rumours of illicit dumping and are sometimes reluctant to publicize incidents. In addition, it seems clear that some groups and individuals are seeking to use the communications procedure to bring broad allegations of environmental damage and human rights violations

[73] Ibid., 7. The subject matter of this complaint led to a lawsuit being filed against one of the US oil companies in a United States federal court, based on the Alien Tort Claim Act, 28 USC sec. 1350. See *Doe v Unocal*, 963 F.Supp. 880 (C.D. Cal. 1997).

caused by foreign investment. The lack of alternative procedures probably accounts for this effort, but unless care is taken to exclude those communications clearly outside the jurisdiction of the Special Rapporteur, the procedure is likely to suffer in credibility and effectiveness, especially given the divided vote over its creation in the first place.

1. Human Rights Instruments and Jurisprudence

In the absence of widespread mention of environmental rights in international human rights agreements, other human rights have been invoked when threatened by environmental harm. The rights to life, association, expression, information, political participation, personal liberty, equality and legal redress, all contained in international legal instruments, can be and have been invoked to further environmental goals. Economic and social rights including the right to health, the right to decent living conditions and the right to a decent working environment are also implicated. International organs and tribunals have expanded or reinterpreted some of these guarantees in light of environmental concerns.

(a) The right to information

Parallel to environmental agreements, human rights texts generally contain a right to freedom of information or a corresponding state duty to inform. European states are generally bound by Article 10 of the European Convention on Human Rights, which guarantees 'the freedom to receive information'. This provision has been interpreted to mean that a state is prohibited from restricting the right of a person to receive information that others are willing to give.[74] The former European Commission on Human Rights and the European Court of Human Rights have taken different views on the scope of state obligations under Article 10. The Commission has found that the right to receive information envisages not only access to general sources of information, which may not be restricted by state authorities, but also the right to receive information not generally accessible that is of particular importance to the individual.[75] The Court, in contrast, has given strict interpretation to Article 10. In the case of *Leander v Sweden*, the applicant alleged violation of Article 10 after he was denied access to a file that was used to deny him employment. The Court unanimously stated:

> the right to receive information basically prohibits a Government from restricting a person from receiving information that others wish or may be willing to impart to

[74] See S. Weber, 'Environmental Information and the European Convention on Human Rights', 12 *Hum Rts LJ* (1991) 177.

[75] *X v Federal Republic of Germany* (1980) 17 DR 227, 228–9.

him. Article 10 does not, in circumstances such as those of the present case, confer on the individual a right to access to a register containing information on his personal position, nor does it embody an obligation on the Government to impart such information to the individual.[76]

The restrictive approach to Article 10 has been applied in environmental cases. In *Anna Maria Guerra and 39 others v Italy*[77] the applicants complained of pollution resulting from operation of the chemical factory, 'ENICHEM Agricoltura', situated near the town of Manfredonia; the risk of major accidents at the plant; and the absence of regulation by the public authorities. Invoking Article 10 of the European Convention on Human Rights, the applicants asserted in particular the government's failure to inform the public of the risks and the measures to be taken in case of a major accident, prescribed by the domestic law transposing the EC 'Seveso' directive.[78]

The European Commission on Human Rights admitted the complaint in so far as it alleged a violation of the right to information. It did not accept the claim of pollution damage. The Commission found on largely uncontested facts that the company enjoyed almost complete impunity to pollute despite existing national law. In addition to the government's failure to hold the company responsible for the pollution it caused, the government failed to take any measure, between the adoption of the 'Seveso' law and the cessation of chemical production by the factory in 1994, to inform the population of the situation or to make operational a contingency plan.

The decision centred on the interpretation of state duties under Article 10. The applicants sought information from the government that was not otherwise available to them. The government claimed that the law protected industrial secrets, prohibiting authorities from divulging such information in their possession. By a large majority, the Commission concluded that Article 10 imposes on states an obligation not only to disclose to the public available information on the environment, but also the positive duty to collect, collate, and disseminate information which would otherwise not be directly accessible to the public or brought to the public's attention. In arriving at its conclusion, the Commission relied upon 'the present state of European law' (l'état actuel du droit européen) which it said confirmed that public information represents one of the essential instruments for protecting the well-being

[76] *Leander v Sweden* ECHR (1987) Series A, No. 117, para. 74. See also *Gaskin v United Kingdom* ECHR (1987) Series A, No. 160 (government did not breach Convention in failing to allow access to a personal file of former foster child).

[77] Case 14967/89.

[78] Directive on the Major Accident Hazards of Certain Industrial Activities, 82/501/EEC, 1982 OJ 230. Amended by 87/216/EEC, 19 March 1987. The 'Seveso' law required disclosure of the production process; the substances present and their quantities; possible risks for employees, workers, the population and the environment; security measures, and rules to follow in case of accident. Other laws supplemented the right to environmental information.

and health of the populace in situations of environmental danger. The Commission referred specifically to the Chernobyl resolution, adopted by the Parliamentary Assembly of the Council of Europe, which it said recognized, at least in Europe, a fundamental right to information concerning activities that are dangerous for the environment or human well-being.

The case was referred to a Grand Chamber of the European Court of Human Rights which issued its judgment 19 February 1998. It reversed the Commission on its expanded reading of Article 10, but unanimously found a violation of Article 8, the right to family, home and private life.[79] The Court reaffirmed its earlier case law holding that Article 10 generally only prohibits a government from restricting a person from receiving information that others wish or may be willing to impart. According to the Court, '[t]hat freedom cannot be construed as imposing on a State, in circumstances such as those of the present case, positive obligations to collect and disseminate information of its own motion'.[80] Although Article 10 was found to be not applicable to the case, eight of the twenty judges indicated through separate opinions a willingness to consider positive obligations to collect and disseminate information in some circumstances.

The right to information is also contained in the Inter-American Declaration of the Rights and Duties of Man,[81] the American Convention on Human Rights,[82] the Universal Declaration of Human Rights,[83] and the African Charter on the Rights and Duties of Peoples.[84]

(b) The right to participate in governance

As noted in Part II, the right to information is a prerequisite to effective participation in decisions affecting individuals and groups. Human rights instruments, like environmental texts, generally guarantee a right to participate in government,[85] as a means of self-government and self-realization. This produces yet another set of relationships, one between human rights, environment

[79] See below, at 229–30.

[80] *Guerra and Others v Italy* ECHR Judgment of 19 February 1998, Reports 1998–I para. 53.

[81] Article IV ('Every person has the right to freedom of investigation, of opinion, and of the expression and dissemination of ideas, by any medium whatsoever').

[82] Article 13 ('Everone has the right to freedom of thought and expression. This right includes freedom to seek, receive and impart information and ideas of all kinds, regardless of frontiers, either orally, in writing, in print, in the form of art, or through any medium of one's choice').

[83] Article 19 ('Everyone has the right to freedom of opinion and expression; this right includes freedom to hold opinions without interference and to seek, receive and impart information and ideas through any media and regardless of frontiers').

[84] Article 9 ('Every individual shall have the right to receive information').

[85] Universal Declaration of Human Rights, Art. 21; International Covenant on Civil and Political Rights, Art. 25; European Convention on Human Rights, Protocol I, Art. 3; American Declaration of the Rights and Duties of Man, Arts 20, 24; American Convention on Human Rights, Art. 23; African Charter of Human and Peoples' Rights, Art. 13.

and political democracy. Some argue that democratic governance is itself an emerging right.[86] Like the question of a right to environment, this proposition raises questions about the scope and content of such a right, beyond the free and fair elections expressly required by human rights law. Broadly conceived, and directly related to environmental rights, is the notion of an ongoing and active participation in governance and institutions of civil society,[87] involving the empowerment of individuals and groups with respect to social decisions that condition life in the society.[88]

The provisions of various human rights instruments generally grant citizens the right to take part, directly or through representatives, in the conduct of public affairs and government, without specifying the modalities or scope of the right. It is notable that this right is limited to citizens, especially in light of the participatory rights granted by environmental law to all affected persons, without regard to nationality. Indeed, equality of access to participation in decision-making and remedies is a cornerstone of international environmental justice.

None of the human rights provisions identify how persons are to take part in the conduct of public affairs. Here, again, environmental law fills the gap in mandating and detailing participatory environmental impact procedures and other means of public participation.

(c) The right to a remedy

The right to a remedy when a right is violated is itself a right expressly guaranteed by universal and regional human rights instruments. The Universal Declaration of Human Rights provides that:

> Everyone has the right to an effective remedy by the competent national tribunals for acts violating the fundamental rights granted him by the constitution or laws.[89]

The International Covenant on Civil and Political Rights also obligates states to provide remedies. According to Article 2(3):

> Each State Party to the . . . Covenant undertakes:
>
> (a) To ensure that any person whose rights or freedoms as . . . recognized [in the Covenant] are violated shall have an effective remedy notwithstanding that the violation has been committed by persons acting in an official capacity.
> (b) To ensure that any person claiming such a remedy shall have the right thereto determined by competent judicial, administrative or legislative authorities, or by any

[86] See Franck, 'The Emerging Right to Democratic Governance', 86 *AJIL* (1992) 46; Fox, 'The Right to Political Participation in International Law', 17 *Yale LJ Int'l L* (1992) 539; Steiner, 'Political Participation as a Human Right,' 1 *Harv Hum Rts Y'bk* (1988) 78.

[87] See H. Steiner and P. Alston, *International Human Rights in Context* (1996) 659.

[88] Roth, 'Democratic Progress: A Normative Theoretical Perspective,' 9 *Ethics & Int'l Affairs* (1995) 55.

[89] Universal Declaration of Human Rights, Art. 8.

other competent authority provided for by the legal system of the State, and to develop the possibilities of judicial remedy.
(c) To ensure that the competent authorities shall enforce such remedies when granted.[90]

The Human Rights Committee, established pursuant to the Covenant, has identified the kinds of remedies required, depending on the type of violation and the victim's condition. The Committee has indicated that the state which has engaged in human rights violations, in addition to treating and financially compensating the victim, must undertake to investigate the facts, take appropriate action, and bring those found responsible to justice.

Among treaties adopted by the specialized agencies, the ILO Convention concerning Indigenous and Tribal Peoples in Independent Countries[91] refers to 'fair compensation for damages' (Article 15(2)), 'compensation in money' (Article 16(4)), and full compensation for 'any loss or injury' (Article 16(5)). Several treaties also expressly refer to the right to legal protection for attacks on privacy, family, home or correspondence, or attacks on honour and reputation.[92] This last protection is important, because many cases of environmental harm have been considered as attacks on the right to respect for the home.

Declarations, resolutions and other non-treaty texts also proclaim or discuss the right to a remedy. In some instances, the issue is raised by human rights organs as part of the mechanism of issuing General Comments. The third General Comment of the Committee on Economic, Social and Cultural Rights concerns the nature of state obligations pursuant to Article 2(1) of the Covenant on Economic, Social and Cultural Rights. The Committee finds that appropriate measures to implement the Covenant might include the provision of judicial remedies with respect to rights which may be considered justiciable. It specifically points to the non-discrimination requirement of the treaty and cross-references to the right to a remedy in the Covenant on Civil and Political Rights. A number of other rights are also cited as 'capable of immediate application by judicial and other organs'.[93]

Regional instruments also contain provisions regarding legal remedies for violations of rights. Article XVII of the American Declaration of the Rights

[90] International Covenant on Civil and Political Rights, Art. 2(3).

[91] Convention Concerning Indigenous and Tribal Peoples in Independent Countries, ILO No. 169, 27 June 1989, in force 5 September 1991, 28 *ILM* 1382 (1989).

[92] See Universal Declaration of Human Rights, Art. 12; International Covenant on Civil and Political Rights, Art. 17; Convention on the Rights of the Child, Art. 16; American Declaration of the Rights and Duties of Man, Art. V; American Convention on Human Rights, Art. 11(3); European Convention on Human Rights, Art. 8; African Charter on Human and Peoples Rights, Art. 5.

[93] United Nations, Compilation of General Comments and General Recommendations Adopted by Human Rights Treaty Bodies, HRI/GEN/1/Rev.3, 63, para. 5.

and Duties of Man guarantees every person the right to resort to the courts to ensure respect for legal rights and protection from acts of authority that violate any fundamental constitutional rights.

The American Convention goes further, entitling everyone to effective recourse for protection against acts that violate the fundamental rights recognized by the constitution 'or laws of the state or by the Convention', even where the act was committed by persons acting in the course of their official duties (Article 25).[94] The States Parties are to ensure that the competent authorities enforce remedies that are granted. The Inter-American Court has commented on the obligation of states to make available effective internal remedies, stating:

> Under the Convention, States Parties have an obligation to provide effective judicial remedies to victims of human rights violations (Article 25), remedies that must be substantiated in accordance with the rules of due process of law (Article 8(1)), all in keeping with the general obligation of such States to guarantee the free and full exercise of the rights recognized by the Convention to all persons subject to their jurisdiction (Article 1).[95]

The Court concluded that the obligation of Convention parties to ensure rights generally requires that remedies include due diligence efforts by the state to prevent, investigate and punish any violation of the rights recognized by the Convention.[96]

The Inter-American Commission has further elaborated on the duty to provide a remedy. It views Article 8 as requiring due process during procedures to determine rights, including determination of the matter in question by a competent, independent and impartial judicial body. The Commission interpreted Article 25 to encompass the right to 'effective' judicial protection. According to the Commission, this means the tribunal 'must reach a reasoned conclusion on the claim's merits, establishing the appropriateness or inappropriateness of the legal claim that, precisely, gives rise to the judicial recourse'.[97]

[94] American Convention on Human Rights, Art. 25.

[95] *Velasquez Rodriguez Case (Preliminary Exceptions)* IACtHR (1987) Series C, No. 1, para. 91.

[96] *Velasquez Rodriguez Case (Merits)* IACtHR (1988) Series C, No. 4 para. 166.

[97] Report No. 30/97, *Gustavo Carranza v. Argentina*, IACHR, *Annual Report of the Inter-American Commission on Human Rights 1997*, OEA/Ser.L/V/II.98, December 7 rev. (1998) 266–7. The Commission cites Report 5/96 in which it held that: 'the right to a recourse set forth in Article 25, interpreted in conjunction with the obligation in Article 1(1) and the provisions of Article 8(1), must be understood as the right of every individual to go to a tribunal when any of his rights have been violated (whether a right protected by the Convention, the constitution, or the domestic laws of the state concerned), to obtain a judicial investigation conducted by a competent, impartial, and independent tribunal that will establish whether or not a violation has taken place and will set, when appropriate, adequate compensation'.

In the European system, Article 6,[98] which provides judicial guarantees of a fair trial, has been construed to include a right to a tribunal for the determination of rights and duties.[99] Applicability of Article 6 depends upon the existence of a dispute concerning a right recognized in the law of the state concerned, including those created by licences, authorizations and permits that affect the use of property or commercial activities.[100] In *Oerlemans v Netherlands*[101] Article 6 was deemed to apply in a case involving a Dutch citizen who could not challenge a ministerial order designating his land as a protected site.

In *Zander v Sweden*,[102] Article 6 of the European Convention provided the basis for a complaint that the applicants had been denied a remedy for threatened environmental harm. The applicants owned property next to a waste treatment and storage area. Local well water showed contamination by cyanide from the dump site. The municipality prohibited use of the water and furnished temporary water supplies. Subsequently, the permissible level of cyanide was raised and the city supply was halted. When the company maintaining the dump site sought a renewed and expanded permit, the applicants argued that the threat to their water supply would be sufficiently high that the company should be obliged to provide free drinking water if pollution occurred. The board granted the permit, but denied the applicants' request. They sought but could not obtain judicial review of the decision. The European Court held that Article 6 applied and was violated. The applicability of Article 6 was based on the Court's finding that the applicants 'could arguably maintain that they were entitled under Swedish law to protection against the water in their well being polluted as a result of VAFAB's activities on the dump'.[103] According to the Court:

> As regards the character of the right at issue, the Commission notes that the right related to the environmental conditions of the applicants' property and that existence of environmental inconveniences or risks might well be a factor which affects the value of a property. Consequently the right at issue must be considered to be a civil right to which Article 6, para 1 of the Convention applies.[104]

The right to a remedy extends to compensation for pollution. In *Zimmerman and Steiner v Switzerland*,[105] the Court found Article 6 applicable to a complaint about the length of proceedings for compensation for

[98] Article 6, para. 1 states: 'In the determination of his civil rights and obligations or of any criminal charge against him, everyone is entitled to a fair and public hearing within a reasonable time by an independent and impartial tribunal established by law.'

[99] *Golder v United Kingdom* ECHR (1975) Series A, No. 18; *Klass v Germany* ECHR (1978) Series A, No. 28.

[100] *Benthem v Netherlands* ECHR (1985) Series A, No. 97.

[101] *Oerlemans v Netherlands* ECHR (1991) Series A, No. 219.

[102] *Zander v Sweden* ECHR (1993) Series A, No. 279B.

[103] Ibid., para. 24.

[104] Ibid., para. 45 (Commission opinion).

[105] *Zimmerman and Steiner v Switzerland* ECHR (1983) Series A, No. 66.

injury caused by noise and air pollution from a nearby airport. Article 6 does not, however, encompass a right to judicial review of legislative enactments. In *Braunerheilm v Sweden*,[106] the Commission denied a claim that Article 6 was violated when the applicant could not challenge in court a new law that granted fishing licences to the general public in waters where the applicant previously had exclusive rights.

Finally, the African Charter contains several provisions relevant to the right to a remedy. In Article 7, the Charter provides that every individual shall have the right to have his cause heard, including the right to an appeal to competent national organs against acts violating his fundamental rights as recognized and guaranteed by conventions, laws, regulations and customs in force. It also refers to 'the right to adequate compensation' in regard to the spoliation of resources of a dispossessed people.[107] Article 26 imposes a duty on States Parties to the Charter to guarantee the independence of the courts and allow the establishment and improvement of appropriate national institutions entrusted with the promotion and protection of rights and freedoms guaranteed by the Charter. The Commission's mandate also calls on it to draw inspiration in its work from international human rights law including the Universal Declaration of Human Rights, other instruments adopted by the United Nations and its specialized agencies, and instruments adopted by African countries. This cross-referencing in Article 60 allows the Commission to draw upon the right to a remedy contained in other human rights texts.

Humanitarian law also contains norms relating to remedies in case of a breach. Article 3 of the Hague Convention Regarding the Laws and Customs of Land Warfare obliges contracting parties to indemnify in case of a violation of the regulations. Protocol I to the Geneva Conventions of 12 August 1949 and Relating to the Protection of Victims of International Armed Conflicts states that any party to a conflict who violates the provisions of the Geneva Conventions or the Protocol 'shall . . . be liable to pay compensation'.

(d) Violations of substantive human rights

Despite the lack of explicit reference to environmental rights in most human rights instruments, global and regional tribunals—the UN Human Rights Committee, the Inter-American Commission on Human Rights, the European Commission and Court of Human Rights, the European Court of Justice, and the African Commission on Human Rights—have developed a jurisprudence that recognizes and enforces rights linked to environmental protection. Substantive rights that have been invoked in regard to environmental

[106] *Braunerheilm v Sweden*, App. No. 11764/85 (9 March 1989). See Dejeant-Pons, 'Le Droit de l'homme a l'environnement, droit fondamental au niveau européen dans le cadre du Conseil de l'Europe, et la Convention européenne de sauvegarde des droits de l'homme et des libertés fondamentales', 4 *Revue jur. de l'environnement* (1994).

[107] African Charter on Human and Peoples' Rights, Art. 21(2).

issues are principally those of the right to life, the right to respect for one's private life and home, the right to health, the right to culture and the right to the peaceful enjoyment of one's possessions.

The UN Human Rights Committee has indicated that state obligations to protect the right to life can include positive measures designed to reduce infant mortality and protect against malnutrition and epidemics.[108] In the context of the periodic reporting procedure of the International Covenant on Economic, Social and Cultural Rights, states sometimes report on environmental issues as they affect guaranteed rights. In 1986, Tunisia reported to the Commission on Economic, Social and Cultural Rights, in the context of Article 11 on the right to an adequate standard of living, on measures taken to prevent degradation of natural resources, particularly erosion, and about measures to prevent contamination of food.[109] Similarly, the Ukraine reported in 1995 on the environmental situation consequent to the explosion at Chernobyl, in regard to the right to life.[110]

Committee members sometimes request specific information about environmental harm that threatens human rights. Poland, for example, was asked to provide information in 1989 about measures to combat pollution, especially in upper Silesia.[111] Members of the Committee on the Elimination of Racial Discrimination and the Committee on the Rights of the Child have also posed questions of States Parties concerning environmental matters related to the guarantees of the treaties they monitor.

Pursuant to the Optional Protocol, the Human Rights Committee has received several complaints concerning environmental damage as a violation of one or more civil and political rights. First, a group of Canadian citizens alleged that the storage of radioactive waste near their homes threatened the right to life of present and future generations. The Committee found that the case raised 'serious issues with regard to the obligation of States parties to protect human life', but declared the case inadmissible due to failure to exhaust local remedies.[112] The Committee has also received complaints, discussed below, concerning violation of the rights of indigenous groups and minorities to protection of their traditional cultures.

On the regional level, human rights commissions in Europe, the Americas and Africa have dealt with alleged violations of human rights linked to environmental harm. In the Inter-American system, claims linked to environmental

[108] See the General Comment on Article 6 of the Civil and Political Covenant, issued by the United Nations Human Rights Committee, in Compilation of General Comments and General Recommendations adopted by Human Rights Treaty Bodies, UN Doc. HRI/GEN/1/Rev.3 (1997) 6–7 [hereinafter Compilation].

[109] E/1986/3/Add.9.

[110] CCPR/C/95/Add. 2, 20 July 1994, paras 53–5.

[111] E/1989/4/Add.12.

[112] Communication No. 67/1980, *EHP v Canada*, 2 Selected Decisions of the Human Rights Committee (1990), 20.

harm have generally asserted that the right to life is threatened, or that the rights of indigenous groups have been violated. The cases submitted to the African system have generally invoked the right to health, protected by Article 16 of the African Charter, rather than the right to environment contained in the same document. In Communications 25/89, 47/90, 56/91 and 100/93 against Zaire the Commission held that failure by the government to provide basic services such as safe drinking water constituted a violation of Article 16. The Commission currently has pending a communication involving the Ogoni region of Nigeria which presents complex issues of the right to life, health and environment.

In Europe, most of the victims have invoked either the right to information, discussed above, or the right to privacy and family life (Article 8). Article 8(1) of the European Convention on Human Rights and Fundamental Freedoms provides that 'everyone has the right to respect for his private life, his home and his correspondence'. The second paragraph of the Article sets forth the permissible grounds for limiting the exercise of the right.[113] A related provision, Article 1 of Protocol 1, ensures that 'every natural or legal person is entitled to the peaceful enjoyment of his possessions'. The former European Commission accepted that pollution or other environmental harm may result in a breach of Article 1 of Protocol 1, but only where such harm results in a substantial reduction in the value of the property and that reduction is not compensated by the state. The Commission added that the right to peaceful enjoyment of possessions 'does not, in principle, guarantee the right to the peaceful enjoyment of possessions in a pleasant environment'.[114]

Decisions of the European Commission on Human Rights indicate that environmental harm attributable to state action or inaction which has significant injurious effect on a person's home or private and family life constitutes a breach of Article 8(1). The harm may be excused, however, under Article 8(2) if it results from an authorized activity of economic benefit to the community in general, as long as there is no disproportionate burden on any particular individual; i.e. the measures must have a legitimate aim, be lawfully enacted, and be proportional. States enjoy a margin of appreciation in determining the legitimacy of the aim pursued. The Court, in recent decisions, seems to balance the competing interests of the individual and the community more overtly than did the Commission, at the same time affording the state a certain margin of appreciation.

[113] Paragraph 2 provides: 'There shall be no interference by a public authority with the exercise of this right except such as is in accordance with the law and is necessary in a democratic society in the interests of national security, public safety or the economic well-being of the country, for the prevention of disorder or crime, for the protection of health and morals, or for the protection of the rights and freedoms of others.'

[114] *Rayner v United Kingdom* (1986) 47 DR 5, 14.

Most of the European privacy and home cases involve noise pollution. In *Arrondelle v United Kingdom*,[115] the applicant complained of noise from Gatwick Airport and a nearby motorway. The application was declared admissible and eventually settled with the payment of £7,500. *Baggs v United Kingdom*, a similar case, was also resolved by friendly settlement.[116] The settlement of the cases left unresolved numerous issues, some of which were addressed in *Powell and Rayner v United Kingdom* at the Court.[117] The Court found that aircraft noise from Heathrow Airport constituted a violation of Article 8, but was justified under Article 8(2) as 'necessary in a democratic society' for the economic well-being of the country. Noise was acceptable under the principle of proportionality, if it did not 'create an unreasonable burden for the person concerned', a test that could be met by the state if the individual had 'the possibility of moving elsewhere without substantial difficulties and losses'. In contrast, in the *Vearncombe* case, the Commission found that the level and frequency of the noise did not reach the point where a violation of Article 8 could be made out and therefore the application was inadmissible.[118]

The European Commission and the Court often accept that the economic well-being of the country will excuse a certain amount of environmental harm, following the *Powell and Rayner* case.[119]

In *G and E v Norway*,[120] two members of the Sami people alleged a violation of Article 8 due to a proposed hydroelectric project that would flood part of their traditional reindeer grazing grounds. The Commission accepted that traditional practices could constitute 'private and family life' within the meaning of Article 8. It questioned, however, whether the amount of land to be flooded was enough to constitute an 'interference' and found that in any case, the project was justified as necessary for the economic well-being of the country. The application was therefore inadmissible.

The major decision of the Court on environmental harm as a breach of the right to private life and the home is *Lopez-Ostra v Spain*.[121] The applicant and her daughter suffered serious health problems from the fumes of a tannery waste treatment plant which operated alongside the apartment building where they lived. The plant opened in July 1988 without a required licence

[115] *Arrondelle v United Kingdom* (1980) 19 DR 186; (1982) 26 DR 5.

[116] *Baggs v United Kingdom* (1985) 44 DR 13; (1987) 52 DR 29.

[117] *Powell and Rayner v United Kingdom* ECHR (1990) Series A, No. 172.

[118] *Vearncombe et al v United Kingdom and Federal Republic of Germany* (1989) 59 DR 186.

[119] See also *S v France* (1990) 65 DR 250 (application inadmissible: nuisance due to nuclear power station built 300 metres from applicant's house constituted a breach of Article 8(1), but was justified under Article 8(2) because the economic well-being of the country made it necessary in a democratic society and there was no unreasonable burden placed on the applicant because compensation was paid).

[120] *Joined Applications 9278/81 and 9415/81* (1984) 35 DR 30.

[121] *Lopez-Ostra v Spain* ECHR (1994) Series A, No. 303C.

and without having followed the procedure for obtaining such a licence. The plant malfunctioned when it began operations, releasing gas fumes and contamination which immediately caused health problems and nuisance to people living in the district. The town council evacuated the local residents and rehoused them free of charge in the town centre during the summer. In spite of this, the authorities allowed the plant to resume partial operation. In October the applicant and her family returned to their flat where there were continuing problems. The applicant finally sold her house and moved in 1992.

The decision is significant for several reasons. First, the Court did not require the applicant to exhaust administrative remedies to challenge operation of the plant under the environmental protection laws, but only to complete remedies applicable to enforcement of basic rights. Mrs Lopez exhausted the latter remedies when the Supreme Court of Spain denied her appeal on a suit for infringement of her fundamental rights and her complaint with the Constitutional Court was dismissed as manifestly ill-founded. Two sisters-in-law of Mrs Lopez, who lived in the same building as her, followed the procedures concerning environmental law. They brought administrative proceedings alleging that the plant was operating unlawfully. On 18 September 1991 the local court, noting a continuing nuisance and that the plant did not have the licences required by law, ordered that it should be closed until they were obtained. However, enforcement of this order was stayed following an appeal. The case was still pending in the Supreme Court in 1995 when the European Court issued its judgment. The two sisters-in-law also lodged a complaint, as a result of which a local judge instituted criminal proceedings against the plant for an environmental health offence. The two complainants joined the proceedings as civil parties.

The European Human Rights Court noted that severe environmental pollution may affect individuals' well-being and prevent them from enjoying their homes in such a way as to affect their private and family life adversely, without, however, seriously endangering their health. It found that the determination of whether this violation had occurred should be tested by striking a fair balance between the interest of the town's economic well-being and the applicant's effective enjoyment of her right to respect for her home and her private and family life. In doing this, the Court applied its 'margin of appreciation' doctrine, allowing the state a 'certain' discretion in determining the appropriate balance, but finding in this case that the margin of appreciation had been exceeded. It awarded Mrs Lopez 4,000,000 pesetas, plus costs and attorneys' fees.

In *Maria Guerra v Italy*, in regard to Article 8, the Court reaffirmed that it can impose positive obligations on states to ensure respect for private or family life. Citing the *Lopez-Ostra* case, the Court reiterated that 'severe environmental pollution may affect individuals' well-being and prevent

them from enjoying their homes in such a way as to affect their private and family life'.[122] Noting that the individuals waited throughout the operation of fertilizer production at the company for essential information 'that would have enabled them to assess the risks they and their families might run if they continued to live at Manfredonia, a town particularly exposed to danger in the event of an accident at the factory' the Court found a violation of Article 8.

The Court's decision is strained, resulting from the Court's reluctance to overturn its prior case law interpreting Article 10. The basis of the complaint was the government's failure to provide environmental information, not pollution like that found in the *Lopez-Ostra* case. The Court also declined to consider whether the right to life guaranteed by Article 2 had been violated, considering it unnecessary in light of its decision on Article 8. The decision seems unwarranted, given that deaths from cancer had occurred in the factory and this would have a clear bearing on damages. In regard to the latter, the Court found that applicants had not proved pecuniary damages but were entitled to 10,000,000 lire each for non-pecuniary damage. The applicants also sought a clean-up order, which the Court declined to give on the ground that it lacks the power to issue orders.

It must be recognized that existing human rights guarantees are primarily useful when the environmental harm consists of pollution. Issues of resource management and nature conservation or biological diversity are more difficult to bring under the human rights rubric, absent a right to a safe and ecologically-balanced environment. A 1974 opinion of the European Commission on Human Rights indicates the attitude of some human rights bodies and the limits of the human rights approach. In an application challenging the refusal to allow an Icelandic resident to have a dog as a violation of the right of privacy and family life guaranteed by Article 8 of the European Convention on Human Rights, the Commission stated:

> The Commission cannot however accept that the protection afforded by Article 8 of the Convention extends to relationships of the individual with his entire immediate surroundings, in so far as they do not involve human relationships and notwithstanding the desire of the individual to keep such relationships within the private sphere. No doubt the dog has had close ties with man since time immemorial. However, given the above considerations this alone is not sufficient to bring the keeping of a dog into the sphere of the private life of the owner.[123]

Several recent cases in the European human rights system mark renewed efforts to address issues of nature protection through human rights. All of the cases were brought against France and concerned a French law imposing an obligation on certain owners of small areas of land to belong to the local

[122] *Maria Guerra v Italy*, supra n. 80, para. 60.

[123] *Application 6825/74 (X v Iceland)*, 5 DR 86.

hunting association and to permit hunting on their property. The applicants opposed hunting and complained that the French legal obligations violated the right to peaceful enjoyment of their possessions, the right to freedom of association, and the right to freedom of conscience. They also maintained that the obligations were discriminatory. They relied on Article 1 of Protocol No. 1 and Articles 9 and 11 of the Convention, separately and in conjunction with Article 14 of the Convention.

The Commission issued its report on the first of the cases, *Marie-Jeanne Chassagnou, René Petit and Simone Lasgrezas v France*, on 30 October 1997.[124] It found a violation of all the rights except freedom of conscience, which it decided it need not address because of the other findings. The report was submitted to the Committee of Ministers. The second two cases, *Leon Dumont and others v France* and *Josephine Montion v France*, involved identical issues and were submitted by the Commission to the Court in March 1998.

2. The Right to Environment

A growing number of global and regional instruments and national constitutions include a right to environment among human rights guarantees. Nonetheless the issue continues to be debated. As noted earlier, human rights and environmental protection represent different, but overlapping social values, sharing a core of common interests and objectives, while also having potentially conflicting areas of independent concern. Given the goal of international human rights law, expressed in the Universal Declaration of Human Rights and the Covenants as 'freedom, justice and peace in the world', the issue becomes whether recognition of a right to environment is necessary to achieving this goal. Scientifically, the integrated biosphere, and each interrelated and interdependent sector of it, must be protected to ensure human survival. It thus constitutes a fundamental common interest of humanity.

Environmental protection can be viewed as a precondition for or integral part of the exercise of existing human rights, with protection sought through enforcement of the current rights catalogue. However, such protection is unlikely ever to be adequate to achieve the level of environmental protection necessary to remedy current problems and prevent future ones. Procedural guarantees of information and participation may prove insufficient to protect the environment if the majority of a fully informed society decides to sacrifice environmental quality to advance economic or cultural considerations, however great may be the harm to the minority or to those outside its borders. Procedural environmental rights can effectively protect the environment only

[124] *Marie-Jeanne Chassagnou, René Petit and Simone Lasgrezas v France*; http://www.dhcommhr.coe.fr/fr/25088R31.F.html.

if coupled with substantive international regulation, which leads to the question of the right to environment. Many of the arguments supporting and opposing the right to environment are described in Part I. In addition to those, some argue against any addition to the human rights catalogue out of fear that the addition of claims will devalue existing human rights.[125] In spite of these concerns, various treaties and other international instruments have been drafted to include a right to an environment of a specified quality, the problem being deemed sufficiently important to fit within the human rights framework.

At the United Nations, the Human Rights Commission and Sub-Commission have both addressed the issue of the right to environment. During its 1989 session, the United Nations Sub-Commission on the Prevention of Discrimination and Protection of Minorities adopted a decision calling for consideration of a possible study of the problem of the environment and its relation to human rights.[126] The Human Rights Commission, influenced in part by preparations for UNCED, approved the Sub-Commission decision on 15 March 1990.[127] The Sub-Commission thereupon appointed a Special Rapporteur who presented reports on the subject between 1991 and 1994.[128] In her 1993 report, the Special Rapporteur left open the question of the preparation of a new international instrument on the right to a satisfactory environment or environmental rights. However, the report acknowledged such a right in its discussion, integrating it with a right to development, with action to ensure the enjoyment of all human rights, and with a right to prevention of environmental harm.

In a final report in 1994, the Special Rapporteur included in an Annex a set of Draft Principles on Human Rights and the Environment. The Preamble to the Declaration grounds it in human rights law, including humanitarian law, and international environmental law. It proclaims the indivisibility, universality and interdependence of all human rights (Preamble, Principles I and II). The Draft Declaration sets forth the environmental dimension of recognized human rights and also explicitly states that:

All persons have the right to a secure, healthy and ecologically-sound environment. (Principle II)

[125] See M.A. Glendon, *Rights Talk: The Impoverishment of Political Discourse* (1991). See also, Alston, 'Conjuring Up New Human Rights: A Proposal for Quality Control', 78 *AJIL* (1984) 607.

[126] UN Doc. E/CN.4/Sub.2/1989/L.23 (1989).

[127] The United States and Japan both abstained on the resolution, stating that environmental issues should be dealt with exclusively by environmental bodies.

[128] Human Rights and the Environment: Preliminary Report, UN Doc. E/CN.4/Sub.2/1991/8, 2 August 1992; First Progress Report, UN Doc. E/CN.4/Sub.2/1992/7, 2 July 1992; Second Progress Report, UN Doc. E/CN.4/Sub.2/1993/7, 26 July 1993.

The Principles reaffirm the right to be free from discrimination in regard to actions and decisions that affect the environment (Principle 3). Part II details the substantive aspects of environmental human rights, including the right to freedom from pollution, environmental degradation and activities that adversely affect the environment, threaten life, health, livelihood, well-being or sustainable development (Principle 5); the right to protection and preservation of environmental milieu and 'the essential processes and areas necessary to maintain biological diversity and ecosystems' (Principle 6); the right to the highest attainable standard of health free from environmental harm (Principle 7); and the right to safe and healthy food and water adequate to well-being (Principle 8). Rights to safe and healthy home and working environments are also guaranteed (Principles 9, 10). Cultural rights are included in Principle 13, which provides that everyone has the right to benefit from the conservation and sustainable use of nature and natural resources, including ecologically sound access to nature and the right to preservation of unique sites. Indigenous rights are especially mentioned. Part III of the Draft concerns the procedural aspects of environmental human rights and includes rights of information and participation and the right to a remedy. Unlike many human rights instruments, the Declaration also details in Part IV the duties owed by humans, legal persons, and states beginning with a duty to protect and preserve the environment.

The Human Rights Commission decided to request a report of the Secretary-General on the issues raised by the study and the Draft Principles. The Secretary-General submitted reports in 1997 and 1998, based on the comments of states, intergovernmental and non-governmental organizations. At its 1998 session, the Commission decided to appoint a review committee to submit a revised version of the Draft Declaration for possible adoption.

On the regional level, the African Charter on Human and Peoples' Rights was the first international human rights instrument to contain an explicit guarantee of environmental quality. Its Article 24 recognizes the right of '[a]ll peoples' to a generally 'satisfactory environment favourable to their development'. The inclusion of the right to environment as a peoples' right reflects the widespread nature of most environmental harm and the indivisibility and interdependence of the biosphere, where harm to one milieu often transfers to another and may cause long-term and unforeseen consequences. Unlike most human rights violations, it would be an extremely rare case where environmental degradation would affect only a single individual or small group.

In 1988, the Organization of American States adopted the Protocol on Economic, Social and Cultural Rights to the American Convention on Human Rights.[129] Article 11, entitled 'Right to a healthy environment', provides: (1)

[129] Protocol of San Salvador, 14 November 1988, OASTS No. 69, reprinted in 28 *ILM* (1989) 156.

'Everyone shall have the right to live in a healthy environment and to have access to basic public services.' This right is complemented in paragraph 2 by imposing a duty on States Parties to promote the protection, preservation and improvement of the environment.

The operative parts of the Protocol affirm the progressive nature of the obligations. Article 1 requires states to cooperate on an international level and to adopt all necessary measures 'to the extent allowed by their available resources, and taking into account their degree of development' to protect the guaranteed rights. In addition, the parties must adopt domestic legislation or take other measures as necessary to make those rights a reality. The Protocol does not grant the right of individual petition for violations of the right to environment[130] but the Inter-American Commission on Human Rights may formulate observations and recommendations on the status of the rights contained in the Protocol in all or some of the member states.[131]

In comparing the OAU and OAS texts, different emphases on environmental protection can be seen. In the African Charter, the right to environment is grounded in concerns for development: economic, social and personal development. The Protocol of San Salvador focuses instead on health. The phrase can be read either to require an environment adequate for human health or more broadly to mean that the environment itself must remain healthy, i.e. ecologically-balanced, sustainable and free from pollution. The latter is more in keeping with the separate inclusion of a right to environment.[132]

In Europe, neither the European Convention[133] nor the European Social Charter[134] contain a right to environmental quality and the European Commission on Human Rights has held that such a right cannot be directly inferred from the Convention. During the 1970s the Council of Europe considered proposals to provide for a human right to a healthy environment. Some objected in principle to including the right to a healthy environment in the catalogue of human rights. Others questioned whether it should be considered a political, civil or social right. A Draft Protocol to the European Convention on Human Rights attempted to address these concerns, but it was never adopted. In 1990, renewed efforts resulted in a Recommendation to the Parliamentary Assembly of the Council of Europe on the Formulation

[130] Protocol of San Salvador, 14 November 1988, OASTS No. 69, reprinted in 28 *ILM* 156 (1989), Art. 19(6). Protocol Art. 19(6) permits individual complaints to be filed with the Inter-American Commission on Human Rights only for violations of Articles 8(a) (trade union freedoms) and 13 (right to education).

[131] Ibid., Art. 19(7).

[132] The right to health is guaranteed in Article 10 of the Protocol.

[133] European Convention for the Protection of Human Rights and Fundamental Freedoms, ETS No. 5, 213 UNTS 221.

[134] European Social Charter, ETS No. 35, 529 UNTS 89.

of a European Charter and a European Convention on Environmental Protection.[135]

To date, no general charter or convention has been adopted, but the Council of Europe authored a Convention for the Protection of Human Rights and Dignity of the Human Being with Regard to the Application of Biology and Medicine.[136] Concerned with human dignity and respect for the human being, the Convention requires prior informed consent before there is any intervention in the health field. The Convention establishes that States Parties shall protect the dignity and identity of human beings, referring to the latter as a human right to be respected along with other rights and fundamental freedoms. This is reinforced by Article 15 which provides that scientific research in the field of biology and medicine is subject to the provisions of the Convention and 'the other legal provisions ensuring the protection of the human being'. This suggests that all existing human rights norms govern research and treatment, whether undertaken by the state or by private actors. Article 2 explicitly states that the interests and welfare of the human being shall prevail over the sole interest of society or science. Free and informed consent is the subject of a chapter in the agreement, providing a basic principle for 'intervention.' Unfortunately, the Convention contains no definitions of terms. One problematic provision is Article 7, which concerns the mentally ill. It allows non-consensual treatment, without substantive limits on the nature or extent of the intervention, where 'without such treatment, serious harm is likely to result to his or her health'. It would have been preferable had the treaty imposed a requirement that the least harmful or dangerous treatment be utilized, and excluded permanently disabling or personality-crippling 'treatments' such as lobotomies and electroshock.

The provisions on the human genome are progressive. Article 13 provides that an intervention seeking to modify the human genome may only be undertaken for preventive, diagnostic or therapeutic purposes and only if its aim is not to introduce any modification in the genome of any descendants. No testing or alterations are permitted for gender selection or other preferences (Articles 12, 14). The creation of human embryos for research purposes is prohibited (Article 18(2)) and the human body and its parts are not to be used for financial gain (Article 21). The treaty foresees enforcement through injunctions, compensation and punishment.

The Convention also contains no direct ban on human cloning. Due to concerns over this omission, the European states negotiated a protocol to this

[135] See van Dyke, 'A Proposal to Introduce the Right to a Healthy Environment into the European Convention Regime', 13 *Va. Envt'l LJ* (1993) 323; and Hodvka, 'Is There a Right to a Healthy Environment in the International Legal Order?', 7 *Conn J Int'l. L* (1991) 65.

[136] Convention on Human Rights and Biomedicine (Oviedo, 4 April 1997), ETS No. 164 reprinted in 36 *ILM* (1997) 817. For other texts on this topic, see Part IV below.

effect.[137] The Committee of Ministers presented the draft, prepared at its request by the Steering Committee on Bioethics, to the Parliamentary Assembly, which prepared an opinion recommending adoption of the draft protocol. The Preamble calls cloning 'contrary to human dignity' and in Article 1, its only substantive provision, the draft prohibits 'any intervention seeking to create a human being genetically identical to another human being, whether living or dead'.

In national law, the constitutions of more than 60 countries, including virtually every constitution adopted or revised since 1970, either state the principle that an environment of a specified quality constitutes a human right or impose environmental duties upon the state. Article 50 of the Constitution of the Ukraine, adopted 28 June 1996, is an example. It states that 'every person has the right to a safe and healthy environment and to compensation for damages resulting from the violation of this right'. Other constitutions refer to a decent, healthy (Hungary, South Africa, Nicaragua, Korea, Turkey), pleasant (Korea), natural, clean, ecologically-balanced (Peru, Philippines, Portugal), or safe environment or one free from contamination (Chile). In some states, courts have allowed lawsuits to enforce the constitutional right to environmental quality, while other courts have found that the right is non-justiciable. This widespread state practice supports the view that the right to environment is an emerging norm likely to continue to develop in international law.

IV INDIGENOUS PEOPLES AND LOCAL COMMUNITIES

1. Indigenous Peoples

There are over 200 million indigenous people in the world, many of them living in extremely vulnerable ecosystems: the Arctic and tundra, tropical rainforests, the boreal forests, riverine and coastal zones, mountains and semi-arid rangelands. These lands have come under increasing pressure from economic exploitation. Governments, development banks, transnational corporations and entrepreneurs see the territories used and occupied by indigenous peoples as important repositories of mineral deposits, hydroelectric potential, hardwoods, oil and new farm and pasture lands. Indigenous peoples[138] are particularly

[137] Council of Europe, Draft Additional Protocol to the Convention on Human Rights and Biomedicine on the Prohibition of Cloning Human Beings with Explanatory Report and Parliamentary Assembly Opinion, Doc. DIR/JUR (97) 9, 36 *ILM* (1997) 1415.

[138] Although there is no clear definition of the term 'indigenous peoples', a certain number of criteria have emerged in the course of discussions in the Working Group on Indigenous Populations. Indigenous peoples are the descendants of the original inhabitants of territories since colonized by foreigners; they have distinct cultures which set them apart from the dominant society; many have, until comparatively recently, had a high degree of control over their development; indigenous peoples have a strong sense of self-identity.

affected by environmental harm. As found by the Special Papporteur on human rights and the environment:

Indigenous peoples have a special relationship with the land and the environment in which they live. In nearly all indigenous cultures, the land is revered; 'Mother Earth' is the core of their culture. The land is the home of the ancestors, the provider of everyday material needs, and the future held in trust for coming generations. According to the indigenous view, land should not be torn open and exploited—this is a violation of the Earth—nor can it be bought, sold or bartered. Furthermore, indigenous peoples have, over a long period of time, developed successful systems of land use and resource management. These systems, including nomadic pastoralism, shifting cultivation, various forms of agro-forestry, terrace agriculture, hunting, herding and fishing, were for a long time considered inefficient, unproductive and primitive. However, as world opinion grows more conscious of the environment and particularly of the damage being done to fragile habitats, there has been a corresponding interest in indigenous land-use practices. The notion of sustainability is the essence of both indigenous economies and their cultures.[139]

Forest-dwelling indigenous people have often been forced from their traditional homelands by deforestation, mining and invasion of non-indigenous settlers. In the most extreme cases, they have contracted diseases against which they have no immunity. Outside the forests, farmers in many regions suffer from desertification, a phenomenon which is most often the result of human misuse of soil.

Environmental law recognizes the importance of indigenous peoples and local communities, particularly their traditional knowledge about environmentally-sustainable practices. Principle 22 of the Rio Declaration refers to indigenous peoples, stating:

Indigenous people and their communities, and other local communities, have a vital role in environmental management and development because of their knowledge and traditional practices. States should recognize and duly support their identity, culture and interests and enable their effective participation in the achievement of sustainable development.

This formulation fails to mention indigenous rights, in keeping with the general tenor of the texts adopted at the Rio Conference. The chapter of Agenda 21 on indigenous populations mentions existing treaties and the draft universal declaration on indigenous rights. However, no reference is made to the ILO Indigenous and Tribal Peoples Convention (No. 169) which contains environmental rights for the indigenous populations, requiring States Parties to take special measures to safeguard the environment of indigenous peoples (Article 4). In particular governments must provide for environmental impact studies of planned development activities and take measures, in cooperation with the peoples concerned, to protect and preserve the environment of the

[139] See Preliminary Report, supra n. 128, at para. 25.

territories they inhabit. In contrast, Agenda 21 provides that indigenous people and their communities 'may require, in accordance with national legislation, greater control over their lands, self-management of their resources, participation in development decisions affecting them, including, where appropriate, participation in the establishment or management of protected areas'.

Among environmental agreements, the most innovative in regard to indigenous rights and responsibilities is the Declaration on the Establishment of the Arctic Council.[140] A major feature of the Council is the involvement of indigenous peoples as Permanent Participants, based on 'recognition of the special relationship and unique contributions to the Arctic of indigenous peoples and their communities' (Preamble). Three organizations, the Inuit Circumpolar Conference, the Sami Council and the Association of Indigenous Minorities of the North, Siberia and the Far East of the Russian Federation, are specifically included in the Declaration. Other groups may participate, up to one fewer than the number of member states, if they meet the criteria set forth in Article 2 of the Declaration including having a majority Arctic indigenous constituency. The category of Permanent Participation is created, according to the Declaration 'to provide for active participation and full consultation with the Arctic indigenous representatives within the Arctic Council'.

Indigenous groups may also invoke human rights instruments. The provisions of the Covenant on Civil and Political Rights, in particular the guarantee of minority rights, can help to protect indigenous land and culture from environmental degradation. The United Nations Human Rights Committee has interpreted Article 27[141] of the Covenant on Civil and Political Rights in a broad manner:

> With regard to the exercise of the cultural rights protected under Article 27, the Committee observes that culture manifests itself in many forms, including a particular way of life associated with the use of land resources, especially in the case of indigenous peoples. That right may include such traditional activities as fishing or hunting and the right to live in reserves protected by law. The enjoyment of those rights may require positive legal measures of protection and measures to ensure the effective participation of members of minority communities in decisions which affect them. . . . The protection of these rights is directed towards ensuring the survival and continued development of the cultural, religious and social identity of the minorities concerned, thus enriching the fabric of society as a whole.[142]

[140] Canada–Denmark–Finland–Iceland–Norway–the Russian Federation–Sweden–United States, Declaration on the Establishment of the Arctic Council, Ottawa, 19 September 1996, reprinted in 35 *ILM* (1996) 1382.

[141] CCPR Article 27 provides that members of minority groups 'shall not be denied the right, in community with other members of their group, to enjoy their own culture, to profess and practise their own religion, or to use their own language'.

[142] General Comment 23 paras 7, 9 in Compilation at 41. See *Kitok v Sweden*, Comm. 197/1985, II Official Records of the Human Rights Committee 1987/88, UN Doc. CCPR/7/Add.1, at 442 (Swedish 1971 Reindeer Husbandry Act held not to violate rights of

The invocation of Article 27 protects the cultural life rather than physical life of indigenous people, even though the survival of the group, *qua* group, may be at stake. In a rare case decided on the merits, the Committee decided that Article 27 was not violated by the extent of stone-quarrying permitted by Finland in traditional lands of the Sami.[143] The applicants, forty-eight Sami reindeer breeders challenged the decision of the Central Forestry Board to permit the quarry. The Committee observed that a state may wish to encourage development or economic activity, but found that the scope of its freedom to do so must be tested by reference to the obligations of the state under Article 27. The Committee explicitly rejected the European doctrine of margin of appreciation, holding that measures whose impact amount to a denial of the right to culture will not be compatible with the Covenant, although those which simply have a 'certain limited impact on the way of life of persons belonging to a minority' will not necessarily violate the treaty. The Committee also referred to its General Comment on Article 27, according to which measures must be taken 'to ensure the effective participation of members of minority communities in decisions which affect them'.

The Committee concluded that the amount of quarrying which had taken place did not constitute a denial of the applicants' right to culture. It noted that they were consulted and their views taken into account in the government's decision. Moreover, the Committee determined that measures were taken to minimize the impact on reindeer herding activity and on the environment. In regard to future activities, 'if mining activities in the Angeli area were to be approved on a large scale and significantly expanded' then it might constitute a violation of Article 27. According to the Committee, '[t]he State party is under a duty to bear this in mind when either extending existing contracts or granting new ones'.[144]

In *Bernard Ominayak and the Lubicon Band v Canada*,[145] the applicants alleged that the government of the province of Alberta had deprived the Band of their means of subsistence and their right to self-determination by selling oil and gas concessions on their lands. The Committee characterized the claim as one of minority rights under Article 27 and found that historic inequities and more recent developments, including the oil and gas

an individual Sami as a reasonable and objective measure necessary for the continued viability and welfare of the minority as a whole).

[143] Communication No. 511/1992, *Ilmari Lansman et al v Finland*, Human Rights Committee, Final Decisions, 74, CCPR/C/57/1 (1996).

[144] Other cases involving Sami reindeer breeders include Communication No. 431/1990, *OS et al v Finland*, decision of 23 March 1994, and Communication No. 671/1995, *Jouni E Lansmann et al v Finland*, decision of 30 October 1996.

[145] Communication No. 167/1984, Decisions of the Human Rights Committee, UN Doc. CCPR/C/38/D/167/1984 (1990).

exploitation, were threatening the way of life and culture of the Band and thus were in violation of Article 27.

In the Inter-American system, the Commission established a link between environmental quality and the right to life in response to a petition brought on behalf of the Yanomani Indians of Brazil. The petition alleged that the government violated the American Declaration of the Rights and Duties of Man[146] by constructing a highway through Yanomani territory and authorizing the exploitation of the territory's resources. These actions led to the influx of non-indigenous people who brought contagious diseases which remained untreated due to lack of medical care. The Commission found that the government had violated the Yanomani rights to life, liberty and personal security guaranteed by Article 1 of the Declaration, as well as the right of residence and movement (Article VIII) and the right to the preservation of health and well-being (Article XI).[147]

Apart from deciding the individual complaints brought to it and discussed above, the Inter-American Commission on Human Rights has the authority to study the human rights situation generally or in regard to specific issues with a member state of the OAS. In two recently published studies, the Commission devoted particular attention to environmental rights of indigenous populations in Ecuador[148] and Brazil[149]

In regard to Ecuador, the Commission noted that it had been examining the human rights situation in the Oriente for several years, in response to claims that oil exploitation activities were contaminating the water, air and soil, thereby causing the people of the region to become sick and to have a greatly increased risk of serious illness.[150] It found, after an on-site visit, that both the government and inhabitants agreed that the environment was contaminated, with inhabitants exposed to toxic by-products of oil exploitation in their drinking and bathing water, in the air, and in the soil. The inhabitants were unanimous in claiming that oil operations, especially the disposal of toxic wastes, jeopardized their lives and health. Many suffered skin diseases, rashes, chronic infections, and gastrointestinal problems. In addition, many

[146] Pan American Union, Final Act of the Ninth Conference of American States, Res. XXX, at 38 (1948), reprinted in OAS, *Basic Documents Pertaining to Human Rights in the Inter-american System* (1996).

[147] Case 7615 (Brazil), Inter-Am.CHR, 1984–1985 Annual Report 24, OEA/Ser.L/V/II.66, doc. 10, rev. 1 (1985).

[148] Inter-Am.CHR., Report on the Situation of Human Rights in Ecuador, OEA/Ser.L/V/II.96, doc. 10 rev. 1 (1997) [hereinafter Report on Ecuador].

[149] Inter-Am.CHR., Report on the Situation of Human Rights in Brazil, OEA/Ser.L/V/II.97, doc. 29, rev. 1 (1997).

[150] Report on Ecuador (supra n. 148) v. The Commission first became aware of problems in this region of the country when a petition was filed on behalf of the indigenous Huaorani people in 1990. The Commission decided that the situation was not restricted to the Huaorani and thus should be treated within the framework of the general country report.

claimed that pollution of local waters contaminated fish and drove away wildlife, threatening food supplies.

The Commission in its discussion of relevant human rights law emphasized the right to life and physical security. It stated that:

> [t]he realization of the right to life, and to physical security and integrity is necessarily related to and in some ways dependent upon one's physical environment. Accordingly, where environmental contamination and degradation pose a persistent threat to human life and health, the foregoing rights are implicated.[151]

In this regard, States Parties may be required to take positive measures to safeguard the fundamental and non-derogable rights to life and physical integrity, in particular to prevent the risk of severe environmental pollution that could threaten human life and health, or to respond when persons have suffered injury.

The Commission also directly addressed concerns for economic development, noting that the Convention does not prevent nor discourage it, but rather requires that it take place under conditions of respect for the rights of affected individuals. Thus, while the right to development implies that each state may exploit its natural resources, 'the absence of regulation, inappropriate regulation, or a lack of supervision in the application of extant norms may create serious problems with respect to the environment which translate into violations of human rights protected by the American Convention'.[152] The Commission concluded that:

> [c]onditions of severe environmental pollution, which may cause serious physical illness, impairment and suffering on the part of the local populace, are inconsistent with the right to be respected as a human being . . . The quest to guard against environmental conditions which threaten human health requires that individuals have access to: information, participation in relevant decision-making processes, and judicial recourse.[153]

This holding can clearly be applied outside the context of indigenous peoples and sets general standards for environmental rights in the Inter-American system. The Commission elaborated on these rights, stating that the right to seek, receive and impart information and ideas of all kinds is protected by Article 13 of the American Convention. According to the Commission, information that domestic law requires to be submitted as part of environmental impact assessment procedures must be 'readily accessible' to potentially affected individuals. Public participation is viewed as linked to Article 23 of the American Convention, which provides that every citizen shall enjoy the right 'to take part in the conduct of public affairs, directly or through freely chosen representatives'. Finally, the right of access to judicial remedies is called 'the fundamental guarantor of rights at the national level'. The Commission

[151] Report on Ecuador at 88. [152] Ibid., at 89. [153] Ibid., at 92, 93.

quotes Article 25 of the American Convention that provides everyone 'the right to simple and prompt recourse, or any other effective recourse, to a competent court or tribunal for protection against acts that violate his fundamental rights recognized by the constitution or laws of the state concerned or by th[e] Convention'.

The Commission called on the government to implement legislation enacted to strengthen protection against pollution and to clean up activities by private licensee companies and to take further action to remedy existing contamination and prevent future recurrences. In particular it recommended that the state take measures to improve systems to disseminate information about environmental issues, and enhance the transparency of and opportunities for public input into processes affecting the inhabitants of development sectors.

The report on Brazil also included a chapter on indigenous rights. Among the problems discussed are those of environmental destruction leading to severe health and cultural consequences. In particular their cultural and physical integrity are said to be under constant threat and attack from invading prospectors and the environmental pollution they create. State protection against the invasions is called 'irregular and feeble' leading to constant danger and environmental deterioration.

United Nations and OAS organs have drafted Declarations on the Rights of Indigenous Peoples. The United Nations Sub-Commission on Prevention of Discrimination and Protection of Minorities adopted a draft on 26 August 1994, which it submitted to the Commission on Human Rights for further action.[154] The Commission decided on 3 March 1995 to establish an intergovernmental working group to review the draft. As of its 1998 session, the Commission had not yet approved the Declaration. The OAS Declaration was adopted in the framework of the Inter-American Commission on Human Rights and submitted to the OAS General Assembly for adoption at its June 1998 session in Bogota, Colombia. Both declarations emphasize the land rights of indigenous peoples, including archaeological and historical sites. Part VI of the UN draft details such rights, including the right of indigenous peoples 'to maintain and strengthen their distinctive spiritual and material relationship with the lands, territories, waters and coastal seas and other resources which they have traditionally owned or otherwise occupied or used, and to uphold their responsibilities to future generations in this regard' (Article 25). Specific protection is also afforded to medicinal plants, animals and minerals. Indigenous peoples have the right to special measures to control, develop and protect their genetic resources, including seeds, medicines, and knowledge of the properties

[154] Resolution 1994/45, Sub-Commission on Prevention of Discrimination and Protection of Minorities, 46th sess. 1994, reprinted in 34 *ILM* (1995) 541. The chair of the Working Group on Indigenous Peoples also prepared a special study on the protection of the cultural and intellectual property of indigenous peoples. See E.-I. Daes, *Discrimination against Indigenous Peoples: Protection of the Heritage of Indigenous People*, E/CN.4/Sub.2/1994/31.

of fauna and flora. Indigenous peoples are given the right to own, develop, control and use the total environment of the lands, air, waters, coastal seas, sea-ice, flora and fauna and other resources which they have traditionally owned or otherwise occupied or used. Restitution of or compensation for lands taken without free and informed consent is required.

Further environmental protection is afforded in Article 28, which provides that indigenous peoples have the right to the conservation, restoration and protection of the total environment and the productive capacity of their lands, territories and resources. Assistance is to be provided for this purpose. Military activities and storage or disposal of hazardous materials is prohibited, although the former may take place with the free consent of indigenous peoples. Part IV of the UN draft contains other procedural rights, including the right of indigenous peoples to participate fully at all levels of decision-making in matters which may affect them.

The UN General Assembly, in the context of the International Decade of the World's Indigenous Peoples (1994–2004), has noted that the goal of the decade is to strengthen international cooperation for the solution of problems faced by indigenous peoples in various areas, including the environment. It has called for increased participation of indigenous peoples in activities for the decade, affirming its conviction of their contribution to environmental advancement of all countries of the world.[155]

Finally, indigenous peoples have sought and received protection for their unique genetic resources, drawing upon both human rights law and international environmental law. The Draft Declaration on Indigenous Rights explicitly states that indigenous peoples' genetic resources are entitled to special protection. More broadly, UNESCO adopted on 11 November 1997 a Declaration on the Human Genome and Human Rights. The Declaration relies upon the Convention on Biological Diversity[156] which itself emphasizes the genetic diversity of humanity, the inherent dignity and equal and inalienable rights of all members of the human family. The Declaration is positive towards research on the human genome, foreseeing 'vast prospects for progress in improving the health of individuals and of humankind as a whole'. It calls for respect for human rights in regard to such research, and calls in particular for non-discrimination on the basis of genetic characteristics. The Declaration in general combines techniques and legal approaches from both human rights and from environmental protection. It demands that all research, treatment or diagnosis be preceded by rigorous and prior assessment of the potential risks and benefits and be based on prior, free and informed consent of the person concerned. Rather than declare a right to genetic

[155] GA Res. 52/108 of 12 December 1997, A/52/641.

[156] Convention on Biological Diversity, 5 June 1992 (Rio de Janeiro), EMuT 992:42, 31 *ILM* (1992) 818.

integrity, the Declaration places its focus on duties, providing in Article 10 that 'no research or research applications concerning the human genome, in particular in the fields of biology, genetics and medicine, should prevail over respect for the human rights, fundamental freedoms and human dignity of individuals or, where applicable, of groups of people'. Article 11 specifically prohibits cloning and other 'practices which are contrary to human dignity'. At the same time, Article 12 calls freedom of research part of freedom of thought. As the group of experts involved in drafting the Declaration came from the scientific and research community, it is incumbent on those concerned with human rights to examine the Declaration carefully to determine whether its protections are adequate.

2. Farmers' Rights

The issue of protecting traditional knowledge and local resources is one that goes beyond indigenous peoples to encompass local communities in general, particularly farmers who have been instrumental in conserving, improving and contributing to plant genetic resources. The international community is divided over whether intellectual property rights or equitable considerations should apply to farmers' developments of plant genetic resources or whether plant genetic resources constitute part of the common heritage of mankind or the sovereign natural resources of states. The FAO Global System for the Conservation and Utilization of Plant Genetic Resources attempts to reconcile competing interests by providing in an International Undertaking that such resources are the common heritage, but subject to the overriding sovereign rights of nations over their genetic resources.

The debate over the place of farmers' rights in this system remains unresolved, in spite of FAO resolution 5/89 that accepts the concept of farmers' rights arising from their contributions, rights it sees as vested in the international community as trustee for present and future generations of farmers, for the purpose of ensuring full benefits to farmers and supporting the continuation of their contributions. At the Fourth International Technical Conference on Plant Genetic Resources, held in 1996, with participants from 150 countries, the issue was particularly contentious. Nonetheless, a reference to farmers' rights, as defined in FAO resolution 5/89 remained in the text. The final text of the Leipzig Declaration on Conservation and Sustainable Utilization of Plant Genetic Resources for Food and Agriculture recognizes 'the needs and individual rights of farmers and, collectively, where recognized by national law, to have non-discriminatory access to germplasm, information, technologies and financial resources'.

V ENVIRONMENTAL RESPONSIBILITIES

Environmental ethics suggest that it is both a right and a duty of all persons to conserve and have conserved the existing global resources. International environmental law has continually stressed that humans have a 'solemn responsibility to protect and improve the environment for present and future generations'.[157] It is perhaps due to this focus that environmental law rarely speaks of human rights. The perception is that humans exercising their rights are largely responsible for the existing environmental problems of the planet.

Declarations of human duties are contained in the World Charter for Nature, in Agenda 21 and other environmental instruments. In human rights, they are contained in the Universal Declaration of Human Rights (Article 29), the American Declaration of the Rights and Duties of Man (Articles 29–37) and the African Charter on Human and Peoples' Rights (Articles 27–9). None of the human rights provisions refer to duties toward nature or the environment.

Recent efforts have sought to provide more detailed lists of human duties. A group of former heads of state, joined in the InterAction Council, proposed such a text, to be adopted on the 50th Anniversary of the adoption of the Universal Declaration of Human Rights. UNESCO also has a text under consideration, drafted by a meeting of philosophers held on 25–8 March 1997. The responsibilities it discusses are little more than an extension of human rights obligations to individuals and other non-state actors. Rather than limiting or 'balancing' the Universal Declaration of Human Rights with a declaration of responsibilities—which could provide a pretext for the state to limit existing rights—it would perhaps be better to attempt to extend the possibility of claiming human rights against non-state entities as well as against state actors.

VI INTERNATIONAL HUMANITARIAN LAW

Related to the right to environment are the humanitarian protections afforded during periods of armed conflict. These protections have become increasingly important as technology offers destructive forces of unprecedented scope. In addition, activities hazardous during peacetime become even more so during armed conflict and can seriously affect many persons not party to the hostilities. It is a long-standing principle that 'the right of belligerents to adopt means of injuring the enemy is not unlimited'.[158]

[157] Principle 1, Stockholm Declaration.

[158] Article XXII, Hague Convention II of 1899, Regarding Laws and Customs of War on Land, replaced by Article IV, Hague Convention IV of 1907. In addition to this rule, Article LV of the 1899 Annex provides that occupying powers can only be regarded as administrator and usufructuary of forests and agricultural works.

Among the most common norms of humanitarian law are those prohibiting destruction of or damage to forests, orchards, fruit trees or vines, and those forbidding the poisoning of wells, springs and rivers.

Rules respecting armed conflict have evolved rapidly in recent years. The Rio Declaration, Principle 24, declares that warfare is inherently destructive of sustainable development. States are to respect international law providing for the environment in times of armed conflict and cooperate in its further development, as necessary.

Several legal instruments concerning the law of armed conflict are relevant to environmental rights:

- the Hague Conventions of 1907;
- the Fourth Geneva Convention of 1949, and its Protocol I;
- the Convention on Military or Any Other Hostile Environmental Modification Techniques ('ENMOD');
- Protocol III to the 1980 Conventional Weapons Convention which restricts incendiary weapons;
- Convention on the Prohibition of the Development, Production, Stockpiling and Use of Chemical Weapons and on their Destruction (Paris, 15 January 1993);
- Protocol II to the Convention on Prohibitions on the Use of Certain Conventional Weapons which may be Deemed to be Excessively Injurious or to have Indiscriminate Effects (Geneva, 3 May 1996);
- Convention on the Prohibition of the Use, Stockpiling, Production and Transfer of Anti-Personnel Mines and on Their Destruction (Oslo, 18 September 1997).

Some of these laws contain provisions and general principles that may be invoked to protect the environment without explicitly mentioning it. Others include environment-specific protections. Several customary international norms provide potentially far-reaching protection for the environment in times of armed conflict without specifically addressing environmental concerns, including the principles of necessity, proportionality and discrimination between military and civilian targets.

The existing laws of armed conflict now contain four provisions which make an explicit reference to either the environment or natural elements: Article I of the 1977 ENMOD Convention; Articles 35(3) and 55(1) of the 1977 Protocol to the Geneva Convention; and Article 2 of the 1981 Protocol III to the United Nations Conventional Weapons Convention.

Protocol I to the 1949 Geneva Convention (Protocol I) protects the environment itself (Article 35.3) and the human population (Article 55). These two articles prohibit wartime damage even when the environment is a military objective or when the military objective outweighs the damage to the

environment. Further, they prohibit actions which are not intended to render destruction but from which damage is nevertheless objectively foreseeable.

Article 35(3) and Article 55 of Protocol I both prohibit only 'widespread, long-term and severe damage', a standard too high to provide any real protection during war. The ENMOD treaty defines 'widespread' to mean several hundred square kilometres, 'long-term' as damage extending beyond a season, and 'severe' to mean serious or significant disruption to human life, natural or economic resources or other assets. Protocol I, in contrast considers 'long-term' in terms of decades rather than seasons. In addition, the Protocol I Conference Committee clearly stated that its terms must be interpreted in accordance with the meaning specified in Protocol I, and not in light of similar terms contained in other instruments, such as ENMOD.

1. The Gulf War

The Gulf War raised substantial questions about environmental protection during armed conflicts and the applicable law on this subject. In January 1991, the Iraqi military occupying Kuwait opened valves at several oil terminals and pumped large quantities of crude oil into the Gulf. Subsequent allied bombing of the terminals halted the flow of oil. Other oil slicks appeared, apparently caused by damage to tankers and oil-storage facilities. During the conflict, Iraqi soldiers also set fire to over 700 well-heads in Kuwait and damaged others by explosive charges, sending oil spilling onto the desert. Oil refineries, oil gathering stations and power and water desalination plants were all damaged or destroyed.[159]

The United Nations Security Council reacted to Iraqi actions in Resolution 687 which affirmed that Iraq:

> is liable under international law for any direct loss, damage, including environmental damage and the depletion of natural resources, or injury to foreign Governments, nationals and corporations, as a result of Iraq's unlawful invasion and occupation of Kuwait (paragraph 16).

Paragraph 18 of the Resolution created a fund for the payment of such claims and established a commission to administer the fund. A portion of the export sales of Iraqi oil is used for the fund.

The United Nations Compensation Commission (UNCC) established its procedures regarding claims in a series of decisions taken by its Governing Council. Decision 7 of the Council provides that payments are to be made for losses or expenses resulting from:

[159] Letter of 12 July 1991 from the chargé d'affaires of the Permanent Mission of Kuwait to the United Nations to the Secretary-General, 15 July 1991; UN Doc. A/45/1035, S/22787, at 2.

(a) Abatement and prevention of environmental damage, including expenses directly relating to fighting oil fires and stemming the flow of oil in coastal and international waters;
(b) Reasonable measures already taken to clean and restore the environment or future measures which can be documented as reasonably necessary to clean and restore the environment;
(c) Reasonable monitoring and assessment of the environmental damage for the purpose of evaluating and abating harm and restoring the environment;
(d) Reasonable monitoring of public health and performing medical screening for the purposes of investigation and combating increased health risks as a result of the environmental damage; and
(e) Depletion of or damage to natural resources.[160]

The list is not exhaustive. The word 'direct' limits the extent of liability for environmental damage, excluding indirect and remote harm. It appears that the two terms 'environmental damage' and 'depletion of or damage to natural resources' were included to provide comprehensive relief, in order to ensure that components of the natural environment having no commercial value as well as those primarily commercial in nature would be encompassed in the claims process.

At the beginning of the Gulf conflict, the United Nations Environment Programme's (UNEP) Governing Council expressed concern over destruction of the environment. The Global Resources Information Database of UNEP and The International Maritime Organization (IMO) conducted an extensive preliminary assessment of the impact of the oil spill on the coastal waters of Kuwait and Saudi Arabia. The IMO responded to a request of Saudi Arabia and other governments in the region, pursuant to the International Convention on Oil Pollution, Preparedness and Cooperation of 1990, and took action to facilitate and coordinate international assistance.

The UNEP Governing Council decided in May 1991 to recommend:

that governments consider identifying weapons, hostile devices and ways of using such techniques that would cause particularly serious effects on the environment and consider efforts in appropriate forms to strengthen international law prohibiting such weapons, hostile devices and ways of using such techniques.

It invited the General Assembly to review the 1977 Convention on the Prohibition of Military or Any Other Hostile Use of Environmental Modification Techniques with a view to strengthening and encouraging accession to it and establishing concrete means of verification of its implementation.[161]

As a final aftermath of the Gulf Conflict, UNEP established a Working Group on Liability and Compensation for Environmental Damage Arising

[160] UNCC, Governing Council Decision 7, para. 35.
[161] UNEP/GC.16/L.53, Part B, 'Environmental Effects of Warfare' (May 1991).

from Military Activities as part of its Montevideo Programme for the Development and Periodic Review of Environmental Law (II–1993). The Report of the Working Group was presented to the UNEP Governing Council in 1997. The Report notes that state responsibility for damage from the Gulf War resulted from the unlawful invasion and occupation of Kuwait. According to the Report, it follows that thresholds of damage established under instruments relating to the laws of war could not be used to reject environmental claims submitted to the United Nations Compensation Commission. According to the Report, a state which has committed an act of aggression cannot rely on the rules of international law allowing for exclusions or exemptions of responsibility and liability.[162] The Working Group also proposed a comprehensive definition of environmental damage and methods of valuation.

2. Development of Environmental Protection Norms for Armed Conflicts

Issues of environmental harm during armed conflict have also arisen in other international organizations. The IAEA General Conference adopted a resolution on 21 September 1990 recognizing that attacks or threats of attack on nuclear facilities devoted to peaceful purposes could jeopardize the development of nuclear energy, affirmed the importance and reliability of its safeguard procedures, and emphasized the need for the Security Council to act immediately should such a threat or attack occur.[163]

The UN General Assembly supported the IAEA with its own resolution 45/58 of 4 December 1990 in which it referred to the IAEA resolution and expressed its conviction of the need to prohibit armed attacks on nuclear installations. It expressed its awareness of the danger that such an attack could result in radioactive releases with grave transboundary consequences. At the first Security Council summit on 31 January 1992, the heads of state present cited risks to international peace and security posed by, *inter alia*, environmental sources.[164] In July 1992, the Secretary-General recommended that ECOSOC be delegated to report to the Security Council on economic and social developments, including environment and development, that might threaten international peace and security.[165]

In spite of long-standing law and recent developments, many claim that humanitarian law is inadequate and further instruments are needed to ensure environmental protection during armed conflicts. Agenda 21 asked the Sixth Committee of the United Nations General Assembly authority to consider action on the issue of environmental protection in times of armed conflict,

[162] UNEP/ENV.LAW/3/info.1, 15 October 1996, reprinted in 27 *EPL* (1997) 134.
[163] IAEA GC (XXXIV)RES/533 (21 September 1990).
[164] UN Doc. S/23500, 31 January 1992.
[165] UN Doc. E/1992/82/Add.1, para. 29.

taking into account the specific competence and role of the International Committee of the Red Cross.[166]

On 25 November 1992, the UN General Assembly adopted Resolution 47/37, expressing its deep concern about environmental damage and depletion of natural resources during recent conflicts. It condemned the destruction of hundreds of oil well-heads and the release and waste of crude oil into the sea and noted that existing provisions of international law prohibit such acts. It stressed that destruction of the environment, not justified by military necessity and carried out wantonly, is clearly contrary to existing international law. The resolution invited the International Committee of the Red Cross (ICRC) to report on activities undertaken by the Committee and other relevant bodies with regard to the protection of the environment in times of armed conflict.

In a report to the Secretary General in 1992, the ICRC argued that existing law was sufficient to protect the environment adequately and that deficiencies were due to improper implementation.[167] The ICRC report discusses the major international legal rules relevant to the protection of the environment in time of armed conflicts, including the rules concerning the protection of property and those concerning the protection of the environment as such, embodied in Additional Protocol I to the Geneva Conventions (Articles 35, 36, 55). It also mentions the 14 May 1954 Convention for the Protection of Cultural Property in the Event of Armed Conflict and the 23 November 1972 UNESCO Convention concerning the Protection of the World Cultural and Natural Heritage. The report recommends that mechanisms provided by Protocol I, such as the designation of Protecting Powers and of the International Fact-Finding Commission (Article 90), should be used for protection of the environment.

The ICRC report calls for application of the Martens clause[168] which states that in cases not covered by specific provisions, civilians and combatants remain under the protection and authority of the principles of international law derived from established customs, from the principles of humanity, and from the dictates of public conscience. It finds this clause indisputably valid in the context of environmental protection during times of armed conflict. In addition, the ICRC advocates applying the precautionary principle to the protection of the environment and the protection of nature reserves. It calls for the drafting of guidelines for military manuals and instructions and stresses that the law of armed conflict must take technical developments of weapons into account and contain their effects. The report concludes by submitting to the General Assembly a list of issues which should be examined by

[166] Agenda 21, para. 39.6.

[167] UN Doc. A/47/328.

[168] See, Preamble, 1907 Hague Convention IV; Article 1, Protocol I of 1977; and Preamble, Protocol II of 1977.

the Sixth Committee: the applicability of international environmental law during armed conflicts; restrictions on the use of mines; protection of cultural sites, nature reserves and parks; and protection of the environment in times of non-international armed conflict. These issues will be the subject of discussion and debate in the coming years.

3. Control of Weapons Systems

In regard to the means and methods of warfare, a Convention on the Prohibition of the Development, Production, Stockpiling and Use of Chemical Weapons and on their Destruction was signed in Paris on 15 January 1993.[169] The Convention contains far-reaching provisions on control of national chemical production facilities and international verification of state obligations. Contracting states must destroy all chemical weapons and all production facilities within 10 years of the agreement's entry into force. Each State Party must provide access to any chemical weapons' destruction facility for the purpose of on-site systematic verification and monitoring. The treaty covers all toxic chemicals and their precursors, listed in three schedules or annexes. Schedule 1 chemicals, including all nerve and mustard gases now in existence, cannot be produced in excess of 10 kilograms per year, and must be done at a single, specially designated facility. Schedules 2 and 3 list chemicals which can be used for both civilian and military purposes. States may produce these chemicals without production limits, but any production of schedule 2 chemicals above a range from one kilogram to one ton triggers a reporting obligation in regard to the producing facility. In addition, there may be on-site inspections. For schedule 3 chemicals, states are required to submit reports for each facility that produces amounts over limits ranging from 30 to 200 tons per year.

Within 30 days of the entry into force of the agreement on 29 April 1997, each state party had to submit to the Organization for the Prohibition of Chemical Weapons (OPCW), a treaty monitoring group based in the Hague, a declaration on its ownership or possession of chemical weapons, the precise location, quantity and detailed inventory of such weapons, and information on the import or export after 1 January 1946 of weapons-producing equipment (Article III(1)). Each state also must provide a general plan for destruction, closure, or conversion of any chemical weapons' production facility it owns or possesses or which is within its jurisdiction or control. Contracting states must forward annual data on the national production, import and export of listed chemicals. The State Party must provide to the Technical Secretariat, for each of its chemical weapons' destruction facilities, the plant operations manuals, the safety and medical plans, the laboratory operations

[169] 13 January 1993, 32 *ILM* 800 (1993).

and quality assurance and control manuals, and the environmental permits that have been obtained (Part IV(A), paragraph 32).

The Convention is the first agreement to apply verification procedures to the civilian chemicals industry. All locations at which chemical weapons are stored or destroyed are subject to systematic verification through on-site inspection and monitoring with on-site instruments. The procedures allow international inspectors to examine chemical facilities on request of another signatory state. More detailed measures concerning the elimination and disposal of chemical reserves will be dealt with by the Organization. The treaty will enter into force 180 days after 65 states have become party to it. As has become the common practice in multilateral regulatory instruments, no reservations are permitted.

Implementation of the agreement will raise significant environmental problems due to the number of weapons and technical difficulties involved. Environmentally sound implementation of the Convention will be costly. Article IV, paragraph 12, obligates States Parties to cooperate and provide information and assistance regarding methods for the safe and efficient destruction of chemical weapons. The Convention includes some specific obligations regarding the environmental implications of the destruction of chemical weapons. Article VII (3) provides that each State Party shall assign the highest priority to ensuring the safety of people and to protecting the environment as the treaty is implemented. Thus, a State Party may not refuse to implement the Convention on environmental grounds, but must reconcile environmental protection with the goals of the Convention to the fullest extent possible. A similar provision was included in the Biological Weapons Convention of 10 April 1972.[170] The latter provides that 'in implementing the provisions of this Article all necessary safety precautions shall be observed to protect populations and the environment' (Article II(2)).

The Chemical Weapons Convention refers to national standards for safety and emissions in regard to the destruction of chemical weapons (Article IV(10)). In principle each State Party may decide how it shall destroy chemical weapons consistent with its obligation to place safety and environmental protection at the forefront. The weapons must be destroyed, however, in designated facilities suited for the task and states may not eliminate chemical weapons through dumping in water, land burial or open-air burning. Old chemical weapons, i.e. those produced before 1925 and those produced between 1925 and 1946 which have deteriorated to such extent that they can no longer be used as chemical weapons, are to be treated as toxic waste under national and international regulation according to paragraph B.6 of Part IV (B) of the Verification Annex. Several bilateral agreements have been concluded that may contribute to the environmentally sound destruction of

[170] 1015 UNTS 163.

chemical weapons. The United States–Russian Agreement Concerning the Safe, Secure and Ecologically Sound Destruction of Chemical Weapons of 30 July 1992, provides that the United States will provide up to $55 million to assist Russian chemical weapons destruction. An agreement of December 1992 between Russia and Germany enabled the construction of a plant which is set to destroy specific materials. Similarly, Sweden agreed to assist Russia by examining the risks associated with the storage and destruction of the Russian chemical stockpile.

Other weapons systems have come under international restrictions because of their indiscriminate effects or the excessive injuries they cause. In particular, nuclear weapons and anti-personnel land mines have been recently targeted by the international community. In 1996, the conference of State Parties to the Convention on Prohibitions or Restrictions on the Use of Certain Conventional Weapons adopted a protocol on the use of mines, booby-traps and other devices.[171] The Protocol applies to international and to internal armed conflicts. It limits the types of weapons that can be used and calls on each contracting party to clear, remove, destroy or maintain all mines, booby-traps and other devices that are permitted. Article 7 prohibits the use of booby-traps and other devices attached to or associated with internationally recognized protective emblems, signs or signals. This could include UNESCO World Heritage Sites, internationally protected wetlands, Antarctic protected areas, and other sites marked or signalled under international law. The same Article protects historic monuments, works of art or places of worship which constitute the cultural or spiritual heritage of people. The environment, per se, is not protected.

Another recent weapons treaty, the Convention on the Prohibition of the Use, Stockpiling, Production and Transfer of Anti-Personnel Mines and on Their Destruction,[172] mentions the environment, although its purpose is to end the casualties caused by land mines. According to Article 5 of the Convention, each State Party must clear all mines in areas under its jurisdiction or control at the latest within ten years of the entry into force of the Convention. Within that time, if a State Party believes it cannot destroy or ensure the destruction of all anti-personnel mines by the end of ten years, it may submit a request for an extension to a meeting of the States Parties or a review conference. The request must contain, *inter alia*, a reference to the environmental implications of the extension (Article 5(4)(c)). The meeting of the States Parties or the review conference will decide by majority vote whether to grant the request, taking into consideration the factors mentioned

[171] Convention on Prohibitions or Restrictions on the Use of Certain Conventional Weapons which may be Deemed to be Excessively Injurious or to have Indiscriminate Effects: Protocol on Prohibitions or Restrictions on the Use of Mines, Booby-Traps and Other Devices (Protocol II), Geneva, 3 May 1996, reprinted in 35 *ILM* (1996) 1206.

[172] Adopted at Oslo, 18 September 1997, reprinted in 36 *ILM* (1997) 1507.

in the agreement, including the environmental implications. The Convention does not require an environmental impact assessment prior to mine clearance activities, although this may be necessary pursuant to other international agreements or national law. Each State Party is required to report to the Secretary-General of the United Nations within 180 days of the entry into force of the Convention for that party on numerous matters related to mines and mined areas. Included in the reporting obligation is information regarding the status of programmes for the destruction of anti-personnel mines, including details of the methods which will be used in destruction, the location of all destruction sites and the applicable safety and environmental standards to be observed (Article 7(1)(f)).

4. Decisions of the International Court of Justice

In a general effort to determine the scope of legal obligations towards the environment during armed conflict or in weapons testing, the International Court of Justice was asked on three occasions after 1993 to consider the legality of nuclear weapons and weapons testing. First, on 6 September 1993, the World Health Organization (WHO) requested an advisory opinion of the International Court of Justice on whether the use of nuclear weapons is a violation of international law, including the WHO Constitution, 'in view of the health and environmental effects' such use would have. The Court decided in 1996 that the request exceeded the competence of the WHO. It viewed the question as being one within the purview of those organs of the United Nations on which had been expressly conferred the responsibility to regulate the use of force and armaments.[173] Perhaps anticipating this result, the United Nations General Assembly presented its own request asking a series of similar questions in 1995.[174] In fact, transnational civil society, in the form of a coalition of non-governmental organizations and individuals calling themselves 'the World Court Project', was behind both requests, having successfully exerted pressure on both the WHO and the General Assembly to go to the Court. The Court decided it had jurisdiction to answer the General Assembly's questions and did so on 8 July 1996,[175] the same date it decided

[173] Legality of the Use by a State of Nuclear Weapons in Armed Conflict (Advisory Opinion of 8 July 1996). For a critical analysis of the Court's opinion, see Weston, 'Nuclear Weapons and the World Court: Ambiguity's Consensus', 7 *Transnational Law and Contemporary Problems* (1997) 371.

[174] Request for an Advisory Opinion from the International Court of Justice on the Legality of the Threat or Use of Nuclear Weapons, GA Res. 49/75K UN GAOR, 49th Sess., Supp. No. 49, at 71, UN Doc. A/4949 (1995).

[175] Legality of the Threat or Use of Nuclear Weapons (Advisory Opinion of 8 July), UN Doc. A/51/218 (1996), reprinted in 35 *ILM* (1996) 809 and 1343. The Court decided to comply with the request by a vote of 13–1; only Judge Oda dissented.

against the WHO request. The third proceeding before the Court was an effort to reopen a contentious case filed by Australia and New Zealand against France, challenging the legality of nuclear testing in the South Pacific.[176] The Court held that the proceedings were closed but noted that its conclusion was 'without prejudice to the obligations of states to respect and protect the natural environment'.[177]

The Court was intensely divided on some issues in the advisory opinion on the legality of nuclear weapons and unanimous in regard to others. Given the complexity of the matter, it is perhaps not surprising that for the first time in its history, every judge sitting in the matter issued a separate declaration or opinion. Several holdings were closely linked to international environmental law. First, the Court found by a vote of 11–3 that neither customary nor conventional international law—including international environmental law—prohibits nuclear weapons *as such*.[178] The dissenters found that nuclear weapons in all their probable uses are so devastating that they would be likely to breach human rights and environmental standards and thus are prohibited as such. The Court unanimously agreed that '[a] threat or use of nuclear weapons should . . . be compatible with . . . the principles and rules of international humanitarian law, as well as with specific obligations under treaties and other undertakings which expressly deal with nuclear weapons'.[179] Thus, international environmental law, like human rights law, must be taken into account in determining the issue under the humanitarian rules of armed conflict. The Court noted that certain treaties prohibit the use of nuclear weapons in specific geographic areas,[180] but none of them prohibit the threat of use of nuclear weapons.

The Court's final holdings were the most divided. The Court's vote was 7–7, necessitating a deciding vote of the president, in holding that 'the threat or use of nuclear weapons would generally be contrary to the rules of international law applicable in armed conflict and, in particular, the principles and rules of humanitarian law'.[181] The Court went on, however, to say that it could not conclude definitively whether or not extreme self-defence in which

[176] See Request for an Examination of the Situation in Accordance with Paragraph 63 of the Court's Judgment of 20 December 1974 in the Nuclear Tests (*New Zealand v France*) Case, Order of 22 September 1995, ICJ Reports 1995.

[177] Ibid., at 306, para. 64.

[178] Advisory Opinion, at 36, para. 105(2)(B).

[179] Ibid., at 36, para. 105(2)(D).

[180] e.g. the 1959 Antarctic Treaty, the 1963 Partial Test-Ban Treaty, the 1967 Outer Space Treaty, the 1967 Treaty of Tlatelolco, the 1971 Sea-Bed Arms Control Treaty, the 1979 Moon Treaty, the 1985 South Pacific Nuclear Free Zone Treaty, the 1995 Treaty on an African Nuclear-Weapon-Free Zone, and the 1995 Treaty on the Southeast Asia Nuclear-Weapon-Free Zone.

[181] Advisory Opinion, at 36, para. 105(2)(E).

the life of the state would be at stake, would allow the threat or use of nuclear weapons.[182]

Among the arguments submitted by the 28 states participating in the proceedings were arguments that any use of nuclear weapons would be unlawful according to international environmental law. Specific references were made to various international treaties,[183] Principle 1 of the Stockholm Declaration and Principle 2 of the Rio Declaration. In contrast, some states argued that international environmental law principally applied in times of peace. The Court itself recognized that 'the use of nuclear weapons could constitute a catastrophe for the environment', the latter representing 'not an abstraction but . . . the living space, the quality of life and the very health of human beings, including generations unborn'. Given this, the Court held that states must take environmental considerations into account in assessing what is necessary and proportionate in the pursuit of military objectives. The Court noted that the provisions of Additional Protocol I embody a general obligation to protect the natural environment against widespread, long-term and severe environmental damage; the prohibition of methods and means of warfare which are intended, or may be expected to cause such damage; and the prohibition of attacks against the natural environment by way of reprisals. Thus, while no specific provision prohibits the use of nuclear weapons, the law indicates that important environmental factors are properly taken into account in the context of the implication of the principles and rules of the law applicable in armed conflict.

VII CONCLUSIONS

Without the link of property, conscience or association, it is difficult to see human rights tribunals moving more broadly into nature protection, given the current human rights catalogue. Neither scenic areas, flora and fauna, nor ecological balance are viewed as part of the rights to which humans are entitled, absent explicit recognition of the right to a specific environment. No doubt debate will continue over whether such a recognition serves to enhance

[182] Note that the three dissenters from the earlier holding also dissented on this point, finding the Court's pronouncement too weak, not too strong. Only four judges, three of them from nuclear power states, felt the Court had gone too far in questioning the legality of the threat of use of nuclear weapons pursuant to international humanitarian law. On the other hand, some of those concurring with the majority clearly seemed to approve mutual deterrence, i.e. the threat of use of nuclear weapons, disagreeing with the view that all threats of use of nuclear weapons are illegal.

[183] The instruments referred to included Additional Protocol I of 1977 to the (four) Geneva Conventions of 1949 and the Convention of 18 May 1977 on the Prohibition of Military or Any Other Hostile Use of Environmental Modification Techniques, Article 1.

environmental protection or simply to further the anthropocentric, utilitarian view that all the world exists to further human well-being.

If a right to environment becomes widely accepted as part of the human rights catalogue, there remains the problem of balancing it with other human rights. The General Assembly itself has pronounced many times on the indivisibility, interdependence, interrelatedness and universality of all human rights.[184] In December 1997 it reiterated its conviction of this reality and emphasized that transparent and accountable governance in all sectors of society, as well as effective participation by civil society, are an essential part of the necessary foundations for the realization of sustainable development.[185] Yet, the possibility of collision or conflict between rights cannot be avoided. For example, among the human rights guaranteed by international law is the right of each family to decide on the number and spacing of their children. Demographic pressures have been recognized as a threat to environmental quality and economic development, leading to demands that national birthrates be lowered to achieve sustainable development.[186] The possibility that some human rights may be limited to achieve the right to environment is seen in the Constitution of Ecuador where Article 19 establishes 'the right to live in an environment free from contamination'. The Constitution invests the state with responsibility for ensuring the enjoyment of this right and 'for establishing by law such restrictions on other rights and freedoms as are necessary to protect the environment'. As noted by the Inter-American Commission on Human Rights, the Constitution thus establishes a hierarchy according to which environmental protection may have priority over other entitlements.[187]

Recently, the concept of environmental justice has come to play an important role in international environmental law and policy as a means of integrating human rights and environmental law, even as the content and scope of the term remains under discussion. It is increasingly recognized that favourable natural conditions are essential to the fulfilment of human desires and goals. Preservation of these conditions is a basic need of individuals and societies. Environmental justice encompasses preserving environmental quality, sustaining the ecological well-being of present and future generations, and reconciling competing interests. There is also an element of distributional justice, as it has become clear that the poor and marginalized of societies, including the global society, suffer disproportionately from environmental harm.

[184] See the Vienna Declaration and Programme of Action, adopted by the World Conference on Human Rights, 25 June 1993, UN Doc. A/CONF.157/24 (Part I).

[185] GA Res. 52/136 of 12 December 1997, UN Doc. A/52/644/Add.2.

[186] See Report of the International Conference on Population and Development (Cairo, 5–13 September 1994), UN Doc. A/CONF. 171/13 (1994) UN Pub. E.95.XIII.18.

[187] Inter-American Commission on Human Rights, Report on the Situation of Human Rights in Ecuador 87.

Environmental justice emphasizes the environment as a social good rather than a commodity or purely economic asset. The focus is on the proper allocation of social benefits and burdens, both in the present and in the future. Thus, it requires the equitable distribution of environmental amenities and environmental risks, the redress and sanctioning of environmental abuses, the restoration and conservation of nature and the fair allocation of resource benefits. The polluter pays principle itself is based on the concept of environmental justice, as it encompasses the notion that those who engage in and profit from activities that damage the environment should be liable for the harm caused. On the most fundamental level, environmental justice can be seen as a term that encompasses the twin aims of environmental protection and international protection of human rights.

7

Peoples' Rights: Their Rise and Fall

PHILIP ALSTON

1. Introduction: A Time to Take Stock

The preceding chapters have provided extensive insights into the current situation in relation to most of the key peoples' rights that continue to be an important part of international human rights discourse. In the present chapter an attempt is made to provide an overview both of the historical evolution of these rights and of their current status. The principal focus is on what are identified as the four phases which have characterized the treatment which international law has given to the concept of peoples and their rights since the 1940s. Some conclusions are then drawn as to the prospects for the future.

2. The Four Phases in the Evolution of the Concept of Peoples' Rights in International Law

The transition in the terminology of international law from the 'peoples' in whose name the Charter of the United Nations was proclaimed, through the right of peoples to self-determination which acquired such importance in the era of decolonization, to the broader concept of peoples' rights which has gained prominence since the late 1970s, could easily be seen to reflect a logical conceptual progression. And so it has been presented by various commentators.[1] But such a characterization is not as straightforward as it might seem at first blush. In particular, it conceals fundamental questions as to the basic concept which is purportedly being developed. If it is presented as a historical narrative and as a way of capturing the sequence of certain historical events it is reasonably accurate, if not especially informative. If it is presented in conceptual terms it will be problematic since the conception of 'peoples' used in each of the phases differs significantly. The biggest question raised, however, is whether it is accurate as a description of the evolution of international human rights law. For the most part, it is not.

[1] The most persistent proponent of the concept of peoples' rights has been Karel Vasak. See most recently Vasak, 'Revisiter la troisième génération des droits de l'homme avant leur codification', in *Héctor Gros Espiell Amicorum Liber: Persona humana y derecho internacional*, Vol. II, (1997) 1649.

In order to see why this is so it is appropriate to review briefly the four phases through which the concept of peoples' rights has evolved in the post-Second World War period. They are: 1940–49—the drafting of the United Nations Charter; 1950–71—the development of the right of self-determination; 1972–89—the promotion of the broader concept of peoples' rights; and 1990–present—the post-Cold War waning of significance.

3. The First Phase: 1940–1949

In the first of these phases the principle of the self-determination of peoples was much discussed in the context of post-war planning undertaken by the allied powers. But although the Atlantic Charter of 1941 affirmed the importance of self-determination, there was no reference either to the principle or to this or any other right of peoples in any of the pre-1945 drafts of the UN Charter.[2] Eventually, however, the symbolism of the term 'peoples' was prominently, even ostentatiously, enshrined in the UN Charter by the proclamation of the Charter in the name of 'We the peoples'. The symbolism of these words is potentially significant but it was immediately neutralized by the phrase with which the very same Preamble concludes which is 'accordingly, our respective Governments, through representatives assembled . . ., who have exhibited their full powers found to be in good and due form, have agreed to the present Charter . . .'.[3] More formal diplomatic or governmental terminology could hardly have been found and the idea that the peoples of the world were taking action in any sense of the word was thus rapidly dispelled.

This is not surprising when we recall that the principal proponent of including this reference to peoples during the drafting of the Charter was General Smuts,[4] one of the architects of the South African system of apartheid. His reference point was the phrase 'We the People' with which the Preamble to the United States Constitution of 1787 begins. But that inspiration in itself tells us that the phrase 'peoples' was not intended to embrace a wide diversity of heterogeneous peoples but rather an aggregation of the people, as in the citizens, of each of the participating states. It was a rhetorical flourish that paid homage to the American victors of the Second World War but which was devoid of the type of symbolism which would give much encouragement to the modern-day proponents of peoples' rights.[5]

[2] See generally R. Russell and J. Muther, *A History of the United Nations Charter* (1958) 62.

[3] UN Charter, paras 1 and 12 of the Preamble.

[4] Russell and Muther, supra n. 2, at 45.

[5] See, for example, the discussion of what is meant by the term 'people' in discussions of popular sovereignty within the United States context in D.T. Rodgers, *Contested Truths: Keywords in American Politics Since Independence* (1987) 84.

[6] UN Charter, Article 1(2).

The Charter also listed among the purposes of the United Nations the development 'of friendly relations among nations based on respect for the principle of equal rights and self-determination of peoples . . .'.[6] But while this phrase also drew on the more populist notions such as those variously propounded by V.I. Lenin and Woodrow Wilson,[7] neither the drafting history nor the formulation finally adopted support any extensive understanding of the phrase. Indeed, the most systematic and careful study that has been done in relation to the right of self-determination concludes that:

> the principle enshrined in the UN Charter boils down to very little; it is only a principle suggesting that States should grant *self-government* as much as possible to the communities over which they exercise jurisdiction.[8]

And most importantly, of course, in its Charter incarnation self-determination was not a right at all but only a principle. Accordingly, the Universal Declaration of Human Rights of 1948 contains no reference at all to self-determination, which seems an odd omission if we are to take at face value the assertion originally put forward in the early post-War years by the Soviet Union,[9] but commonly made even today, that in the absence of the achievement of self-determination other human rights have little meaning. Its elevation to the status of a right was to have to wait until the agitation for self-determination in the context of decolonization raised both the stakes and the normative aspirations of the proponents.

The other major development during this phase was the adoption in 1948, one day before the adoption of the Universal Declaration, of the Convention on the Prevention and Punishment of the Crime of Genocide.[10] This is frequently cited as one of the major international instruments which recognizes a right of peoples—the right to physical existence.[11] The initial draft of the Convention, submitted to the UN General Assembly in 1946 by Saudi Arabia, expressly used the term 'people', but this was fairly quickly eliminated in the process of drafting.[12] While it is clear that the right as reflected in the

[7] A. Cassese, *Self-determination of Peoples: A Legal Reappraisal* (1995), at 14–23.

[8] Ibid., at 42 (emphasis in the original).

[9] For an account of the Soviet position, and its triumph in the context of the process of drafting the International Covenant on Civil and Political Rights, see Cassese, 'The Self-determination of Peoples', in L. Henkin (ed.), *The International Bill of Rights: The Covenant on Civil and Political Rights* (1981) 92.

[10] 78 United Nations Treaty Series 277.

[11] The General Assembly, in initiating the drafting of the Convention stated that '[g]enocide is a denial of the right of existence of entire human groups'. GA Res. 96(I)(1946). The phrase was subsequently incorporated into the African Charter on Human and Peoples' Rights, Article 20(1) of which states that '[a]ll peoples shall have right to existence'. This is directly linked, however, to self-determination since the very next sentence of the same provision notes that '[t]hey shall have the unquestionable and inalienable right to self-determination'.

[12] Under the terms of the draft genocide would have been defined as 'the destruction of an ethnic group, people or nation'. UN Doc. A/C.6/86 (1946).

Convention is a collective one, which makes no sense when formulated in individual terms, it is nevertheless also important to acknowledge the very limited nature of the precedent thereby created in terms of peoples' rights in general. This is because the Convention proceeds primarily by emphasizing the obligations of potential offenders ('whether they are constitutionally responsible rulers, public officials or private individuals')[13] and the need to punish offenders rather than by proclaiming the rights of the groups who are thereby protected. Nevertheless, the Convention represents a significant step in the direction of recognizing certain rights as belonging to certain groups ('national, ethnical, racial or religious'),[14] including peoples.[15]

4. The Second Phase: 1950–1971

This phase can be considered to be the heyday of self-determination. It lasted for some twenty years and the principles which emerged are still ostensibly those that are being applied today in relation to situations in which a denial of the internal or external dimensions of the right of self-determination is alleged. During this phase the status of the concept was elevated to that of a right in the context of developments in three different but closely related areas—the development of principles governing the process of decolonization, the evolution of general principles of international law, and the drafting of the two International Human Rights Covenants. The four landmark documents are the two Covenants, the 1960 Declaration on Granting Independence to Colonial Countries and Peoples[16] and the 1970 Declaration on Principles of International Law concerning Friendly Relations and Cooperation among States in accordance with the Charter of the United Nations.[17] The latter two are not treaties and thus, whatever their status today in terms of customary law, they did not at the time of their adoption represent binding formulations of the right of self-determination. Nonetheless, the 1960 Declaration represented a watershed moment in the transformation of the principle into a right in relation to peoples living in colonial situations.

The 1970 Declaration, adopted by unanimity and self-declared to be 'a landmark in the development of international law',[18] laid the groundwork for the broader development of self-determination beyond the colonial

[13] UN Doc. A/C.6/86 (1946), Article IV. [14] Ibid., Article II.
[15] See generally W. Schabas, *Genocide in International Law* (2000).
[16] GA Res. 1514 (XV)(1960), Annex.
[17] GA Res. 2625 (XXV)(1970), Annex.
[18] Ibid., fourth preambular para.

context.[19] It also consolidated an evolution in the law on the basis of which the International Court of Justice could reverse its earlier decisions in relation to South West Africa[20] and rule in the Namibia case of 1971 that self-determination was no longer a mere guiding principle but a right that could be invoked by the peoples concerned to assert their entitlement to sovereign independence.[21]

The two Covenants contain an identical formulation which was accorded the honour of being included as Article 1 of each treaty. This ranking has, however, turned out to be a mixed blessing in the sense that rather than being treated as *primus inter pares* the right of self-determination has tended to be treated as *sui generis*, a right in some ways apart and distinct from the others recognized in the Covenants.[22] The right is expressed in the following terms:

> 1. All peoples have the right of self-determination. By virtue of that right they freely determine their political status and freely pursue their economic, social and cultural development.
> 2. All peoples may, for their own ends, freely dispose of their natural wealth and resources without prejudice to any obligations arising out of international economic co-operation, based upon the principle of mutual benefit, and international law. In no case may a people be deprived of its own means of subsistence.
> 3. The States Parties to the present Covenant, including those having responsibility for the administration of Non-Self-Governing and Trust Territories, shall promote the realization of the right of self-determination, and shall respect that right, in conformity with the provisions of the Charter of the United Nations.

Both this specific provision and developments that occurred in the second phase as a whole have been much debated and dissected within the literature[23] and in the present volume its significance is analysed in detail by James Crawford.[24] Suffice it to say that the formulation also contains what are sometimes characterized as being additional peoples' rights: the right of a people to dispose freely

[19] Although the only book devoted explicitly to an analysis of the significance of the Declaration manifests a marked hostility to this suggestion. See G. Arangio-Ruiz, *The UN Declaration on Friendly Relations and the System of the Sources of International Law* (1979) 141 where self-determination, except in relation to treaty provisions, is said to remain a matter of *de lege ferenda*, and the notion of peoples being the holders of rights and subjects of international law is dismissed out of hand. 'The international right corresponding to any legal obligation with regard to self-determination would presumably develop—short of a fundamental change in the system—as a right of other States *vis-à-vis* the duty bound one.' Ibid.

[20] *South West Africa cases* [1966] ICJ Reports 3.

[21] *Legal Consequences for States of the Continued Presence of South Africa in Namibia* [1971] ICJ Reports 16.

[22] This is especially the case in terms of the practice of the two supervisory committees set up to monitor compliance by States Parties with their obligations under the Covenant. See generally D. McGoldrick, *The Human Rights Committee: Its Role in the Development of the International Covenant on Civil and Political Rights* (1991), and M. Craven, *The International Covenant on Economic, Social and Cultural Rights* (1995).

[23] For details, see the Bibliography contained in this volume.

[24] See supra Ch. 2.

of their natural wealth and resources, and the right of a people not to be deprived of its own means of subsistence. The former is also explicitly recognized in Article 21 of the African Charter on Human and Peoples' Rights of 1979. Crawford has expressed considerable scepticism as to the viability of the formulation and characterized it as a double-edged sword.[25] In practice, neither of the rights has been invoked to any great effect and they are even omitted from some of the lists of peoples' rights that have been drawn up, on the assumption that they form an integral part of the right of self-determination.

The final development to which reference might be made in this phase is the adoption by the International Labour Organization in 1957 of its first comprehensive convention dealing with the rights of indigenous populations. While it constituted a significant step at the time, it soon came to be seen as reflecting an outdated assimilationist philosophy. It is certainly not appropriately categorized as a peoples' rights document and the right of self-determination was far from being its guiding philosophy.[26]

5. The Third Phase: 1972–1989

It was during this phase that the concept of peoples' rights, broadly defined, blossomed and reached its highpoint. It began in the early 1970s under the impetus of scholarly analyses and proposals by individuals such as Kéba M'Baye,[27] Karel Vasak,[28] François Rigaux, Richard Falk, Stephen Marks[29] and others, [30] and by a variety of conferences organized by universities[31] and international organizations such as UNESCO.[32] These promotional efforts were then given further impetus by various non-governmental initiatives, the

[25] Crawford, 'The Rights of Peoples: "Peoples" or "Governments" ', in J. Crawford (ed.), *The Rights of Peoples* (1988), at 64–5.

[26] ILO Convention No. 107 of 26 June 1957, Convention Concerning the Protection and Integration of Indigenous and Other Tribal and Semi-Tribal Populations in Independent Countries, 328 UNTS 247.

[27] M'Baye, 'Le droit au développement comme un droit de l'homme', 5 *Revue des droits de l'homme* (1972) 503.

[28] Vasak, 'A 30-year Struggle: The Sustained Effort to Give Force of Law to the Universal Declaration of Human Rights', *UNESCO Courier*, November 1977, p. 29; Vasak, 'For the Third Generation of Human Rights: The Rights of Solidarity', Inaugural Lecture to the Tenth Study Session of the International Institute of Human Rights, Strasbourg, 2–27 July 1979; and Vasak, 'Pour une troisième génération des droits de l'homme', in C. Swinarski (ed.), *Studies and Essays on International Humanitarian Law and Red Cross Principles* (1984) 837.

[29] Marks, 'Emerging Human Rights: A New Generation for the 1980s?', 33 *Rutgers Law Review* (1981) 435.

[30] Holleaux, 'Les lois de la "troisième génération" des droits de l'homme', 15 *Revue française d'administration publique* (1980) 45.

[31] e.g. A. Fenet (ed.), *Droits de l'homme, droits des peuples* (1982).

[32] See text accompanying infra n. 111.

most important of which was the adoption of the Algiers Declaration or the Declaration of the Rights of Peoples in 1976.[33] That Declaration in turn gave rise to the founding of the Lelio Basso International Foundation for the Rights and Liberation of Peoples, under whose auspices a Permanent Peoples' Tribunal was established. The stated aim of the Tribunal is to promote the law relating to peoples' rights, and a range of hearings continue to be held.[34] The most recent focused on 'Global Corporations and Human Wrongs' and was held at the University of Warwick in March 2000.[35]

After Algiers increasing attention was given to the intergovernmental forums in which some of the same actors[36] were able to persuade governments to implement at least some parts of the overall peoples' rights agenda. Within the United Nations context the General Assembly's adoption of resolution 32/130 was widely seen as a turning point by many observers. Its assertion that 'all human rights . . . of the human person and of peoples are inalienable' and that the UN should give 'priority to the search for solutions to the mass and flagrant violations of human rights of peoples and persons . . .'.[37] gave a strong impetus to the proponents of peoples' rights and caused considerable anguish for traditionalists, including most Western governments. Starting at this time the rights to development and peace were both strongly promoted by a coalition of developing and Socialist countries. The recognition of the right to development by the UN Commission on Human Rights in 1977[38] was the first step in relation to that right and this was followed by the adoption of the Declaration on the Right to Development less than a decade later, in 1986.[39] This more or less ensured the elevation of one of the 'new' rights of peoples into the pantheon of UN-recognized human rights and launched a debate which continues to have considerable life in it. Similarly, in relation to the right to peace, a resolution was adopted by the General Assembly in 1984, albeit with virtually no prior debate and no advance warning of its content, which proclaimed the Declaration of the Right of Peoples to Peace.[40]

[33] The text of the Declaration and other related papers are contained in A. Cassese and E. Jouve (eds.), *Pour un droit des peuples* (1978).

[34] See < http://www.grisnet.it/filb/filbeng.html>.

[35] See <http://www.law.warwick.ac.uk/lawschool/ppt/default.html>.

[36] For example, Kéba M'Baye chaired the session of the UN Commission on Human Rights at which the first resolution proclaiming the existence of a right to development was adopted. Karel Vasak was the Legal Counsel to UNESCO and one of the Organization's representatives at the UN Commission sessions at this time.

[37] GA Res. 32/130 (1977), para. 1(a) and (e).

[38] See Commission on Human Rights Res. 4 (XXXIII)(1977).

[39] GA Res. 41/128 (1986), Annex.

[40] GA Res. 39/11 (1984), Annex. In a highly unusual move, the Declaration was adopted directly by the plenary session of the General Assembly without prior reference to any of the relevant Committees of the Assembly, or to the Commission on Human Rights.

At the regional level the main development during this period was the adoption of the African Charter on Human and Peoples' Rights in 1981.[41] It entered into force in 1986. In many ways the Charter represents the high-water mark of efforts to achieve the recognition of peoples' rights. It not only puts those rights on the same footing as human rights but does so in an almost ostentatious way by bracketing them together in the title of the Charter. In addition it proclaims a range of rights that had not previously found any recognition in treaty form. The rights of peoples recognized include those to: be equal to all others (Art. 19); existence, self-determination (described as an 'unquestionable and inalienable right'), assistance in their liberation struggle against foreign domination, be it political, economic or cultural (Art. 20); freely dispose of their wealth and natural resources (Art. 21); their economic, social and cultural development (Art. 22); national and international peace and security (Art. 23); and a general satisfactory environment favourable to their development (Art. 24). A great deal has been written about the pros and cons of the approach adopted within the African Charter,[42] and it is not useful to go over those debates here. What remains to be seen, however, is whether the innovative peoples' rights provisions have in practice added a significant dimension to the work of the African Commission when compared to the approaches adopted by equivalent institutions in regions operating on the basis of conventions which do not specifically affirm any of these peoples' rights. We return to this issue below in considering the achievements of the Charter during the fourth phase.[43]

In terms of the rights of indigenous peoples this period represented an especially important one. Various initiatives were launched within the UN and major work was achieved in the drafting of a proposed declaration.[44] And within the framework of the International Labour Organization a path-breaking Convention, No. 169 of 1989, was adopted which effectively repudiated the integrationist thrust of the earlier ILO Convention No. 107 (1957), moved beyond the language of individual rights in affirming the value of indigenous groups and cultures, and used the word 'peoples' in its title.[45]

[41] 21 *IML* (1982) 58.

[42] See, for example, F. Ouguergouz, *La Charte africaine des droits de l'homme et des peuples: une approche juridique des droits de l'homme entre tradition et modernité* (1993); J. Matringe, *Tradition et modernité dans la Charte africaine des droits de l'homme et des peuples: étude du contenu normatif de la Charte et de son apport à la théorie du droit international des droits de l'homme* (1996); E. Ankumah, *The African Commission on Human and Peoples' Rights* (1996); U. Oji Umozurike, *The African Charter on Human and Peoples' Rights* (1997); and Mutua, 'The African Human Rights Court: A Two-Legged Stool?', 21 *Human Rights Quarterly* (1999) 342.

[43] See text accompanying infra n. 144.

[44] This work is described below. See text accompanying infra n. 92.

[45] ILO Convention No. 169 of 27 June 1989, Convention Concerning Indigenous and Tribal Peoples in Independent Countries reprinted in 28 *ILM* (1989) 1382.

The latter innovation, however, came only at the price of a statement in the text to the effect that the term should not be construed 'as having any implications as regards the rights which may attach to the term under international law'.[46] In other words, there was no endorsement of the implication which might otherwise flow from the usage of the term in the ILO Convention that the right of self-determination attached to indigenous peoples.[47]

By the end of this phase there was considerable reason for confidence that the concept of peoples' rights was firmly entrenched in international human rights law. One indicator of the inroads that the concept appeared to have made was the strength of the opposition that it generated. It was one of the factors cited by the United States in withdrawing from membership of the United Nations Educational, Scientific and Cultural Organization (UNESCO) in 1984 and it led a significant number of mainstream human rights commentators, at least in the West, to issue dire warnings of the consequences of accepting the concept. To take but one example, Paul Sieghart compared the notion with other abstractions such as 'the one true faith', 'the nation', 'the State' and the 'masses', in the names of whom some of the worst human rights violations have historically been perpetrated. 'A people' he warned, 'is no less of an abstraction than any of these: it cannot in reality consist of anything more than the individuals who compose it.'[48]

One indication of the extent to which the concept was expected to 'take-off' as a result of the activism during this third phase is contained in the pages of an omnibus textbook published under the auspices of UNESCO entitled *International Law: Achievements and Prospects*,[49] the fourth and final part of which is devoted to 'Human Rights and Rights of Peoples'. It contains an extensive introduction dealing with peoples' rights,[50] a shorter introduction on the same theme,[51] and separate chapters on the right to development,[52] the right to decolonization,[53] and the right to peace.[54] Several aspects of this approach are striking. The first is that peoples' rights are given as much if not more prominence than human rights *per se*. The second is that the terminology varies from author to author, ranging from a focus on peoples' rights to one on 'community-oriented rights'. The third is that the right to self-determination is not the subject of a separate chapter, whereas the much more

[46] Ibid., Article 1(3).

[47] J. Anaya, *Indigenous Peoples in International Law* (1996), at 47–9.

[48] P. Sieghart, *The International Law of Human Rights* (1983) 368. Rather than dismissing the concept out of hand, his main concern was to ensure that individual rights would never become subservient to the rights of peoples.

[49] M. Bedjaoui (ed.), *International Law: Achievements and Prospects* (1991).

[50] M'Baye, 'Introduction', ibid., at 1043.

[51] Gros Espiell, 'Introduction', ibid., at 1167.

[52] Bedjaoui, 'The Right to Development', ibid., at 1177.

[53] Abdulah, 'The Right to Decolonisation', ibid., at 1216.

[54] Nastase, 'The Right to Peace', ibid., at 1219.

limited and conservatively-formulated so-called 'right to decolonization' is included. Nevertheless, in some respects at least, this approach and the priorities it reflected can be seen to be representative of a certain set of assumptions that came out of the high point of the promotion of the concept of peoples' rights during this third phase.

With such a track record it might reasonably have been expected that the 1990s would be a period of consolidation of the concept which might see, *inter alia*, the recognition of additional peoples' rights at the United Nations level, the reflection of some of the innovative aspects of the African Charter in the work of the two other main regional human rights systems (in Europe and the Americas), the adoption of treaty-based formulations in the form of specialized Conventions dealing with the rights to environment, peace and development within the UN framework, the adoption of a Declaration on the Rights of Indigenous Peoples with a strong focus on peoples' rights, and the reorientation of traditional approaches to human rights in general so as to take account of the assumptions or principles upon which the new focus on peoples' rights was based. In addition, there were even grounds for optimism that the new wave of constitution-making that was unleashed by political developments in the late 1980s would see the widespread recognition of peoples' rights in national constitutions. To this effect Blaustein predicted in 1988 in relation to constitutions likely to be adopted in the following decade that:

> Certainly they will all encompass social, cultural and economic rights. Many will also include the new Third Generation of human rights: the right to peace, the right to a clean environment and the right to development.[55]

But as we shall see in looking at the record achieved in the course of the next phase, not a single one of these expectations was fulfilled.

6. The Fourth Phase (1990–present)

The fourth phase, and the one that currently prevails, began in about 1990 with the end of the Cold War. A number of developments came together to undermine the forces which had until this time given the greatest impetus to the movement for the recognition of a broad-based conception of peoples' rights. Many of the principal liberation movements, whose struggles had been an important background factor encouraging the focus on peoples during the previous phases, were transformed either into government (as in Namibia, South Africa and Eritrea) or into a different 'state in-waiting' status (as in

[55] Blaustein, '"Human Rights in the World"'s Constitutions' in M. Nowak, D. Steurer and H. Tretter (eds), *Progress in the Spirit of Human Rights* (1988) 602.

Palestine and East Timor). The importance of other liberation movements, such as that of the Polisario in Western Sahara, waned as the end of the Cold War reduced their importance to the big powers. Sympathy for the plight of other peoples, such as the Kurds, was also a casualty of this development. The break-up of the former Union of Soviet Socialist Republics into a large number of independent states and the collapse of the former Yugoslavia into its various constituent parts not only relieved some of the pressures to recognize the rights of the various peoples concerned but also made other governments increasingly wary of the risks of 'excessive fragmentation' as more and more groups within existing state borders were tempted to think that secession might suddenly be a viable option. The UN Secretary-General, whose predecessors had generally been seen as supporters of the rights of the various liberation movements, reflected the new thinking accurately in 1992 when he warned that:

> [I]f every ethnic, religious or linguistic group claimed statehood, there would be no limit to fragmentation, and peace, security and economic well-being for all would become even more difficult to achieve.[56]

Concern to protect minority rights was put back onto the agenda at both the global and regional levels, especially in Europe but, as observed below, in practice these efforts actually run counter to the recognition of peoples' rights in any strong sense of the term since they are concerned much more with promoting respect for the human rights of the members of the relevant groups than with the promotion of their status as peoples.

Globalization, with its much remarked tendencies towards both centralization and fragmentation,[57] has also had an impact in convincing governments of the importance of reinforcing approaches that uphold state sovereignty and the integrity of their existing arrangements.[58] The virtual elimination of the East–West divide and the prevalence of free market approaches have also removed the incentives that previously existed for certain countries to promote various conceptions of peoples' rights. Thus the Non-Aligned Movement is increasingly anachronistic and the old alliances within the Group of 77 are only a shadow of their former selves.

The best way to get a sense of the greatly diminished significance of peoples' rights during this fourth phase, and of their failure to live up to any of the more ambitious expectations that their proponents harboured in the preceding phase, is to consider briefly developments in some of the key policy arenas in which the claims had previously been most strongly pushed. These are

[56] B. Boutros-Ghali, *An Agenda for Peace: Preventive Diplomacy, Peace-making and Peace-keeping*, UN Doc. A/47/277 (1992), para. 17.

[57] See, for example, R. Falk, *Predatory Globalization: A Critique* (1999).

[58] See generally Kingsbury, 'Sovereignty and Inequality', 9 *EJIL* (1998) 599.

self-determination, minority rights, indigenous peoples' rights, the right to peace, the right to environment and the right to development. Consideration is then given to the achievements of the African Charter during this period and to some more broadly focused efforts to revive the focus on peoples and their rights.

(a) Self-determination

While the scholarly literature on self-determination during this period retained the ambivalence that characterized earlier analyses, much of it also took a very significant turn towards a post-Cold War direction of a right to democracy. The balance began to swing in relation to the longstanding distinction between internal and external self-determination, in favour of the former, although not in the way that might have been expected. Efforts in that direction during the third phase, even appearing in the work of the Human Rights Committee[59] and building upon the acknowledgement in the 1970 Declaration that the principles of national unity and territorial integrity might have to give way in the absence of a government 'representing the whole people belonging to the territory without distinction as to race, creed or colour',[60] had come to relatively little outside the realms of theory. But by the beginning of the fourth phase this changed dramatically. Thomas Franck, Gregory Fox and others[61] wrote about an emerging norm of democratic governance, the underpinnings of which drew in part on the right of self-determination. While they did not suggest that the new norm replaced the old one, there seems little doubt that one of the implications is that the existence of a system of democratic governance would render a claim for self-determination much less compelling, if not entirely redundant.

During this post-Cold War phase some commentators tended to combine a reaffirmation of secession as a possibly legitimate means by which to assert the right of groups to self-determination with an insistence that the onus of proof on the group in question would be very difficult to meet. Thus, for example, Tomuschat countenanced the possibility of secession but only in cases where the state 'turns itself into an apparatus of terror which persecutes specific groups of the population'.[62] Hannum suggested two possibilities, the first of which required an extremely high threshold and the second a

[59] See M. Nowak, *U.N. Covenant on Civil and Political Rights: CCPR Commentary* (1993) 5.

[60] GA Res. 2625 (XXV)(1970), Annex. UN Doc. A/8028 (1970) 121, 124.

[61] Franck, 'The Emerging Right to Democratic Governance', 86 *AJIL* (1992) 46; Fox, 'The Right to Political Participation in International Law', 17 *Yale Journal of International Law* (1992) 539. For critiques see B. Roth, *Governmental Illegitimacy in International Law* (1999) and S. Marks, *The Riddle of All Constitutions: International Law, Democracy, and the Critique of Ideology* (2000).

[62] Tomuschat, 'Self-determination in a Post-Colonial World', in C. Tomuschat (ed.), *Modern Law of Self-determination* (1993) 1, at 9.

surprisingly low one. The first would apply in cases of 'massive, discriminatory human rights violations, approaching the scale of genocide', while the second would kick in whenever 'reasonable demands for local self-government or minority rights have been arbitrarily rejected by a central government—even without accompanying large-scale violence'.[63] While the latter is surprisingly open-ended, the former is more in line with the general disposition of the times.

Other commentators, however, sought to ring the death knell for the right of self-determination by consigning it essentially to the history of the struggle for decolonization.[64] Thus, for example, Helen Quane contends that 'when many States affirmed the right of peoples everywhere to self-determination they did not intend to affirm the universality of the right as commonly understood'.[65] Their intention, in her view, was solely to offer a one-time only option for peoples in non-self-governing situations. All other attempts to 'define people on the basis of personal criteria such as ethnicity or language have been unsuccessful'. While this is too pessimistic a conclusion if applied to developments in international law generally, it is difficult to contest it in relation to the current status of the self-determination debate.

Western governments pursued the 'democracy, not secession' line with predictable enthusiasm. Thus for example the US Deputy Secretary of State in the Clinton administration used what he discerned to be a globalization-driven trend toward decentralization within states to argue that 'the rise of interdependence among states offers a remedy for conflicts within states that is better than secession'. His solution was to combine the promotion of democracy within the state as a whole with 'an effort to help would-be breakaway areas benefit from cross-border economic development and political cooperation'.[66] At the end of his analysis he adopted a formulation which is very much in line with scholarly trends and which could readily be interpreted as effectively superseding self-determination with a focus on democracy: '[d]emocracy is the political system most explicitly designed to ensure self-determination'.[67]

[63] Hannum, 'The Specter of Secession: Responding to Claims for Ethnic Self-determination', 77/2 *Foreign Affairs* (1998) 13, at 16.

[64] This is quite apart from those who continued to deny altogether the existence of the right. See Rubin, 'Secession and Self-determination: A Legal, Moral, and Political Analysis', 36 *Stanford Journal of International Law* (2000) 253 ('Since there is no holder of such a right and no standing in any state to speak for the national or other minority or majority of another, and all states deny such a right to their own secessionist movements, it is doubted that this category, although much discussed and asserted loudly, exists' ibid.).

[65] Quane, 'The United Nations and the Evolving Right to Self-determination', 47 *ICLQ* (1998) 537, at 571.

[66] Talbott, 'Self-determination in an Interdependent World', *Foreign Policy* (Spring 2000), 152, at 153.

[67] Ibid., at 159.

While developing countries have had reservations about this turn of events, they have certainly not sought to resurrect a more rounded conception of the right of self-determination. Thus, for example, wherever the right is mentioned in the Programme of Action adopted by the Group of 77 Summit meeting held in Cuba in April 2000, it is immediately followed by the phrase: 'in particular of peoples living under colonial or other forms of alien domination or foreign occupation'.[68] Consistent with this approach, the only reference to the concept on the annual agenda of the UN Commission on Human Rights is under an item entitled 'the right of peoples to self-determination and its application to peoples under colonial or alien domination or foreign occupation.[69] Indeed, within the United Nations context as a whole the self-determination debate has reached a parlous state.

It is perhaps best illustrated by the annual resolution adopted by the General Assembly on the subject, which is little more than a sad relic of a bygone golden era. In 1999,[70] and again in 2000,[71] the resolution reaffirms the importance of 'the universal realization of the right of all peoples, including those under colonial, foreign and alien domination, to self-determination', but proceeds to move from any conception of universal applicability of the right to focus exclusively on 'acts of foreign military intervention, aggression and occupation, since these have resulted in the suppression of the right of peoples to self-determination and other human rights in certain parts of the world'. Given the extent to which threats to the enjoyment of the right are internally generated in a great many situations, this narrow focus deprives the resolution of any claim to give an accurate representation of the threats that exist to the enjoyment of the right of self-determination. The resolution is 'underpinned' each year by a 'report of the Secretary-General' which is devoid of all content other than to recall initiatives taken by the Commission in regard to Western Sahara and Palestine, and the use of mercenaries to impede the exercise of the rights of peoples to self-determination.[72]

Two other trends may be mentioned, although they will not be explored in any depth. The first is the reignition of the debate on humanitarian intervention which was occasioned by the Kosovo crisis of the late 1990s. Some commentators raised the issue of self-determination but the great majority treated it as being of marginal relevance at best.[73] Governments, for their part, strenuously

[68] See <http://www.g77.org/summit/ProgrammeofAction_G77Summit.htm>, (2000), para. 11.

[69] UN Doc. E/CN.4/2001/1 (2000), item 5.

[70] GA Res. 54/155 (1999).

[71] See UN Doc. A/C.3/55/L.22 (2000), final text of resolution not available at the time of writing.

[72] UN Doc. A/55/176 (2000), para. 5.

[73] See, for example, Cassese, '*Ex iniuria ius oritur*: Is International Legitimation of Forcible Humanitarian Countermeasures Taking Shape in the World Community?', 10 *EJIL* (1998) 23, at 24 where he cites with approval the statement by O. Schachter, *International Law in*

avoided any use of the term in this connection, and nor did they refer to the rights of minority groups. While they did speak generously of the need for 'a substantially greater degree of autonomy' and for 'meaningful self-administration',[74] these terms are all the more significant for present purposes because they were clearly chosen as a means to avoid reference to any form of peoples' rights.

The second trend is the extent to which the principle of *uti possidetis* is now commonly invoked by prominent international lawyers to insist that the territorial integrity of states, presented as a principle which is indispensable for international stability, qualifies the right of self-determination, thus greatly reducing the potential scope of the right.[75] While strong arguments have been used to challenge this approach,[76] the argument is symptomatic of a general trend towards the downgrading of the right of self-determination.

In general, therefore, the fourth phase has seen a number of developments which constitute important steps away from a focus on self-determination in non-colonial situations and on conceptions of group autonomy and their replacement by a concern with democratic legitimacy and more limited forms of autonomy.

(b) Minority rights

The perceived ineffectiveness of the innovative regime established by the League of Nations to protect the rights of minority groups within Europe resulted in a considerable wariness in relation to this issue on the part of the drafters of both the UN Charter and the Universal Declaration of Human Rights. Rather than recognizing group or collective rights, the various formulations subsequently adopted reflected an essentially individual rights-based non-discrimination framework. Throughout the prolonged Cold War years the UN was able to do little other than conduct conceptual studies on the matter and these led to few conclusions other than that the matter was best dealt with pragmatically.[77] Efforts launched in the late 1970s to draft a

Theory and Practice (1991) 128 that '[I]nternational law does not, and should not, legitimize the use of force across national lines except for self-defence (including collective self-defence) and enforcement measures ordered by the Security Council. Neither human rights, democracy or self-determination are acceptable legal grounds for waging war . . .'.

[74] Statement by the Contact Group established in the context of negotiations over Bosnia-Herzegovina, which included representatives of France, Germany, Italy, the Russian Federation, the United Kingdom and the United States, made in London, 9 March 1998, and reproduced at <http://www.ohr.int>.

[75] e.g. Pellet, 'Quel avenir pour le droit des peuples à disposer d'eux-mêmes?', in *Le droit international dans un monde en mutation: Mélanges Jiménez de Aréchaga* (1994) 255, at 259–61.

[76] Corten, 'Droit des peuples à disposer d'eux-mêmes et uti possidetis: deux faces d'une même médaille?', [1998] *Revue belge de droit international* 161.

[77] e.g. F. Capotorti, *Study of the Rights of Persons Belonging to Ethnic, Religious and Linguistic Minorities,* UN Doc. E/CN.4/Sub.2/384/Rev.1 (1979); J. Deschênes, *Proposal*

Declaration on the Rights of Persons belonging to National or Ethnic, Religious or Linguistic Minorities were characterized by marked reluctance until 1990 when the situation changed very significantly and enabled the completion of the task in 1992.[78] Based on a consensus among governments, the Declaration was far from path-breaking and contained no implementation arrangements. Subsequently the Sub-Commission on the Prevention of Discrimination and the Protection of Minorities (which, despite its name tag, had previously been unable to do a great deal in relation to the latter issue) was authorized to establish a Working Group on Minorities.[79] Its tasks, however, clearly indicated that the promotion of the rights of peoples could not be considered to have been among the reasons for which it had been created. In its work to date it has concentrated on the drafting of a commentary on the Declaration and issues of group rights and peoples' rights have, notwithstanding occasional attempts to the contrary, been assiduously avoided.[80] At one point during its session in 2000 the Group's Chairman sought to reassure participants that, unlike the rights of indigenous peoples, 'the rights of minorities were individual'.[81]

Similarly, in interpreting the provisions of Article 27 of the International Covenant on Civil and Political Rights which recognizes the rights of 'persons belonging to' minority groups, the Human Rights Committee has insisted very much on the individual as the holder. In so far as its interpretation has been progressive in nature it has largely consisted of an emphasis on the possible need for affirmative acts on the part of governments. The language it has chosen to use acknowledges in only a very oblique way the inevitable interplay between the individual and the group in any consideration of minority rights.[82]

Concerning a Definition of the Term 'Minority', UN Doc. E/CN.4/Sub.2/1985/31 (1985); and generally P. Thornberry, *International Law and the Rights of Minorities* (1991).

[78] GA Res. 47/135 (1992), Annex.

[79] Commission on Human Rights Res. 1995/24 and Economic and Social Council Res. 1995/31.

[80] Thus when the representative of Pakistan sought to assert 'that a minority community could acquire a collective right to exercise self-determination if its collective right and identity were being suppressed and where the Government of the State in question did not fulfil the requirements for respecting its territorial integrity', the Group's Chairman sought to put the issue beyond the scope of its work by pointing out that 'the Declaration on Minorities neither extended nor limited the right of peoples to self-determination. . . . Neither the Working Group nor the commentary intended to pass any judgement on the scope of the right to self-determination . . .'. Report of the Working Group on Minorities on its sixth session, UN Doc. E/CN.4/Sub.2/2000/27 (2000), paras 19, 20.

[81] Ibid., para. 29.

[82] General Comment No. 23 (1994) on Article 27. UN Doc. HRI/GEN/1/Rev.4 (2000) 115, 117, para. 6.2.

It is difficult to conclude that efforts at the international level to encourage the protection of minority rights have benefited much, if at all, from being put forward under the rubric of peoples' rights. While non-governmental organizations, such as the Unrepresented Nations and Peoples Organization (UNPO)[83] have worked under such an umbrella, it is doubtful if this dimension of their activities has been especially helpful or important. Indeed the most successful efforts on behalf of minorities may well have been accomplished at the regional level, but even most of these successes have added little to the lustre of the concept of peoples' rights. One example is the quasi-diplomatic, quasi-legal nature of the work of the High Commissioner on National Minorities established by the Organization for Security and Co-operation in Europe in 1992. The High Commissioner may be requested by an organ of the OSCE or the country concerned to undertake a mission, but the decision to do so is his own, and his reports are essentially confidential. His recommendations address both short-term policy towards minorities and longer-term measures to encourage a continuing dialogue between the government and minority members. But his involvement is premised upon the existence of an actual or potential conflict among states and his focus is on confidence-building and mediation rather than on the vindication of rights *per se*. In practice his approach has been characterized by a perhaps inevitable element of pragmatism and his discourse has been located at a level which is distant from that of peoples' rights.[84]

Other regional examples within the European context are the European Charter for Regional or Minority Languages of 1992 and the Framework Convention for the Protection of National Minorities of 1995, neither of which makes even the least concession to the concept of group, let alone peoples', rights.[85] The same is true of the vast majority of bilateral treaties drawn up in the post-Cold War era with a view to protecting national minorities in the Central and Eastern European states.[86] Finally, the European Court of Human Rights has, with a very small number of exceptions, taken a notably cautious approach to the rights of minorities. This was illustrated in a recent series of five cases involving the treatment of gypsies in the United

[83] Established in 1991, UNPO consists of 50 different 'nations and peoples . . . who are not represented as such in the world's principal international organizations'. They include 'occupied nations, indigenous peoples, minorities, and even oppressed majorities who currently struggle to regain their lost countries, preserve their cultural identities, protect their basic human and economic rights and safeguard the natural environment'. See <http://www.unpo.org/>.

[84] For an excellent recent survey of his activities, techniques used, and impact see Ratner, 'Does International Law Matter in Preventing Ethnic Conflict?', 32 *NYU Journal of Int'l Law and Politics* (2000) 591.

[85] Hofmann, 'Minority Rights: Individual or Group Rights? A Comparative View on European Legal Systems', 40 *German Yearbook of International Law* (1997) 357, at 380.

[86] Ibid.

Kingdom.[87] In deciding to give priority to rather inchoate planning considerations over the rights of the minority group the majority of the Court effectively opted out of any responsibility to give effect to what it conceded to be 'an emerging international consensus' within the Council of Europe 'recognizing the special needs of minorities and an obligation to protect their security, identity and lifestyle'.[88] It did so on the highly debatable grounds that it was 'not persuaded that the consensus is sufficiently concrete for it to derive any guidance as to the conduct or standards which Contracting States consider desirable in any particular situation'. As a result, it interpreted its own role as being 'a strictly supervisory one', or in other words, it insisted on being highly deferential and was unprepared to attach any significant weight to minority rights.[89]

Similarly, the discourse of peoples' rights has been notably absent from some impressive breakthroughs on minority rights that have taken place at the national level. Thus the formulations included in constitutions or bills of rights adopted in India, Canada, South Africa, and the arrangements concluded in situations such as Papua-New Guinea or Fiji in the wake of challenges to minority rights have been far-reaching but not premised upon the existence of a category of peoples' rights.

As in the case of self-determination, the impact of the fragmentationist tendencies of the Cold War era, combined with some of the consequences of globalization, have led many commentators to stress the need to move away from the old rhetoric of collective, group, or peoples' rights for minorities. The following analysis by John Packer represents a classic exposition of the case:

> In our increasingly complex, interdependent world . . . the separatist logic of the nation-state . . . offers few if any solutions. Indeed, its pursuit causes conflicts . . . The challenge, therefore, is to find means of reconciling competing interests and aspirations in a multicultural and multilingual world that is increasingly open, mobile, interconnected, multi-layered, and dynamic. To a large extent, this can be achieved through a concerted effort to ensure respect for the human rights of everyone everywhere, including opportunities for the maintenance and development of cultural identities.[90]

[87] *Beard v The United Kingdom*, Application No. 24882/94, 18 January 2001; *Coster v The United Kingdom*, Application No. 24876/94, 18 January 2001; *Lee v The United Kingdom*, Application No. 25289/94, 18 January 2001; *Jane Smith v The United Kingdom*, Application No. 25154/94, 18 January 2001; and *Chapman v The United Kingdom*, Application No. 27238/95, 18 January 2001,

[88] Ibid., para. 93.

[89] Ibid., para. 94.

[90] Packer, 'Making International Law Matter in Preventing Ethnic Conflict: A Practitioner's Perspective', 32 *NYU Journal of Int'l Law and Politics* (2000) 715, at 719–20.

(c) Indigenous peoples' rights

This is one of the most specific contexts in which the right of self-determination and peoples' rights more broadly have been consistently invoked.[91] The current draft of a proposed UN Declaration on the Rights of Indigenous Peoples includes a formulation which is carefully designed to mirror precisely Article 1 of the International Covenant on Civil and Political Rights. Thus, while the latter refers to 'all peoples', the former speaks of 'indigenous peoples' who are said to have the right to self-determination, by virtue of which 'they freely determine their political status and freely pursue their economic, social and cultural development'.[92] The adoption of this formulation would represent a significant victory for indigenous peoples and would enable them to reclaim the ground lost in the drafting of ILO Convention No. 169.[93] In an effort to make the formulation both more explicit and perhaps potentially more palatable to governments fearing secessionist tendencies, the draft later provides that '[I]ndigenous peoples, as a specific form of exercising their right to self-determination, have the right to autonomy or self-government in matters relating to their internal and local affairs . . .'.[94]

The terminological struggles and acrobatics which have characterized the twenty-five years or so during which the United Nations human rights mechanisms have been considering these issues provides a perfect illustration of the hopes and fears that have been vested in the use of the term 'peoples'. The story began in 1971 when a Special Rapporteur of the UN Sub-Commission on Prevention of Discrimination and Protection of Minorities was appointed to study the issue. At that time the use of the term 'peoples' was anathema to governments which assumed that it carried with it the implication of an entitlement to secession. Hence the title of the study dealt neither with rights nor peoples: its more limited focus was on 'the problem of discrimination against indigenous populations'.[95]

A decade later, when the time was ripe to establish the first institutional arrangements to deal with the issues raised in the study, the same cautious approach was adopted and the forum was called the Working Group on Indigenous Populations. One of its first acts, however, was to announce that

[91] See generally Wiessner, 'Rights and Status of Indigenous Peoples: A Global Comparative and International Legal Analysis', 12 *Harvard Human Rights Journal* (1999) 57; Turpel, 'Indigenous Peoples' Rights of Political Participation and Self-determination; Recent International Legal Developments and the Continuing Struggle for Recognition', 25 *Cornell International Law Journal* (1992) 579; and Corntassel and Primeau, 'Indigenous "Sovereignty" and International Law: Revised Strategies for Pursuing "Self-determination"', 17 *Human Rights Quarterly* (1995) 343.

[92] UN Doc. E/CN.4/Sub.2/1994/2, Article 3.

[93] See text accompanying supra n. 46.

[94] Draft declaration, supra n. 92, Article 31.

[95] UN Docs E/CN.4/Sub.2/1986/7 and Add.1–4; and *Conclusions, Proposals and Recommendations* (UN Publication, Sales No. E.86.XIV.3).

it would embark upon the drafting of a UN Declaration on the Rights of Indigenous Peoples, thus seeking to confront the issue directly. At one stage it even sought to use the terminology of a draft Universal Declaration on the subject, but for this it was rebuked by its parent body, the UN Commission on Human Rights. When its drafting work was completed,[96] it was sent to the Commission which set up its own working group to consider the matter. The new working group was given a cumbersome title which was specifically designed to avoid the use of the term 'peoples' and instead referred to the fact that it would focus on the Sub-Commission draft, thereby avoiding any advance commitment on the part of the Commission to the terminology used.[97]

Unsurprisingly, one of the most contentious issues to be discussed by the working group is the applicability of the right of self-determination to indigenous peoples. In 1999 an extended debate was held on this subject. The representatives of indigenous groups were almost unanimous in insisting that the right was fundamental and integral to the self-respect and enjoyment of other human rights by those concerned. Governmental responses were, for the most part, predictably closed. The exceptions were those governments such as Pakistan[98] which consider that they have little if anything to lose by adopting a progressive stance. In contrast, governments of countries in which indigenous peoples reside were almost uniformly reluctant. For example, the representative of the United States of America not only claimed that 'there was no international practice or instrument that accorded indigenous groups everywhere the right to self-determination', but also insisted 'there was not yet international consensus', despite views to the contrary 'expressed by some Governments and academics, that the right to self-determination included both an external and an internal aspect and that the latter applied to groups within existing States'.[99] The Canadian representative accepted the existence of such a right provided that its implementation 'respected the political, constitutional and territorial integrity of democratic States'.[100] And Australia rejected the inclusion of the term 'self-determination' in the draft declaration 'because for many people it implied the establishment of separate nations and laws'.[101] In short, the spirit that infused the peoples' rights initiatives of the third phase was hardly alive and kicking in the fourth phase even in one of the contexts in which it might have been assumed to be most likely to be accepted.

[96] The draft is annexed to Sub-Commission Res. 1994/45.

[97] On the progress achieved to date see Foster, 'Articulating Self-determination in the draft Declaration on the Rights of Indigenous Peoples' 12 *EJIL* (2001) 140.

[98] UN Doc. E/CN.4/2000/84 (1999), para. 67.

[99] Ibid., para. 49.

[100] Ibid., para. 50.

[101] Ibid., para. 62.

The most recent step in this saga is the decision by the UN Economic and Social Council in July 2000 to establish a permanent forum in which issues relating to the rights of indigenous peoples can be discussed. Consistent with longstanding governmental reticence to embrace the terminology of 'peoples', the new sixteen-member forum will be known as the 'permanent forum on indigenous issues'.[102]

(c) The right to peace

During the fourth phase there has been no follow-up whatsoever by the United Nations itself to the General Assembly's 1984 Declaration on the Right of Peoples to Peace in which, *inter alia*, it 'solemnly proclaim[ed] that the peoples of our planet have a sacred right to peace'.[103] In effect the entire proposition, having been championed by the then Communist Government of Poland, has simply been dropped like a stone. The generally accepted position today is probably best expressed in the following terms:

> The collective (peoples') right to peace . . . does not have a clear legal meaning and cannot be translated into meaningful action. However, many individual rights can be exercised with the view of defending peace . . .[104]

That did not prevent Federico Mayor, the former Director-General of UNESCO, from championing the right in the late 1990s, some years after most observers considered it to be a concept whose time had long since passed. Having failed to persuade the General Conference of the organization to take action in 1997 in response to a declaration made in his own name,[105] he then sought to build support for a renewed attempt the following year by convening an 'international consultation of governmental experts on the right to peace'.[106] The experts were presented with a draft 'Declaration on the

[102] ESC Res. 2000/22.

[103] GA Res. 39/11 (1984), Annex, para. 1.

[104] Dimitrijevic, 'Human Rights and Peace', in J. Symonides (ed.), *Human Rights: New Dimensions and Challenges* (1998) 47, at 64. It is consistent with this analysis that those who continue to advocate the relevance of this right provide no definition of any use. Thus, for example, the 'People's Movement for Human Rights Education', which has a webpage devoted to the right says only that 'The human right of all persons to peace and disarmament is inextricably linked to all other human rights . . .'. See <http://www.pdhre.org/rights/peace.html>. The earliest and probably still the clearest definition of this right was provided by Immanuel Kant, but he made it clear that it was a right possessed not by individuals or peoples but by states: 'The rights of peace are as follows: firstly the right to remain at peace when nearby states are at war . . . ; secondly, the right to secure the continued maintenance of peace once it has been concluded . . . ; and thirdly, the right to form alliances or confederate leagues of several states for the purpose of communal defence . . .': I. Kant, *The Metaphysics of Morals* (1797) section 59, reprinted in M. Ishay (ed.), *The Human Rights Reader* (1997) 161, 169.

[105] 'The Human Right to Peace, Declaration by the Director-General', UNESCO Doc. SHS–97/WS/6 (1997).

[106] Report by the Director-General on the Results of the International Consultation of Governmental Experts on the Right to Peace, UNESCO Doc. 154 EX/40 (1998).

Human Right to Peace as the Foundation of the Culture of Peace' which was notable only for being platitudinous and vacuous. It consisted of 19 preambular paragraphs followed by six 'substantive' paragraphs. The two key provisions speak eloquently about the hollowness of the initiative:

Every human being has the right to peace, which is inherent in the nature of the human person; it must be recognized, respected and implemented without any discrimination in either internal or international contexts by all states and other members of the international community.

Violence in all its forms is intrinsically incompatible with the right of every human being to peace; since inequalities, exclusion and poverty are liable to lead to violations of international peace and internal peace, the right of every human being to peace requires the promotion of social justice through appropriate national and international policies aimed at sustainable human development.[107]

The governmental experts 'amended' the proposal so as to remove all mention of the right to peace in the operative part of the draft.[108] In his report on the outcome the Director-General tried in vain to put a positive gloss on the debacle by observing that the 'vast majority of countries firmly support the human right to peace as a moral principle that is binding only in so far as a country has had it adopted by its parliament and incorporated into its legal system'.[109] Perhaps unsurprisingly, Mr Mayor's successor, Koichiro Matsuura, has subsequently shown no interest in pursuing the matter.[110] It is noteworthy, nonetheless, that for more than twenty years UNESCO has been the single most consistent and enthusiastic proponent of the concept of peoples' rights, starting with a meeting in Paris in 1978, and featuring subsequent meetings in 1980 in Mexico City, 1985 in Zimbabwe, 1989 in Paris, 1991 in Budapest, and 1998 in Spain.[111] When the United States withdrew from the organization in 1984 it cited several reasons for doing so but prominent among them was UNESCO's efforts in relation to peoples' rights. The US feared that 'the thrust in UNESCO would give international legitimacy to abuses of individual rights by authoritarian states. Abuses justified by appealing to a supposedly higher or equally

[107] UNESCO Doc. 154 EX/40 (1998), Annex II, paras 3, 4.

[108] Ibid., Annex V.

[109] Ibid., para. 4.

[110] See, for example, his speech 'The Culture of Peace: An Idea in Action', UNESCO Doc. DG/2000/40 of 24 November 2000.

[111] See International Meeting of Experts on Further Study of the Concept of the Rights of Peoples, convened by UNESCO, Paris, 27–30 November 1989, UNESCO Doc. SHS89/CONF.602/7; Final Report of UNESCO Expert Meeting on Human Rights, Human Needs and the Establishment of a New International Economic Order, Paris 19–23 June 1978, UNESCO Doc. SS-78/CONF. 630/12; Final Report of a Colloquium on the New Human Rights, Mexico City, 12–15 August 1980, UNESCO Doc. SS-80/CONF. 806/4. Other meetings are listed in UNESCO, UNESCO and Human Rights: Standard-Setting Instruments, Major Meetings and Publications (2nd edn., 1999) 491–8.

valid set of collective rights'.[112] Even as recently as 1998 it published an entire volume devoted, in effect, to yet another exploration of the various rights of peoples.[113] While the organization and its officials have been praised for 'courage and intellectual rigour' in probing these issues,[114] there has in fact been all too little of the latter in most of UNESCO's work on peoples' rights.

But as with any such idea, the eventual loss of interest on the part of the initial proponents of the right to peace did not necessarily signify an end to the matter. In recent years Pope John Paul II has consistently sung the praises of the right to peace, both in general terms[115] and in specific situations.[116] Perhaps more revealing of the impact of these efforts by UNESCO and others, however, is that a search of 'right to peace' sites on the World Wide Web yields almost nothing which sheds any light on the issue but instead reveals a great number devoted to the right to peace and quiet![117] While it remains to be seen whether the next global arms build-up will provoke more enthusiasm for this concept, it seems fair to say that it has definitively failed to capture the global imagination and that it has done little, if anything, to strengthen the concept of peoples' rights as a separate category of rights.

(e) The right to environment

This right has been the subject of extensive debate and analysis at both the national and international levels, and like the right to development, seems to have an instinctive appeal which guarantees it a continuing place on the human rights agenda. Nevertheless, as Chapter 6 above has made clear, there is very limited support in international law for the existence of such a right seen as a freestanding human right, attaching either to individuals or to peoples. During the fourth phase the main push for the recognition of such a right came from the work done under the auspices of what is now the Sub-Commission on Promotion and Protection of Human Rights. The

[112] Statement of Hon. Edmund Hennelly, Chairman, US Delegation to the 1983 UNESCO General Conference, in *U.S. Withdrawal from UNESCO*, Hearings before the Subcommittee on Human Rights and International Organizations of the Committee on Foreign Affairs, House of Reps., 98th Cong., 2nd Sess. (1984) 12, 13.

[113] Symonides supra n. 104.

[114] M. Kirby, 'UNESCO, Human Rights and Courage', Paris, 7 June 1999, at <http://www3.lawfoundation.net.au/resources/kirby/papers/19990607_unesco7june99.html>. Justice Kirby mistakenly refers to UNESCO's work on the right to self-determination but in fact it was the 1989 meeting in Paris on peoples' rights in general in which he was involved.

[115] 'Message for Peace', <http://www.jubil2000.org/papa/mes11.uk.html> (2000) ('In a sense, promoting the right to peace ensures respect for all other rights . . .').

[116] Ioannes Paulus PP. II, 'Ethiopia and Eritrea have a right to peace and solidarity', <http://www.catholic-forum.com/churches/kidanemehret/ethiopia_solid.html>, 23 May 2000.

[117] e.g. Bronzaft, 'Assert Your Right to Peace and Quiet!', 25 *Hearing Rehabilitation Quarterly* (2000), <http://www.lhh.org/hrq/25-1/right.htm>.

Sub-Commission appointed Ms F. Ksentini as Special Rapporteur to study 'human rights and the environment' and she concluded that 'recognition of the right to a satisfactory environment as a human right' was confirmed by developments at both the universal and regional levels.[118] Accordingly, her final report contained a set of Draft Principles which referred *inter alia* to 'the right of a satisfactory environment' and a right to a 'secure, healthy and ecologically sound environment'.[119] The suggestion that such a right already exists was based upon a loose amalgam of non-binding formulations, aspirational analyses by non-governmental groups and references to instruments such as the African Charter on Human and Peoples' Rights. But the practice in relation to the latter has not been such as to provide much support for the proposition that there has emerged a meaningful new right which goes beyond existing individual rights. In supervising compliance with the provision the African Commission seems to have focused essentially on ensuring that polluting activities are curtailed rather than adopting an interpretation of the scope of the 'right to a general satisfactory environment' which would be consistent with the concept of a far-reaching new peoples' right to environment.[120]

Another development which might be invoked in support of progress on this front during the fourth phase is the entry into force in late 1999 of the Protocol of San Salvador which recognizes the right to 'live in a healthy environment'.[121] But this is not expressed as a peoples' right and it is directly linked to the right to have access to basic public services which would suggest a somewhat limited scope for the right. While the provision has the potential to be interpreted broadly, the failure of the Inter-American Commission to take very seriously the existing provisions of the American Convention which deal with economic, social and cultural rights[122] provides little basis for expecting a more radical approach in relation to a right which is formulated in such broad and open-ended terms.

It is not surprising then that the vast majority of scholarly assessments of the right to environment reach a negative conclusion as to both the existence and the potential significance of such a right.[123] Instead, their focus is consistently on the synergies which can be achieved by linking the two subject areas

[118] UN Doc. E/CN.4/Sub.2/1994/9, para. 242. [119] Ibid., Annex 1, para. 261.

[120] Churchill, 'Environmental Rights in Existing Human Rights Treaties', in A. Boyle and M. Anderson (eds), *Human Rights Approaches to Environmental Protection* (1996) 89, at 106.

[121] Additional Protocol to the American Convention on Human Rights in the Area of Economic, Social and Cultural Rights of 1988, reprinted at 28 *ILM* (1989) 161.

[122] Craven, 'The Protection of Economic, Social and Cultural Rights under the Inter-American System of Human Rights', in D. Harris and S. Livingstone (eds), *The Inter-American System of Human Rights* (1998) 289.

[123] For an excellent overview of the current state of the debate in this respect see Handl, 'Human Rights and Protection of the Environment', in A. Eide, C. Krause and A. Rosas (eds), *Economic, Social and Cultural Rights: A Textbook* (2nd edn., forthcoming).

in creative ways and by using existing human rights provisions in both substantive and procedural ways to promote different parts of the environmental agenda. In practice the United Nations human rights organs have adopted a similar focus as illustrated by the preparedness of the Commission on Human Rights to examine the issue of the 'adverse effects of the illicit movement and dumping of toxic and dangerous products and wastes on the enjoyment of human rights'[124] but its apparent unwillingness to take any concrete initiatives in response to the proposed Draft Principles sent on to it by the Sub-Commission which would involve recognition of the right to environment.

(f) The right to development

At first glance the right to development, the current status of which is dealt with in depth in Chapter 5 above, would seem to be the sole exception to the general proposition that the concept of peoples' rights is in a phase of serious decline. It features prominently on the agenda of the various UN human rights organs and continues to be the subject of a great deal of diplomatic, bureaucratic and scholarly activity. But in fact even the prospects of this particular peoples' right seem to depend significantly on eliminating for all practical purposes the collective rights dimension and of defining the concept in such a way that it blends seamlessly into mainstream human rights analysis.

The misfortune of the right to development is that it has been constructed upon foundations which simultaneously impel it in two opposite directions. The result, perhaps unsurprisingly when we see the real nature of the dynamics that have been at work, is an almost stationary, even stagnant, state of affairs. The first impulse has been generated by those who view the right to development as a conceptual tool by which to break free of the restraints which limit the potential of international human rights discourse and practice to transcend the unimaginative, heavily negotiated, relatively conservative, and by some accounts destructively bureaucratized, approach which they would suggest currently prevails. This group includes a few governments which, for varying reasons, see in existing approaches few solutions which might be capable of addressing the principal challenges which they consider should be central to the international human rights agenda.

In the same vein a number of valiant attempts have been made within the scholarly literature both to provide a sound legal and conceptual foundation for this right and to breathe life into it in terms of its practical implications. Mention can be made in particular of the analyses undertaken by Georges

[124] See Shelton, supra Ch. 6, n. 69.

Abi-Saab,[125] Mohammed Bedjaoui,[126] Upendra Baxi,[127] and Boaventura de Sousa Santos.[128]

But at the same time as this progressive vision has been unfolding, the great majority of governments have used the right to development as an arena of last refuge in which to relocate many of the old ideological and political struggles which are left over from the days of the New International Economic Order and related debates of decades past. While there are valid concerns underlying many of the perspectives put forward in this regard, the debates themselves have become sterile and repetitive and bear a diminishing resemblance to evolving realities.

Against this background it is unsurprising that very few constructive, carefully thought-through proposals have been put forward within the context of the principal intergovernmental arena, that of the UN Commission on Human Rights. Its attempts to develop a clearer understanding of the concept have been largely confined to a succession of working groups, of varying composition, which over a period of twenty years have produced an endless succession of reports.[129] Rather than enlighten or energize the debate these reports have succeeded in doing little more than recording the fundamental incompatibility of the various positions which they had been asked to reconcile. Some ten years ago it was suggested that the only possible way out of the impasse in which these groups have inevitably found themselves was the provision of high-level analytical policy inputs into the debate by an independent expert consultant with the necessary expertise to carry some weight with the Commission and to formulate politically palatable proposals as a basis for further negotiation.[130] In 1998 the Commission acted along these lines and appointed a distinguished Indian development economist, Arjun Sengupta, for that purpose.[131]

The reports by the 'independent expert' have sought to steer a middle path through the competing interests of different groups of states. In definitional terms, he has introduced Amartya Sen's ideas about the importance of focusing

[125] G. Abi-Saab, 'The Legal Formulation of a Right to Development', in Hague Academy Of International Law, *The Right to Development at The International Level* (1980) 159.

[126] Bedjaoui, supra n. 52.

[127] Baxi, 'The Development of the Right to Development', in Symonides, supra n. 104, at 99.

[128] B. de Sousa Santos, *Toward a New Common Sense: Law, Science and Politics in the Paradigmatic Transition* (1995) 356.

[129] The details of the composition and mandates of the different groups and the text of their reports can be found at <http://www.unhchr.ch/html/menu2/10/e/wgrtd.htm>.

[130] Alston, 'Revitalising United Nations Work on Human Rights and Development', 18 *Melbourne University Law Review* (1991) 216, at 250 and 254.

[131] CHR Res. 1998/72, para. 10(b) provides for 'the appointment by the Chairman of the Commission on Human Rights of an independent expert with high competence in the field of the right to development, with a mandate to present to the working group at each of its sessions a study on the current state of progress in the implementation of the right to development as a basis for a focused discussion . . .'.

on entitlements and capabilities, while at the same time retaining, in practice if not in theory, the view that the right to development is a synthesis of all existing rights.[132] Although he insists that the right to development and the so-called 'rights approach to development' are not the same thing,[133] his analysis seems to tie them together to the point where the distinction becomes rather difficult to maintain.[134] His economic analysis is predicated upon the need for growth but also the inability of most developing countries to realize the right to development without the assistance of international cooperation. The bottom line of his analysis is that there is a duty on the part of the rich countries to cooperate to facilitate the right to development of the developing countries and that this includes both resource transfers and measures to give the latter 'an equitable share in the fruits of international transactions'.[135] While acknowledging that externally imposed conditionality has rarely worked, he nevertheless makes the entitlement to this assistance conditional upon the elaboration of 'development compacts' which would be negotiated among donors and recipients and be monitored, primarily by national human rights commissions.[136] It is unlikely, however, that even this form of conditionality will be acceptable to the developing countries engaged in the debate.[137]

But for present purposes the principal question is, what has happened to the language of peoples' rights which provided much of the impetus for the concept in the third phase and was explicitly reflected in the 1986 Declaration on the Right to Development?[138] While Sengupta's report to the General Assembly in 2000 records this formulation[139] he goes to some lengths in his analysis to avoid using the term 'peoples' and instead refers to the 'people of the developing countries' and even 'indigenous people', always in the

[132] Thus, after observing that it 'is not just an umbrella right or the sum of a set of rights', he goes on to define it as 'the right to a particular process of development that allows the realization of economic, social and cultural rights, as well as civil and political rights and all fundamental freedoms, by expanding the capabilities and choices of the individual'. UN Doc. A/55/306 (2000), paras 22 and 64 respectively.

[133] Ibid., para. 21.

[134] e.g. ibid., para. 54 ('The human rights approach . . . is not just an end in itself, helping to realize the human right to development' but it is also 'instrumental to improving the realization of the right to development').

[135] Ibid., para. 59.

[136] Ibid., paras 69–72.

[137] See, e.g. the analysis presented to the Commission on Human Rights by Algeria, Bhutan, China, Cuba, Egypt, India, Iran, Malaysia, Myanmar, Nepal, Pakistan, Sri Lanka, Sudan and Viet Nam, which stated that '[t]he "rights" based approach to developoment undermines human rights by creating conditionalities to "development" which is itself a basic human right' (UN Doc. E/CN.4/1999/120, para. 103(c)) and thus by definition, according to this view, cannot be subjected to any conditionality.

[138] 'The right to development is an inalienable human right by virtue of which every human person *and all peoples* are entitled . . .'. General Assembly Res 41/128, Annex, Article 1(1) (emphasis added).

[139] Supra n. 132, para. 26(e).

singular.[140] The Commission on Human Rights adopts an identical approach.[141] The General Assembly, however, appears to have dropped the terminology altogether in its 1999 resolution in which it reaffirmed 'the importance of the right to development for every human person and *all people* in all countries, in particular the developing countries . . .'.[142] This clear overall trend accords with the view forcefully expressed by the United States according to which the right to development 'is focused on the individual' and 'is not a collective right of groups or States'.[143]

(g) The African Charter on Human and Peoples' Rights

As noted earlier, this is the instrument which, on its face, seemed to offer the greatest prospect of changing the international community's attitude to and way of thinking about peoples' rights. But despite the strong arguments that have been mounted to show why African history, culture, and social realities militated in favour of a more collectivist, or peoples-oriented, approach to the implementation of rights,[144] the relevant provisions have come to little in practice. First and foremost this is because the drafters, rather than resolving the dilemma as to whether the holders of peoples' rights are individuals, the state, or separate collective entities, chose to avoid the issue of definitions. This omission has since been compounded by the failure of both African governments and the African Commission on Human and Peoples' Rights to bite the same bullet. This fact, combined with the highly constrained possibilities open to the Commission to take the initiative in some areas and the singular lack of transparency flowing from the continuing confidentiality of much of the Commission's work, have ensured that there is very little evidence of any forward movement in terms of giving substance to the concept of peoples' rights.[145]

[140] Supra n. 132, paras 34, 39 and 67.

[141] CHR Res. 2000/5.

[142] GA Res. 54/175 (1999), para. 2 (emphasis added). Note, however, that the equivalent draft considered in 2000 proposed the restoration of the plural 'peoples'. See UN Doc. A/C.3/55/L.57 (2000).

[143] UN Doc. E/CN.4/2000/97 (1999) 2, para. 2.

[144] See wa Mutua, 'The Banjul Charter and the African Cultural Fingerprint: An Evaluation of the Language of Duties', 35 *Virginia Journal of International Law* (1995) 339; and Swanson, 'The Emergence of New Rights in the African Charter', 12 *New York Law School Journal of International and Comparative Law* (1991) 307.

[145] The lack of 'a body to make authoritative determination(s) of specific' abuses under the Charter and its failure to give a 'truly judicial mandate' to the Commission has long been the subject of criticism. See Okoth-Ogendo, 'Human and Peoples' Rights: What Point is Africa Trying to Make?', in R. Cohen *et al.* (eds), *Human Rights and Governance in Africa* (1993) 74, at 80; and Gittleman, 'The Banjul Charter on Human and Peoples' Rights: A Legal Analysis', in C. Welch and R. Meltzer (eds), *Human Rights and Development in Africa* (1984) 152. More recent analyses have been equally critical of the transparency of the Commission's work. See Churchill, supra n. 120, and Anthony, 'Beyond the Paper Tiger: The Challenge of a Human Rights Court in Africa', 32 *Texas International Law Journal* (1997) 511, at 518.

Indeed the approach reflected in the Charter is such that there is no incentive for governments to encourage a focus on any intermediate group of rights holders such as ethnic or other minority groups within their countries. The longstanding emphasis within the Organization of African Unity on the principles of state sovereignty, non-interference and the maintenance of inherited colonial boundaries, all point in the direction of the likely downplaying of any meaningful conception of peoples' rights and its replacement with a strong statist orientation. By the same token, individuals wishing to assert their rights in the African context are unlikely to want to place too much reliance upon the concept of the rights of peoples since it has the potential in many circumstances to undermine their claim by pitting it against a conflicting characterization of the collective interest. In short there is no reason to expect that the African Charter will prove in the years ahead to be a force for the progressive development of peoples' rights, despite the occasional invocation of the concept for rhetorical purposes.

(h) Other examples

Various other initiatives relating to peoples or peoples' rights during the fourth phase also warrant a brief mention. Thus, picking up on the prediction by Blaustein that many constitutions would acknowledge the new peoples' rights, [146] a few have, but they have done so in a way that has done nothing to transform traditional approaches. In 1994 Ethiopia, for example, adopted a new constitution which included the right to environment and the right to development. The latter provision was proclaimed to belong to 'The Peoples of Ethiopia as a whole'. But the provision rapidly moves to speak about 'Ethiopia's right to sustainable development' and when it addresses individuals the 'basic aim of development activities' is said to be 'to enhance the capacity of citizens for development and to meet their basic needs'.[147] As a result, the formulation could hardly be said to mark a step forward in terms of either human rights in general or of peoples' rights in particular.

Some initiatives by non-governmental organizations during this fourth phase have also sought to give life to the 'new' rights. The most sustained and noteworthy endeavour was the proclamation of an Asian Human Rights Charter by the Asian Human Rights Commission.[148] But while the drafters go out of their way to refer to it as a 'people's charter' which seeks 'to create in Asia a popular culture on human rights', and to argue that internationally recognized human rights are best 'pursued through a broader conceptualization', which the Charter seeks to provide, the various formulations put forward

[146] Supra n. 55.

[147] The Ethiopian Constitution of 8 December 1994, Article 43, <http://www.uni-wuerzburg.de/law/et00000_.html>. See generally Nahum, 'Ethiopia: Constitution for a Nation of Nations', 60 *The Review of the International Commission of Jurists* (1998) 91.

[148] <http://www.ahrchk.net/charter/final_1.html>.

carefully avoid characterizing the rights as peoples' rights. Thus, for example, the right to peace is held by 'all persons' and it gives 'every individual and group' an entitlement 'to protection against all forms of state violence'.[149] The 'right to development and social justice' provides that '[e]very individual has the right to the basic necessities of life and to protection against abuse and exploitation' and elaborates upon the meaning of 'development, for individuals and states'.[150]

The final example is more symbolic than substantive and concerns the 'Millennium Summit' organized by the UN in September 2000 which was attended by the heads of state or government of almost sixty countries. A major report prepared for the occasion by the UN Secretary-General was entitled simply 'We the Peoples'.[151] The choice was symbolic since it not only evoked the opening words of the UN Charter but also sought to reach beyond governments and embrace civil society. In response the Millennium Declaration which was adopted mentions 'peoples' only once, in calling for the strengthening of the United Nations in order, *inter alia*, to 'fight for development for all the peoples of the world . . .'. While there was no mention of peoples' rights as such, some emphasis was accorded to the right to development and the right to self-determination was reaffirmed, but only in relation to 'peoples which remain under colonial domination and foreign occupation'.[152] In many respects the report and the Declaration are symptomatic of the current situation. The symbolism of peoples remains important but the substance is simply absent.

7. Some Conclusions

In 1985 Michel Virally described the evolution of the concept of peoples' rights in international law as 'undoubtedly one of the most significant developments to have occurred in that field since 1945'.[153] In 1988 James Crawford reinforced this assessment when he concluded the first sustained study of the subject by asserting that peoples' rights had clearly been established as a 'separate category' in international law.[154] The thrust of the present analysis, however, is that since these assessments were made various developments have cast doubt on the continuing validity of the conclusions reached by those distinguished commentators. In essence, while the discourse

[149] <http://www.ahrchk.net/charter/final_1.html>, Article 4.1.

[150] Ibid., Article 7.

[151] See <http://www.un.org/millennium/sg/report/key.htm>.

[152] GA Res. 55/1 (2000) Part I, para. 4.

[153] Virally, 'Panorama du droit international contemporain', 192 *Collected Courses of the Hague Academy of International Law* (1985) 57.

[154] Crawford, 'Some Conclusions', in J. Crawford (ed.), supra n. 25, at 159, 166.

of peoples' rights continues to thrive in a few settings,[155] the situation in both law and practice today is characterized by a systematic reluctance on the part of governments to attach any significance to this dimension of human rights. This might not be unduly problematic were it not for the fact that most other actors in the human rights field have also adopted a comparable approach.

The preceding analysis shows that, in historical terms, the movement to secure the recognition of a significantly expanded conception of peoples' rights reached its peak in the 1980s with their recognition in treaty form in the African Charter of 1981 and the ILO Convention (No. 169) of 1989, and the adoption of several important non-binding instruments such as the Declaration on the Right of Peoples to Peace of 1984 and the Declaration on the Right to Development of 1986. Since that time, however, what has been described above as the fourth phase in the evolution of the concept, has witnessed an almost relentless succession of developments in which governments have sought to downplay the importance or even the existence of various peoples' rights. This trend has been reinforced by the fact that the great majority of scholars and human rights groups have also conspicuously avoided using the terminology.

As noted above,[156] the 'resolution' of several of the principal *causes célèbres* in the realm of self-determination, combined with the demise of Cold War-driven support for other claims, has led to the right of self-determination being all but superseded by the discourse of civil and political rights, and in particular a right to democratic governance and the enhanced relevance of minority rights. But neither of these 'surrogates' has been promoted in a way which accords any real significance to an actual or even potential peoples' rights dimension of the relevant issues and the valiant efforts of some publicists to keep alive the core of the right have done equally little in this regard.

The post-Cold War tendency towards fragmentation of the international order, combined with the perceived promise and risks of the centralizing impetus of globalization, have dampened the enthusiasm for viewing minority rights as peoples' rights in any meaningful sense. In those contexts in which minority rights have experienced something of a revival, such as in the work of the Organization for Security and Cooperation in Europe or the membership conditions being outlined by the European Community in relation to would-be new members,[157] a focus on individual rights and the accommodation of group rights within that framework have been the dominant themes. In this respect, the continuing reluctance of the European Court of Human Rights to modify its reticence in relation to group rights, even in the face of major European initiatives on the rights of minorities, is symptomatic. In the one

[155] See Symonides, supra n. 104.

[156] See text preceding supra n. 56.

[157] See Pentassuglia, 'The EU and the Protection of Minorities: The Case of Eastern Europe', 12 *EJIL* (2001) 1.

area in which the terminology of peoples' rights continues to be crucial, that of the right of indigenous peoples, their asserted right of self-determination continues to be heavily contested and seems likely only to be generally accepted by governments to the extent that its potential implications are heavily diluted.

The new rights of peoples that emerged in the 1970s have fared at least as badly as the old ones, despite the extensive attention accorded to them in some contexts. Despite UNESCO's somewhat maverick efforts over a lengthy period to resuscitate it, the right to peace has proven to have virtually no support within the work of international organizations and neither its conceptual nor its legal foundations have been developed in a convincing manner. The right to environment has been rhetorically important but, in so far as it has made a contribution to the overall debate on the interaction between these two areas, it has not been in terms of any distinctively collective or peoples' rights dimension. Indeed, of the various new claimants, only the right to development has succeeded in establishing a prominent place for itself within the broad compass of international human rights discourse. It occupies a prominent, and in some respects increasingly important, place on the agenda of international organizations.

Ironically, however, it is in relation to the vibrant debate over the right to development that the unmistakable decline, if not demise, of the concept of peoples' rights becomes most apparent. This is because whatever influence the concept exerts today is based upon one or other of the ways in which it has been conceptualized and promoted, and neither of them is consistent with its purported label as a right of peoples. The first is as a right of states and not peoples. Bedjaoui, for example, leaves no doubt that in his view it is primarily a right belonging to states and he analyses its implications in terms of the needs of the state and its entitlement to a 'fair share of what belongs to all'.[158] But despite the various legal and diplomatic formulae that have been proposed in an effort to reconcile the two different dimensions, they are, unless heavily qualified, conceptually incompatible. As Crawford wrote in 1988, '[a]ny insistence that peoples' rights are vested in governments disqualifies the right in question from being regarded as a peoples' right'.[159] Characterization of the right as attaching to states makes the underlying issues no less important and the need to find constructive solutions no less pressing, but the quest must be undertaken within the general framework of international law rather than that of human rights.

The second is as the sum or synthesis of existing human rights held by individuals. This is the line that has been promoted at the outset, such as in the only comprehensive analysis of the issue undertaken by the Secretary-General

[158] Bedjaoui, supra n. 52, 1177, at 1192.

[159] Crawford, 'Some Conclusions', in Crawford, supra n. 25, at 167.

in 1978,[160] and continues to be reflected in virtually all of the statements issued by the current UN High Commissioner for Human Rights, Mary Robinson. While it is conceptually coherent and politically palatable to a wide range of governments, it too effectively neutralizes the claim that the right to development is essentially a peoples' right. There is no reason why the sum total of a host of rights, almost every one of which is explicitly vested in the individual, should when aggregated automatically metamorphose into a right possessed primarily not by individuals but by peoples.

What then went wrong with the effort to expand and entrench a separate category of peoples' rights? Why has the movement to proclaim a wider range of such rights apparently come to so little? In part, history was not on the side of the proponents. The collectivist connotations of the rights, and the enthusiastic support they garnered from communist governments, ensured that they would be treated with great suspicion after the post-Cold War victory of liberalism and the free market. But, at least on its own, this explanation is too easy, especially if it distracts attention from the shortcomings of the way in which the peoples' rights project was pursued, particularly over the past quarter of a century.

Much of the fault lies with the way in which the proponents of these rights sought to dispense with any phase of progressive development of the relevant body of law and instead tried to vault over the *acquis* and establish a new paradigm which was, at best, poorly rooted in what had gone before. Neither the first nor the second phases had really laid the groundwork for the ambitious and far-reaching attempts which were subsequently made in the third phase. Thus, rather than building upon a set of conceptual foundations or some solid precedents that had been established, as the proponents of group rights purported to do, they were actually seeking to superimpose a radically different approach upon the relatively conservative existing structure of international human rights law. The result, felt most strongly in the 1990s, was a legacy in relation to peoples' rights which was unstable and, as it turned out, politically unsustainable.

Another shortcoming was the lack of modesty or perspective of the initiative. This is perhaps best illustrated by the highly over-ambitious and heavily prescriptive draft, 'Third International Covenant on Solidarity Rights' introduced by Karel Vasak in the 1980s and recycled yet again in the 1990s.[161] The proposal was so all-encompassing, so many crucial issues were

[160] UN Doc. E/CN.4/1334 (1978).

[161] See supra n. 1, Annex II, 1673. In addition to the rights dealt with in the present analysis the draft Covenant also recognized the right to respect for the common heritage of mankind and the right to humanitarian assistance. The latter formulation is said to have been drawn up in the context of a 1986 seminar devoted to the consequences of the Chernobyl nuclear reactor disaster, but it purports to be applicable to all situations in which life and health are severely threatened. Ibid., 1678, n. 28.

left unexplained, and so many proposals rested on dubious or problematic foundations, that the inevitable response was to throw the baby out with the bath water. This had a significant negative effect on efforts in other contexts to develop the concept of peoples' rights in ways designed to ensure a more sophisticated and sympathetic consideration of the rights of collectivities of different types. The right of self-determination and minority rights might have been able to evolve in more satisfactory ways had they not had cast over them the shadow of a conception of peoples' rights which effectively attributed rights to states and which raised the prospect of unqualified, undefined, and open-ended obligations to transfer resources from some states to others.

What then does the future hold for the concept of peoples' rights? There are good grounds for concluding that it is not very bright. The term will continue to diminish in importance in relation to all of the rights considered above with the sole exception of indigenous peoples' rights. While the right to development and the right of self-determination will continue to be staple parts of the international discourse of rights, their origins as rights attaching to peoples, in the sense of distinctive groups separate from the state or the territorial entity in question, will become ever less relevant in practice.

In some respects, there will not be a lot of cause to mourn in response to these developments. The world is unlikely to be a less peaceful place as a result of the failure to find a meaningful formulation of the right to peace, and the right of self-determination will continue to have the power to move the world in many of the types of situations in which it has been significant in the past. In other respects, however, this gloomy prognosis will be highly detrimental if it also involves the demise of two of the principal concerns that gave much of the impetus to the concept over recent years. The first is the central importance of seeking to develop a sophisticated understanding of human rights which is capable, in the appropriate circumstances, of transcending the insistence that there can be no place whatsoever for collective or group rights considerations. In part, a more contextual vision of human rights is indispensable if the relevant body of international law is going to have the strength and depth to respond adequately to the concerns coming from perspectives as diverse as communitarianism, cultural relativism and post-modernism. It goes without saying that these issues take us very far beyond the focus of this volume, but a conception of human rights which has banished all dimensions of group and peoples' rights will be a greatly impoverished one and one which is ill-equipped to deal with some of the major challenges that are certain to confront it in the years ahead.

The second concern is the need to give substance to the much-quoted but studiously-ignored notion reflected in Article 28 of the Universal Declaration of Human Rights according to which '[e]veryone is entitled to a social and international order in which the rights and freedoms set forth in this

Declaration can be fully realized'.[162] The connotations of solidarity, of a duty to cooperate, and of the need for mechanisms to achieve an ongoing international redistribution of wealth linked to human rights obligations, have for too long been anathema to Western governments. As the growing inequalities accompanying globalization become ever more evident,[163] it will be more and more essential to engage in a sustained debate which clarifies the nature of these obligations and promotes their acceptance. It will be tragic if the steady move away from the notion of peoples' rights is mistakenly thought to have disposed of the need to engage actively and urgently in this task.

[162] For an analysis of some of the possible implications of this provision see Pogge, 'Human Flourishing and Universal Justice', in E. F. Paul *et al.* (eds), *Human Flourishing* (1999) 333.

[163] See, for example, Ghai, 'Rights, Social Justice, and Globalization in East Asia', in J. Bauer and D. Bell (eds), *The East Asian Challenge for Human Rights* (1999) 241; I. Shapiro and L. Brilmayer (eds), *Global Justice* (1999), and Weissbrodt and Hoffman, 'The Global Economy and Human Rights: A Selective Bibliography', 6 *Minn J Global Trade* (1997) 189.

Peoples' Rights: A Bibliography

PHILIP ALSTON AND JAMES HEENAN

Peoples' Rights and Collective Rights in General

Alston P., 'A Third Generation of Solidarity Rights: Progressive Development or Obfuscation of International Human Rights Law?', *Netherlands International Law Review,* Vol. 29 (1982), 307.

—— 'Conjuring Up New Human Rights: A Proposal for Quality Control', *American Journal of International Law,* Vol. 77 (1984), 607.

Anaya S., 'On Justifying Special Ethnic Group Rights: Comments on Pogge', in I. Shapiro and W. Kymlicka (eds), *Ethnicity and Group Rights* (New York: New York University Press, 1997), 222.

Ankumah E., *The African Commission on Human and Peoples' Rights. Practice and Procedures* (The Hague, Boston: Martinus Nijhoff, 1996).

Basso L., *Droits de l'homme et droits des peuples: textes présentés au séminaire international d'études, 27–29 juin 1980, République de Saint-Marin, sous le patronage du Ministère de la culture et de la justice* (Republic of San Marino: Fondation internationale Lelio Basso pour le droit et la libération des peuples, 1983).

Brilmayer L., 'Groups, Histories, and International Law', *Cornell International Law Journal* Vol. 25(3) (1992), 555.

Brölmann C., Lefeber R. and Zieck M. (eds), *Amsterdam International Law Conference: Peoples and Minorities in International Law* (Dordrecht, Boston: Martinus. Nijhoff, 1993).

Brownlie I., 'The Rights of Peoples in Modern International Law', in J. Crawford (ed.), *The Rights of Peoples* (Oxford: Oxford University Press, 1988), 1.

Buyun, L., 'On Individual and Collective Human Rights', in P. Baehr, F. van Hoof, L. Nanlai, and T. Zhenghua (eds), *Human Rights: Chinese and Dutch Perspectives* (The Hague: Martinus Nijhoff, 1996), 119.

Cassese A. and Jouve E. (eds), *Pour un droit des peuples: essais sur la Déclaration d'Alger* (Paris: Berger-Levrault, 1978).

Churchill W., *The People's Rights* (London: Jonathan Cape, 1970).

Corten O., 'Droit des peuples à disposer d'eux-mêmes et uti possidetis: deux faces d'une même médaille?', *Revue Belge de droit international* (1998), 161.

Crawford J. (ed.), *The Rights of Peoples* (Oxford: Clarendon Press, 1988).

—— 'The Rights of Peoples: "Peoples" or "Governments"?', in J. Crawford (ed.), *The Rights of Peoples* (Oxford: Clarendon Press, 1988), 55.

—— 'Some Conclusions', in J. Crawford (ed.), *The Rights of Peoples* (Oxford: Clarendon Press, 1988), 159.

Das V., 'Cultural Rights and the Definition of Community', in O. Mendelsohn and U. Baxi (eds), *The Rights of Subordinated Peoples* (New Delhi: Oxford University Press, 1994), 117–58.

Dinstein Y., 'Collective Human Rights of Peoples and Minorities', *International and Comparative Law Quarterly*, Vol. 25 (1976), 102.

Ermacora F., 'The Protection of Minorities before the United Nations', in *Recueil des Cours: Collected Courses of the Hague Academy of International Law* (Dordrecht: Martinus Nijhoff, 1984), 247–370.

Falk R., 'The Rights of Peoples (in Particular Indigenous Peoples)', in J. Crawford (ed.), *The Rights of Peoples* (Oxford: Clarendon Press, 1998), 17.

Felice W., 'The Case for Collective Human Rights: The Reality of Group Suffering', *Ethics and International Affairs*, Vol. 10, (1996), 47–62.

—— *Taking Suffering Seriously: The Importance of Collective Human Rights* (Albany, NY: State University of New York Press, 1996).

Fenet A. (ed.), *Droits de l'homme, droits des peuples* (Paris: Presses universitaires de France, 1982).

Fottrell D. and Bowring B., *Minority and Group Rights in the New Millennium* (The Hague: Kluwer, 1999).

Franck T., 'Clan and Superclan: Loyalty, Identity and Community in Law and Practice', *American Journal of International Law*, Vol. 90 (1996), 359.

Galenkamp M., *Collective Rights* (Utrecht: Netherlands Institute of Human Rights, 1995).

Glazer N., 'Individual Rights against Group Rights', in E. Kamenka and A. Erh-Soon Tay (eds), *Human Rights* (Port Melbourne, Australia: Edward Arnold, 1978), 87–103.

Horowitz D., *Ethnic Groups in Conflict* (Berkeley, CA: University of California Press, 1985).

Huaraka T., 'The African Charter on Human and Peoples' Rights: A Significant Contribution to the Development of International Human Rights Law', in M. Tom (ed.), *Essays on the Concept of a Right to Live: In Memory of Y. Khushalani* (Brussels: Bruylant, 1988), 191–204.

Jones P., 'Human Rights, Group Rights, and Peoples' Rights', *Human Rights Quarterly*, Vol. 21(1) (1999), 80.

Kamenka E., 'Human Rights: People's Rights', in J. Crawford (ed.), *The Rights of Peoples* (Oxford: Clarendon Press, 1988), 130.

Kingsbury B., 'Claims by Non-State Groups in International Law', *Cornell International Law Journal*, Vol. 25 (1992), 481–513.

—— 'Whose International Law?: Sovereignty and Non-State Groups', in *The American Society of International Law: Proceedings of the 88th Annual Meeting* (Washington, DC: American Society of International Law, 1994).

Kymlicka W., 'Individual and Community Rights', in J. Baker (ed.), *Group Rights* (Toronto: University of Toronto Press, 1994), 17–33.

Makinson D., 'Rights of Peoples: A Logician's Point of View', in J. Crawford (ed.), *The Rights of Peoples* (Oxford: Clarendon Press, 1988), 69.

Malik M., 'Communal Goods as Human Rights', in C. Gearty and A. Tomkins (eds), *Understanding Human Rights* (London: Mansell Publishing, 1996), 115–37.

Marie J., 'Relations between Peoples' Rights and Human Rights: Semantic and Methodological Distinctions', *Human Rights Law Journal*, Vol. 7 (1986), 195–204.

M'Baye K., 'Human Rights and Rights of Peoples', in M. Bedjaoui (ed.), *International Law: Achievements and Prospects* (Paris: UNESCO, 1991), 1043–60.

Nettheim G., 'Peoples and Populations', in J. Crawford (ed.), *The Rights of Peoples* (Oxford: Clarendon Press, 1988), 107.

Nickel J., 'Group Agency and Group Rights', in I. Shapiro and W. Kymlicka (eds), *Ethnicity and Group Rights* (New York: New York University Press, 1997), 235.

Partsch K., 'Recent Developments in the Field of Peoples' Rights', *Human Rights Law Journal*, Vol. 7 (1986), 177–82.

Pellet A., 'Quel avenir pour le droit des peuples à disposer d'eux-mêmes?', in *El derecho internacional en un mundo en transformacion Liber amicorum en homenaje al Profesor Jiménez de Aréchaga* (Montevideo, Uruguay: Fundación de Cultura Universitaria, 1994), 255.

—— 'Le «bon droit» et l'ivraie: plaidoyer pour l'ivraie', in C. Chaumont, *Le droit des peuples à disposer d'eux-mêmes, méthodes d'analyse du droit international: mélanges offerts à Charles Chaumont* (Paris: A. Pedone, 1984), 465–93.

Pogge T., 'Group Rights and Ethnicity', in I. Shapiro and W. Kymlicka (eds), *Ethnicity and Group Rights* (New York: New York University Press, 1997), 187.

Prott L., 'Cultural Rights as Peoples' Rights in International Law', in J. Crawford (ed.), *The Rights of Peoples* (Oxford: Clarendon Press, 1988), 93.

Ramcharan B., 'Peoples' Rights and Minorities' Rights', *Nordic Journal of International Law*, Vol. 56(1) (1987), 9–38.

Réaume D., 'Common-Law Constructions of Group Autonomy: A Case Study', in I. Shapiro and W. Kymlicka (eds), *Ethnicity and Group Rights* (New York: New York University Press, 1997), 257.

Rich R., 'The Right to Development: A Right of Peoples?', in J. Crawford (ed.), *The Rights of Peoples* (Oxford: Clarendon Press, 1988), 39–54.

Rigaux F., 'The Rights of Peoples as Inalienable Rights', in D. Prémont (ed.), *Non-Derogable Rights and States of Emergency* (Brussels: Bruylant, 1996), 537–48.

Roback J., 'Plural but Equal: Group Identity and Voluntary Integration', in E. Paul, F. Miller and J. Paul (eds), *Reassessing Civil Rights* (Cambridge, UK: Blackwell Publishers, 1991), 60–80.

Rosas A., 'So-Called Rights of the Third Generation', in A. Eide, C. Krause and A. Rosas (eds), *Economic, Social and Cultural Rights: A Textbook* (Dordrecht: Martinus Nijhoff, 1995), 243–6.

Shapiro I. and Kymlicka W. (eds), *Ethnicity and Group Rights* (New York: New York University Press, 1997).

Triggs G., 'Peoples' Rights and Individual Rights: Conflict or Harmony?', in J. Crawford (ed.), *The Rights of Peoples* (Oxford: Clarendon Press, 1988), 141.

Umozurike U., *The African Charter on Human and Peoples' Rights* (The Hague: Martinus. Nijhoff, 1997).

—— *Five years of the African Commission on Human and Peoples' Rights being the 1992 NSIA lecture* (Ile-Ife, Oyo State, Nigeria: Nigerian Society of International Affairs & Vantage Publishers, Ibadan, 1992).

UNESCO, *Colloquium on the New Human Rights: Final Report*, SS-80/CONF.806/4, 12–15 August (UNESCO: Mexico City, 1980).

van Boven T., 'The Relations between Peoples' Rights and Human Rights in the African Charter', *Human Rights Law Journal*, Vol. 7 (1986), 183–94.

van Dyke V., 'The Cultural Rights of Peoples', *Universal Human Rights*, Vol. 2(2) (1980), 1–21.

van Dyke V., *Human Rights, Ethnicity and Discrimination* (Westport, CT: Greenwood Press, 1985).

—— 'Human Rights and the Rights of Groups', *American Journal of Political Science*, Vol. 18 (1974), 725–41.

—— 'Justice as Fairness: For Groups?', *American Political Science Review*, Vol. 69 (1975), 607–14.

Vasak K., *For the Third Generation of Human Rights: The Rights of Solidarity, Leçon inaugurale* (International Institute of Human Rights: Strasbourg, 1979).

Wellman C., 'Solidarity, the Individual, and Human Rights', *Human Rights Quarterly*, Vol. 22(3) (2000), 639.

Right to Self-Determination

Abdulah F., 'The Right to Decolonization', in M. Bedjaoui (ed.), *International Law, Achievements and Prospects* (Paris: UNESCO/Martinus. Nijhoff Publishers, 1991), 1216.

Addo M., 'Political Self-Determination within the Context of the African Charter of Human and Peoples' Rights', *Journal of African Law*, Vol. 32 (1988), 182.

Allott P., 'Self-Determination: Absolute Right or Social Poetry?', in C. Tomuschat (ed.), *Modern Law of Self-Determination* (Dordrecht: Martinus Nijhoff, 1993), 177.

An-Na'im A., 'The National Question, Secession and Constitutionalism: The Mediation of Competing Claims to Self-Determination', in D. Greenberg, S. Katz, M. Oliviero and S. Wheatley (eds), *Constitutionalism and Democracy: Transitions in the Contemporary World* (New York: Oxford University Press, 1993), 105.

Barkin J., 'The Evolution of the Constitution of Sovereignty and the Emergence of Human Rights Norms', *Millennium Journal of International Studies*, Vol. 27(2) (1998), 229.

Barsh R., 'The Challenge of Indigenous Self-Determination', *University of Michigan Journal of Law Reform*, Vol. 26 (2 Winter) (1993), 277.

Bibó I., 'Self-Determination as Opposed to the Territorial Integrity of States', in I. Bibó, *The Paralysis of International Institutions and the Remedies: A Study of Self-Determination, Concord among the Major Powers, and Political Arbitration* (New York: John Wiley & Sons, 1976), 70.

Blay S., 'Changing African Perspectives on the Right of Self-Determination in the Wake of the Banjul Charter on Human and Peoples' Rights', *Journal of African Law*, Vol. 29(2) (1985), 147.

Bos M., 'Self-Determination by the Grace of History', *Netherlands International Law Review*, Vol. 15(4) (1968), 362.

Bowett D., 'Problems of Self-Determination and Political Rights in Developing Countries', *Proceedings of the American Society of International Law* (1966), 134.

Bowring B., 'The Rule of Law as an Instrument of Oppression?: Self-Determination and Human Rights in the New Latvia', *Law and Critique*, Vol. 5(1) (1994), 69.

Brilmayer L., 'Secession and Self-determination: A Territorial Interpretation', *Yale Journal of International Law*, Vol. 16 (1991), 177.

Bring O., 'Kurdistan and the Principle of Self-Determination', *German Yearbook of International Law*, Vol. 35 (1992), 157.

Brossard J., 'Le droit du peuple québécois de disposer de lui-même au regard du droit international', *Canadian Yearbook of International Law*, Vol. 15 (1977), 84.

Buchanan A., 'Self-Determination and the Right to Secede', *Journal of International Affairs*, Vol. 45 (1992), 347.

Buchheit L., *Secession: The Legitimacy of Self-determination* (New Haven CT.: Yale University Press, 1978).

Cassese A., 'The International Court of Justice and the Right of Peoples to Self-determination', in V. Lowe and M. Fitzmaurice (eds), *Fifty Years of the International Court of Justice: Essays in Honour of Sir Robert Jennings* (Cambridge: Grotius Publications, 1996), 351.

—— 'Political Self-Determination: Old Concepts and New Developments', in A. Cassese (ed.), *UN Law/Fundamental Rights: Two Topics in International Law* (Alphen aan den Rijn, Netherlands: Sijthoff and Noordhoff, 1979), 137.

—— 'The Self-determination of Peoples', in L. Henkin (ed.), *The International Bill of Rights: The Covenant on Civil and Political Rights* (New York: Columbia University Press, 1981), 92.

—— *Self-Determination of Peoples: A Legal Reappraisal* (Cambridge: Cambridge University Press, 1995).

Chen L., 'Self-Determination: An Important Dimension of the Demand for Freedom', *Proceedings of the American Society of International Law* (1994), 88.

Chinkin C. and Wright S., 'The Hunger Trap: Women, Food, and Self-Determination', *Michigan Journal of International Law*, Vol. 14 (1993), 262.

Clark D., Williamson R. and Blakeney A., *Self-determination: International Perspectives* (Houndmills, Basingstoke, Hampshire, New York, NY: Macmillan Press. St. Martin's Press, 1996).

Corntassel J. and Primeau T. 'Indigenous "Sovereignty" and International Law: Revised Strategies for Pursuing "Self-Determination" ', *Human Rights Quarterly*, Vol. 17 (1995), 343.

Crawford J., 'The General Assembly, the International Court and Self-determination', in R. Jennings, V. Lowe and M. Fitzmaurice (eds), *Fifty Years of the International Court of Justice: Essays in Honour of Sir Robert Jennings* (Cambridge, New York: Cambridge University Press, 1996), 585.

Cristescu A., *The Right to Self-Determination: Historical and Current Development on the Basis of United Nations Instruments*, E.80.XIV.3 (New York: United Nations, 1981).

Danspeckgruber W. and Watts A. (eds), *Self-determination and Self-administration: A Sourcebook* (Boulder, CO: Lynne Rienner Publishers, 1997).

Diaz A., 'Permanent Sovereignty over Natural Resources', *Environmental Policy and Law*, Vol. 24(4) (1994), 157–73.

Duursma J., *Fragmentation and the International Relations of Micro-States: Self-Determination and Statehood* (Cambridge, New York: Cambridge University Press, 1996).

Eide A., 'In Search of Constructive Alternatives to Secession', in C. Tomuschat (ed.), *Modern Law of Self-Determination* (Dordrecht: Martinus Nijhoff, 1993), 139–76.

Emerson R., 'Self-Determination', *American Journal of International Law*, Vol. 65 (1971), 459–75.

Falk R., 'Problems and Prospects for the Kurdish Struggle for Self-Determination after the End of the Gulf and Cold Wars', *Michigan Journal of International Law*, Vol. 15 (Winter) (1994), 591–603.

Finger S. and Singh G., 'Self-Determination: A United Nations Perspective', in Y. Alexander and R. Friedlander (eds), *Self-Determination: National, Regional and Global Dimensions* (Boulder, CO: Westview Press, 1981), 333–46.

Foster C., 'Articulating Self-determination in the Draft Declaration on the Rights of Indigenous Peoples', *European Journal of International Law*, Vol. 12 (2001), 140.

Freeman M., 'The Right of Self-Determination in International Politics: Six Theories in Search of a Policy', *Review of International Studies*, Vol. 25(3) (1999), 355.

French S. and Gutman A., 'The Principle of National Self-Determination', in V. Held, S. Morgenbesser and T. Nagel (eds), *Philosophy, Morality, and International Affairs* (New York: Oxford University Press, 1974), 138–53.

Friedlander R., 'Self-Determination: A Legal-Political Inquiry', in Y. Alexander and R. Friedlander (eds), *Self-Determination: National, Regional and Global Dimensions* (Boulder, CO: Westview Press, 1981), 307–31.

Gayim E., *The Principle of Self-Determination: A Study of Its Historical and Contemporary Legal Evolution* (Oslo: Norwegian Institute of Human Rights, 1990).

George D., 'National Identity and National Self-Determination', in S. Caney, D. George and P. Jones (eds), *National Rights, International Obligations* (Boulder, CO: Westview Press, 1996), 13–33.

Gros Espiell H., *The Right to Self-Determination: Implementation of United Nations Resolutions* (New York: United Nations, 1980).

Hannum H., *Autonomy, Sovereignty and Self-Determination: The Accommodation of Conflicting Rights* (Philadelphia: University of Pennsylvania Press, 1990).

—— 'The Limits of Sovereignty and Majority Rule: Minorities, Indigenous Peoples, and the Right to Autonomy', in E. Lutz, H. Hannum and K. Burke (eds), *New Directions in Human Rights* (Philadelphia: University of Pennsylvania Press, 1989), 3–24.

—— 'Minorities, Indigenous Peoples, and Self-Determination', in L. Henkin and J. Hargrove (eds), *Human Rights: An Agenda for the Next Century* (Washington, DC: American Society of International Law, 1994), 1–16.

—— 'Rethinking Self-Determination', *Virginia Journal of International Law*, Vol. 34 (1 Fall) (1993), 1–69.

—— 'The Right of Self Determination in the Twenty-First Century', *Washington and Lee Law Review*, Vol. 55(3) (1998), 773.

—— 'The Specter of Secession: Responding to Claims for Ethnic Self-Determination', *Foreign Affairs*, Vol. 77(2) (1998), 13.

Heraclides A., *The Self-determination of Minorities in International Politics* (London: Cass, 1991).

Horowitz D., 'Self-Determination: Politics, Philosophy, and Law', in I. Shapiro and W. Kymlicka (eds), *Ethnicity and Group Rights* (New York: New York University Press, 1997), 421.

International Centre for Human Rights and Democratic Development, *People or Peoples, Equality, Autonomy and Self-Determination: The Issues at Stake of the International Decade of the World's Indigenous People* (Montreal: International Centre for Human Rights and Democratic Development, 1996).

Jayawickrama N., 'The Right of Self-Determination: A Time for Reinvention and Renewal', *Saskatchewan Law Review*, Vol. 57(1) (1993), 1–19.

Johnson H. and Singh B., 'Self-Determination and World Order', in Y. Alexander and R. Friedlander (eds), *Self-Determination: National, Regional and Global Dimensions* (Boulder, CO: Westview Press, 1981), 349–71.

Karsai F., 'The Right of Self-Determination in Africa: A Contribution', *Africana Gandensia*, Vol. 6 (1989), 75–103.

Kim M., 'The New World Order: Sovereignty, Human Rights, and the Self-Determination of Peoples', *Harvard International Law Journal*, Vol. 39(1) (1998), 304.

Kimminich O., 'A Federal Right of Self-Determination?', in C. Tomuschat (ed.), *Modern Law of Self-Determination* (Dordrecht: Martinus Nijhoff, 1993), 83–100.

Kingsbury B., 'Claims by Non-State Groups in International Law', *Cornell International Law Journal*, Vol. 25 (1992), 481–513.

—— 'Whose International Law?: Sovereignty and Non-State Groups', in *The American Society of International Law: Proceedings of the 88th Annual Meeting* (Washington, DC: American Society of International Law, 1994).

Klabbers J. and Lefeber R., 'Africa: Lost between Self-Determination and Uti Possidetis', in C. Brohmann, R. Lefeber and M. Zieck (eds), *Peoples and Minorities in International Law* (Dordrecht: Martinus Nijhoff, 1993), 37–76.

Koskenniemi M., 'National Self-Determination Today: Problems of Legal Theory and Practice', *International and Comparative Law Quarterly*, Vol. 43 (April) (1994), 241–69.

Mayall J., 'Sovereignty, Nationalism, and Self-Determination', *Political Studies*, Vol. 47(3) (1999), 474.

McCorquodale R., 'Self-Determination: A Human Rights Approach', *International and Comparative Law Quarterly*, Vol. 43 (1994), 857–86.

—— 'Self-Determination beyond the Colonial Context and its Potential Impact on Africa', *African Journal of International and Comparative Law*, Vol. 4(3) (1992), 592–608.

—— 'South Africa and the Right of Self-Determination', *South African Journal on Human Rights*, Vol. 10(1) (1994), 4–30.

Morphet S., 'The Palestinians and their Right to Self-Determination', in R. Vincent (ed.), *Foreign Policy and Human Rights: Issues and Responses* (Cambridge: Cambridge University Press, 1986), 85–104.

Murswief D., 'The Issue of a Right of Secession Reconsidered', in C. Tomuschat (ed.), *Modern Law of Self-Determination* (Dordrecht: Martinus Nijhoff, 1993), 21–40.

Nielsen K., 'Liberal Nationalism, Liberal Democracies, and Secession', *University of Toronto Law Journal*, Vol. 48(2) (1998), 253.

Nowak M., 'The Right of Self-Determination and the Protection of Minorities in Central and Eastern Europe in Light of the Case-Law of the Human Rights Committee', *International Journal of Groups Rights*, Vol. 1 (1993), 7–16.

Oloka-Onyango J., 'Heretical Reflections on the Right to Self-Determination: Prospects and Problems for a Democratic Global Future in the New Millennium', *American University International Law Review*, Vol. 15 (1999), 151–280.

Pellet A., 'The Opinions of the Badinter Arbitration Committee: A Second Breath for the Self-Determination of Peoples', *European Journal of International Law*, Vol. 3 (1992), 178–85.

Pomerance M., *Self-Determination in Law and Practice: The New Doctrine in the UN* (The Hague: Martinus Nijhoff, 1982).

Quane H., 'The UN and the Evolving Right to Self-Determination', *International and Comparative Law Quarterly*, Vol. 47(3) (1998), 537.

Ramose M., 'Self-Determination in Decolonisation', in W. Twining (ed.), *Issues of Self-Determination* (Aberdeen: Aberdeen University Press, 1991), 25–32.

Reisman M., 'Coercion and Self-Determination: Construing Charter Article 2(4)', *American Journal of International Law*, Vol. 78 (1984), 642.

Rivera-Ramos E., 'Self-Determination and Decolonisation in the Society of the Modern Colonial Welfare State', in W. Twining (ed.), *Issues of Self-Determination* (Aberdeen: Aberdeen University Press, 1991), 115–32.

Rodriquez Orellana M., 'Human Rights Talk . . . and Self-Determination, too!', *The Notre Dame Law Review*, Vol. 73(5) (1998), 1391.

Ronen D., *The Quest for Self-Determination* (New Haven, CT: Yale University Press, 1979).

Rosas A., 'Internal Self-Determination', in C. Tomuschat (ed.), *Modern Law of Self-Determination* (Dordrecht: Martinus Nijhoff, 1993), 225–52.

—— 'The Right of Self-Determination', in A. Eide, C. Krause and A. Rosas (eds), *Economic, Social and Cultural Rights: A Textbook* (Dordrecht: Martinus Nijhoff, 1995), 79.

Räikkä J., 'On National Self-Determination: Some Problems of Walzer's Definition of Nation', in W. Twining (ed.), *Issues of Self-Determination* (Aberdeen: Aberdeen University Press, 1991), 20–4.

Salmon J., 'Internal Aspects of the Right to Self-Determination: Towards a Democratic Legitimacy Principle?', in C. Tomuschat (ed.), *Modern Law of Self-Determination* (Dordrecht: Martinus Nijhoff, 1993), 253–82.

Sanders D., 'Self-Determination and Indigenous Peoples', in C. Tomuschat (ed.), *Modern Law of Self-Determination* (Dordrecht: Martinus Nijhoff, 1993), 55–82.

'Self-Determination', *Global Journal on Human Rights Law*, Vol. 2(2) (1998), 111.

Svenson T., 'Right to Self-Determination, A Basic Human Right Concerning Cultural Survival: The Case of the Sami and the Scandinavian State', in A. An-Na'im (ed.), *Human Rights in Cross-Cultural Perspectives: A Quest for Consensus* (Philadelphia: University of Pennsylvania Press, 1992), 363–86.

Talbott S., 'Self-Determination in an Interdependent World', *Foreign Policy*, Vol. Spring (2000), 152.

Thornberry P., 'The Democratic or Internal Aspect of Self-Determination, with Some Remarks on Federalism', in C. Tomuschat (ed.), *Modern Law of Self-Determination* (Dordrecht: Martinus Nijhoff, 1993), 101–38.

Tomuschat C. (ed.), *Modern Law of Self-Determination* (Dordrecht, Martinus. Nijhoff, 1993).

—— 'Self-Determination in a Post-Colonial World', in C. Tomuschat (ed.), *Modern Law of Self-Determination* (Dordrecht: Martinus Nijhoff, 1993), 1–20.

Türk D., 'Minorities, Self-Determination and Other Crucial Issues of Human Rights in Europe', in Z. Kedzia, A. Korula and M. Nowak (eds), *Perspectives of an All-European System of Human Rights Protection: The Role of the Council of Europe, the CSCE and the European Communities* (Kehl am Rhein, Germany: N. P. Engel Verlag, 1991), 279–90.

Turpel M., 'Indigenous Peoples' Rights of Political Participation and Self-Determination: Recent International Legal Developments and the Continuing Struggle for Recognition', *Cornell International Law Journal*, Vol. 25 (1992), 579–602.

White R., 'Self-Determination: Time for a Re-Assessment?', *Netherlands International Law Review*, Vol. 28 (1981), 147–70.

Wilkinson D., 'The Meaning of Self Determination', *Quadrant*, Vol. 43(3) (1999), 23.

Minority Rights

Alfredsson G. and de Zayas A., 'Minority Rights: Protection by the United Nations', *Human Rights Law Journal*, Vol. 14 (1–2 February) (1993), 1.

—— and Türk D., 'International Mechanisms for the Monitoring and Protection of Minority Rights: Their Advantages, Disadvantages and Interrelationships', in A. Bloed, L. Leicht, M. Nowak and A. Rosas (eds), *Monitoring Human Rights in Europe: Comparing International Procedures and Mechanisms* (Dordrecht: Martinus Nijhoff, 1993), 169.

Anghie A., 'Human Rights and Cultural Identity: New Hope for Ethnic Peace?', *Harvard International Law Journal*, Vol. 33 (2 Spring) (1992), 341.

Attanasio J., 'The Rights of Ethnic Minorities: The Emerging Mosaic', *Notre Dame Law Review*, Vol. 66(5) (1991), 1195.

Beyani C., 'The Prerequisites of Education', in *Education Rights and Minorities* (London: The Minority Rights Group, 1994), 14.

Bilder R., 'Can Minorities Treaties Work?', in Y. Dinstein and M. Yoram (eds), *The Protection of Minorities and Human Rights* (Dordrecht: Martinus Nijhoff, 1992), 59.

Black M., *Children and Families of Ethnic Minorities, Immigrants and Indigenous Peoples: Summary Report of Innocenti Global Seminar* (Florence: UNICEF Innocenti Research Centre, 1997), 55.

Blishchenko I. and Abashidze A., 'National Minorities and International Law', in A. Rosas and J. Helgesen (eds), *Human Rights in a Changing East/West Perspective* (London: Pinter Publishing, 1990), 202.

Bloch A., 'Minorities and Indigenous Peoples', in A. Eide, C. Krause and A. Rosas (eds), *Economic, Social and Cultural Rights: A Textbook* (Dordrecht: Martinus Nijhoff, 1995), 309.

Bloed A. and van Dijk P. (eds), *Protection of Minority Rights through Bilateral Treaties: The Case of Central and Eastern Europe* (The Hague: Kluwer, 1999).

Bricker D., 'Autonomy and Culture: Will Kymlicka on Cultural Minority Rights', *The Southern Journal of Philosophy*, Vol. 36(1) (1998), 47.

Bruhác J., 'The Special Place of the Rights of Minorities in the International Regime of Human Rights', *Acta Juridica Hungarense*, Vol. 35 (1993), 249–55.

Capotorti F., *Study on the Rights of Persons Belonging to Ethnic, Religious and Linguistic Minorities*, E.78.XIV.1 (New York: United Nations, 1992).

Cator J. and Niessen J. (eds), *The Use of International Conventions to Protect the Rights of Migrants and Ethnic Minorities* (Brussels: Churches' Commission for Migrants in Europe, 1994).

Chopard J., *Minorities and Prevention of Conflicts: The Role of National Red Cross and Red Crescent Societies* (Geneva: Henri Dunant Institute, 1993).

Chowdhury A., *Study on Discriminatory Treatment against Members of Racial, Ethnic, Religious or Linguistic Groups at the Various Levels in the Administration of Criminal Justice Proceedings*, UN Doc. E/CN.4/Sub.2/1982/7 (United Nations, 1982).

Coulmas F. (ed.), *Linguistic Minorities and Literacy: Language Policy Issues in Developing Countries* (Berlin: Mouton, 1984).

Cullen H., 'Education Rights or Minority Rights?', *International Journal of Law and the Family*, Vol. 7 (1993), 143–77.

Daes E., *Human Rights and Scientific and Technical Developments: Preliminary Report of the Sub-Commission on the Prevention of Discrimination and the Protection of Minorities*, UN Doc. E/CN.4/Sub.2/474 (New York: United Nations, 1981).

Davies C., 'The Protection of Minority Cultures and Religions within State Boundaries', in N. Lowe and G. Douglas (eds), *Families across Frontiers* (The Hague: Martinus Nijhoff, 1996), 407–16.

de Azcárate P., *League of Nations and National Minorities* (Washington, DC: Carnegie Endowment for International Peace, 1945).

de Varennes F., *Language, Minorities, and Human Rights* (Dordrecht: Martinus Nijhoff, 1994).

Deschênes J., *Proposal Concerning a Definition of the Term 'Minority'*, E/CN.4/Sub.2/1985/31 (Geneva: United Nations, 1985).

Dinstein Y., 'Collective Human Rights of Peoples and Minorities', *International and Comparative Law Quarterly*, Vol. 25 (1976), 102.

—— and Tabory M. (eds), *The Protection of Minorities and Human Rights* (Dordrecht: Martinus Nijhoff, 1992).

Eide A., *Ethno-nationalism and Minority Protection: The Need for Institutional Reforms*, A/CONF.157/LACRM/6, 15 December (Geneva: United Nations, 1992).

—— 'Human Rights, Minority Rights and the Search for the National Contract', in P. Baehr, C. Flinterman and M. Senders (eds), *Innovation and Inspiration: Fifty Years of the Universal Declaration of Human Rights* (Amsterdam: Royal Netherlands Academy of Arts and Sciences, 1999), 71.

—— 'National Movements, Protection of Minorities and the Prevention of Discrimination', in A. Eide and J. Helgesen (eds), *The Future of Human Rights Protection in a Changing World, Fifty Years since the Four Freedoms Address: Essays in Honour of Torkel Opsahl* (Oslo: Norwegian University Press, 1991), 213–32.

Ermacora F., 'The Protection of Minorities before the United Nations', in *Collected Courses of the Hague Academy of International Law* (Dordrecht: Martinus Nijhoff, 1984), 247–370.

Fottrell D. and Bowring B., *Minority and Group Rights in the New Millennium* (The Hague: Kluwer, 1999).

Giordan H. (ed.), *Les minorités en Europe: droits linguistiques et droits de l'homme* (Paris: Kimé, 1992).

Green L., 'Internal Minorities and their Rights', in J. Baker (ed.), *Group Rights* (Toronto: University of Toronto Press, 1994), 100–17.

Gurr T. and Scarritt J., 'Minorities Rights at Risk: A Global Survey', *Human Rights Quarterly*, Vol. 11 (1989), 375.

Heraclides A., 'Secessionist Minorities and External Involvement', *International Organization*, Vol. 44 (3 Summer) (1990), 341.

Hofmann R., 'Minority Rights: Individual or Group Rights? A Comparative View on European Legal Systems', *German Yearbook of International Law*, Vol. 40 (1997), 357.

—— 'The Protection of Minorities in Europe: The Current Situation in International and Constitutional Law', *Heidelberg Journal of International Law*, Vol. 52 (1992), 66–9.

Keller P., 'Rethinking Ethnic and Cultural Rights in Europe', *Oxford Journal of Legal Studies*, Vol. 18(1) (1998), 29.

Khubchandani L., '"Minority" Cultures and their Communication Rights', in T. Skutnabb-Kangas, M. Rannut and R. Phillipson (eds), *Linguistic Human Rights: Overcoming Linguistic Discrimination* (Berlin: de Gruyter, 1995), 478.

Klabbers J. and Lefeber R., 'Africa: Lost between Self-Determination and Uti Possidetis', in C. Brohmann, R. Lefeber and M. Zieck (eds), *Peoples and Minorities in International Law* (Dordrecht: Martinus Nijhoff, 1993), 37–76.

Leuprecht P., 'Le Conseil de l'Europe et les droits des minorités', *Les cahiers de droit*, Vol. 27 (1986), 203.

Martín Estébanez M., 'The Protection of National or Ethnic, Religious and Linguistic Minorities', in N. Neuwahl and A. Rosas (eds), *The European Union and Human Rights* (The Hague: Martinus Nijhoff, 1996), 133–64.

Merle J., 'Cultural Minority Rights and the Rights of the Majority in the Liberal State', *Ratio Juris*, Vol. 11(3) (1998), 259.

Nowak M., 'The Right of Self-Determination and the Protection of Minorities in Central and Eastern Europe in Light of the Case-Law of the Human Rights Committee', *International Journal of Groups Rights*, Vol. 1 (1993), 7–16.

Orentlicher D., 'Separation Anxiety: International Responses to Ethno-Separatist Claims', *Yale Journal of International Law*, Vol. 23(1) (1998), 1–78.

Packer J., 'On the Definition of Minorities', in J. Packer and K. Myntti (eds), *The Protection of Ethnic and Linguistic Minorities in Europe* (Turku/Åbo, Finland: Institute for Human Rights, Åbo Akademi University, 1993), 23–66.

—— 'United Nations Protection of Minorities in Time of Public Emergency: The Hard-core of Minority Rights', in D. Prémont (ed.), *Non-Derogable Rights and States of Emergency* (Brussels: Bruylant, 1996), 501–22.

—— and Myntti K. (eds), *The Protection of Ethnic and Linguistic Minorities in Europe* (Turku/Åbo, Finland: Institute for Human Rights, Åbo Akademi University, 1993).

Pentassuglia G., 'Monitoring Minority Rights in Europe: The Implementation Machinery of the Framework Convention for the Protection of National Minorities—With Special Reference to the Role of the Advisory Committee', 6 *International Journal on Minority and Group Rights* (1999) 417.

Phillips A. (ed.), *Education Rights and Minorities* (London: Minority Rights Group, 1994).

—— and Rosas A. (eds), *Universal Minority Rights* (Turku/Åbo, Finland: Institute for Human Rights, Åbo Akademi University, 1995).

Plant R., *Land Rights and Minorities* (London: Minority Rights Group International, 1994).

Ramcharan B., 'Peoples' Rights and Minorities' Rights', *Nordic Journal of International Law*, Vol. 56(1) (1987), 9–38.

Röben V., 'A Report on Effective Protection of Minorities', *German Yearbook of International Law*, Vol. 31 (1988), 621–38.

Rodley N., 'Conceptual Problems in the Protection of Minorities: International Legal Developments', *Human Rights Quarterly*, Vol. 17 (1 February) (1995), 48–71.

Rosas A., 'The Protection of Minorities in Europe: A General Overview', in J. Packer and K. Myntti (eds), *The Protection of Ethnic and Linguistic Minorities in Europe* (Turku/Åbo, Finland: Institute for Human Rights, Åbo Akademi University, 1993), 9–14.

Roth S., 'Comments on the CSCE meeting on National Minorities and its Concluding Document', *Human Rights Law Journal*, Vol. 12(8–9) (1991), 330–4.

Steiner H., 'Ideals and Counter-Ideals in the Struggle over Autonomy Regimes for Minorities', *Notre Dame Law Review*, Vol. 66(5) (1991), 1539–68.

Stone J., *Regional Guarantees of Minority Rights* (New York: Macmillan Press, 1933).

Storey A., 'Economics and Ethnic Conflict: Structural Adjustment in Rwanda', *Development Policy Review*, Vol. 17 (1999), 43–63.

Terstal S. and Huber K. 'The Functioning of the CSCE High Commissioner on National Minorities', *New Community*, Vol. 20 (3 April) (1994), 502–8.

Thomas H., 'Perestroika in the Western Wing: Nationalism and National Rights within the European Community', in W. Twining (ed.), *Issues of Self-Determination* (Aberdeen: Aberdeen University Press, 1991), 149–60.

Thornberry P., *International Law and the Rights of Minorities* (Oxford, Clarendon Press, 1991).

—— *Minorities and Human Rights Law* (London: Minority Rights Group, 1987).

—— 'Self-Determination, Minorities, Human Rights: A Review of International Instruments', *International and Comparative Law Quarterly*, Vol. 38 (1989), 867.

—— and Estebanez M., *The Council of Europe and Minorities* (Strasbourg: Council of Europe, 1994).

Türk D., 'Minorities, Self-Determination and Other Crucial Issues of Human Rights in Europe', in Z. Kedzia, A. Korula and M. Nowak (eds), *Perspectives of an All-European System of Human Rights Protection: The Role of the Council for Europe, the CSCE and the European Communities* (Kehl am Rhein, Germany: N. P. Engel Verlag, 1991), 279–90.

United Nations, *The International Protection of Minorities under the League of Nations*, E/CN.4/Sub.2/6 (New York: United Nations, 1947).

—— *Definition and Classification of Minorities: Memorandum by the Secretary-General*, 1950.xiv.3 (New York: United Nations, 1950).

Wrench J., *The EU, Ethnic Minorities and Migrants at the Workplace* (London: Kogan Page, 1998).

Wright Q., *Mandates under the League of Nations* (Chicago: University of Chicago Press, 1930).

Yacoub J., *Les minorités: quelle protection?* (Paris: Desclée de Brouwer, 1995).

Indigenous Peoples

Alston P., 'Individual Complaints: Historical Perspectives and the International Covenant on Economic, Social and Cultural Rights', in S. Pritchard (ed.) *Indigenous Peoples, the United Nations and Human Rights* (London: Zed Books, 1998), 81.

Anaya S., *Indigenous Peoples in International Law* (New York: Oxford University Press, 1996).

—— 'Indigenous Rights Norms in Contemporary International Law', *Arizona Journal of International and Comparative Law*, Vol. 8 (1991), 1.

—— and Crider S., 'Indigenous Peoples, the Environment, and Commercial Forestry in Developing Countries: The Case of Awas Tingni, Nicaragua', *Human Rights Quarterly*, Vol. 18 (2 May) (1996), 345.

Barsh R., 'The Challenge of Indigenous Self-Determination', *University of Michigan Journal of Law Reform*, Vol. 26 (2 Winter) (1993), 277.

Bay C., 'Human Rights and Indigenous Peoples', in IPSA Study Group on Human Rights, *Human Rights from Theory to Practice: Round-Table Discussion* (Geneva: Centre for Applied Studies in International Negotiations, 1981), 113.

Black M., *Children and Families of Ethnic Minorities, Immigrants and Indigenous Peoples: Summary Report of Innocenti Global Seminar* (Florence: UNICEF Innocenti Research Centre, 1997), 55.

Bloch A., 'Minorities and Indigenous Peoples', in A. Eide, C. Krause and A. Rosas (eds), *Economic, Social and Cultural Rights: A Textbook* (Dordrecht: Martinus Nijhoff, 1995), 309.

Buhl, C., *A Citizen's Guide to the Multilateral Development Banks and Indigenous Peoples* (Washington, DC: World Bank, 1995).

Corntassel J. and Primeau T., 'Indigenous "Sovereignty" and International Law: Revised Strategies for Pursuing "Self-Determination"', *Human Rights Quarterly*, Vol. 17 (1995), 343.

Daes E., 'Equality of Indigenous Peoples under the Auspices of the United Nations: Draft Declaration on the Rights of Indigenous Peoples', *St. Thomas Law Review*, Vol. 7 (Summer) (1995), 493–519.

Das V., 'Cultural Rights and the Definition of Community', in O. Mendelsohn and U. Baxi (eds), *The Rights of Subordinated Peoples* (New Delhi: Oxford University Press, 1994), 117–58.

Davis S., 'Conclusion', in S. Davis (ed.) *Land Rights and Indigenous Peoples: The Role of the Inter-American Commission on Human Rights* (Cambridge: Cultural Survival, 1989), 63–6.

Douglas R. and Douglas T., 'The Rights of the Indigenous Child: Reconciling the United Nations Convention on the Rights of the Child and the (Draft) Declaration on the Rights of Indigenous People with Early Education Policies for Indigenous Children', *International Journal of Children's Rights*, Vol. 3 (1995), 197–211.

Enslaved Peoples in the 1990s, No. 83 (Copenhagen: Anti-Slavery International, International Working Group for Indigenous Affairs, 1997).

Fabra A., 'Indigenous Peoples, Environmental Degradation and Human Rights: A Case Study', in A. Boyle and M. Anderson (eds), *Human Rights Approaches to Environmental Protection* (Oxford: Clarendon Press, 1996), 245–64.

Falk R., 'The Rights of Peoples (in Particular Indigenous Peoples)', in J. Crawford (ed.), *The Rights of Peoples* (Oxford: Clarendon Press, 1998), 17.

Feder G. and Feeny D., 'Land Tenure and Property Rights: Theory and Implications for Development Policy', *World Bank Economic Review*, Vol. 5 (1991).

Foster C., 'Articulating Self-determination in the Draft Declaration on the Rights of Indigenous Peoples', *European Journal of International Law*, Vol. 12 (2001) 140.

Galey M., 'Indigenous Peoples, International Consciousness-Raising and the Development of International Law on Human Rights', *Revue des droits de l'homme*, Vol. 8 (1975), 21–39.

Gupta R., 'Indigenous Peoples and the International Environmental Community, Accommodating Claims through a Cooperative Legal Process: Note', *New York University Law Review*, Vol. 74 (1999), 1741–85.

Hamel R., 'Indigenous Education in Latin America: Policies and Legal Frameworks', in T. Skutnabb-Kangas, M. Rannut and R. Phillipson (eds), *Linguistic Human Rights: Overcoming Linguistic Discrimination* (Berlin: de Gruyter, 1995), 271.

Hannum H., 'The Limits of Sovereignty and Majority Rule: Minorities, Indigenous Peoples, and the Right to Autonomy', in E. Lutz, H. Hannum and K. Burke (eds), *New Directions in Human Rights* (Philadelphia: University of Pennsylvania Press, 1989), 3–24.

—— 'Minorities, Indigenous Peoples, and Self-Determination', in L. Henkin, and J. Hargrove (eds), *Human Rights: An Agenda for the Next Century* (Washington, DC: American Society of International Law, 1994), 1–16.

—— 'New Developments in Indigenous Rights', *Virginia Journal of International Law*, Vol. 28 (1988), 649–78.

Hitchcock R., 'International Human Rights, the Environment, and Indigenous Peoples', *Colorado Journal of International Law and Politics*, Vol. 1 (1994), 1.

Hornberger N., 'Language Policy, Language Education, Language Rights: Indigenous, Immigrant, and International Perspectives', *Language in Society*, Vol. 27(4) (1998), 439.

International Centre for Human Rights and Democratic Development, *People or Peoples, Equality, Autonomy and Self-Determination: The Issues at Stake of the International Decade of the World's Indigenous People* (Montreal: International Centre for Human Rights and Democratic Development, 1996).

Iorns C., 'Indigenous Peoples and Self Determination: Challenging State Sovereignty', *Case Western Reserve Journal of International Law*, Vol. 24 (1992), 199–348.

Ivison D., Patton P. and Sanders W. (eds), *Political Theory and the Rights of Indigenous Peoples* (Cambridge: Cambridge University Press, 2000).

Kemf E. (ed.), *The Law of the Mother. Protecting Indigenous Peoples and Protected Areas* (San Francisco: Sierra Club Books, 1993).

Kingsbury B., 'Operational Policies of International Institutions as Part of the Law-Making Process: The World Bank and Indigenous Peoples', in G. Goodwin-Gill and S. Talmon (eds), *The Reality of International Law: Essays in Honour of Ian Brownlie* (Oxford: Clarendon Press, 1999), 323–42.

Macduff I., 'Biculturalism, Partnership and Parallel Systems: The Context of Maori Rights', in W. Twining (ed.), *Issues of Self-Determination* (Aberdeen: Aberdeen University Press, 1991), 102–14.

McNeil K., *Common Law Aboriginal Title* (Oxford: Clarendon Press, 1989).

Martinez Cobo J., *The Problem of Discrimination against Indigenous Populations*, UN Doc. E/CN.4/Sub.2/1986/7 & Add.1–3 (Geneva: United Nations, 1986).

Nunes K., '"We can do . . . better": The Rights of Singular Peoples and the United Nations Draft Declaration on the Rights of Indigenous Peoples', *St. Thomas Law Review*, Vol. 7 (Summer) (1995), 521–55.

Pallemaerts M., 'Development, Conservation, and Indigenous Rights in Brazil', *Human Rights Quarterly* (1986), 374–400.

Plant R., *Issues in Indigenous Poverty and Development* (Washington, DC: Inter-American Development Bank, Sustainable Development Department, Indigenous Peoples and Community Development Unit, 1998).

—— *Land Rights for Indigenous and Tribal Peoples in Developing Countries: A Survey of Law and Policy Issues, Current Activities, and Proposal for an Inter-Agency Programme of Action* (International Labour Organization: Geneva, 1991).

Posey D., *Traditional Resource Rights: International Instruments for Protection and Compensation for Indigenous Peoples and Local Communities* (Gland, Switzerland: World Conservation Union, 1996).

Sanders D., 'Self-Determination and Indigenous Peoples', in C. Tomuschat (ed.), *Modern Law of Self-Determination* (Dordrecht: Martinus Nijhoff, 1993), 55–82.

—— 'The UN Working Group on Indigenous Populations', *Human Rights Quarterly*, Vol. 11 (1989), 406.

Shutkin W., 'International Human Rights Law and the Earth: The Protection of Indigenous Peoples and the Environment', *Virginia Journal of International Law*, Vol. 31 (1991), 479.

Swepston L., 'Indigenous and Tribal Populations: A Return to Centre Stage', *International Labour Review*, Vol. 126 (4 July–August) (1987), 447–55.

—— 'A New Step in the International Law on Indigenous and Tribal Peoples: ILO Convention 169 of 1989', *Oklahoma City University Law Review*, Vol. 15 (1990), 677

—— and Plant R., 'International Standards and the Protection of the Land Rights of Indigenous and Tribal Populations', *International Labour Review*, Vol. 124 (1 January–February) (1985).

Tomei M. and Swepston L., *A Guide to ILO Convention No. 169 on Indigenous and Tribal Peoples* (Geneva: International Labour Organization, 1995).

Tully J., 'Aboriginal Property and Western Theory: Recovering a Middle Ground', *Social Philosophy and Policy*, Vol. 11(2) (1994), 139–52.

Turpel M., 'Indigenous Peoples' Rights of Political Participation and Self-Determination: Recent International Legal Developments and the Continuing Struggle for Recognition', *Cornell International Law Journal*, Vol. 25 (1992), 579–602.

United Nations, *Working Group on Indigenous Populations*, UN Docs E/CN.4/Sub.2/1982/33; E/CN.4/Sub.2/1983/22; E/CN.4/Sub.2/1984/20; E/CN.4/Sub.2/1985/22 & Add.1; E/CN.4/Sub.2/1987/22 & Add.1; E/CN.4/Sub.2/1988/24 & Add.1; E/CN.4/Sub.2/1989/36; E/CN.4/Sub.2/1990/42; E/CN.4/Sub.2/1991/40; E/CN.4/Sub.2/1992/33 & Add. 1; E/CN.4/Sub.2/1993/29 & Add.1; E/CN.4/Sub.2/1994/30; E/CN.4/Sub.2/ 1995/24; E/CN.4/Sub.2/1996/22; E/CN.4/Sub.2/1997/14; E/CN.4/Sub.2/1998/16; E/CN.4/Sub.2/1999/19; and E/CN.4/Sub.2/2000/24.

Vakatale T., 'Multiculturalism vs Indigenous Cultural Rights', in M. Wilson and P. Hunt (eds), *Culture, Rights, and Cultural Rights: Perspectives from the South Pacific* (Wellington, New Zealand: Huia Publishers, 2000), 69.

Weiss G. (ed.), *Trying to Get it Back: Indigenous Women, Culture and Education* (Waterloo, Ontario, Canada: Wilfrid Laurier University Press, 1999).

Wiessner S., 'Rights and Status of Indigenous Peoples: A Global Comparative and International Legal Analysis', *Harvard Human Rights Journal*, Vol. 12 (1999), 57.

Right to Development

Abi-Saab G., 'Le droit au développement', *Schweizerisches Jahrbuch Für Internationalrecht*, Vol. 44 (1988), 9.

—— 'The Legal Formulation of a Right to Development', in R. Dupuy (ed.), *The Right to Development at the International Level* (Alphen aan den Rijn, Netherlands: Sijthoff and Noordhoff, 1981), 163.

Aguda T., *Human Rights and the Right to Development in Africa* (Lagos: Nigerian Institute of International Affairs, 1989).

Alfredsson G., 'The Right to Development: Perspectives from Human Rights Law', in L. Rehof and C. Gulmann (eds), *Human Rights in Domestic Law and the Development Assistance Policies of the Nordic Countries* (Dordrecht: Martinus Nijhoff, 1989), 83.

Alston P., 'Making Space for New Human Rights: The Case of the Right to Development', *Harvard Human Rights Yearbook*, Vol. 1 (1988), 1–38.

—— 'The Right to Development', in *Evaluating the Vienna Declaration: Advancing the Human Rights Agenda* (Washington, DC: The American University, 1994), 51–7.

—— 'The Right to Development at the International Level', in Hague Academy of International Law, *Collected Papers of a Colloquium on the Right to Development* (The Hague: Sijthoff and Noordhoff, 1981), 99–114.

Alston P., 'The Right to Development at the International Level', in F. Snyder and S. Sathirathai (eds), *Third World Attitudes toward International Law: An Introduction* (Dordrecht: Martinus Nijhoff, 1987), 811.

—— 'The Shortcomings of a "Garfield the Cat" Approach to the Right to Development', *California Western International Law Journal*, Vol. 15 (1985), 510 .

—— 'Some Notes on the Concept of the Right to Development', in *Essais sur le concept de 'droit de vivre' en mémoire de Yougindra Khushalani* (Brussels: Bruylant, 1988), 73–84.

Arts K., 'Implementing the Right to Development?: An Analysis of European Community Development and Human Rights Policies', in P. Baehr, L. Sadiwa and J. Smith (eds), *Human Rights in Developing Countries: Yearbook 1996* (The Hague: Kluwer Law International, 1996).

Barsh R., 'The Right to Development as a Human Right: Results of the Global Consultation', *Human Rights Quarterly*, Vol. 13 (1991), 321.

Baxi U., 'The Development of the Right to Development', in J. Symonides (ed.), *Human Rights: New Dimensions and Challenges* (Aldershot, Brookfield, VT: Ashgate. UNESCO, 1998), 99.

Bedjaoui M., 'Propos libres sur le droit au développement', in *International Law at the Time of its Codification: Essays in Honour of Roberto Ago* (Milan: Giuffré, 1987), 15.

—— 'The Right to Development', in M. Bedjaoui (ed.), *International Law: Achievements and Prospects* (Paris: UNESCO, 1991), 1177.

Cançado Trindade A., 'Environment and Development: Formulation and Implementation of the Right to Development as a Human Right', in A. Cançado Trindade (ed.), *Human Rights, Sustainable Development and the Environment* (San José, Costa Rica: Inter-American Institute of Human Rights, 1992), 39.

Charlesworth H., 'The Public/Private Distinction and the Right to Development in International Law', *Australian Year Book of International Law*, Vol. 12 (1992), 190–204.

Chowdhury R., Denters E. and de Waart P. (eds), *The Right to Development in International Law* (Dordrecht: Martinus Nijhoff, 1992).

Colliard L., 'L'adoption par l'Assemblée générale des Nations unies de la Déclaration sur le droit au développment', *Annuaire français de droit international*, Vol. 33 (1987), 614–28.

Commission of International Development, *Partners in Development: Report of the Commission of International Development* (Praeger: New York, 1969).

de vey Mestdagh K., *The Right to Development*, UN Doc. HR/Geneva/1980/WP.7 (Geneva: United Nations, 1980).

Dias, C. 'Realizing the Right to Development: The Importance of Legal Resources', in International Commission of Jurists, *Development, Human Rights and the Rule of Law* (The Hague: Pergamon Press, 1981), 187–98.

Dimitrijevic V., 'Development as a Right', *Review of International Affairs*, Vol. 33 (June 20) (1982), 51–3.

Donnelly J., 'Development Rights Trade-offs: Needs and Equality', in J. Donnelly, *Universal Human Rights in Theory and Practice* (Ithaca, NY: Cornell University Press, 1989), 163–83.

—— 'The Human Rights Priorities of the UN: A Rejoinder to Alston', *International Organization*, Vol. 37 (1983), 547–50.

—— 'The "Right to Development": How not to Link Human Rights and Development', in C. Welch and R. Meltzer (eds), *Human Rights and Development in Africa* (Albany, NY: State University of New York Press, 1984), 261–83.

Dupuy, R., 'Le droit au développement au plan international', in *Colloque de l'Académie de droit international* (Alphen aan den Rijn, Netherlands: Sijthoff and Noordhoff, 1981).

Eide A., *Consideration of the Impact of the Arms Race in the Realization of the Right to Development and Peace: Analysis of the Concrete Measures for the full Enjoyment of Human Rights, Particularly the Right to Development*, UN Doc. HR/New York/1981/BP.1 (Geneva: United Nations, 1981).

Feuer G. and Cassan H., *Droit international du développement* (Paris: Dalloz, 1991).

Ginther K., 'The Domestic Policy Function of a Right of Peoples to Development: Popular Participation, a New Hope for Development and Challenge for the Discipline', in S. Chowdhury, E. Denters and P. de Waart (eds), *The Right to Development in International Law* (Dordrecht: Martinus Nijhoff, 1992), 61–82.

Gros Espiell H., 'The Right of Development as a Human Right', *Texas International Law Journal*, Vol. 16 (1981), 189–205.

James P., 'Law, Socialism and the Human Right to Development in Third World Countries', *Review of Socialist Law*, Vol. 7 (1981), 235–41.

Kjeldgaard H., *The International Elaboration of the Right to Development as a Human Right*, UN Doc. HR/Geneva/1980/WP.16 (Geneva: United Nations, 1980).

'Legal Dimensions of the Right to Development as a Human Right: Some Conceptual Aspects', *Revista Interamericana De Derechos Humanos*, Vol. 12 (1991), 81.

M'Baye K., 'De droit au développement comme un droit de l'homme', *Revue des droits de l'homme*, Vol. 5(2–3) (1972), 503–34.

—— *Emergence of the Right to Development as a Human Right in the Context of a New International Economic Order*, UNESCO Doc. SS-78/CONF.630/8 (UNESCO: Paris, 1978).

Mansell W. and Scott J., 'Why Bother about a Right to Development?', *Journal of Law and Society*, Vol. 2(1–2) (1994), 171–92.

Mavungu J.-P., 'The Right to Development as a Human Right', in International Commission of Jurists and African Development Bank (eds), *Report of a Regional Seminar on Economic, Social, and Cultural Rights* (Geneva: International Commission of Jurists, 1999), 33.

Munoz A., 'Estado actual de los derechos económicos, sociales y culturales y del derecho al desarrollo en el derecho internacional', in Terre des Hommes (ed.), *El derecho a la equidad: etica y mundializacion social* (Barcelona: Icaria Antrazyt, 1997), 53.

Nanda V., Shepherd G. and McCarthy-Arnold E. (eds), *World Debt and the Human Condition: Structural Adjustment and the Right to Development* (Westport, CT: Greenwood Press, 1993).

Nieman M., 'Regional Integration and the Right to Development in Africa', in E. McCarthy-Arnolds, D. Penna and D. Sobrepena (eds), *Africa, Human Rights, and the Global System: The Political Economy of Human Rights in a Changing World* (Westport, CT: Greenwood Press, 1994), 107–27.

Pellet A., *Le droit international de développement* (Paris: Presses Universitaires de France, 1987).

Petersmann H., 'The Right to Development in the United Nations, an Opportunity for Strengthening Popular Participation in Development: Programs and Prospect', in J. Jekewitz, K. Klein, J. Kuhne and H. Petersmann (eds), *Das Menschenrecht zwischen Freiheit und Verantwortung: Festschrift für Karl Josef Partsche* (Berlin: Duncker und Humbolt, 1989), 125–40.

Pindic D., *The Right to Development: A New Approach to the Problems of Human Rights Based on a Conception for Establishment of the New International Economic Order*, UN Doc. HR/Geneva/1980/WP.5 (Geneva: United Nations, 1980).

Prakash N., *The Right to Development and the International Economic Order*, UN Doc. HR/Geneva/1980/WP.13 (Geneva: United Nations, 1980).

Ramcharan B., 'The Role of the Development Concept in the UN Declaration on the Right to Development and in the UN Covenant', in P. de Waart, P. Peters and E. Denters (eds), *International Law and Development* (Dordrecht: Martinus Nijhoff, 1988).

Rich R., 'The Right to Development: A Right of Peoples?', in J. Crawford (ed.), *The Rights of Peoples* (Oxford: Clarendon Press, 1988), 39–54.

Saksena K., 'Human Rights and the Right to Development', *International Studies* (1991), 41–53.

Salcedo C., 'El derecho al desarrollo como un derecho humano', *Revista Espanola De Derecho Internacional*, Vol. 25 (1972), 119–25.

Sengupta A., 'Realising the Right to Development', *Development and Change*, Vol. 31 (2000), 553–78.

Smith R., *The Right to Development: A Perspective*, HR/Geneva/1980/WP.10 (Geneva: United Nations, 1980).

Stewart F., *Basic Needs Strategies, Human Rights and the Right to Development* (Oxford: International Development Centre, University of Oxford, 1988).

'Symposium: Development as an Emerging Human Right', *California Western International Law Journal* (1985), 429.

'Symposium: Nuclear Weapons and the Right to Survival, Peace and Development', *Denver Journal of International Law and Policy*, Vol. 19 (1 Fall) (1990), 1.

Türk D., 'The Human Right to Development', in P. Van Dijk, F. Van Hoof, A. Koers and K. Mortelmans (eds), *Restructuring the International Economic Order: The Role of Law and Lawyers* (Deventer: Kluwer Law, 1986), 85.

Udombana N., 'The Third World and the Right to Development: Agenda for the Next Millenium', *Human Rights Quarterly*, Vol. 22(3) (2000), 753–87.

United Nations, *The International Dimensions of the Right to Development as a Human Right in Relation with Other Human Rights Based on International Co-operation, Including the Right to Peace, Taking into Account the Requirements of the New International Economic Order and Fundamental Human Needs: Report by the Secretary-General*, UN Doc. E/CN.4/1334 (1979).

—— *The Regional and National Dimensions of the Right to Development as a Human Right: Study by the Secretary-General*, Part 1: UN Doc. E/CN.4/1421 (1980); Parts 2, 3 and Conclusions: E/CN.4/1488 (1981).

—— *Working Group of Governmental Experts on the Right to Development*, UN Docs E/CN.4/1489 (1982); E/CN.4/1983/11; E/CN.4/1984/13; E/CN.4/1985/11; E/CN.4/1987/10; E/CN.4/1988/10; E/CN.4/1989/10; E/CN.4/1994/21; E/CN.4/1995/11; E/CN.4/1996/10; and E/CN.4/1996/24.

—— *Working Group of Intergovernmental Experts on the Right to Development*, UN Docs E/CN.4/1997/22; and E/CN.4/1998/29.

—— *Open-ended Working Group on the Right to Development*, UN Doc. E/CN.4/2000/21.

—— *Reports of the Independent Expert on the Right to Development*, UN Docs E/CN.4/1999/118; A/54/401 (1999); and A/55/306 (2000).

—— *Concrete Proposals for the Effective Implementation and Promotion of the Declaration on the Right to Development*, UN Doc. E/CN.4/Sub.2/1989/19.

—— *The Realization of the Right to Development: Global Consultation on the Right to Development as a Human Right*, UN Doc. E/CN.4/1990/9/Rev.1.

—— *Report of the Secretary-General on Promoting the Right to Development in the Context of the United Nations Decade for the Elimination of Poverty (1997–2006)*, UN Doc. E/CN.4/Sub.2/1999/30.

—— *Report of the Secretary-General on the Impact of the Activities and Working Methods of Transnational Corporations on the Full Enjoyment of All Human Rights, in Particular Economic, Social and Cultural Rights and the Right to Development*, UN Doc. E/CN.4/Sub.2/1996/12.

—— *Report of the Secretary-General on the Implementation of the Declaration on the Right to Development*, UN Doc. E/CN.4/1997/21.

—— *Report of the Secretary-General on the Question of the Realization of the Right to Development*, UN Doc. E/CN.4/1998/28.

—— *Report of the Secretary-General on the Right to Development*, UN Doc. A/54/319 (1999).

—— *The Right to Development: Report of the High Commissioner for Human Rights Submitted in Accordance with Commission on Human Rights Resolution 1999/79*, UN Doc. E/CN.4/2000/20.

—— *The Right to Development: Report of the Secretary-General Submitted in Accordance with Commission on Human Rights Resolution 1998/72*, UN Doc. E/CN.4/1999/20.

Uribe Vargas D., 'La formulacion del derecho al desarrollo', in *Héctor Gros Espiell Amicorum Liber: Persona humana y derecho internacional* (Brussels: Bruylant, 1997), 1605–12.

van Boven T., 'The Right to Development and Human Rights', *Review of the International Commission of Jurists*, Vol. 28 (1982), 49–56.

van Dijk P., 'The Right to Development and Human Rights: A Matter of Equality and Priority', *Israel Yearbook on Human Rights*, Vol. 14 (1984), 221–48.

Verwey W., *The Establishment of a New International Economic Order and the Realization of the Right to Development and Welfare: A Legal Survey*, UN Doc. HR/Geneva/1980/BP.3 (Geneva: United Nations, 1980).

—— 'The New International Economic Order and the Realization of the Right to Development and Welfare: Legal Survey', *Indian Journal of International Law*, Vol. 21 (1981), 1–178.

Virally M., 'Vers un droit international du développement', *Annuaire français de droit international*, Vol. 11 (1965), 3–12.

Weeramantry C., 'The Right to Development', *Indian Journal of International Law*, Vol. 25 (1985), 482–505.

Yusuf A., 'Differential Treatment as a Dimension of the Right to Development', in R. Dupuy, *The Right to Development at the International Level: Colloquium, The Hague, 16–18 October 1979* (Alphen aan den Rijn, Netherlands: Sijthoff and Noordhoff, 1980).

Right to Environment

Alfredson G. and Ovsiouk A., 'Human Rights and the Environment', *Nordic Journal of International Law*, Vol. 60 (1991), 19.

Anaya S. and Crider S., 'Indigenous Peoples, the Environment, and Commercial Forestry in Developing Countries: The Case of Awas Tingni, Nicaragua', *Human Rights Quarterly*, Vol. 18 (1996), 345.

Anderson M., 'Individual Rights to Environmental Protection in India', in A. Boyle and M. Anderson (eds), *Human Rights Approaches to Environmental Protection* (Oxford: Clarendon Press, 1996), 199.

Bartlett S. (ed.), *Cities for Children: Children's Rights, Poverty and Urban Management* (London: Earthscan, 1999).

Batty H. and Gray T., 'Environmental Rights and National Sovereignty', in S. Caney, D. George and P. Jones (eds), *National Rights, International Obligations* (Boulder, CO: Westview Press, 1996), 149.

Boisson de Chazournes L., 'Non-derogable Rights and the Need to Protect the Environment', in D. Prémont (ed.), *Non-Derogable Rights and States of Emergency* (Brussels: Bruylant, 1996), 463.

Boyle A., 'The Role of International Human Rights Law in the Protection of the Environment', in A. Boyle and M. Anderson (eds), *Human Rights Approaches to Environmental Protection* (Oxford: Clarendon Press, 1996), 43.

—— and Anderson M. (eds), *Human Rights Approaches to Environmental Protection* (Oxford, New York: Clarendon Press. Oxford University Press, 1996).

Bryant B. and Mohai P., *Race and the Incidence of Environmental Hazards: A Time for Discourse* (Boulder, CO: Westview Press, 1992).

Bullard R., *Dumping in Dixie: Race, Class, and Environmental Quality* (Boulder, CO: Westview Press, 1994).

Cahalan S., 'NIMBY, Not in Mexico's Back Yard?: A Case for the Recognition of a Human Right to Healthy Environment in the American States', *Georgia Journal of International and Comparative Law*, Vol. 23 (1993), 409.

Cançado Trindade A., 'Human Rights and the Environment', in J. Symonides (ed.), *Human Rights: New Dimensions and Challenges* (Aldershot, Brookfield, VT: Ashgate. UNESCO, 1998), 117.

—— 'Environment and Development: Formulation and Implementation of the Right to Development as a Human Right', in A. Cançado Trindade (ed.), *Human Rights, Sustainable Development and the Environment* (San José, Costa Rica: Inter-American Institute of Human Rights, 1992), 39.

Churchill R., 'Environmental Rights in the Existing Human Rights Treaties', in A. Boyle and M. Anderson (eds), *Human Rights Approaches to Environmental Protection* (Oxford: Clarendon Press, 1996), 89.

Civic M., 'Discovering and Enforcing a Human Right to Environmental Protection', *Journal of Natural Resources and Environmental Law*, Vol. 13(1) (1997), 123.

Cullet P., 'Definition of an Environmental Right in a Human Rights Context', *Netherlands Quarterly of Human Rights*, Vol. 13 (1995), 25.

Davis R., 'Weather Warfare: Law and Policy', *Arizona Law Review*, Vol. 14 (1972), 659.

Dejeant-Pons M., *La Méditerranée en droit international de l'environnement* (Marseille, Paris: Centre d'études et de recherches internationales et communautaires, Université d'Aix-Marseille III. Economica, 1990).

—— 'The Right to Environment in Regional Human Rights Systems', in K. Mahoney and P. Mahoney (eds), *Human Rights in the Twenty-first Century: A Global Challenge* (Dordrecht, Boston: M. Nijhoff, 1993), 595.

Desgagne R., 'Integrating Environmental Values into the European Convention on Human Rights', *American Journal of International Law*, Vol. 89 (1995), 263.

Diaz A., 'Permanent Sovereignty over Natural Resources', *Environmental Policy and Law*, Vol. 24(4) (1994), 157–73.

Downs J., 'A Healthy and Ecologically Balanced Environment: An Argument for a Third Generation Right', *Duke Journal of Comparative and International Law*, Vol. 3 (1993), 351.

Eaton J., 'The Nigerian Tragedy, Environmental Regulation of Transnational Corporations and the Human Right to a Healthy Environment', *Boston University International Law Journal*, Vol. 15 (1997), 261.

Eleftheriadis P., 'The Future of Environmental Rights in the European Union', in P. Alston, M. Bustelo and J. Heenan (eds), *The EU and Human Rights* (Oxford: Oxford University Press, 1999), 529–49.

Fabra A., 'Indigenous Peoples, Environmental Degradation and Human Rights: A Case Study', in A. Boyle and M. Anderson (eds), *Human Rights Approaches to Environmental Protection* (Oxford: Clarendon Press, 1996), 245–64.

Falk R., 'Environmental Warfare and Ecocide', *Bulletin of Peace Proposals*, Vol. 4 (1973), 1.

Fernandes E., 'Constitutional Environmental Rights in Brazil', in A. Boyle and M. Anderson (eds), *Human Rights Approaches to Environmental Protection* (Oxford: Clarendon Press, 1996), 265–84.

Fernandez J., 'State Constitutions, Environmental Rights Provisions, and the Doctrine of Self-Execution: A Political Question?', *Harvard Environmental Law Review*, Vol. 17 (1993), 333–87.

Fitzmaurice M., 'The Right of the Child to a Clean Environment', *Southern Illinois University Law Journal*, Vol. 23 (1999), 611.

Friends of the Earth, *The IMF: Selling the Environment Short* (Washington, DC: Friends of the Earth, 1999).

Gelobter M., 'The Meaning of Urban Environmental Justice', *Fordham Urban Law Journal*, Vol. 21 (1994), 841.

Gibson N., 'The Right to a Clean Environment', *Saskatchewan Law Review*, Vol. 54 (1990), 5.

Glazewski J., 'Environmental Rights and the New South African Constitution', in A. Boyle and M. Anderson (eds), *Human Rights Approaches to Environmental Protection* (Oxford: Clarendon Press, 1996), 177–98.

Glick R., 'Environmental Justice in the United States: Implications of the International Covenant on Civil and Political Rights', *Harvard Environmental Law Review*, Vol. 19 (1995), 69.

Goldblat J., 'Environmental Warfare Convention: How Meaningful Is It?', *Ambio*, Vol. 6 (1977), 216.

Green L., 'The Environment and the Law of Conventional Warfare', *Canadian Yearbook of International Law*, Vol. 29 (1991), 222.

Gupta R., 'Indigenous Peoples and the International Environmental Community, Accommodating Claims through a Cooperative Legal Process: Note', *New York University Law Review*, Vol. 74 (1999), 1741–85.

Handl G., 'Human Rights and Protection of the Environment: A Mildly "Revisionist" View', in A. Cançado Trindade (ed.), *Human Rights, Sustainable Development and the Environment* (San José, Costa Rica: Inter-American Institute of Human Rights, 1992), 117.

Hitchcock R., 'International Human Rights, the Environment, and Indigenous Peoples', *Colorado Journal of International Law and Politics*, Vol. 1 (1994), 1.

Hodkova I., 'Is There a Right to a Healthy Environment in the International Legal Order?', *Connecticut Journal of International Law*, Vol. 7 (1991), 65.

Hoog G. and Steinmetz A., *International Conventions on Protection of Humanity and Environment* (Berlin, New York: W. de Gruyter, 1993).

Kane M., 'Promoting Political Rights to Protect the Environment', *Yale Journal of International Law*, Vol. 18 (1993), 389.

Kiss A., 'Le droit à la conservation de l'environnement', *Revue universelle des droits de l'homme*, Vol. 1 (1990), 445.

Koppen I. and Ladeur K., 'Environment Rights', in A. Cassese, A. Clapham and J. Weiler (eds), *Human Rights and the European Community: The Substantive Law* (Baden-Baden: Nomos Verlagsgesellschaft, 1991), 1–47.

Kromarek P., *Le droit à un environnement sain et équilibre*, UNESCO Doc. SS-80/CONF.806/11 (UNESCO: Paris, 1980).

Lazarus R., 'Pursuing "Environmental Justice": The Distributional Effects of Environmental Protection', *Northwestern University Law Review*, Vol. 87 (1993), 787.

Liebler A., 'Deliberate Wartime Environmental Damage: New Challenges for International Law', *California Western International Law Journal*, Vol. 23 (1992), 67.

Lyster R., 'The Protection of Environmental Rights', *South African Law Journal* (1992), 518–28.

McClymonds J., 'The Human Right to a Healthy Environment: An International Legal Perspective', *New York Law School Law Review*, Vol. 37 (1992), 583.

Ovsiouk A., 'Interrelationship between the Right to Life, Environment and Disarmament in the United Nations System', in D. Prémont and F. Montant (eds), *Proceedings of the Symposium on the Right to Life: Forty Years after the Adoption of the Universal Declaration of Human Rights, Evolution of the Concept, Norms and Case-Law* (Geneva: Consultants internationales des droits de l'homme, 1992), 17.

Pallemaerts M., 'Development, Conservation, and Indigenous Rights in Brazil', *Human Rights Quarterly* (1986), 374–400.

Percival R. and Alevizatos D., *Law and the Environment: A Multidisciplinary Reader* (Philadelphia: Temple University Press, 1997).

Plant G. (ed.), *Environmental Protection and the Law of War: A Fifth Geneva Convention on the Protection of the Environment in the Time of Armed Conflict* (London, New York: Belhaven Press, 1992).

Popovic N., 'In Pursuit of Environmental Human Rights: Commentary on the Draft Declaration of Principles on Human Rights and the Environment', *Columbia Human Rights Law Review*, Vol. 27 (1996), 487.

Portney K., 'Environmental Justice and Sustainability: Is There a Critical Nexus in the Case of Waste Disposal or Treatment Facility Siting?', *Fordham Urban Law Journal*, Vol. 21 (1994), 827.

Prakash S., 'The Right to the Environment: Emerging Implications in Theory and Praxis', *Netherlands Quarterly of Human Rights*, Vol. 4 (1995), 403–33.

Roberts A., 'Environmental Destruction in the 1991 Gulf War', *International Review of the Red Cross*, Vol. 291 (1992), 538.

Russo C., 'Le droit de l'environnement dans les décisions de la Commission des droits de l'homme et dans la jurisprudence de la Cour européenne', in *Mélanges en hommage à Louis Edmond Pettiti* (Brussels: Bruylant, 1998).

Schafer B., 'The Relationship between the International Law of Armed Conflict and Environmental Protection: The Need to Reevaluate What Types of Conduct Are Permissible during Hostilities', *California Western International Law Journal*, Vol. 19 (1989), 287.

Scott I., 'Note. The Inter-American System of Human Rights: An Effective Means of Environmental Protection?', *Virginia Journal of International Law*, Vol. 19 (2000), 197.

Shelton D., 'Human Rights, Environmental Rights, and the Right to Environment', *Stanford Journal of International Law*, Vol. 28 (1991), 103.

—— 'The Right to Environment', in A. Eide and J. Helgesen (eds), *The Future of Human Rights Protection in a Changing World* (Oslo: Norwegian University Press, 1991), 197.

—— 'What Happened in Rio to Human Rights?', *Yearbook of International Environmental Law*, Vol. 4 (1994), 75.

Shutkin W., 'International Human Rights Law and the Earth: The Protection of Indigenous Peoples and the Environment', *Virginia Journal of International Law*, Vol. 31 (1991), 479.

Steiger H., 'The Fundamental Right to a Decent Environment', in M. Bothe (ed.), *Trends in Environmental Policy and Law* (Gland, Switzerland: International Union for Conservation of Nature and Natural Resources, 1980), 5.

Symonides J., 'The Human Right to a Clean, Balanced and Protected Environment', in T. Tonchia (ed.), *Diritti dell'uomo e ambiente la partecipazione dei cittadini alle decisioni sulla tutela dell'ambiente* (Padova: CEDAM, 1990), 239.

Thorme M., 'Establishing Environment as a Human Right', *Denver Journal of International Law and Policy*, Vol. 19 (1991), 302.

Tomaševski K., 'Environmental Rights', in A. Eide, C. Krause and A. Rosas (eds), *Economic, Social and Cultural Rights: A Textbook* (Dordrecht: Martinus Nijhoff, 1995), 257.

van Dyke B., 'A Proposal to Introduce the Right to a Healthy Environment into the European Convention Regime', *Virginia Journal of International Law*, Vol. 13 (1993), 323.

Wagner J. and Popovic N., 'Environmental Injustice on United States Bases in Panama: International Law and the Right to Land Free from Contamination and Explosives', *Virginia Journal of International Law*, Vol. 38 (1999), 401.

Weber S., 'Environmental Information and the European Convention on Human Rights', *Human Rights Law Journal*, Vol. 12 (1991), 117.

Weiss E., *Environmental Change and International Law: New Challenges and Dimensions* (Tokyo: United Nations University Press, 1992).

Westing A., *Cultural Norms, War and the Environment* (New York: Oxford University Press, 1988).

—— (ed.), *Environmental Hazards of War: Releasing Dangerous Forces in an Industrialized World* (London, Newbury Park: SAGE Publications, 1990).

—— (ed.), *Environmental Warfare: A Technical, Legal, and Policy Appraisal* (London, Philadelphia: Taylor & Francis, 1984).

—— *Explosive Remnants of War. Mitigating the Environmental Effects* (London, Philadelphia: Taylor & Francis, 1985).

—— *Global Resources and International Conflict. Environmental Factors in Strategic Policy and Action* (Oxford: Oxford University Press, 1986).

—— *Threat of Modern Warfare to Man and his Environment: An Annotated Bibliography Prepared under the Auspices of the International Peace Research Association* (Paris: UNESCO, 1979).

Westing A., *Warfare in a Fragile World: Military Impact on the Human Environment* (London; New York: Taylor & Francis, 1980).
—— *Weapons of Mass Destruction and the Environment* (London, New York: Taylor & Francis, 1977).
Westra L. and Wenz P., *Faces of Environmental Racism. Confronting Issues of Global Justice* (Lanham, MD: Rowman & Littlefield, 1995).
Wiggins A., 'Indian Rights and the Environment', *Yale Journal of International Law*, Vol. 18 (1993), 345.
World Health Organization, *Health and Environmental Effects of Nuclear Weapons*, WHO Doc. A46/30, 26 April 1993 (Geneva: World Health Organization, 1993).

Right to Peace

Aguiar A., 'Les profils éthiques et normatifs du droit de l'homme à la paix', in *Boutros Boutros-Ghali amicorum discipulorumque liber: Paix, développement, démocratie* (Brussels: Bruylant, 1998).
Alston P., 'Peace as a Human Right', *Bulletin of Peace Proposals*, Vol. 11(4) (1980), 319.
—— 'Peace, Disarmament and Human Rights', in G. Fischer (ed.), *Armement, développement, droits de l'homme, désarmement* (Brussels: Bruylant, 1985), 324.
Ball N. and Halevy T., *Making Peace Work: The Role of the International Development Community* (Washington, DC: Overseas Development Council, 1996).
Bay C., 'Positive Peace and Rational Human Rights Priorities', *Bulletin of Peace Proposals*, Vol. 2 (1977), 160.
Bedjaoui M., 'Quelques considerations sur les perspectives de paix et de développement à l'aube de l'an 2000', in *Héctor Gros Espiell Amicorum Liber: Persona humana y derecho internacional* (Brussels: Bruylant, 1997), 93.
Dimitrejevic V., 'Human Rights and Peace', in J. Symonides (ed.), *Human Rights: New Dimensions and Challenges* (Aldershot, Brookfield, VT: Ashgate. UNESCO, 1998), 47.
Eide A., *Consideration of the Impact of the Arms Race in the Realization of the Right to Development and Peace: Analysis of the Concrete Measures for the Full Enjoyment of Human Rights, Particularly the Right to Development*, UN Doc. HR/New York/1981/BP.1 (Geneva: United Nations, 1981).
Forsythe D., *Human Rights and Peace: International and National Dimensions* (Lincoln, NE: University of Nebraska Press, 1993).
Gimenez J., 'Por la vida de una infancia en justicia y en paz', in *Héctor Gros Espiell Amicorum Liber: Persona humana y derecho internacional* (Brussels: Bruylant, 1997), 1379–90.
Ikram A., *Some Significant 21st Century Trends and Issues: Poverty, Population, Peace, and Sustainability* (Islamabad: Pakistan Futuristics Foundation and Institute, 1998).
Kudryavtsev V., *Human Rights, Peace and Development*, UN Doc. HR/New York/1981/BP.2 (Geneva: United Nations, 1981).
Marks S., 'Development and Human Rights: Some Reflections on the Study of Development, Human Rights, and Peace', *Bulletin of Peace Proposals*, Vol. 8(3) (1977), 236–46.
—— 'The Peace–Human Rights-Development Dialectic', *Bulletin of Peace Proposals*, Vol. 11(4) (1980).
Mayor F., *The Human Right to Peace: Declaration by the Director-General* (Paris: UNESCO, 1997).

Nastase A., 'The Right to Peace', in M. Bedjaoui (ed.), *International Law: Achievements and Prospects* (Paris: UNESCO, 1991), 1219–32.

Richard P., 'De l'utilité du concept de droit de vivre en matière de désarmement et de sécurité internationale', in D. Prémont and F. Montant (eds), *Proceedings of the Symposium on the Right to Life: Forty Years after the Adoption of the Universal Declaration of Human Rights, Evolution of the Concept, Norms and Case-Law* (Geneva: CID, 1992), 25.

Rosas A. and Sandvik M., 'Armed Conflicts', in A. Eide, C. Krause and A. Rosas (eds), *Economic, Social and Cultural Rights: A Textbook* (Dordrecht: Martinus Nijhoff, 1995), 341–54.

Russett B., 'Disarmament, Human Rights and Basic Needs', *Bulletin of Peace Proposals*, Vol. 10(3) (1979), 275–80.

Sohn L., *The Human Rights Movement: From Roosevelt's Four Freedoms to the Interdependence of Peace, Development and Human Rights* (Cambridge, MA: Human Rights Program, Harvard Law School, 1995).

Stark B., 'Nurturing Rights: An Essay on Women, Peace, and International Human Rights', *Michigan Journal of International Law*, Vol. 13 (1 Fall) (1991), 144–60.

'Symposium: Nuclear Weapons and the Right to Survival, Peace and Development', *Denver Journal of International Law and Policy*, Vol. 19 (1 Fall) (1990), 1.

Tichonov A., *The Right to Peace*, UNESCO Doc. SS-78/CONF.630/10 (UNESCO: Paris, 1978).

UNESCO, *UNESCO and a Culture of Peace: Promoting a Global Movement* (Paris: UNESCO, 1995).

Uribe Vargas D., 'El derecho a la paz', in D. Bardonnet and A. Cançado Trindade (eds), *Derecho internacional y derechos humanos* (San José, Costa Rica: Instituto Interamericano de Derechos Humanos, 1996), 177–96.

Virally M. (ed.), *Le droit international au service de la paix, de la justice et du développement* (Paris: A. Pedone, 1991), 273–9.

Index

Lightning Source UK Ltd.
Milton Keynes UK
UKOW04f1601161013

219182UK00004B/31/A